The Matter with Ireland

Second Edition

THE FLORIDA BERNARD SHAW SERIES

Florida A&M University, Tallahassee
Florida Atlantic University, Boca Raton
Florida Gulf Coast University, Ft. Myers
Florida International University, Miami
Florida State University, Tallahassee
University of Central Florida, Orlando
University of Florida, Gainesville
University of North Florida, Jacksonville
University of South Florida, Tampa
University of West Florida, Pensacola

THE MATTER
WITH IRELAND

SECOND EDITION

Bernard Shaw

edited by Dan H. Laurence and David H. Greene

University Press of Florida

GAINESVILLE · TALLAHASSEE · TAMPA · BOCA RATON

PENSACOLA · ORLANDO · MIAMI · JACKSONVILLE · FT. MYERS

First edition published in 1962 by Hill and Wang
Text of First Edition: copyright 1962, The Public Trustee as Executor of the Estate
of George Bernard Shaw; copyright 1990, The Trustees of the British Museum, The
Governors and Guardians of the National Gallery of Ireland and Royal Academy of
Dramatic Art.
Preface to *Immaturity:* copyright 1930, G. Bernard Shaw; copyright 1958, The Public
Trustee as Executor of the Estate of George Bernard Shaw.
Preface to *John Bull's Other Island:* copyright 1907, 1913, 1930, 1941, G. Bernard Shaw;
copyright 1957, The Public Trustee as Executor of the Estate of George Bernard Shaw.
Previously unpublished Bernard Shaw material: copyright 2001, The Trustees of the
British Museum, The Governors and Guardians of the National Gallery of Ireland and
Royal Academy of Dramatic Art.

Frontispiece: Photograph of Bernard Shaw, copyright 1904, by Frederick Evans.
Courtesy of the Laurence Collection, University of Guelph, Ontario, Canada.

Library of Congress Cataloging-in-Publication Data
Shaw, Bernard, 1856–1950.
The matter with Ireland / Bernard Shaw; edited by Dan H. Laurence and David H.
Greene—2nd ed., 1st University Press of Florida ed.
p. cm.—(The Florida Bernard Shaw series)
Includes index.
ISBN 0-8130-1886-2 (alk. paper)
1. Ireland—History. I. Laurence, Dan H. II. Greene, David H. (David Herbert), 1913– .
III. Title. IV. Series.
DA913 .S45 2001
941.50819—dc21   2001016182

The University Press of Florida is the scholarly publishing agency for the State
University System of Florida, comprising Florida A&M University, Florida Atlantic
University, Florida Gulf Coast University, Florida International University, Florida
State University, University of Central Florida, University of Florida, University of
North Florida, University of South Florida, and University of West Florida.

University Press of Florida
15 Northwest 15th Street
Gainesville, FL 32611–2079
http://www.upf.com

The Florida Bernard Shaw Series
Edited by R. F. Dietrich

This series is devoted to works of and about Shaw, Shaw's literary production, and Shavian topics of interest. While supportive of traditional approaches, the series also aims to encourage scholars with new critical paradigms to engage Shaw's works.

Pygmalion's Wordplay: The Postmodern Shaw, by Jean Reynolds (1999)
Shaw's Theater, by Bernard F. Dukore (2000)
Bernard Shaw and the French, by Michel W. Pharand (2000)
The Matter with Ireland, second edition, edited by Dan H. Laurence and David H. Greene (2001)

In Memory of
Sean O'Casey

One charge alone we give to youth,
Against the sceptered myth to hold
The golden heresy of truth.
—A.E., "On Behalf of Some Irishmen Not Followers of Tradition"

CONTENTS

FOREWORD

When Shaw had Professor Higgins say, "Making life means making trouble," he was simply applying to the world something he had said a few months earlier in a speech about Ireland, to be found in this volume of Shaw's essays on Ireland: "I do not want a peaceful Ireland. . . . I want a turbulent Ireland. All free and healthy nations are full of the turbulence of controversy, political, religious, social: all sorts of controversy. Without it you can have no progress, no life." But when Shaw suggested that certain Irish institutions needed to be exploded, he meant with words, not literal dynamite. The sort of trouble Shaw favored excluded the *literal* bullets and bombs of "the Troubles." And thus much more of Shaw's talk was devoted to trying to make peace in Ireland than to making trouble, however paradoxical and ironic that talk was. Some understood him, but many did not. Representing those who did was Senator W. B. Yeats, who, near the end of his long misunderstanding with Shaw, realized with some surprise that Shaw was one of the traditional types he admired, the type of the public-spirited statesman-poet, like Swift. In fact, you will find many ironic "modest proposals" in this collection. And paradoxes galore. Shaw pointed out, for instance, that if Ireland actually achieved independence from England and had to govern herself, it would mean that "her troubles are beginning, not ending."

The often complex ironies and paradoxes that Shaw brought to the "Irish question" made people wonder which side he was on. As usual, he didn't see things as usual. Such as his view that the "sides" were not as most thought they were. And he confused people with his journalistic tactic of "slanting both ways" and his orator's tactic of overstating the case to get people's attention. As he tried to balance out overstatements on one side of the Irish question with overstatements on the other side, this juggling act often left the literal-minded far behind.

On the one hand, one finds him confessing that, despite his expatriate status and internationalist perspective, "the mere geographical accident of my birth . . . this fact that I am an Irishman—has always filled me with a wild and inextinguishable pride." He pitied the poor English when they would have to do without Irish brains and talent to run the empire. And if anyone should warn that he as a Protestant was in danger of persecution from an independent Catholic Ireland, Shaw would reply, "I would rather be burnt at the stake by Irish Catholics than protected by Englishmen."

On the other hand, one finds him excoriating the Irish for not supporting England in its fight to the death with Germany in two world wars and ridiculing the "romantic nationalism" that sought to revive Gaelic and to retreat to an idealized past. Summing up his paradoxical view, he advised that if and when Ireland achieved its wholly independent parliament, it should at once freely join the British Commonwealth on an equal footing with other commonwealths and agitate for "Home Rule for England," England being the commonwealth most in need of home rule. The Irish might also give some thought to teaching the English how to speak English, a rapidly disappearing tongue in England but crucial to that world state—the commonwealth of nations—he hoped would replace the British Empire.

Despite the misunderstandings, there are small signs that the Irish may yet reclaim the "fatherlandless" Shaw, such as the fairly recent conversion of his boyhood "downstart" home into a museum, ironically now part of an upscale neighborhood. That the only major, long-standing theatre festival in the world devoted to Shaw is in Ontario, not in Ireland, more convincingly speaks to Ireland's neglect of him. If Shaw's repatriation *were* accomplished, it might signal that Ireland was at last becoming what Shaw always wanted it to become, a leading citizen of the world. But one suspects that, since he would really be at home only in a country that put the world before the nation, Shaw might have to wait a bit still for the country of his dreams to materialize. How long, O Lord?

Nevertheless, at this juncture of history, when the possibility of peace in Northern Ireland seems more promising than ever and may actually have been realized by the time this book is printed, it is salutary to look back on the ancient quarrel and note its lessons. The schoolmaster in Shaw was fond of pointing them out, as he saw them, and the introduction and annotations provided here by Dan H. Laurence and David H. Greene complement Shavian instruction so well that *The Matter with Ireland* serves as an excellent review of the subject. And should the promise *not* be realized, the reasons for that and the lessons of that will be found in this volume as well.

In anticipation of the better rather than the worse fate, this second edition of *The Matter with Ireland* is intended as a commemorative summation of one of the most important "matters" of modern times. It serves as well as an updating of the history, for much has happened since the 1962 first edition. And, revealing new dimensions in Shaw's relation to his native land, thirteen new essays have been added to fill in the picture. A surprising number of the essays are off the Irish question altogether, such as his promotion of Ireland as a land worth visiting and as capable of sustaining a film industry. He even entertained plans to establish an Irish film company himself. The Florida Bernard Shaw Series is grateful to Dan Laurence and David Greene for making this remarkable review possible.

And while we are on the subject of gratitude, it should be acknowledged that the Florida Bernard Shaw Series would not have been so well launched without the generosity of the David and Rachel Howie Foundation, which played an especially crucial part in the production of this book. We want the Howies to know how thankful we are for the booster rocket they have provided this series.

R. F. Dietrich
University of South Florida

INTRODUCTION

I

When he reached the age of ninety, Shaw was asked by an interviewer for an Irish newspaper to what extent he thought his mental makeup had been colored by the fact that he had been born in Ireland. He replied, "To the extent of making me a foreigner in every other country. But the position of a foreigner with complete command of the same language has great advantages. I can take an objective view of England, which no Englishman can. I could not take an objective view of Ireland."

The reader of this volume of writings—taken from the flood of articles, pamphlets, books, texts of speeches, and letters to the press which were Shaw's contribution to solving the Irish question—is likely to find that statement inaccurate on one count at least. During the period of more than fifty years in which these selections were written and in which Ireland was the scene of bitter political agitation, bloodshed, and civil war, not many Irishmen, whether participants in those events or merely commentators on them, showed as much objectivity as Shaw did.

Most of these pieces are, in effect, political journalism, occasioned by the urgency of the moment, inspired by the feelings that the moment provoked, and written under the hazards that implies. It is all the more remarkable, therefore, that Shaw, who believed he could not be objective on the subject of his native country, could be not only objective but temperate and wise in an atmosphere of rabid partisanship. The reader, knowing that very few of the books that made Shaw famous deal with Ireland, will also be surprised to learn how concerned he was about the problems of his native country and how much of his time and energies was devoted to studying and writing about them.

Shaw lived in Ireland for only twenty of his ninety-four years. But, as he once pointed out, the twenty came first and the mark they left upon him was indelible. Ireland, he wrote, was a country of easy living and easy dying, but he was unhappily ambitious. Dublin, he felt, offered him only poverty and obscurity, and since he could not conquer it he abandoned it.

It was a long time before he came back—twenty-nine years—and even then he admitted he returned only to please his wife, Charlotte. Whatever the motivation for his later visits might have been, they would seem to have occurred coincidentally with periods of intense political crisis. His last visit was in the summer of 1923, the year that saw the end of the Irish Civil War. After that, except for Eamon de Valera's insistence upon Irish neutrality during World War II, on which Shaw had a contrary opinion, he found little in Ireland to get excited about. One cannot help feeling that despite his repeated insistence upon the fact of his being Irish—"eternal is the fact that the human creature born in Ireland and brought up in its air is Irish"—we would have been less aware of it if Ireland itself had not attracted so much interest through its political problems, and if Dublin, the city Shaw abandoned because it offered nothing to an aspiring writer, had not become for a while the literary center of the English-speaking world.

Two years after Shaw left Dublin in 1876, Standish O'Grady published his *History of Ireland: The Bardic Period*, a book that has been described as the prelude to the literary movement known as the Irish Renaissance. If Shaw had stayed to witness the rediscovery of the Irish language and the resurgence of Gaelic nationalism, would he too have been swept up in the Irish literary revival? He once admitted the possibility: "If I had gone to the hills nearby to look back upon Dublin and to ponder upon myself, I too might have become a poet like Yeats, Synge, and the rest of them." But this is at best wistful conjecture. One doesn't become a different person merely by leaving home, and one cannot imagine a different Shaw from the one we have.

Shaw's fellow Dubliner James Joyce left Ireland at a similarly early age and for a similar reason, because it seemed to be the "center of paralysis." But unlike Shaw, who returned many times after that initial hiatus, Joyce returned only for two brief visits. And whereas Shaw considered his native country a fit setting for only one major play out of the many that he wrote—and that one was "commissioned" by Yeats for the Abbey Theatre—Joyce's entire body of creative work deals with nothing outside Ireland. If there is any conclusion to be drawn from this parallel it is that, whether an Irish writer leaves Ireland or stays there to dream on the hills, the material he uses for his art comes not from where he lives but where his thoughts are.

II

The Ireland that Shaw left in the 1870s had already taken the first important steps toward achieving effective political expression. In 1870 the Irish Home Rule Party was founded and would eventually weld the country's representatives at Westminster into a solid phalanx devoted to the securing of home rule for Ireland. In 1879 the Land League, an organization of tenants, was founded. Six years later the fruit of these two movements, both under the brilliant leadership of Charles Stewart Parnell, was the first of three Home Rule Bills. If it had not been defeated by a vote of 343 to 313, it would have given Ireland its own parliament and the management of most of its own affairs.

By the time the second Home Rule Bill was introduced seven years later, only to be defeated in the House of Lords, Parnell had been removed from power because of the scandal in his private life and was in his grave. An aging Gladstone was too tired to take the issue of Irish Home Rule to the country and retired from public office in 1894. With the two men who might yet have given Ireland its freedom out of the way and the Irish Home Rule Party no longer the force it had been at Westminster, the Irish question ceased to be an important issue in English politics.

The years following the Parnell scandal and the collapse of Ireland's hopes were years of bitterness and depression for the Irish. But it was out of this period of utter despondency that the energies of young Irishmen were turned to literature and the arts. "It was the death of Parnell," wrote W. B. Yeats, "that convinced me that the moment had come for work in Ireland, for I knew that for a time the imagination of young men would turn from politics." The Parnellite shock may not have been the only condition that produced "the miracle that raised a language from the dead" and gave us the literary revival, but it certainly contributed.

For twenty-six years after the death of Parnell the Irish Party continued to work for home rule, but the Irish people no longer hoped for anything from it, and the influence of the party waned steadily. There were other things that gave hope, like the Sinn Féin movement, which advocated abstention from Westminster, and the Gaelic League, at first merely a cultural movement but later a force for rebellion.

When the third Home Rule Bill was introduced by Prime Minister Herbert Henry Asquith's government in 1912, the ugly head of partition began to rear itself, and the whole issue became hopelessly complicated by the fact that Ireland itself was divided. When the bill was passed in 1914 and its operation suspended because of the First World War, a good many Irish people could not have cared less. In 1916 the Easter Rising, as dramatic as it was futile, finished the Irish Home Rule Party for good and emphasized the fact that Irishmen would no longer place their faith in parliamentary methods. In the next few years it became apparent that a large number of the people would settle for nothing short of an independent republic. What they actually got—in the treaty of 1921, which concluded the three-year period of assassination and reprisal known as the Anglo-Irish War—was the Irish Free State. In many ways it represented a more complete victory than Parnell had ever dreamed of, but it included only twenty-six of the thirty-two counties, and for the first time in its history Ireland was now two countries.

It soon developed that the Free State itself was divided, for when the terms of the treaty—specifically partition and the oath of allegiance to the king—proved to be unacceptable to Éamon de Valera and a large minority in Dáil Eireann, the assembly of the republic, Ireland was thrown into a civil war between Republicans and Free Staters. A year later the Republicans laid down their arms, de Valera found himself in an Irish jail for a change, and peace came permanently to a country distressed by the bloodshed it had witnessed and still far from happy with its new freedom. Arthur Griffith and Michael Collins, the two most important Free State leaders, were dead, the first from a heart attack brought on by Republican harassment, according to his personal physician, Oliver St. John Gogarty, and the second from Republican bullets in an ambush in County Cork.

With the separation of Northern Ireland and the Free State made final in 1925, the Irish question became one of gradually removing the few remaining ties that still bound the Free State to England. In 1927 de Valera and his Republicans agreed to take the distressful oath, affirming like Hippolytus that the tongue had sworn but not the heart, and took the seats in the Dáil to which they had been elected. In 1932 de Valera's party obtained a majority, and he became prime minister. Except for a brief period between 1948 and 1951, when his party failed to get a clear majority and John Costello became head of a coalition government, de Valera remained in power until his retirement from politics to the presidency in 1959.[1]

In 1937 a new constitution, approved by the Dáil and enacted by means of a plebiscite, did away with the name Free State and replaced it with the ancient name of Eire. A year later an agreement was reached enabling Ireland to make a final payment in commutation of the land annuities made necessary by various land acts. England in turn agreed to relinquish its rights to naval bases and airfields in Ireland, a decision England had reason to regret when war came and Ireland insisted upon remaining neutral.

The last constitutional links between Ireland and England were severed in 1949, when the government of John Costello declared Ireland a republic. But the step had been taken only after the Irish prime minister had assured the English prime minister that no ill will was intended toward the Crown or the Commonwealth. The English prime minister then assured the Irish prime minister that England would continue to consider the citizens of the new republic as English citizens also. To political scientists the final act of the seven-hundred-year-old drama may have seemed rich in ambiguities, but to laymen it must have seemed more like comic opera.

Shaw celebrated the new Republic of Ireland on his ninety-fourth birthday by writing a sprightly letter to *The Times*, London, hailing the appointment of the first Irish ambassador to the Court of St. James. It was his last public utterance on the subject of Ireland. But the Republic embraced only twenty-six counties. The king's writ continued to run in six counties somewhat inexactly described as Ulster—the traditional Ulster consisted of nine counties—and as Northern Ireland, although Donegal is farther north than any of the "northern" counties. In 1973 the regional parliament of Northern Ireland at Stormont was dissolved, and the six counties came completely under direct rule from Westminster.

1. The president of Ireland has some limited powers but as head of state is required to be nonpolitical.

III

The fifty-year period since Shaw's death has brought a wave of prosperity to the Irish Republic, which has been described as having the fastest growing economy in western Europe. Most of this boom undoubtedly is the result of its membership in the European Community. But in the same period the traditional enmity between Protestant Unionist or Loyalist— the terms are virtually interchangeable—and Catholic Nationalist continued to exist in the north of Ireland, with considerable bloodshed on both sides. Since 1966 more than 3,500 men, women, and children have died violent deaths by bombs or bullets, the body count not significantly favoring either side.

The cease-fire, which was declared in 1994, revoked in 1996, and reinstated in 1997, took soldiers off the streets and brought people out of their houses. But peace continued to be elusive despite the efforts of the British prime minister, the president of the United States, and a respected American senator.

One of the ironies of the Northern Ireland problem was that when each of the leaders of the two largest adversarial parties—John Hume of the Socialist Democratic Labor Party (SDLP) and David Trimble of the Ulster Unionist Party (UUP)—was awarded a Nobel Prize in 1998, with the hopeful expectation, one assumes, that the international recognition would encourage them to resolve their differences of opinion and reach a final agreement for peace, Mr. Hume's prize was welcomed by his fellow Nationalists. However, many Unionists looked on Mr. Trimble's prize as a bribe to make him more susceptible to accepting proposals they would consider a betrayal of the Protestant cause. The pressure they were able to exert on him apparently forced Mr. Trimble to take a more unyielding position than he had before, which probably explains his sudden and unexpected insistence that the IRA surrender its arms before its political representatives in Sinn Féin would be allowed to participate in the new government. Gerry Adams, leader of Sinn Féin, responded by arguing that an agreement was an agreement and that although the agreement exhorted the parties to work toward a decommissioning by May 2000, it did not require decommissioning as a necessary condition for the elected members of Sinn Féin taking their places in the cabinet. Accepting such a condition could open the way to more such conditions.

The document that is the basis for the present agreement and that was accepted by both UUP and Sinn Féin is known as the Good Friday Agreement (1998). Its proposals were submitted to public referendum on both sides of the border in May 1998 and received overwhelming endorsement from the people, with 94.4 percent of the vote in the Republic of Ireland and 71.1 percent in Northern Ireland in favor. The referendum called for the establishment of a government for Northern Ireland based upon the principle of power sharing between Protestant and Catholic with a 108-member Assembly similar to the regional parliaments granted not long before to Scotland and Wales under Prime Minister Tony Blair's policy of devolution. The government would have a ten-member executive made up of Protestants and Catholics, a first minister and his deputy —one Protestant and one Catholic—with the direct involvement of the Irish Republic through a number of north-south councils of ministers to deal with cross-border concerns. It was agreed that prisoners serving terms for sectarian crimes would be released (this measure has now been implemented) and that the Royal Irish Constabulary, which is almost completely Protestant and has been widely discredited among Catholics, would recruit more Catholics and work toward the day when it would be unarmed like the police in other parts of the United Kingdom and in the Republic of Ireland.

Much has been done to create the new government. Members of the Assembly and executive were elected, with David Trimble (UUP) first minister and Seamus Mallon (SDLP) deputy minister. In the last week of November 1999, the UUP dropped its demand that the IRA disarm before being permitted to participate in the new government. The IRA on its part agreed to join the independent commission set up by the Good Friday Agreement to determine how disarmament would be carried out. As a result of the compromises by both sides, Westminister speedily passed the necessary legislation and on 2 December 1999 relinquished the direct control it had exercised over Northern Ireland for more than a quarter of a century. The new government came into existence and held its first meetings. Then David Trimble suddenly threw up a second roadblock by announcing that if the IRA had not made substantial progress toward total disarmament by February, he and his colleagues would resign from their positions of leadership and shut down the government.

Sinn Féin's response to this unexpected ultimatum was to argue that disarmament should not be thus forced and that in any case Sinn Féin did not have the power to order the IRA to disarm under such circumstances.

IV

Before Trimble and his colleagues would have had to follow through on their threat to resign, the secretary of state for Northern Ireland announced on 11 February 2000 that Westminster would resume the direct rule of Northern Ireland. The government of Northern Ireland had lasted just ten weeks. But when, on 25 March 2000, Trimble held off a strong challenge to his leadership of the UUP from Martin Smyth, former grand master of the Orange Order, by 57 percent of the votes of the Party Council, the British government decided to make another attempt at self-rule for Northern Ireland. On 5 June the Northern Ireland Assembly met for the first time since the suspension of home rule in February. The meeting, which was televised and shown on almost all continents, featured a lengthy debate on the question of whether the Union Jack or the Irish Tricolor—or both—should fly over government buildings.

Despite all the bitterness that had scuttled so many other agreements and proposals of the past thirty years—Sunningdale (1973), the Anglo-Irish Agreement (1985), the Downing Street Declaration (1993), the Framework Document (1995), and the Good Friday Agreement (1998)—and despite continued incidents of violence, the worst of which killed twenty-nine people in a bombing in County Tyrone by a group calling themselves the "Real IRA," the cease-fire between the main former combatants still holds.

Such is the road Ireland travelled from Home Rule to the Good Friday Agreement. If Shaw had lived through the past fifty years, he would undoubtedly have given as much guidance and advice to his countrymen as he had given them during the previous fifty years. His countrymen did not listen to him much of the time, but that is of the nature of things. Outside his country, the prophet was not without an audience, undoubtedly a larger one than any other Irishman of the day could command. That audience listened to what he had to say about virtually every important question in Ireland's political and social life. His protests against injustice were frequently futile, his solutions sometimes impractical, and his prophecies occasionally quaint, but he was never irrelevant or uninteresting, and the record will show that if he was not always right, neither was anyone else.

He defended home rule, but not just for Ireland, for he believed that Scotland and Wales also had a right to their own parliaments—something that has now happened. He renounced nationalism per se and ridiculed the nationalist myth that the Irish were God's chosen people and the English were monsters. While acknowledging his own alliance with Protestant Ireland, he preferred the claims of Roman Catholic Ireland and preached against intolerance, bigotry, and class warfare. He thought partition was evil but believed—wrongly, as it has so far turned out—that economic forces would be the death of it. He had little sympathy for the artificial resuscitation of the Irish language and was fond of saying that he could not speak Irish *because* he was an Irishman. He was, however, not the only Irishman of his day to hold such a view; he was proved right when the Irish government discontinued the program of Compulsory Irish, which it had never more than halfheartedly supported, and in 1973 announced that knowledge of Irish would no longer be required for graduation from high school or for employment in the civil service.

He was unhappy, as Yeats was, about Irish literary censorship—fortunately for Irish writers today a thing of the past—although his objections were directed not to the restrictions against imaginative literature so much as to books on birth control. When Ireland preferred to remain neutral in World War II, Shaw believed the nation was misguided, though within its rights, to remain so. Finally, he was eloquent in defending individual Irishmen of courage and good conscience, whether it was Parnell dethroned because of adultery, the Dublin strikers of 1913 locked out by management, the leaders of the Easter Rebellion condemned to be shot for their heroism, Sir Roger Casement condemned to be hanged for high treason, or Michael Collins killed by his own countrymen.

Ireland has not always honored or even listened to its greatest writers. But in this Ireland is not alone among nations—only more noticeable because its writers are so famous. And one is tempted to ask, as Shaw did when the English insisted that their presence in Ireland was necessary to keep the Irish from cutting one another's throats, Who has a better right to cut them? (Shaw's version of "Brits Out.") Though Ireland did not always listen to Shaw, he rarely stopped listening to Ireland. What he heard and saw sometimes exasperated and frequently amused him, but his criticism was always constructive and his laughter always kind. As Yeats had once written to him in regard to *John Bull's Other Island*: "You have laughed at the things that are ripe for laughter, and not where the ear is still green."

David H. Greene
Dan H. Laurence
September 2000

EDITORS' NOTE

In the present work, which complements Shaw's Standard Edition (1931–51), the editors have sought to follow Shaw's dicta in regard to spelling, punctuation, and the omission of accents within his texts, as well as in matters of general style and design. Except for the correction of obvious misprints and of minor errors of grammar in verbatim reports of speeches not submitted to Shaw for his approval before their original publication, the texts are faithfully reproduced, with editorial emendations inserted in square brackets. House style is deferred to in the foreword, introduction, headnotes, footnotes, and index.

The extracts from the prefaces to *Immaturity* (London: Constable, 1930; New York: William H. Wise, 1930) and *John Bull's Other Island* (London: Constable, 1907; New York: Brentano, 1907)—the only materials that have previously appeared among Shaw's collected writings—have been included in this volume to provide a more fully rounded picture of Shaw's background and his attitude toward Ireland and are reprinted with the kind permission of the Estate of George Bernard Shaw and the Society of Authors.

The unsigned writings in *The Star* and *The Pall Mall Gazette* were identified from Shaw's diaries and those in *The New Statesman* from marked files of that journal, confirmed by Shaw's unpublished correspondence.

Although in the preparation of this book the work was initially divided between us—Professor Greene's principal responsibility being to provide the Irish historical materials embodied in the introduction and the footnotes, while Professor Laurence identified and collected the texts and provided the Shavian biographical data—the final work is a collaboration for which we take joint responsibility.

As in the first edition, we would like to acknowledge those individuals, living or deceased, who assisted us in preparing this book: Blanche Patch, T. J. Brown, Frank Singleton, librarian of *The Guardian*, Stanley Pryor, librarian of *The Star* and *News Chronicle*, Owen Edwards, Felix F. Strauss, Owen Sheehy Skeffington, Mrs. W. B. Yeats, S. Geduld, Sir Rupert

Hart-Davis (our original publisher), and the staffs of the National Library of Ireland and the British Newspaper Library, Colindale.

For invaluable aid in the preparation of the new edition we extend our thanks to include Nicholas Grene, Maureen Halligan and her Irish tribe (Josie MacAvin, Sunniva Sheridan, Ann Simmons, and Michele Whelan), Alice Kersnowski, Daniel J. Leary, and Craig S. Likness, Assistant Director for Public Services, and the reference staff of the Coates Library, Trinity University, San Antonio.

D.H.L.
D.H.G.

The Matter with Ireland

PREFACE: FRAGMENTS OF
AUTOBIOGRAPHY

I

From the preface, written in 1921, to Shaw's first novel, *Immaturity*, written in 1879 and first published in 1930

The Shaws were younger sons from the beginning, as I shall shew when I reveal my full pedigree. Even the baronetcy was founded on the fortunes of a fifth son who came to Dublin and made that city his oyster. Let who will preen himself on his Mother Hubbard's bare cupboard, and play for sympathy as an upstart: I was a downstart and the son of a downstart. But for the accident of a lucrative talent I should today be poorer than Spinoza; for he at least knew how to grind lenses, whereas I could not afford to learn any art. Luckily, nature taught me one.

The social *dégringolade* never stops in these islands. It produces a class which deserves a history all to itself. Do not talk of the middle class: the expression is meaningless except when it is used by an economist to denote the man of business who stands in the middle between land and capital on the one hand, and labor on the other, and organizes business for both. I sing my own class: the Shabby Genteel, the Poor Relations, the Gentlemen who are No Gentlemen. If you want to know exactly where I came in, you will get at such facts as that of my many uncles only one, the eldest, contrived to snatch a university education. The rest shifted as best they could without it (rather better than he, mostly). One distinguished himself as a civil servant. He had a gun, and went shooting. One made a fortune in business, and attained to carriage horses; but he lost the fortune in a premature attempt to develop the mineral resources of Ireland without waiting for the new railways produced by the late war. Two emigrated to Tasmania, and like Mr Micawber, made history there. One was blind and dependent on his brothers: another became blind later, but remained independent and capable. One aunt married the rector of St Bride's (now demolished) in Dublin. The others married quite prosperously, except the eldest, whose conception of the family dignity was so prodigious (the family snobbery being unmitigated in her case by the family sense of humor) that she would have refused an earl because he was not a duke, and so died a very ancient virgin. Dead or alive, there were fourteen of them; and they all, except perhaps the eldest, must have had a very straitened time of it in their childhood after their father died, leaving my grandmother to bring up an unconscionable lot of children on very inadequate means. The baronet came to the rescue by giving her a quaint cottage, with Gothically pointed windows, to live in at Terenure (we called the place Roundtown). It stands in, or rather creeps picturesquely along, its little walled garden near the tram terminus to this day, though my grandfather's brass helmet and sword (he was in the Yeomanry or Militia as a gentleman amateur soldier) no longer hang in the hall. Professionally, he was some sort of combination of solicitor, notary public, and stockbroker that prevailed at that time. I suspect that his orphans did not always get enough to eat; for the younger ones, though invincibly healthy and long-lived, were not athletic, and exhibited such a remarkable collection of squints (my father had a stupendous squint) that to this day a squint is so familiar to me that I notice it no more than a pair of spectacles or even a pair of boots.

On the whole, they held their cherished respectability in the world in spite of their lack of opportunity. They owed something, perhaps, to the confidence given them by their sense of family. In Irish fashion they talked of themselves as the Shaws, as who should say the Valois, the Bourbons, the Hohenzollerns, the Hapsburgs, or the Romanoffs, and their world conceded the point to them. I had an enormous contempt for this family snobbery, as I called it, until I was completely reconciled to it by a certain Mr Alexander Mackintosh Shaw, a clansman who, instead of taking his pedigree for granted in the usual Shaw manner, hunted it up, and published one hundred copies privately in 1877. Somebody sent me a copy, and my gratification was unbounded when I read the first sentence of the first chapter, which ran: "It is the general tradition, says the Rev Lachlan Shaw [bless him!], that the Shaws are descended of McDuff, Earl of Fife." I hastily skipped to the chapter about the Irish Shaws to make sure that they were my people; and there they were, baronet and all, duly traced to the third son of that immortalized yet unborn Thane of Fife who, invulnerable to normally accouched swordsmen, laid on and slew

Macbeth. It was as good as being descended from Shakespear, whom I had been unconsciously resolved to reincarnate from my cradle.

Years after this discovery I was staying on the shores of Loch Fyne, and being cooked for and housekept by a lady named McFarlane, who treated me with a consideration which I at first supposed to be due to my eminence as an author. But she undeceived me one day by telling me that the McFarlanes and the Shaws were descended from the Thanes of Fife, and that I must not make myself too cheap. She added that the McFarlanes were the elder branch.

My uncles did not trouble about Macduff: it was enough for them that they were Shaws. They had an impression that the Government should give them employment, preferably sinecure, if nothing else could be found; and I suppose this was why my father, after essaying a clerkship or two (one of them in an ironworks), at last had his position recognized by a post in the Four Courts, perhaps because his sister had married the brother of a law baron. Anyhow, the office he held was so undeniably superfluous that it actually got abolished before I was born, and my father naturally demanded a pension as compensation for the outrage. Having got it, he promptly sold it, and set up in business as a merchant dealing wholesale (the family dignity made retail business impossible) in flour and its cereal concomitants. He had an office and warehouse in Jervis-street in the city, and he had a mill in Dolphin's Barn on the country side of the canal, at the end of a rather pretty little village street called Rutland-avenue. The mill has now fallen to pieces, but some relics of it are still to be seen from the field with the millpond behind Rutland House at the end of the avenue, with its two stone eagles on the gateposts. My father used to take me sometimes to this mill before breakfast (a long walk for a child), and I used to like playing about it. I do not think it had any other real use, for it never paid its way; and the bulk of my father's business was commissioned: he was a middleman. I should mention that as he knew nothing about the flour business, and as his partner, a Mr [George] Clibborn, having been apprenticed to the cloth trade, knew if possible less, the business, purchased readymade, must have proceeded by its own momentum, and produced its results, such as they were, automatically in spite of its proprietors. They did not work the industry: it worked them. It kept alive, but did not flourish. Early in its history the bankruptcy of one of its customers dealt it such a blow that my father's partner broke down in tears, though he was fortified by a marriage with a woman of property, and could afford to regard his business as only a second string to his bow. My father, albeit ruined, found the magnitude of the catastrophe so irresistibly amusing that he had to retreat hastily from the office to an empty corner of the warehouse, and laugh until he was exhausted. The business struggled on and even supported my father until he died, enabling him to help his family a little after they had solved a desperate financial situation by emigrating to London: or, to put it in another way, by deserting him. His last years were soothed and disembarrassed by this step. He never, as far as I know, made the slightest movement towards a reunion, and none of us ever dreamt of there being any unkindness in the arrangement. In our family we did not bother about conventionalities or sentimentalities.

Our ridiculous poverty was too common in our class, and not conspicuous enough in a poor country, to account wholly for our social detachment from my father's family, a large and (for Ireland) not unprosperous one. In early days the baronet, being a bachelor, was clannishly accessible: he entertained even his second cousins at Bushy Park, and was specially attentive to my mother. I was never at Bushy Park myself except once, on the occasion of his funeral (the Shaw funerals were prodigies of black pomp); but if my father had been able to turn his social opportunities to account, I might have had a quite respectable and normal social training. My mother, socially very eligible, was made welcome in all directions. She sang very well, and the Shaws were naturally a musical family. All the women could "pick out tunes" on the piano, and support them with the chords of the tonic, subdominant, dominant, and tonic again. Even a Neapolitan sixth was not beyond them. My father played the trombone, and could vamp a bass on it to any tune that did not modulate too distractingly. My eldest uncle (Barney: I suppose I was called Bernard after him, but he himself was Uncle William) played the ophicleide, a giant keyed brass bugle, now superseded by the tuba. Berlioz has described it as a chromatic bullock, but my uncle could make it moo and bellow very melodiously. My aunt Emily played the violoncello. Aunt Shah (Charlotte), having beautiful hands, and refinements of person and character to match them, used the harp and tambourine to display them.

Modern readers will laugh at the picture of an evening at Bushy Park, with the bachelor Sir Robert and his clan seated round an ottoman on which my uncle Barney stood, solemnly playing Annie Laurie on the ophicleide. The present distinguished inheritor of the title may well find it incredible. But in those days it was the fashion for guests to provide their own music and gentlemen to play wind instruments as a social accomplishment: indeed that age of brass is still remembered and regretted by the few makers of musical instruments whose traditions go back far enough.

And now you will ask why, with such unexceptional antecedents and social openings, was I not respectably brought up? Unfortunately or fortunately (it all depends on how you look at it), my father had a habit which eventually closed all doors to him, and consequently to my mother, who could not very well be invited without him. If you asked him to dinner or to a party, he was not always quite sober when he arrived; and he was invariably scandalously drunk when he left. Now, a convivial drunkard may be exhilarating in convivial company. Even a quarrelsome or boastful drunkard may be found entertaining by people who are not particular. But a miserable drunkard—and my father, in theory a teetotaler, was racked with shame and remorse even in his cups—is unbearable. We were finally dropped socially. After my early childhood I cannot remember ever paying a visit at a relative's house. If my mother and father had dined out, or gone to a party, their children would have been much more astonished than if the house had caught fire.

How my mother rescued herself from this predicament by her musical talent I will tell elsewhere.[1] My father reduced his teetotalism from theory to practice when a mild fit, which felled him on our doorstep one Sunday afternoon, convinced him that he must stop drinking or perish. It had no worse effect, but his reform, though complete and permanent, came too late to save the social situation; and I, cut off from the social drill which puts one at one's ease in private society, grew up frightfully shy and utterly ignorant of social routine. My mother, who had been as carefully brought up as Queen Victoria, was too humane to inflict what she had suffered on any child; besides, I think she imagined that correct behavior

---

1. See preface to *London Music in 1888–89* (London, 1937).

is inborn, and that much of what she had been taught was natural to her. Anyhow, she never taught it to us, leaving us wholly to the promptings of our blood's blueness, with results which may be imagined.

⤞ ⤝

However that may be, I decided, at thirteen or thereabouts, that for the moment I must go into business and earn some money and begin to be a grown-up man. There was at that time, on one of the quays in Dublin, a firm of cloth merchants, by name Scott, Spain, and Rooney. A friend of ours knew Scott, and asked him to give me a start in life with some employment. I called on this gentleman by appointment. I had the vaguest notion of what would happen: all I knew was that I was "going into an office." I thought I should have preferred to interview Spain, as the name was more romantic. Scott turned out to be a smart handsome man, with moustachios; and I suppose a boy more or less in his warehouse did not matter to him when there was a friend to be obliged: at all events, he said only a few perfunctory things and was settling my employment, when, as my stars would have it, Rooney appeared. Mr Rooney was much older, not at all smart, but long, lean, grave, and respectable.

The last time I saw the late Sir George Alexander (the actor) he described to me his own boyhood, spent in a cloth warehouse in Cheapside, where they loaded him with bales, and praised him highly for his excellent conduct, even rewarding him after some years to the extent of sixteen shillings a week. Rooney saved me from the bales. He talked to me a little, and then said quite decisively that I was too young, and that the work was not suitable to me. He evidently considered that my introducer, my parents, and his young partner had been inconsiderate; and I presently descended the stairs, reprieved and unemployed. As Mr Rooney was certainly fifty then at least, he must be a centenarian if, as I hope, he still lives. If he does, then I offer him the assurance that I have not forgotten his sympathy.

A year later, or thereabouts, my uncle Frederick, an important official in the Valuation Office, whom no land agent or family solicitor in London could afford to disoblige, asked a leading and terribly respectable firm of land agents, carrying on business at 15 Molesworth-street, to find a berth for me. They did so; and I became their office boy (junior clerk I called myself) at eighteen shillings a month. It was a very good opening for anyone with a future as a land agent, which in Ireland at that time was a business of professional rank. It was utterly thrown away on me. However, as the office was overstaffed with gentlemen apprentices, who had paid large fees for the privilege of singing operatic selections with me when the principals were out, there was nothing to complain of socially, even for a Shaw; and the atmosphere was as uncommercial as that of an office can be. Thus I learnt business habits without being infected with the business spirit. By the time I had attained to thirty shillings a month, the most active and responsible official in the office, the cashier, vanished; and as we were private bankers to some extent, our clients drawing cheques on us and so forth, someone had to take his place without an hour's delay. An elder substitute grumbled at the strange job, and, though an able man in his way, could not make his cash balance. It became necessary, after a day or two of confusion, to try the office boy as a stopgap whilst the advertisements for a new cashier of appropriate age and responsibility were going forward. Immediately the machine worked again quite smoothly. I, who never knew how much money I had of my own (except when the figure was zero), proved a model of accuracy as to the money of others. I acquired my predecessor's very neat handwriting, my own being too sloped and straggly for the cash book. The efforts to fill my important place more worthily slackened. I bought a tailed coat, and was chaffed about it by the apprentices. My salary was raised to £48 a year, which was as much as I expected at sixteen and much less than the firm would have had to pay to a competent adult: in short, I made good in spite of myself, and found, to my dismay, that Business, instead of expelling me as the worthless impostor I was, was fastening upon me with no intention of letting me go.

Behold me therefore in my twentieth year, with a business training, in an occupation which I detested as cordially as any sane person lets himself detest anything he cannot escape from. In March 1876 I broke loose. I gave a month's notice. My employers naturally thought I was discontented with my salary (£84 I think, by that time), and explained to me quietly that they hoped to make my position more eligible. My only fear was that they should make it so eligible that all excuse for throwing it up would be taken from me. I thanked them and said I was resolved to go; and I had, of course, no reason in the world to give them for my resolution. They were a little hurt, and explained to my uncle that they had done their best, but that I seemed to have made up my mind. I had. After enjoying for a few days the luxury of not having to go to the office, and being, if not my own master, at least not anyone else's slave, I packed a carpet bag, boarded the North Wall boat, and left the train next morning at Euston, where on hearing a porter cry, in an accent quite strange to me (I had hardly ever heard an *h* dropped before) "Ensm, faw weel?" which I rightly interpreted as "Hansom or four wheel?" I was afraid to say hansom, because I had never been in one and was not sure that I should know how to get in. So I solemnly drove in a growler through streets whose names Dickens had made familiar to me, London being at its spring best, which is its very best, to Victoria Grove, where the driver accepted four shillings as a reasonable fare for the journey.

I did not set foot in Ireland again until 1905, and not then on my own initiative. I went back to please my wife; and a curious reluctance to retrace my steps made me land in the south and enter Dublin through the back door from Meath rather than return as I came, through the front door on the sea. In 1876 I had had enough of Dublin. James Joyce in his Ulysses has described, with a fidelity so ruthless that the book is hardly bearable, the life that Dublin offers to its young men, or, if you prefer to put it the other way, that its young men offer to Dublin. No doubt it is much like the life of young men everywhere in modern urban civilization. A certain flippant futile derision and belittlement that confuses the noble and serious with the base and ludicrous seems to me peculiar to Dublin, but I suppose that is because my only personal experience of that phase of youth was a Dublin experience; for when I left my native city I left that phase behind me, and associated no more with men of my age, until, after about eight years of solitude in this respect, I was drawn into the Socialist revival of the early eighties, among Englishmen intensely serious and burning with indignation at very real and very fundamental evils that affected all the world; so that the reaction against them bound the finer spirits of all the nations together instead of making them cherish hatred of oneanother as a national virtue. Thus, when I left Dublin I left (a few private friendships apart) no society that did not disgust me. To this day my sentimental regard for Ireland does not include the capital. I am not enamored of failure, of poverty, of obscurity, and of the ostracism and contempt which these imply; and these were all that Dublin offered to the enormity of my unconscious ambition. The cities a man likes are the cities he has conquered. Napoleon did not turn from Paris to sentimentalize over Ajaccio, nor Catherine from St Petersburg to Stettin as the centre of her universe.

On this question of ambition let me say a word. In the ordinary connotation of the word I am the least ambitious of men. I have said, and I confirm it here, that I am so poor a hand at pushing and struggling, and so little interested in their rewards, that I have risen by sheer gravitation, too industrious by acquired habit to stop working (I work as my father drank), and too lazy and timid by nature to lay hold of half the opportunities or a tenth of the money that a conventionally ambitious man would have grasped strenuously. I never thought of myself as destined to become what is called a great man: indeed I was diffident to the most distressing degree; and I was ridiculously credulous as to the claims of others to superior knowledge and authority. But one day in the office I had a shock. One of the apprentices, by name C. J. Smyth, older than I and more a man of the world, remarked that every young chap thought he was going to be a great man. On a really modest youth this commonplace would have had no effect. It gave me so perceptible a jar that I suddenly became aware that I had never thought I was to be a great man simply because I had always taken it as a matter of course. The incident passed without leaving any preoccupation with it to hamper me; and I remained as diffident as ever because I was still as incompetent as ever. But I doubt whether I ever recovered my former complete innocence of subconscious intention to devote myself to the class of work that only a few men excel in, and to accept the responsibilities that attach to its dignity.

Now this bore directly on my abandonment of Dublin, for which many young Irishmen of today find it impossible to forgive me. My business in life could not be transacted in Dublin out of an experience confined to Ireland. I had to go to London just as my father had to go to the Corn Exchange. London was the literary centre for the English language, and for such artistic culture as the realm of the English language (in which I proposed to be king) could afford. There was no Gaelic League[2] in those

2. An organization founded in Dublin in 1893 by Douglas Hyde and others for the purpose of preserving the Gaelic language and literature of Ireland. The League encouraged the study of Gaelic by sponsoring classes of instruction in that language and, at the same time, attempted to eradicate illiteracy among native Gaelic speakers.

days, nor any sense that Ireland had in herself the seed of culture. Every Irishman who felt that his business in life was on the higher planes of the cultural professions felt that he must have a metropolitan domicile and an international culture: that is, he felt that his first business was to get out of Ireland. I had the same feeling. For London as London, or England as England, I cared nothing. If my subject had been science or music I should have made for Berlin or Leipsic. If painting, I should have made for Paris: indeed, many of the Irish writers who have made a name in literature escaped to Paris with the intention of becoming painters. For theology I should have gone to Rome, and for Protestant philosophy to Weimar. But as the English language was my weapon, there was nothing for it but London. In 1914 the Germans, resenting my description of their Imperial political situation as Potsdamnation, denounced me as a father-landless fellow. They were quite right. I was no more offended than if they had called me unparochial. They had never reproached me for making pilgrimages to Bayreuth when I could as easily have made them to the Hill of Tara. If you want to make me homesick, remind me of the Thuringian Fichtelgebirge, of the broad fields and delicate airs of France, of the Gorges of the Tarn, of the Passes of the Tyrol, of the North African desert, of the Golden Horn, of the Swedish lakes, or even the Norwegian fiords where I have never been except in my imagination, and you may stir that craving in me as easily—probably more easily—as in any exiled native of these places. It was not until I went back to Ireland as a tourist that I perceived that the charm of my country was quite independent of the accident of my having been born in it, and that it could fascinate a Spaniard or an Englishman more powerfully than an Irishman, in whose feeling for it there must always be a strange anguish, because it is the country where he has been unhappy and where vulgarity is vulgar to him. And so I am a tolerably good European in the Nietzschean sense, but a very bad Irishman in the Sinn Fein[3] or Chosen People sense.

3. Irish, meaning "We Ourselves." The name of the Irish nationalist movement in the period between 1900 and 1922. Today it is the name of a political party identified with the IRA and led by Gerry Adams.

II

The Evening Post, Bristol, 3 December 1946

In my boyhood in the 1860s there were two theatres in Dublin. The Royal, in Hawkins-street, was notably spacious, lofty, beautifully proportioned, and in every architectural way worthy of the arts which were its home. There were four circles: the five-shilling dress circle of courtly splendor, the three-and-sixpenny undress for genteel persons in everyday attire, the eighteenpenny middle gallery for the lower middle class, but frequented by respectable but impecunious ladies who could not afford the circles nor appear in the pit, and the sixpenny top gallery or "gods" for the riffraff.

Stalls not having then been invented, the pit, furnished with hard wood forms, ran right up to the orchestra. Women were not seen there. Admission was two shillings except during the opera season when it was four shillings, and the "gods" sat in their shirt sleeves and tried to keep up a musical entertainment of their own between the acts, mostly very unsuccessfully. I used to come out of the opera-pit crush with all my front buttons down the middle of my back; but I got a front seat at that price. Queues were undreamt of.

The acting was provided by stars on tour who were supported by the stock company, and used the old stock scenery with its wings and flats and drop scenes which were changed in full view of the audience. The old stock scenery was bearable because it dated from the days of Telbin, Stanfield, and de Loutherbourg.

One in particular, with Big Ben as its centre, was quite cosmopolitan and served for all places and periods, figuring impartially as a street in modern London, in Don Giovanni, and in Richard III. What was really intolerable was the stock company. One got tired of them with their one-step dance, one combat (sixes), and their invariable treatment of every part in every play; for each of them had his "line" and, having a new part to swallow every week or so, had no time for studying anything beyond his cues.

The notion that they all became versatile is the wildest of delusions. Versatility was the much-needed quality of which they became quite incapable. There was the leading juvenile and the walking gentleman, the heavy (for villains), the first and second low comedians, and fathers, noble and vulgar, with their feminine counterparts the leading lady, the singing chambermaid, the heavy, the first and second old women, &c. &c. A few of them were favorites, especially the comedians Mrs Huntley and Sam Johnson; and there was one first-rate actor, Peter Granby, whose Kent in King Lear I have never seen approached, nor his Polonius surpassed; but on the whole and in the lump, every trick of the stock lines, every gesture, every tone became so familiar that they could not produce any illusion; and when the new touring London companies with their modern drawing-room sceneries began to arrive, the change was an enormous relief and the stock company perished, unwept, unhonored, and unsung.

The highlights of the season were the Christmas pantomime, the Opera with the pit at four shillings and the titanic unqueued struggle to get in, and the visits of Barry Sullivan, a very great Shakespearean star actor, who always played to full houses, and preferred making £300 a week in the provinces and leaving £100,000 at his death, to playing in London for thirty years as Irving did and having to take to the road penniless at the end.

There was one other theatre, the Queen's in Brunswick-street (it may be there still); but respectable people did not then frequent it, as it served not only as a theatre for crude melodrama but as a market for ladies who lived by selling themselves, and who flaunted their profession in Dublin to a degree that astonished all travelers.

Suddenly all this was upset by a certain Michael Gunn, who kept a music shop at 61 Grafton-street: a handsome man with a tall consumptive brother John. The two built a new theatre in King-street that was as unlike the old Royal as any theatre could well be. The Royal, with its carriage yard, was built as if land could be had in Hawkins-street for a penny an acre. The new theatre, the Gaiety, was built so as to cram into the space it occupied the utmost possible number of saleable seats. It had stalls. It had next to no boxes: rows of cushioned seats took their places.

To compare the new theatre with the old was like comparing a bandbox with the Parthenon. But it held more money per square foot of ground than the classical Royal, and it was decidedly more comfortable. For half a century after, until Herbert Tree ordered the rebuilding of Her Majesty's Theatre in London as His Majesty's, every new theatre built in

Britain was a bandbox theatre like the Gaiety; and [C. J.] Phipps was the master theatre architect of the day.

The Gaiety had no stock company, although one remembers as a very frequent performer there Edward Royce, irresistible supernumerary funny man and a wonderful dancer, the only perfect harlequin I have ever seen. I made my first acquaintance with Gilbert and Sullivan at the Gaiety in Trial by Jury, and remember very well how astonishingly "churchy" Sullivan's music sounded after Offenbach.

The bandbox theatres will never be the People's theatres. They belong to a passing epoch, though they will still have their uses. The next step forward in Dublin will be the municipal theatre, larger than the old Royal and much more comfortable, spacious, and splendid, and holding enough people to pay its way with prices from threepence or sixpence to half a crown, with perhaps one evening and one matinée reserved every week at prices from half a crown to half a guinea for people who travel first class and will not travel at all unless there are first-class carriages or Rolls-Royce cars available.

It is folly to call the Abbey shelter a National Theatre: it has a heroic history; but it never was a theatre and never will be. Compared to the National Library and the National Gallery it is an insult to dramatic art. I look forward to the day when a municipal theatre will be as much a matter of course in every Irish city as a town hall is now.

THE MAKING OF THE IRISH NATION

Unsigned review of J. A. Partridge's *The Making of the Irish Nation.*
The Pall Mall Gazette, London, 16 September 1886

A calm, orderly, and impartial review of the Irish question being at this moment impossible, a spirited plea for Home Rule[1] by an excited but competent advocate is perhaps the next most instructive document available. This Mr Partridge gives us in a volume in which the cover—more than three-fourths green and less than one-fourth orange—indicates the bias of its contents. In point of arrangement and literary finish his work bears marks of premature delivery, for which Mr Fisher Unwin, the publisher, is probably responsible. History, having broken from her old stately march to take a short breather after Lord Randolph Churchill, would not wait for Mr Unwin;[2] and Mr Unwin dared not wait for the author's finishing touches. This, though but a surmise, uninformed by private knowledge, shall be Mr Partridge's excuse here for having set down events in the order in which they were shaken out of his sheaf of memoranda rather than in that of their occurrence, and for his occasional substitution of passionate rhetoric for carefully reasoned composition.

1. The Home Rule movement, which attempted to secure the government of Ireland by a local Irish parliament instead of by the Parliament at Westminster, began in 1871 but did not become a key issue in British politics until 1885, when Ireland returned a majority of M.P.'s to Westminster pledged to this objective. From that time on, the cause of Irish Home Rule was identified with the Liberal Party. Under Gladstone's leadership in 1886 and in 1893, and under Asquith's leadership in 1912, Home Rule Bills were introduced. The first two were defeated. The third was passed in 1913 over the veto of the House of Lords, but its operation was postponed because of the outbreak of World War I, and it never actually became law. The movement in Ireland was strictly a constitutional one, and was led successively by Isaac Butt, Charles Stewart Parnell, and John Redmond.

2. The First Home Rule Bill received its final reading and was defeated on 7 June 1886. Gladstone's chief opponent, who had inflamed the northeastern part of Ireland with his fiery speeches against the bill, was Randolph Churchill. In the general election that followed in July and in which the chief issue was Home Rule for Ireland, the Liberal Party was defeated and the Tories under Lord Salisbury took over. Ireland had the prospect of waiting nearly seven years before Home Rule could be revived.

His own eloquence is supported by vehement repetitions of the utterances of Grattan, O'Connell, and many minor orators. If the reader be not convinced, he will at least be most strenuously persuaded.

Mr Partridge is an advocate of Imperial Federation. As much, however, may be said of many persons with whom he would certainly not shake hands, for there are two distinct varieties of English Imperialism. The appetite for new markets abroad, cheap native labor, and official appointments, civil and military, in newly annexed districts (cleared by the machine gun), has been dubbed "Imperial Instinct" by Lord Salisbury, who carries on his late leader's business of phrase-making much as Wordsworth's son was supposed by the peasants of the Lake country to carry on the business of poem-making. Gentlemen rich in this instinct, and impatient to be rich in solider metal, are at present rallying to the standard of Imperial Federation, and keeping away many honest people who suspect any cause, however worthy, that brings them into bad company. Then there is your philosophic Imperialist who recognizes that Federation is a step higher in social organization, and that we must inevitably and quite desirably come to it unless we are content to go backward. Of the same stamp, but a lazier thinker, is the poet who longs for "the Parliament of Nations, the Federation of the World." Mr Partridge is not an annexationist: he is philosophic and poetic. He insists very strongly that an empire must be a federation of nations, each subject only to the whole empire, and not to the nucleus or strongest member of it. Thus he is at once Irish Nationalist and British Imperialist, claiming for Ireland absolute political independence of England, while admitting and advocating her subjection to the Empire of Great Britain, Ireland, Canada, Australia, and the colonies. He suggests, too, that the Imperial Senate might fill in the public eye the blank to be left by the abolition of the House of Lords. The rest of his book is historical. It tells the story of the 1783–1801 College-green Parliament; describes in the spirit of Fox, Grattan,[3] and Mr Gladstone the provoked rebellion and purchased

3. Charles James Fox, English statesman, was a close ally of Edmund Burke in his appeals for justice in the American colonies, India, and Ireland. Henry Grattan, Irish statesman, was a leading member of the Irish parliament known to history as Grattan's Parliament during its brief existence from 1783 to 1800. A patriot who fought for Irish independence and Catholic emancipation, he was famed for his eloquence.

Union;[4] deals at some length with O'Connell's agitation; mentions Isaac Butt; and, after a rapid survey of recent history under Mr Parnell's dictatorship, leaves the sympathetic reader on the brink of the future, with his soul in arms and eager for the fray.

The unpolicied reviewer, writing without editorial responsibility, may perhaps be permitted to opine that neither history from the Nationalist nor sociology from the Imperialist point of view will assuage Ireland's longing for separation. History so written is a sensational tale of an atrocious wrong done by England: sociology so considered is a plea for leaving matters as they are until the Imperial project is ripe for execution. The one makes the Irishman grind his teeth and hide a pike under his straw mattress; the other tempts Englishmen to postpone a question that will not wait. Why does not some Democratic Internationalist declare the fact, unseen by the indignant Nationalist and overlooked by the future-dreaming Imperialist, that the people of England have done the people of Ireland no wrong whatever? What voice in the councils of the younger Pitt had the English yoke-fellows of the '98 rebels? What were the sufferings against which the Irish then rose compared with those which led to the first abortive Factory Act of 1802? Surely the English people, in factory, mine, and sweater's workshop, had reason to envy the Irish peasant, who at the worst starved on the open hillside instead of rotting in a fetid tenement rookery. Irish landlords may have shewn themselves "vultures with bowels of iron"; but are there not extant in factory inspectors' reports, Royal Commissioners' reports, philanthropic protests, "Bitter Cries," and utterances of our Shaftesburys and Oastlers (not to mention Mrs Reaney),[5] records of rapacious and cruel English capitalists whose little fingers were thicker than the loins of the real masters of Ireland? Allusions to these matters are suppressed in polite society, and they are consequently seldom made except by the orators of the street corner; but when book after book from the press, and speech after speech from the

4. The Act of Union (1800), which abolished the Dublin parliament and gave Ireland representation at Westminster, was accomplished by widespread bribery.

5. Anthony Ashley Cooper, Seventh Earl of Shaftesbury, a statesman and prominent reformer, was parliamentary leader of the factory reform movement. Richard Oastler was a leader of agitation against factory employment of children and in favor of a ten-hour working day. Isabel (Mrs. G. S.) Reaney, author of popular novels and reformist tracts, was a champion of the working class.

platform, lay upon all England the odium of misdeeds that no Irishman can contemplate without intense bitterness—that too many cannot think of without bloodthirsty rage—it is surely expedient to point out to that most distressful country that she has borne no more than her share of the growing pains of human society, and that the mass of the English people are not only guiltless of her wrongs, but have themselves borne a heavier yoke.

In short, the main fault in Mr Partridge's book is in this sentence, quoted from page xxi of the preface: "Politics based on property and things are used for property and things, and that is what we have been doing in Ireland—farming out law, land, religion, and nation on behalf of property and pretences, and against the national manhood and life."

The inference from the words "in Ireland" is that we have not been doing all this elsewhere. Yet there is not a civilized country in the world of which it is not equally true. Remind the Irish of that, and perhaps they will be patient with Sir Redvers and Lord Randolph yet a little while.[6]

6. General Sir Redvers Buller, active in many British military campaigns, became quartermaster general to the war office in 1887. Shaw's reference to him in the present context is unclear. Lord Randolph Churchill had been deeply involved in Irish politics for some years (his father, the Seventh Duke of Marlborough, was Lord-Lieutenant of Ireland 1876–80). He was a strong Unionist, but firmly opposed to coercion.

THE COERCION BILL

In June 1887 Shaw undertook to provide two thousand words a month
of "European Correspondence" for the New York journal *The Epoch*,
but he cancelled the agreement after submitting the first two contributions.
Pertinent extracts are reproduced here.

I

Written on 2 June 1887; published on 17 June

The Whitsuntide holidays have not, this year, distracted public attention
from politics. The obstinate fight in the House of Commons upon the
Criminal Law Amendment [Ireland] Act, always spoken of as the Coercion Bill,[1] is too exciting to be lost sight of, even in London, during so
short a recess. The newspapers, it is true, have broken off, for the time,
their day-to-day narrative of scenes in committee, which, whatever may
be their merit as exhibitions of statesmanship, are undeniably lively reading.

The indefatigable worrying of the bill, line by line, on the part of Mr
Tim. Healy and his colleagues, the lively insolence of Dr Tanner, and the
heavy, spiritless descent, at frequent intervals, of Mr W. H. Smith with
the closure, never fail to amuse. The unfortunate Chairman, who, unlike

1. This newest of several amendment acts levelled against the Irish Nationalists
was labelled a "Coercion Bill" because it attempted to suppress agrarian disorder by
doing away with trial by jury and habeas corpus and by granting British authorities
in Ireland special powers of arbitrary arrest. Timothy M. Healy, Irish Nationalist
M.P. for North Longford 1887–92, had broken with Parnell a year earlier and
strongly supported Gladstone in advocating home rule. Dr. Charles Tanner was a
hotheaded defiant Nationalist M.P. elected in 1885 to represent Cork (Mid Division).
William Henry Smith, son of the well-known news agent, was M.P. for the Strand
Division (London) and in 1887 Conservative leader in the Commons. The chairman
of the House was the Rt. Hon. Leonard Courtney; the speaker was the four times
elected (and unopposed) Arthur Wellesley (First Viscount) Peel. Despite the Irish
Party allying itself with the Liberals and indulging in unprecedented parliamentary
obstruction, the Conservatives succeeded in achieving passage of the act on the eve
of Victoria's Golden Jubilee ceremonies.

the Speaker, has succeeded in preserving his reputation for impartiality, has sleeplessly to watch for and demand the withdrawal of such epithets as "cad," liar" and "coward," with the usual profane qualifications, besides listening to an occasional appeal to heaven to turn a deaf ear to the Conservatives in their last hour, even as they themselves are now turning one to the peasants of Ireland.

These entertainments are suspended for the present in Parliament; but the actual war has broken out again in Ireland in the recommencement of evictions at Bodyke [a small town northeast of Limerick], with its striking incident of the sheriff's officer falling in convulsions beneath the ban of the parish priest. . . .

II

Written on 2 July 1887; published on 22 July

By way of contrast to the jubilee proceedings, the "Jubilee Coercion Bill" has been made perpetual, and passed through the report stage with a rush. The tug of war between the Irish members and the Government seemed at its height when the Opposition suddenly relinquished its hold of the rope, and the Ministers pulled it through heels over head. The question today is what they will do with their new powers when the bill becomes law, and how the Irish will meet it. The obstinate section of Irish landlords, convinced that the tenants can afford to pay if they please, will insist on the Government—which is abjectly weak in everything except voting power—proceeding to the utmost limit of its coercive license during the six years which remain of its lease of office, a course which may bring about almost anything that is possible in the way of mischief. The Irish members talk of organizing their constituents to break the law, when it is proclaimed, as one man. . . .

A BALFOUR BALLAD

Unsigned verses in *The Star*, London, 23 January 1888,
inspired by news reports of arrests and forcible stripping in Ireland under
the regime of Arthur James Balfour, Tory Chief Secretary for Ireland

I am a statesman bold,
And I've frequently been told
There are other ways of killing dogs than hanging 'em;
And my plan to make it hot
For the Irish patriot
Is subtler far than bludgeoning and banging him.

When the hero of the West
Isnt strong about the chest
I cultivate his tendency to phthisis
By giving him a cell
In my Tullamore hotel
Where the balmy air in winter time like ice is.

And the manager and waiters
In the morning grab his gaiters,
His ulster, and his trousers, and his cardigan;
And he cuddles in his quilt,
And reflects upon his guilt,
Vowing never to put in for three months' hard again.

The nature of his bed
Makes his shoulder blades all red,
Till he longs to have some padding for his skeleton;
And the story of his woes
So long and poignant grows,
That he finds the prison slate too small to tell it on.

And the hacking of his cough
As his coil he shuffles off,
Never strikes me through with shudders of repentance,
Nor spoils my wine and wassail
At the Four Courts and the Castle;
No! consumption wasnt mentioned in my sentence.

Though the dogs may make a fuss
They cant find fault with us
If a higher Power relieves the land they lumbered;
And we reverently say,
"He gave. He took away.
Every hair we left upon their heads was numbered."

THE TORIES AND IRELAND

Unsigned leader in *The Star*, London, 30 April 1888. This attribution was disputed by Stanley Rypins, who, until his death in 1971, was editing the Shaw diaries. Insisting the transliteration from Shaw's shorthand was "leaderette," not "leader," Rypins opted for an art notice published on 1 May. When Stanley Weintraub succeeded Rypins as editor, he retained the ascription, despite Shaw's painstaking distinctions in the diary in which he consistently confined "leader" and "sub-leader" to political subjects, "leaderettes" to social topics, and "notes," "notices," and "paragraphs" to music, drama, and art. We remain convinced that Shaw was the draftsman of the unsigned leader, although it may have undergone amendment at the hands of editor T. P. O'Connor or subeditor H. W. Massingham.

The Irish leaders and the Irish people have now a great opportunity to which we believe they will not be unequal. Their political independence has been attacked. A number of English Tories, acting under the inspiration and the patronage of a Tory Government, have obtained from the head of the Church to which the majority of them belong, a document denouncing their political action.[1] This attack has come upon them when Ireland stands with her back to the wall, fighting the most brutal and one of the most perilous assaults ever made on her life, hopes, and liberties. Such an attack might be allowed to pass by without other comment than a smile if the times were ordinary. But it has come in the moment of Ireland's agony. Nay, this is not putting it strongly enough. It is no exag-

---

1. One of the most brilliant achievements of British secret diplomacy was to get Pope Leo XIII, on 23 April 1888, to use a rescript condemning as unlawful the practice of "boycotting"—the only effective weapon that the Roman Catholic masses of Ireland had devised as a defense against oppressive landlords and their agents. The pope ostensibly had acted as a result of an investigation made in Ireland by his emissary Monsignor Persico, but as the issuing of the papal rescript was announced (and its specific terms outlined) in the English press several days before the Irish hierarchy even were notified of the papal action, most observers concluded that the Vatican had been used in the game of politics. This appears to have been the conclusion of the Irish hierarchy, most of whom declared that the pope had been misled and that his decree was inapplicable.

geration to say that out of the battle which Ireland is now waging she comes a political corpse or a living and an immortal nation. If ever, then, there was a time when a blow was cruel, perilous, wanton, it is at such a moment.

We shall never, perhaps, be able to discover the methods by which this attack on Ireland has been brought about. Of course, the Tory Government is at the bottom of it. What promises they have held out, what *quid pro quo* they are prepared to give, we have as yet no means of knowing; and if questions were put in the House of Commons the answers would be evasive or mendacious. But we all know what are the main facts of the case; and we may sum up their substance by saying that the liberties of Ireland have been sacrificed to a base Tory intrigue. If Ireland were to submit to such things, then Ireland would shew herself but little worthy of the freedom which in a few years will be bestowed upon her by the hands of Englishmen whom Ireland's heroic and obstinate struggle has turned from enemies to loving friends.

And now the people of England have also a duty to perform. We have a right to know what has been the conduct of our own Government in this matter. One of the many dishonest and untrue statements which the Tories have propagated most widely in opposition to the rights of Ireland has been the statement that a self-governed Ireland meant danger to the religious liberty of the Protestant minority. Are the gentlemen who thus used the Pope as a convenient and useful bogy now themselves entering into negotiations with the Pope for the purpose of giving him a return for value received? It would be just like the present Government of broken pledges and promises false as dicers' oaths to pursue a policy of that kind.

Mr John Morley did not put it too strongly when he said that the Unionist party in Ireland were with one hand beating the hateful Orange drum, and with the other plucking stealthily at the sleeve of Monsignor Persico. On the very day when the Pope was transmitting this attack on Ireland the Unionist party from Ireland were preaching in the House of Commons that the Irish were unfit for self-government precisely because they happened to be so faithful sons of the Roman Catholic Church. Thus it has always been with Ireland. The enemies who have persecuted the religious faith of Ireland have triumphed; the people who have faced imprisonment and the scaffold and terrible penal law have been attacked.

It is time for the people of England and the people of Ireland to speak out; for the people of England to denounce these unworthy and dishonest intrigues by their own Ministry; and for the people of Ireland to declare that they accept advice and counsel in their political concerns from no power on earth but the political leaders they themselves have chosen.

A CRIB FOR HOME RULERS

Unsigned review of Robert Oliver's *Unnoticed Analogies: A Talk on the Irish Question. The Pall Mall Gazette,* London, 25 September 1888

This book of Mr Robert Oliver's is 233 pages long. It is the record of a single conversation on a single subject between James and Andrew. For three hours and a quarter, as one calculates, these two gentlemen debate the question of Home Rule with a self-control, a strict keeping to the point, and an undulled sense of literary form that are beyond all praise. Weaker men would have sacrificed propriety to dramatic opportunity, but not these. James does not sneer nor Andrew swear. There are none of those gusts of wrath in which the raised voice and scornful accent arrest the passer-by with promise of a fight. The result is that James and Andrew personally impress the reader as a pair of well-conducted and well-informed members of the middle class, whose arguments and analogies will serve at secondhand in private wranglings over the question of the hour. Indeed, with Andrew's speeches at his tongue's end, a man might become a finished Gladstonian. But he might also become a finished bore. For the truth is, Andrew, though conclusive, is not convincing. One feels that James, the nether millstone of the debate, might make short work of him by quoting Hegel's dictum that all mistakes are made for good reasons.

To the mere literary reviewer, admiring from his study windows the omniscience, the readiness, the energy of his political contemporaries, it seems a strange thing that any human being should discuss Home Rule as if its accomplishment depended on the upshot of a utilitarian discussion of its probable results. Nationalism is surely an incident of organic growth, not an invention. A man discusses whether he shall introduce a roasting jack into his kitchen, but not whether he shall introduce an eye tooth into his son's mouth or lengthen him as he grows older. If men did discuss such things, the result would undoubtedly be a consensus of opinion to the effect that thirty teeth are quite sufficient for modern purposes, and that every inch of stature above five feet six inches is a waste of the world's industry in providing clothing fabrics, carrying power, uselessly high rooms, and so on. But as it is clear that this decision, however scrupulously rational, would not have the slightest effect on the proceedings of the power which arranges our teeth and our inches for us, we have to accept the inevitable average son of five-feet-eight, with thirtytwo teeth, and provide for him accordingly. We shall have to accept the growth of nationalism in exactly the same way. In any purely abstract utilitarian discussion, where the historical method is excluded, and political and social institutions are treated as inventions of the roasting-jack order, Home Rule must stand condemned, as Mr Chamberlain or any utilitarian-materialist-republican can shew.[1] Is not federation the most economical—the most social course? Is it not an advance in complexity of structure and order of organism—a step further towards the Parliament of Man, the Federation of the World? The conviction that all these questions must be answered in the affirmative lurks disquietingly in the consciousness of many a Home Ruler who was wont, when Ireland was not the theme, to indulge imperial dreams of a federated Greater Britain.

In the meantime, Ireland and Poland are as deaf to academic discussion as Italy was in her evil days. Go to the Cork mechanic and point out to him that the condition of the Parisian *ouvrier* who works as a Frenchman under a French Republic is in no way superior to his own under the tyranny of the Castle. Shew him that when he works as an Irishman under an Irish Republic, and Irish industry develops by leaps and bounds, he will assuredly find the bread of freedom as bitter and scarce under King Capital as ever it has been under Mr Balfour. Then advise him to vote against Mr Parnell and Mr Maurice Healy[2] at the next election. He will be about as much impressed as Garibaldi would have been by a discourse on the advantages of a united Austria and Italy. What Mr Oliver calls an "unnoticed analogy" is to be found in the slavery struggle in America. The advantages of being a chattel slave were proved over and over again by the friends of the South. The master who bought a man valued him as something in which his capital was locked up. Just as a tramway company now takes more care of its horses than of its men, so did the planter take more

1. Joseph Chamberlain, Liberal M.P., split with Gladstone over Irish Home Rule and led a group who voted against the First Home Rule Bill.

2. Nationalist M.P., member of the Irish Party, representing Cork in Parliament for more than thirty years. Like his brother Timothy, Maurice Healy turned against Parnell and voted with the majority to terminate Parnell's leadership at the famous meeting in the Parliamentary Committee Room on 6 December 1890.

care of his slave than the employer of his free wage worker. Slaves were cared for in their old age instead of being abandoned to the discomfort and disgrace of a pauper ward. In short, who would not be a slave rather than a free proletarian? Who indeed, except a man in whom the instinct towards personal liberty was as a burning fire shut up in his bones, so that he was weary with forbearing and could not stay? History tells us that it is useless to cross these instincts—tells us so dogmatically, and will not argue the point for a moment, with James or Andrew or anyone else. The slave, equally unreasonable, sees nothing ahead of him but his freedom. He may be a moth flying towards a candle; but he has the moth's power of making it impossible for us to attend to our own business if we undertake the task of keeping him out of the candle by any other means than killing him.

Here, then, we have to face an inevitable order of social growth. First, the individual will have his personal liberty, in pursuit of which he will at last weary out and destroy feudal systems, mighty churches, medieval orders, slave-holding oligarchies, and what else may stand in his way. Then he will enlarge his social consciousness from his individual self to the nation of which he is a unit; and he will have his national liberty as he had his personal liberty, nor will all the excellent reasons in the world avail finally against him. He will rarely take the two steps at a time: he will never take the second before the first, or the third before the second. The third step is the federation of nationalities; but you cannot induce him to forgo the achievement of national independence on the ground that international federation is a step higher. He knows by instinct that if his foot missed that one rung of the ladder, he would not reach the higher rung, but would rather be precipitated into the abyss; and so it comes that there is no federating nationalities without first realizing them. And as the slave destroyed great hierarchies in his fight for freedom, so the conquered subject races will destroy great empires when their time comes, if the empires persist in opposing them.

It may be that Providence has specially exempted the British Empire from these readjustments to social growth. The English middle class has always been more or less of that opinion. Indeed, history teaches us that the middle class always held that opinion. History also teaches us that the middle class is invariably wrong. For, to quote another Hegelian dictum, we learn from history that men never learn anything from history.

THE PARNELL FORGER

Unsigned notes on Richard Pigott, the forger of letters ostensibly
written by Charles Stewart Parnell implicating Parnell in the Phoenix
Park murders. When a British parliamentary commission undertook
an investigation, Pigott confessed and shortly afterward committed
suicide. *The Star,* London, 19 February 1889

Your portrait of Mr Pigott obeying the order to leave the Court the other
day reminded me—I think by a certain cock of the single eyeglass depicted in it—of a few seasons I spent some twentyfive years ago on the
shores of Killiney Bay, the southern corner of Dublin Bay, declared by
Irish enthusiasts to surpass in beauty the Bay of Naples and all other picturesque bays, known or unknown, on the face of the globe. At the north
horn of the bay, at a place called Dalkey, I found a little colony of amateur musicians, headed by a singing master named [George John, later
Vandeleur] Lee, who subsequently came to London and settled in a house
in Park-lane, where he died a few years ago. Among the non-performing
members of the group was a spry-looking gentleman, with a single eyeglass, who was spoken of indifferently as "the Major" and "Dick Pigott,"
so that at first I supposed him to be a retired officer. But I soon learnt that
this was only part of the chaff current in the colony, to which "the Major"
was attached as amateur photographer.

One of Mr Pigott's characteristics was an insatiable appetite for sea
bathing. He was a good swimmer, and one day he got a navvy out of the
water just as the unfortunate man had resigned himself to a watery grave.
Oddly enough, the navvy recorded his thanks in a newspaper advertisement, which he addressed to "Major Pigott," having heard his deliverer
spoken of in the usual fashion among the bystanders. Mr Lee, the sing-
ing-master, whom I have mentioned, spoke to me of this many years
afterwards in London, and added, "Pigott took it into his head that the
advertisement was a practical joke of mine. He never believed my assurances to the contrary, and he never forgave me."

Mr Pigott was, no doubt, a deeper man than he appeared. His opinions
were not of a kind to be safely talked about at large in the 1860–70 period

in Ireland. His two imprisonments, both of which, if I recollect aright, were for contempt of court in commenting in his paper, The Irishman, on sentences pronounced on Fenians,[1] did not cause his friends much concern. Mr Balfour was not grown-up then, and Mr Pigott's health was positively so much benefited by his incarceration that his sister was accustomed to declare that it had saved his life. In later years he lost his jolly air, and became the fully-bearded, portly, bald, and somewhat heavy figure familiar to the Commission. But the single eyeglass still connects him with "the Major" of 1863.

1. Popular name of the Irish Republican Brotherhood, a secret revolutionary society that instigated the rising of 1867. The name was derived from *fiann* or *féinne* (Irish), a legendary band of warriors in the heroic age of Ireland.

SHALL PARNELL GO?[1]

I

To *The Star*, London, 20 November 1890

Sir,—May I go so far as to express my feeling that the "He Must Go" letter from the anchorite of Westbourne-park Chapel[2] is nonsense. In my opinion, which is quite as representative on this point as Dr Clifford's, the relation between Mr Parnell and Mrs O'Shea was a perfectly natural and right one; and the whole mischief in the matter lay in the law that tied the husband and wife together and forced Mr Parnell to play the part of clandestine intriguer, instead of enabling them to dissolve the marriage by mutual consent, without disgrace to either party. Dr Clifford has no right to speak of Mr Parnell as "convicted of immorality"; it is the law that has been convicted of immorality. If "the conscience of the nation is aroused," so much the better; but I doubt it. Dr Clifford's letter does not shew much sign of it. Until our marriage laws are remodeled to suit men

---

1. At the height of his career as leader of the Irish Home Rule Party, Parnell was cited as co-respondent in a divorce action brought by Captain William Henry O'Shea, Home Rule M.P. from Clare, whose wife, Katharine, had been living with Parnell for some years, an arrangement that O'Shea had acquiesced in and exploited to gain Parnell's political patronage. The court rendered its verdict in O'Shea's favor on 17 November 1890. At a meeting of the Irish Party several days later, in Committee Room 15, with Parnell in the chair, the majority voted their confidence in him, but many of those who did so believed that Parnell would then gracefully resign as leader. For days a debate raged, with the party deeply divided. Finally, on 6 December, after repeated calls for Parnell's resignation, the majority of forty-four members voted with their feet by walking out of the meeting, convening elsewhere under the chairmanship of Justin McCarthy, M.P., journalist, and chairman of the anti-Parnell Irish Parliamentary Party, declaring themselves to be the Irish Party. With the "Chief" thus dethroned and the Irish people divided into two irreconcilable camps, the Liberal Party, no longer depending on Irish support to return it to power, withdrew its promise of Home Rule for Ireland. Parnell wed Katharine O'Shea, by whom he had had two children, on 25 June 1891; he died less than four months later.

2. Rev. John Clifford, Baptist minister and author of many books on social problems.

and women and to further the happiness and health of the community, instead of to conform to an ideal of "purity," no verdict in a divorce case will force any man to retire from public life if it appears that he behaved no worse than the law forced him to. Mr Parnell's business is simply to sit tight and let the pure people talk.

G. Bernard Shaw.

II

To The Star, London, 27 November 1890

Sir,—The appearance of Mr Gladstone in the Parnell controversy calls for another word of protest from those who refuse to be bluffed out of their commonsense by the promulgation as "English public opinion" of the inhuman and ridiculous views of Mr [William T.] Stead, Mr Hugh Price Hughes,[3] and the morbidly sexual members of the community in general. It is not surprising that these gentlemen have terrorized the Liberal press for the moment. Mr Stead has always had the courage of his monstrous opinions; and the rest are emboldened by the fact that they have a considerable following in the quarters to which the Liberal party now looks for pecuniary support against the Tories on the one hand and the working classes on the other. But if a line is to be drawn anywhere, it must be drawn at the views of Mr Gladstone, who recently gave to the world in a magazine article a statement of his ideas on sexual morality, which I do not hesitate to describe as more repugnant to popular feeling than Mormonism is. Mr Stead would ostracize Mr Parnell because he has committed adultery; but Mr Gladstone would ostracize Captain O'Shea because he has committed the sin of divorcing the woman with whom he took the sacrament of marriage for better for worse. If Mr Parnell had been the petitioner instead of the co-respondent, Mr Gladstone would nonetheless have condemned him. Nay, if he had merely been guilty of marrying a widow, like the late Lord Beaconsfield, he would have fallen equally under the ban of the Gladstonian ideal. In short, Mr Gladstone is in this, as in most other open questions, the least representative man in the country. For example, there are beyond doubt people—mostly land-

---

3. Stead (onetime editor of *The Pall Mall Gazette*) and Hughes were journalists interested in ecclesiastical matters.

lords—who share his view that the system of country gentleman, tenant farmer, and agricultural laborer is destined to be eternal in England by sheer force of fitness; and I myself know men who agree with him that "thrift is the true solution of the social problem for railway employees earning from sixteen shillings to a guinea a week." But on the marriage question he is practically alone—alone in the rear. Mr Parnell may safely leave his opinion out of account.

As to the large number of people who have written to the papers to explain that they do not in the least mind adultery, but that what they cannot bear is deceit, I would put the following cases to them:—The Coercion Act has forced upon many members of the Irish party the alternative of either spending all their time in prison and giving up public meeting in Ireland, or else practicing repeated deceptions upon the constabulary.[4] In Russia, in the same way, constitutional reformers are driven to employ all the devices of criminals—disguises, false passports, aliases, bribes, and so on. Suppose, I say, that the character of these reformers cannot be cut into two halves—that the man who deceives a policeman will deceive his political followers—that there cannot be two standards of morality, one for your conduct towards your sovereign and the other for your conduct towards the people! Again, in the old days, when the law hung men who stole articles of a greater value than forty shillings, juries kept on declaring the value of stolen articles to be under that sum, no matter what they were really worth, until the law was altered. Suppose, I say, that these men were liars, and therefore unfit for public life. Will the persons who are revolted by Mr Parnell's resort to aliases and to the fire escape (with its irresistibly humorous sequel) support me in these idiotic contentions? If not, what becomes of their cognate argument?

In France and in some of the American States, when a marriage turns out unhappily, and the position of the parties becomes insufferable, they can, on making due provision for any responsibilities they may have incurred by their mistake, free oneanother and marry again if they wish. In this country there is no release. All the suffering which is now being

4. Under the Crimes Act of 1897, which supplemented a number of Coercion Acts already on the statute books, various associations and assemblies were declared illegal in Ireland, and scores of Irish leaders were jailed for any activities considered to be dangerous to the government.

inflicted on Mr Parnell and his "accomplice" (as Dr Clifford would call her) and all the disastrous consequences threatened to the Irish Nationalist party would have happened equally had Mr Parnell forced Captain O'Shea to take proceedings years ago by openly defying the law. Whether you walk proudly down the front stairs or are ignominiously caught on the fire-escape, Messrs Clifford, Price Hughes, and Frederic Harrison (from whom I should have expected better things) are equally ready to stone you at the foot. I contend that whilst the law remains in that wicked and silly condition its verdicts and decrees nisi can produce no genuine conviction of its victims' unfitness for public life, in spite of the utmost hubbub that can be raised by the men who are prepared to stick at nothing in their determination to "purify public life."

I therefore again urge Mr Parnell to "sit tight." Nine days hence my argument for the reform of the marriage laws will be as sound as it is today, whilst nothing will remain of the denunciations of Mr Price Hughes and Mr Harrison except a fading reminiscence of their controversial style. The "public opinion" which they represent on this subject is so thoroughly ill-conditioned and thoughtless that Mr Parnell will set a most wholesome example by defying it. It is indeed precisely by his inflexible indifference to the unsympathetic and unintelligent clamors which rise every now and then from the nurseries of English prejudice that Mr Parnell has struck the popular imagination and created the Parnell myth. I hope he will not now let himself be cowed by an indecent threat from faint-hearted and treacherous allies to support Lord Hartington, actively or passively, at the next election.

G. Bernard Shaw.

OSCAR WILDE

Die Neue Freie Presse, Vienna, 23 April 1905, in a translation by Siegfried Trebitsch. As Shaw's original text apparently has not survived, the essay was re-translated into English by Felix F. Strauss and Dan H. Laurence.

There are three European capitals which have not yet advanced beyond the first quarter of the XIX century. Paris is the most backward of these three cities, followed by Vienna; the most modern is Dublin—my and Oscar Wilde's native city. In Vienna I wont be understood for at least another hundred years because I belong to the XX century; but the Viennese will, to some extent, feel a kinship with me because of my style, which is Augustan Irish classical English, in use in Dublin when I was a boy.

Vienna, however, will take more easily to the style of Oscar Wilde because he was endowed not only with the artistic culture of the XVIII century, but also with an extremely worldly predilection for opulence and elegance. He valued his position as that of a gentleman and repeatedly reproached his opponents (especially Whistler) for their vulgarity; and although he went so far as to claim De Profundis[1] to be the *enfant de son siècle,* he was nonetheless in all questions concerning art a belated Romanticist of the school of Baudelaire and Théophile Gautier and was satisfied with this because he believed that it placed him among the *avant garde.* Oscar Wilde's attitude towards women was gallant and deferential; it is difficult to believe that the author of An Ideal Husband was a contemporary of Ibsen, Strindberg, Wagner, Tolstoi, or myself. He was in every respect, except for his ideas on morality, an old-fashioned Irish gentleman—old-fashioned in his Gautierism, in his gallantry, in his romanticism, in his patriotism, in his choice of dress, and in his custom of living beyond his means. Since Vienna is, after Paris, Europe's most old-fashioned city and yet considers itself to be an *enfant de son siècle par excellence,* Vienna should be able to esteem Oscar Wilde more than would ever be possible in any German or English city.

I need not speak of Wilde as a man of imagination and as an innately

1. Oscar Wilde's *De Profundis* was first published on 23 February 1905.

skilful dramatist. Every talented Irish poet is thus gifted. But no other Irishman has yet produced as masterful a comedy as De Profundis. In spite of the unspeakable horrors of the circumstances under which this work was written, it stimulated me to laughter more than any other of Wilde's works. The man was so completely unbroken, so untouched by misery, hunger, punishment, and shame; he was so consummately successful and sincere in his magnificent attitude of doleful superiority—in the face of a society which had behaved so weakly, narrowly, and unjustly towards the great man—that pity and sentimentality would amount to weakmindedness and bad taste, and one is moved to rejoice over the kind of unsurpassable genius that he was. Wilde shouldered every disgrace and every torment with which England burdened him; he rejected every excuse which England tried to find for him. He made England appear insignificant and stupid, and himself noble, tragic, and superior. In his forbidding convicts' dress he was exhibited to the London crowd on a train platform for half an hour during the busiest time of day. Instead of being shamed into silence, he heaped dishonor upon his tormentors by describing this scene in a manner more affecting than the description of the exhibition of Christ in the pretorium. While in prison, he was visited by a friend who assured the prisoner that he fervently believed him innocent of the crime of which he was accused; but Wilde would not have it so. "You are mistaken," he replied, "my life was fully dedicated to perverse pleasures. The charges levelled against me are essentially correct; I am neither as innocent as you believe, nor am I reformed." With these words he compelled his affectionate friend to apologize and to shake his hand.

This has occasional overtones of comedy. However great Wilde's capacity was for experiencing joy and pain, his talent for unhappiness was so negligible that—in spite of the aim to develop his book as an indictment of society (because of its ignorant repulsion and loathsome dread of him)—he forgot this purpose for pages on end, and, digressing, turned it into a Gautier-like essay on Christ which was a pure streak of *belles-lettres*. Then he became suddenly aware of this and, recognizing the humor of it all, remarked somewhere by way of clarification for his exclusive audience:[2] "I was given enough to eat recently." I broke out in

2. The reference presumably is to Lord Alfred Douglas, to whom Wilde's "Epistola" was addressed.

loud guffaws. An Englishman would have shed a tear upon this page and exclaimed, "Poor devil." From the grave Wilde still makes fools of them, these enemies of his country and of his originality.

My personal relationship with Oscar Wilde is difficult to describe. We both amused the English to a point where they were unwilling to take us seriously. The English consider dulness the hallmark of profound people. Now, I knew very well that Oscar Wilde was a gifted man and he recognized me as the same. The few times we met I made it a point to treat him with marked esteem and warm friendship. He treated me likewise. The result was that we utterly confused each other. We disconcerted one another in a most ludicrous fashion, and we both realized it and recognized the inherent comedy. For this reason we met rarely, unless by chance. His only recorded remark about me was: "Shaw has no enemies and none of his friends like him." This is one of those subtle compliments which most people take for malicious barbs. Only a nonentity has friends who like him unconditionally; Wilde's remark would stem only from a man who knew, himself, the pangs of conscience which all men of talent experience over the pain which is at times inflicted by that talent, especially upon their friends.

On the whole, Wilde's tastes were basically different from mine. He loved luxury, and the salon and the *atelier* were his domain; while I was a man of the street, an agitator, a vegetarian, a teetotaler, incapable of enjoying the life of the drawing room and the chatter of the studio. Furthermore, Wilde was interested in men, I in women; and while he was endlessly pleasure-bent, I found amusements, except for rare and unexpected moments, the emptiest of all useless endeavors. Consequently I write about him without possession of that authority which others have derived from long personal intimacy.

His originality lay in his superiority to the delusive morality of our time; this gave him his high degree of self-esteem, his pride, his seemingly absurd self-confidence, and his epigrammatical talent. Unfortunately, every genius is imprisoned in an ordinary body and an ordinary brain, which discredit it through follies and improprieties. Wilde's genius was imprisoned in the body of a giant (pathologically, giantism is a disease), and this giant had perverse appetites. He had a desire for that which Wilde himself called in his heroic letter of defence (in which he excused himself for having invoked the law for his protection) a senseless and sensuous life. His deterioration and death following his imprisonment (which probably had done him good physically) were the triumph of the accidentally human over the genius, although even this collapse contained a quietly comical element in view of Wilde's avowal that, though it had altered his character, sorrow had made him more profound. He would have admitted that he was indolent, self-indulgent, and a prattler, although he had worked too hard for anyone to have been justified to apply these terms to him. He had not, as Nietzsche had, thought through his own situation sufficiently to understand himself. Without a precisely mapped-out program of life it is impossible, if not useless, to discard moral concepts. Our present-day morality is a repugnant and, as Wilde would have said, "vulgar" error. It is not even ethical. And Wilde's claim to greatness rests on the fact that our morality could not fool him, and the moralists of his time could neither break nor dishonor him.

He held fast to his pose to the very last, because it was an honest pose. For that very reason it has been unspeakably annoying to English morality which, too, is a pose, but without benefit of the excuse of being an honest one.

PREFACE FOR POLITICIANS

Extracts from the preface to *John Bull's Other Island*, 1907

What Is an Irishman?

When I say that I am an Irishman I mean that I was born in Ireland, and that my native language is the English of Swift and not the unspeakable jargon of the mid-XIX-century London newspapers. My extraction is the extraction of most Englishmen: that is, I have no trace in me of the commercially imported North Spanish strain which passes for aboriginal Irish: I am a genuine typical Irishman of the Danish, Norman, Cromwellian, and (of course) Scotch invasions. I am violently and arrogantly Protestant by family tradition; but let no English Government therefore count on my allegiance: I am English enough to be an inveterate Republican and Home Ruler. It is true that one of my grandfathers was an Orangeman; but then his sister was an abbess; and his uncle, I am proud to say, was hanged as a rebel. When I look round me on the hybrid cosmopolitans, slum poisoned or square pampered, who call themselves Englishmen today, and see them bullied by the Irish Protestant garrison as no Bengalee now lets himself be bullied by an Englishman; when I see the Irishman everywhere standing clearheaded, sane, hardily callous to the boyish sentimentalities, susceptibilities, and credulities that make the Englishman the dupe of every charlatan and the idolater of every numskull, I perceive that Ireland is the only spot on earth which still produces the ideal Englishman of history. Blackguard, bully, drunkard, liar, foul-mouth, flatterer, beggar, backbiter, venal functionary, corrupt judge, envious friend, vindictive opponent, unparalleled political traitor: all these your Irishman may easily be, just as he may be a gentleman (a species extinct in England, and nobody a penny the worse); but he is never quite the hysterical, nonsense-crammed, fact-proof, truth-terrified, unballasted sport of all the bogy panics and all the silly enthusiasms that now calls itself "God's Englishman." England cannot do without its Irish and its Scots today, because it cannot do without at least a little sanity.

The Protestant Garrison

The more Protestant an Irishman is—the more English he is, if it flatters you to have it put that way—the more intolerable he finds it to be ruled by English instead of Irish folly. A "loyal" Irishman is an abhorrent phenomenon, because it is an unnatural one. No doubt English rule is vigorously exploited in the interests of the property, power, and promotion of the Irish classes as against the Irish masses. Our delicacy is part of a keen sense of reality which makes us a very practical, and even, on occasion, a very coarse people. The Irish soldier takes the King's shilling and drinks the King's health; and the Irish squire takes the title deeds of the English settlement and rises uncovered to the strains of the English national anthem. But do not mistake this cupboard loyalty for anything deeper. It gains a broad base from the normal attachment of every reasonable man to the established government as long as it is bearable; for we all, after a certain age, prefer peace to revolution and order to chaos, other things being equal. Such considerations produce loyal Irishmen as they produce loyal Poles and Finns, loyal Hindoos, loyal Filipinos, and faithful slaves. But there is nothing more in it than that. If there is an entire lack of gall in the feeling of the Irish gentry towards the English, it is because the Englishman is always gaping admiringly at the Irishman as at some clever child prodigy. He overrates him with a generosity born of a traditional conviction of his own superiority in the deeper aspects of human character. As the Irish gentleman, tracing his pedigree to the conquest of one of the invasions, is equally convinced that if this superiority really exists, he is the genuine true blue heir to it, and as he is easily able to hold his own in all the superficial accomplishments, he finds English society agreeable, and English houses very comfortable, Irish establishments being generally straitened by an attempt to keep a park and stable on an income which would not justify an Englishman in venturing upon a wholly detached villa.

Our Temperaments Contrasted

But, however pleasant the relations between the Protestant garrison and the English gentry may be, they are always essentially of the nature of an *entente cordiale* between foreigners. Personally I like Englishmen much better than Irishmen (no doubt because they make more of me) just as many Englishmen like Frenchmen better than Englishmen, and never go on board a Peninsular and Oriental steamer when one of the ships of the Messageries maritimes is available. But I never think of an Englishman as my countryman. I should as soon think of applying that term to a German. And the Englishman has the same feeling. When a Frenchman fails to make the distinction, we both feel a certain disparagement involved in the misapprehension. Macaulay, seeing that the Irish had in Swift an author worth stealing, tried to annex him by contending that he must be classed as an Englishman because he was not an aboriginal Celt. He might as well have refused the name of Briton to Addison because he did not stain himself blue and attach scythes to the poles of his sedan chair. In spite of all such trifling with facts, the actual distinction between the idolatrous Englishman and the fact-facing Irishman, of the same extraction though they may be, remains to explode those two hollowest of fictions, the Irish and English "races." There is no Irish race any more than there is an English race or a Yankee race. There *is* an Irish climate, which will stamp an immigrant more deeply and durably in two years, apparently, than the English climate will in two hundred. It is reinforced by an artificial economic climate which does some of the work attributed to the natural geographic one; but the geographic climate is eternal and irresistible, making a mankind and a womankind that Kent, Middlesex, and East Anglia cannot produce and do not want to imitate.

How can I sketch the broad lines of the contrast as they strike me? Roughly I should say that the Englishman is wholly at the mercy of his imagination, having no sense of reality to check it. The Irishman, with a far subtler and more fastidious imagination, has one eye always on things as they are. If you compare Moore's visionary Minstrel Boy with Mr Rudyard Kipling's quasi-realistic Soldiers Three, you may yawn over Moore or gush over him, but you will not suspect him of having had any illusions about the contemporary British private; whilst as to Mr Kipling, you will see that he has not, and unless he settles in Ireland for a few years will always remain constitutionally and congenitally incapable of having, the faintest inkling of the reality which he idolizes as Tommy Atkins. Perhaps you have never thought of illustrating the contrast between English and Irish by Moore and Mr Kipling, or even by Parnell and Gladstone. Sir Boyle Roche and Shakespear may seem more to your point. Let

me find you a more dramatic instance. Think of the famous meeting between the Duke of Wellington, that intensely Irish Irishman, and Nelson,
that intensely English Englishman. Wellington's contemptuous disgust at
Nelson's theatricality as a professed hero, patriot, and rhapsode, a theatricality which in an Irishman would have been an insufferably vulgar
affectation, was quite natural and inevitable. Wellington's formula for
that kind of thing was a well-known Irish one: "Sir: dont be a damned
fool." It is the formula of all Irishmen for all Englishmen to this day. It is
the formula of Larry Doyle for Tom Broadbent in my play, in spite of
Doyle's affection for Tom. Nelson's genius, instead of producing intellectual keenness and scrupulousness, produced mere delirium. He was
drunk with glory, exalted by his fervent faith in the sound British patriotism of the Almighty, nerved by the vulgarest anti-foreign prejudice, and
apparently unchastened by any reflections on the fact that he had never
had to fight a technically capable and properly equipped enemy except on
land, where he had never been successful. Compare Wellington, who had
to fight Napoleon's armies, Napoleon's marshals, and finally Napoleon
himself, without one moment of illusion as to the human material he had
to command, without one gush of the "Kiss me, Hardy" emotion which
enabled Nelson to idolize his crews and his staff, without forgetting even
in his dreams that the normal British officer of the time was an incapable
amateur (as he still is) and the normal British soldier a never-do-well (he
is now a depressed and respectable young man). No wonder Wellington
became an accomplished comedian in the art of anti-climax, scandalizing
the unfortunate Croker, responding to the demand for glorious sentiments by the most disenchanting touches of realism, and generally,
pricking the English windbag at its most explosive crises of distension.
Nelson, intensely nervous and theatrical, made an enormous fuss about
victories so cheap that he would have deserved shooting if he had lost
them, and, not content with lavishing splendid fighting on helpless adver-
saries like the heroic De Brueys and Villeneuve (who had not even the
illusion of heroism when he went like a lamb to the slaughter), got himself killed by his passion for exposing himself to death in that sublime
defiance of it which was perhaps the supreme tribute of the exquisite
coward to the King of Terrors (for, believe me, you cannot be a hero
without being a coward: supersense cuts both ways), the result being a
tremendous effect on the gallery. Wellington, most capable of captains,

was neither a hero nor a patriot: perhaps not even a coward; and had it not been for the Nelsonic anecdotes invented for him—"Up guards, and at em" and so forth—and the fact that the antagonist with whom he finally closed was such a master of theatrical effect that Wellington could not fight him without getting into his limelight, nor overthrow him (most unfortunately for us all) without drawing the eyes of the whole world to the catastrophe, the Iron Duke would have been almost forgotten by this time. Now that contrast is English against Irish all over, and is the more delicious because the real Irishman in it is the Englishman of tradition, whilst the real Englishman is the traditional theatrical foreigner.

The value of the illustration lies in the fact that Nelson and Wellington were both in the highest degree efficient, and both in the highest degree incompatible with oneanother on any other footing than one of independence. The government of Nelson by Wellington or of Wellington by Nelson is felt at once to be a dishonorable outrage to the governed and a finally impossible task for the governor.

I daresay some Englishman will now try to steal Wellington as Macaulay tried to steal Swift. And he may plead with some truth that though it seems impossible that any other country than England could produce a hero so utterly devoid of commonsense, intellectual delicacy, and international chivalry as Nelson, it may be contended that Wellington was rather an XVIII-century aristocratic type than a specifically Irish type. George IV and Byron, contrasted with Gladstone, seem Irish in respect of a certain humorous blackguardism, and a power of appreciating art and sentiment without being duped by them into mistaking romantic figments for realities. But faithlessness and the need for carrying off the worthlessness and impotence that accompany it, produce in all nations a gay, skeptical, amusing, blaspheming, witty fashion which suits the flexibility of the Irish mind very well; and the contrast between this fashion and the energetic infatuations that have enabled intellectually ridiculous men, without wit or humor, to go on crusades and make successful revolutions, must not be confused with the contrast between the English and Irish idiosyncrasies. The Irishman makes a distinction which the Englishman is too lazy intellectually (the intellectual laziness and slovenliness of the English are almost beyond belief) to make. The Englishman, impressed with the dissoluteness of the faithless wits of the Restoration and the Regency, and with the victories of the wilful zealots of the patriotic, religious, and revolutionary wars, jumps to the conclusion that wilfulness is the main thing. In this he is right. But he overdoes his jump so far as to conclude also that stupidity and wrongheadedness are better guarantees of efficiency and trustworthiness than intellectual vivacity, which he mistrusts as a common symptom of worthlessness, vice, and instability. Now in this he is most dangerously wrong. Whether the Irishman grasps the truth as firmly as the Englishman may be open to question; but he is certainly comparatively free from the error. That affectionate and admiring love of sentimental stupidity for its own sake, both in men and women, which shines so steadily through the novels of Thackeray, would hardly be possible in the works of an Irish novelist. Even Dickens, though too vital a genius and too severely educated in the school of shabby-genteel poverty to have any doubt of the national danger of fatheadedness in high places, evidently assumes rather too hastily the superiority of Mr Meagles to Sir John Chester and Harold Skimpole. On the other hand, it takes an Irishman years of residence in England to learn to respect and like a blockhead. An Englishman will not respect nor like anyone else. Every English statesman has to maintain his popularity by pretending to be ruder, more ignorant, more sentimental, more superstitious, more stupid than any man who has lived behind the scenes of public life for ten minutes can possibly be. Nobody dares to publish really intimate memoirs of him or really private letters of his until his whole generation has passed away, and his party can no longer be compromised by the discovery that the platitudinizing twaddler and hypocritical opportunist was really a man of some perception as well as of strong constitution, peg-away industry, personal ambition, and party keenness.

English Stupidity Excused

I do not claim it as a natural superiority in the Irish nation that it dislikes and mistrusts fools, and expects its political leaders to be clever and humbug-proof. It may be that if our resources included the armed force and virtually unlimited money which push the political and military figureheads of England through bungled enterprizes to a muddled success, and create an illusion of some miraculous and divine innate English quality that enables a general to become a conqueror with abilities that would not suffice to save a cabman from having his license marked, and a member of

Parliament to become a Prime Minister with the outlook on life of a sporting country solicitor educated by a private governess, I have no doubt we should lapse into gross intellectual sottishness, and prefer leaders who encouraged our vulgarities by sharing them, and flattered us by associating them with purchased successes, to our betters. But as it is, we cannot afford that sort of encouragement and flattery in Ireland. The odds against which our leaders have to fight would be too heavy for the fourth-rate Englishmen whose leadership consists for the most part in marking time ostentatiously until they are violently shoved, and then stumbling blindly forward (or backward) wherever the shove sends them. We cannot crush England as a Pickford's van might crush a perambulator. We are the perambulator and England the Pickford. We must study her and our real weaknesses and real strength; we must practise upon her slow conscience and her quick terrors; we must deal in ideas and political principles since we cannot deal in bayonets; we must outwit, outwork, outstay her; we must embarrass, bully, even conspire and assassinate when nothing else will move her, if we are not all to be driven deeper and deeper into the shame and misery of our servitude. Our leaders must be not only determined enough, but clever enough to do this. We have no illusions as to the existence of any mysterious Irish pluck, Irish honesty, Irish bias on the part of Providence, or sterling Irish solidity of character, that will enable an Irish blockhead to hold his own against England. Blockheads are of no use to us: we were compelled to follow a supercilious, unpopular, tongue-tied, aristocratic Protestant Parnell, although there was no lack among us of fluent imbeciles, with majestic presences and oceans of dignity and sentiment, to promote into his place could they have done his work for us. It is obviously convenient that Mr Redmond should be a better speaker and rhetorician than Parnell; but if he began to use his powers to make himself agreeable instead of making himself reckoned with by the enemy; if he set to work to manufacture and support English shams and hypocrisies instead of exposing and denouncing them; if he constituted himself the permanent apologist of doing nothing, and, when the people insisted on his doing something, only roused himself to discover how to pretend to do it without really changing anything, he would lose his leadership as certainly as an English politician would, by the same course, attain a permanent place on the front bench. In short, our circumstances place a premium on political ability whilst the circumstances of England discount it; and the quality of the supply naturally follows the demand. If you miss in my writings that hero-worship of dotards and duffers which is planting England with statues of disastrous statesmen and absurd generals, the explanation is simply that I am an Irishman and you an Englishman.

Irish Protestantism Really Protestant

When I repeat that I am an Irish Protestant, I come to a part of the relation between England and Ireland that you will never understand unless I insist on explaining it to you with that Irish insistence on intellectual clarity to which my English critics are so intensely recalcitrant.

First, let me tell you that in Ireland Protestantism is really Protestant. It is true that there is an Irish Protestant Church (disestablished some thirtyfive years ago) in spite of the fact that a Protestant Church is, fundamentally, a contradiction in terms. But this means only that the Protestants use the word Church to denote their secular organization, without troubling themselves about the metaphysical sense of Christ's famous pun, "Upon this rock I will build my church." The Church of England, which is a reformed Anglican Catholic Anti-Protestant Church, is quite another affair. An Anglican is acutely conscious that he is not a Wesleyan; and many Anglican clergymen do not hesitate to teach that all Methodists incur damnation. In Ireland all that the member of the Irish Protestant Church knows is that he is not a Roman Catholic. The decorations of even the "lowest" English Church seem to him to be extravagantly Ritualistic and Popish. I myself entered the Irish Church by baptism, a ceremony performed by my uncle in "his own church." But I was sent, with many boys of my own denomination, to a Wesleyan school where the Wesleyan catechism was taught without the least protest on the part of the parents, although there was so little presumption in favor of any boy there being a Wesleyan that if all the Church boys had been withdrawn at any moment, the school would have become bankrupt. And this was by no means analogous to the case of those working class members of the Church of England in London, who sent their daughters to Roman Catholic schools rather than to the public elementary schools. They do so for the definite reason that the nuns teach girls good manners and sweetness of speech, which have no place in the County Council curriculum.

But in Ireland the Church parent sends his son to a Wesleyan school (if it is convenient and socially eligible) because he is indifferent to the form of Protestantism, provided it is Protestantism. There is also in Ireland a characteristically Protestant refusal to take ceremonies and even sacraments very seriously except by way of strenuous objection to them when they are conducted with candles or incense. For example, I was never confirmed, although the ceremony was perhaps specially needed in my case as the failure of my appointed godfather to appear at the font led to his responsibilities being assumed on the spot, at my uncle's order, by the sexton. And my case was a very common one, even among people quite untouched by modern skepticisms. Apart from the weekly church-going, which holds its own as a respectable habit, the initiations are perfunctory, the omissions regarded as negligible. The distinction between churchman and dissenter, which in England is a class distinction, a political distinction, and even occasionally a religious distinction, does not exist. Nobody is surprised in Ireland to find that the squire who is the local pillar of the formerly established Church is also a Plymouth Brother, and, except on certain special or fashionable occasions, attends the Methodist meeting-house. The parson has no priestly character and no priestly influence: the High Church curate of course exists and has his vogue among religious epicures of the other sex; but the general attitude of his congregation towards him is that of Dr Clifford. The clause in the Apostle's creed professing belief in a Catholic Church is a standing puzzle to Protestant children; and when they grow up they dismiss it from their minds more often than they solve it, because they really are not Catholics but Protestants to the extremest practicable degree of individualism. It is true that they talk of church and chapel with all the Anglican contempt for chapel; but in Ireland the chapel means the Roman Catholic church, for which the Irish Protestant reserves all the class rancor, the political hostility, the religious bigotry, and the bad blood generally that in England separates the Establishment from the nonconforming Protestant organizations. When a vulgar Irish Protestant speaks of a "Papist" he feels exactly as a vulgar Anglican vicar does when he speaks of a Dissenter. And when the vicar is Anglican enough to call himself a Catholic priest, wear a cassock, and bless his flock with two fingers, he becomes horrifically incomprehensible to the Irish Protestant Churchman, who, on his part, puzzles the Anglican by regarding a Methodist as tolerantly as an Irishman who likes grog regards an Irishman who prefers punch.

A Fundamental Anomaly

Now nothing can be more anomalous, and at bottom impossible, than a Conservative Protestant party standing for the established order against a revolutionary Catholic party. The Protestant is theoretically an anarchist as far as anarchism is practicable in human society: that is, he is an individualist, a free-thinker, a self-helper, a Whig, a Liberal, a mistruster and vilifier of the State, a rebel. The Catholic is theoretically a Collectivist, a self-abnegator, a Tory, a Conservative, a supporter of Church and State one and indivisible, an obeyer. This would be a statement of fact as well as of theory if men were Protestants and Catholics by temperament and adult choice instead of by family tradition. The peasant who supposed that Wordsworth's son would carry on the business now the old gentleman was gone was not a whit more foolish than we who laugh at his ignorance of the nature of poetry whilst we take it as a matter of course that a son should "carry on" his father's religion. Hence, owing to our family system, the Catholic Churches are recruited daily at the font by temperamental Protestants, and the Protestant organizations by temperamental Catholics, with consequences most disconcerting to those who expect history to be deducible from the religious professions of the men who make it.

Still, though the Roman Catholic Church may occasionally catch such Tartars as Luther and Voltaire, or the Protestant organizations as Newman and Manning, the general run of mankind takes its impress from the atmosphere in which it is brought up. In Ireland the Roman Catholic peasant cannot escape the religious atmosphere of his Church. Except when he breaks out like a naughty child he is docile; he is reverent; he is content to regard knowledge as something not his business; he is a child before his Church, and accepts it as the highest authority in science and philosophy. He speaks of himself as a son of the Church, calling his priest father instead of brother or mister. To rebel politically, he must break away from parish tutelage and follow a Protestant leader on national questions. His Church naturally fosters his submissiveness. The

British Government and the Vatican may differ very vehemently as to whose subject the Irishman is to be, but they are quite agreed as to the propriety of his being a subject. Of the two, the British Government allows him more liberty, giving him as complete a democratic control of local government as his means will enable him to use, and a voice in the election of a formidable minority in the House of Commons, besides allowing him to read and learn what he likes—except when it makes a tuft-hunting onslaught on a seditious newspaper. But if he dared to claim a voice in the selection of his parish priest, or a representative at the Vatican, he would be denounced from the altar as an almost inconceivable blasphemer; and his educational opportunities are so restricted by his Church that he is heavily handicapped in every walk of life that requires any literacy. It is the aim of his priest to make him and keep him a submissive Conservative; and nothing but gross economic oppression and religious persecution could have produced the strange phenomenon of a revolutionary movement not only tolerated by the Clericals, but, up to a certain point, even encouraged by them. If there is such a thing as political science, with natural laws like any other science, it is certain that only the most violent external force could effect and maintain this unnatural combination of political revolution with Papal reaction, and of hardy individualism and independence with despotism and subjugation.

That violent external force is the clumsy thumb of English rule. If you would be good enough, ladies and gentlemen of England, to take your thumb away and leave us free to do something else than bite it, the unnaturally combined elements in Irish politics would fly asunder and recombine according to their proper nature with results entirely satisfactory to real Protestantism.

The Nature of Political Hatred

Just reconsider the Home Rule question in light of that very English characteristic of the Irish people, their political hatred of priests. Do not be distracted by the shriek of indignant denial from the Catholic papers and from those who have witnessed the charming relations between the Irish peasantry and their spiritual fathers. I am perfectly aware that the Irish love their priests as devotedly as the French loved them before the Revolution or as the Italians loved them before they imprisoned the Pope in the Vatican. They love their landlords too: many an Irish gentleman has found in his nurse a foster-mother more interested in him than his actual mother. They love the English, as every Englishman who travels in Ireland can testify. Please do not suppose that I speak satirically: the world is full of authentic examples of the concurrence of human kindliness with political rancor. Slaves and schoolboys often love their masters; Napoleon and his soldiers made desperate efforts to save from drowning the Russian soldiers under whom they had broken the ice with their cannon; even the relations between nonconformist peasants and country parsons in England are not invariably unkindly; in the southern States of America planters are often traditionally fond of negros and kind to them, with substantial returns in humble affection; soldiers and sailors often admire and cheer their officers sincerely and heartily; nowhere is actual personal intercourse found compatible for long with the intolerable friction of hatred and malice. But people who persist in pleading these amiabilities as political factors must be summarily bundled out of the room when questions of State are to be discussed. Just as an Irishman may have English friends whom he may prefer to any Irishman of his acquaintance, and be kind, hospitable, and serviceable in his intercourse with Englishmen, whilst being perfectly prepared to make the Shannon run red with English blood if Irish freedom could be obtained at that price, so an Irish Catholic may like his priest as a man and revere him as a confessor and spiritual pastor whilst being implacably determined to seize the first opportunity of throwing off his yoke. This is political hatred: the only hatred that civilization allows to be mortal hatred.

The Revolt against the Priest

Realize, then, that the popular party in Ireland is seething with rebellion against the tyranny of the Church. Imagine the feelings of an English farmer if the parson refused to marry him for less than £20, and if he had virtually no other way of getting married! Imagine the Church Rates revived in the form of an unofficial Income Tax scientifically adjusted to your taxable capacity by an intimate knowledge of your affairs verified in the confessional! Imagine being one of a peasantry reputed the poorest in the world, under the thumb of a priesthood reputed the richest in the world! Imagine a Catholic middle class continually defeated in the struggle of professional, official, and fashionable life by the superior education of its Protestant competitors, and yet forbidden by its priests to resort to the only efficient universities in the country! Imagine trying to get a modern education in a seminary of priests, where every modern book worth reading is on the index, and the earth is still regarded, not perhaps as absolutely flat, yet as being far from so spherical as Protestants allege! Imagine being forbidden to read this preface because it proclaims your own grievance! And imagine being bound to submit to all this because the popular side must hold together at all costs in the face of the Protestant enemy! That is, roughly, the predicament of Roman Catholic Ireland.

Protestant Loyalty: A Forecast

Now let us have a look at Protestant Ireland. I have already said that a "loyal" Irishman is an abhorrent phenomenon, because he is an unnatural one. In Ireland it is not "loyalty" to drink the English king's health and stand uncovered to the English national anthem: it is simply exploitation of English rule in the interests of the property, power, and promotion of the Irish classes as against the Irish masses. From any other point of view it is cowardice and dishonor. I have known a Protestant go to Dublin Castle to be sworn in as a special constable, quite resolved to take the baton and break the heads of a patriotic faction just then upsetting the peace of the town, yet back out at the last moment because he could not bring himself to swallow the oath of allegiance tendered with the baton. There is no such thing as genuine loyalty in Ireland. There is a separation of the Irish people into two hostile camps: one Protestant, gentlemanly, and oligarchical; the other Roman Catholic, popular, and democratic. The oligarchy governs Ireland as a bureaucracy deriving authority from the king of England. It cannot cast him off without casting off its own ascendancy. Therefore it naturally exploits him sedulously, drinking his health, waving his flag, playing his anthem, and using the foolish word "traitor" freely in its cups. But let the English Government make a step towards the democratic party, and the Protestant garrison revolts at once, not with tears and prayers and anguish of soul and years of trembling reluctance, as the parliamentarians of the XVII century revolted against Charles I, but with acrid promptitude and strident threatenings. When

England finally abandons the garrison by yielding to the demand for Home Rule, the Protestants will not go under, nor will they waste much time in sulking over their betrayal, and comparing their fate with that of Gordon left by Gladstone to perish on the spears of heathen fanatics. They cannot afford to retire into an Irish Faubourg St Germain. They will take an energetic part in the national government, which will be sorely in need of parliamentary and official forces independent of Rome. They will get not only the Protestant votes, but the votes of Catholics in that spirit of toleration which is everywhere extended to heresies that happen to be politically serviceable to the orthodox. They will not relax their determination to hold every inch of the government of Ireland that they can grasp; but as that government will then be a national Irish Government instead of as now an English Government, their determination will make them the vanguard of Irish Nationalism and Democracy as against Romanism and Sacerdotalism, leaving English Unionists grieved and shocked at their discovery of the true value of an Irish Protestant's loyalty.

But there will be no open break in the tradition of the party. The Protestants will still be the party of Union, which will then mean, not the Repeal of Home Rule, but the maintenance of the Federal Union of English-speaking commonwealths, now theatrically called the Empire. They will pull down the Union Jack without the smallest scruple; but they know the value of the Channel Fleet, and will cling closer than brothers to that and any other Imperial asset that can be exploited for the protection of Ireland against foreign aggression or the sharing of expenses with the British taxpayer. They know that the Irish coast is for the English invasion-scaremonger the heel of Achilles, and that they can use this to make him pay for the boot.

Protestant Pugnacity

If any Englishman feels incredulous as to this view of Protestantism as an essentially Nationalist force in Ireland, let him ask himself which leader he, if he were an Irishman, would rather have back from the grave to fight England: the Catholic Daniel O'Connell or the Protestant Parnell. O'Connell organized the Nationalist movement only to draw its teeth, to break its determination, and to declare that Repeal of the Union was not worth the shedding of a drop of blood. He died in the bosom of his Church, not in the bosom of his country. The Protestant leaders, from Lord Edward Fitzgerald to Parnell, have never divided their devotion. If any Englishman thinks that they would have been more sparing of blood than the English themselves are, if only so cheap a fluid could have purchased the honor of Ireland, he greatly mistakes the Irish Protestant temper. The notion that Ireland is the only country in the world not worth shedding a drop of blood for is not a Protestant one, and certainly not countenanced by English practice. It was hardly reasonable to ask Parnell to shed blood *quant. suff.* in Egypt to put an end to the misgovernment of the Khedive and replace him by Lord Cromer for the sake of the English bondholders, and then to expect him to become a Tolstoyan or an O'Connellite in regard to his own country. With a wholly Protestant Ireland at his back he might have bullied England into conceding Home Rule; for the insensibility of the English governing classes to philosophical, moral, social considerations—in short, to any considerations which require a little intellectual exertion and sympathetic alertness—is tempered, as we Irish well know, by an absurd susceptibility to intimidation.

For let me halt a moment to impress on you, O English reader, that no fact has been more deeply stamped into us than that we can do nothing with an English Government unless we frighten it, any more than you can yourself. When power and riches are thrown haphazard into children's cradles as they are in England, you get a governing class without industry, character, courage, or real experience; and under such circumstances reforms are produced only by catastrophes followed by panics in which "something must be done." Thus it costs a cholera epidemic to achieve a Public Health Act, a Crimean War to reform the Civil Service, and a gunpowder plot to disestablish the Irish Church. It was by the light, not of reason, but of the moon that the need for paying serious attention to the Irish land question was seen in England. It cost the American War of Independence and the Irish Volunteer movement to obtain the Irish Parliament of 1782, the constitution of which far overshot the nationalist mark of today in the matter of independence.

It is vain to plead that this is human nature and not class weakness. The Japanese have proved that it is possible to conduct social and political changes intelligently and providentially instead of drifting along helplessly until public disasters compel a terrified and inconsiderate rearrangement. Innumerable experiments in local government have shewn that when men are neither too poor to be honest nor too rich to understand and share the needs of the people—as in New Zealand, for example—they can govern much more providently than our little circle of aristocrats and plutocrats.

The Just Englishman

English Unionists, when asked what they have to say in defence of their rule of subject peoples, often reply that the Englishman is just, leaving us divided between our derision of so monstrously inhuman a pretension, and our impatience with so gross a confusion of the mutually exclusive functions of judge and legislator. For there is only one condition on which a man can do justice between two litigants, and that is that he shall have no interest in common with either of them, whereas it is only by having every interest in common with both of them that he can govern them tolerably. The indispensable preliminary to Democracy is the representation of every interest: the indispensable preliminary to justice is the elimination of every interest. When we want an arbitrator or an umpire, we turn to a stranger: when we want a government, a stranger is the one person we will not endure. The Englishman in India, for example, stands, a very statue of justice, between two natives. He says, in effect, "I am impartial in your religious disputes, because I believe in neither of your religions. I am impartial in your conflicts of custom and sentiment, because your customs and sentiments are different from, and abysmally inferior to, my own. Finally, I am impartial as to your interests, because they are both equally opposed to mine, which is to keep you both equally powerless against me in order that I may extract money from you to pay salaries and pensions to myself and my fellow Englishmen as judges and rulers over you. In return for which you get the inestimable benefit of a government that does absolute justice as between Indian and Indian, being wholly preoccupied with the maintenance of absolute injustice as between India and England.

It will be observed that no Englishman, without making himself ridiculous, could pretend to be perfectly just or disinterested in English affairs, or would tolerate a proposal to establish the Indian or Irish system in Great Britain. Yet if the justice of the Englishman is sufficient to ensure the welfare of India or Ireland, it ought to suffice equally for England.

But the English are wise enough to refuse to trust to English justice themselves, preferring democracy. They can hardly blame the Irish for taking the same view.

In short, dear English reader, the Irish Protestant stands outside that English Mutual Admiration Society which you call the Union or the Empire. You may buy a common and not ineffective variety of Irish Protestant by delegating your powers to him, and in effect making him the oppressor and you his sorely bullied and bothered catspaw and military maintainer; but if you offer him nothing for his loyalty except the natural superiority of the English character, you will—well, try the experiment, and see what will happen! You would have a ten-times better chance with the Roman Catholic; for he has been saturated from his youth up with the Imperial idea of foreign rule by a spiritually superior international power, and is trained to submission and abnegation of his private judgment. A Roman Catholic garrison would take its orders from England and let her rule Ireland if England were Roman Catholic. The Protestant garrison simply seizes on the English power; uses it for its own purposes; and occasionally orders the English Government to remove an Irish secretary who has dared to apply English ideas to the affairs of the garrison. Whereupon the English Government abjectly removes him, and implores him, as a gentleman and a loyal Englishman, not to reproach it in the face of the Nationalist enemy.

Such incidents naturally do not shake the sturdy conviction of the Irish Protestant that he is more than a match for any English Government in determination and intelligence. Here, no doubt, he flatters himself; for his advantage is not really an advantage of character, but of comparative directness of interest, concentration of force on one narrow issue, simplicity of aim, with freedom from the scruples and responsibilities of world-politics. The business is Irish business, not English; and he is Irish. And his object, which is simply to secure the dominance of his own caste and creed behind the power of England, is simpler and clearer than the confused aims of English Cabinets struggling ineptly with the burdens of empire, and biased by the pressure of capital anywhere rather than in Ireland. He has no responsibility, no interest, no status outside his own country and his own movement, which means that he has no conscience in dealing with England; whereas England, having a very uneasy conscience, and many hindering and hampering responsibilities and interests in dealing with him, gets bullied and driven by him, and finally learns sympathy with Nationalist aims by her experience of the tyranny of the Orange party.

Irish Catholicism Forecast

Let us suppose that the establishment of a national government were to annihilate the oligarchic party by absorbing the Protestant garrison and making it a Protestant National Guard. The Roman Catholic laity, now a cipher, would organize itself, and a revolt against Rome and against the priesthood would ensue. The Roman Catholic Church would become the official Irish Church. The Irish Parliament would insist on a voice in the promotion of churchmen; fees and contributions would be regulated; blackmail would be resisted; sweating in conventual factories and workshops would be stopped; and the ban would be taken off the universities. In a word, the Roman Catholic Church, against which Dublin Castle is powerless, would meet the one force on earth that can cope with it victoriously. That force is Democracy, a thing far more Catholic than itself. Until that force is let loose against it, the Protestant garrison can do nothing to the priesthood except consolidate it and drive the people to rally round it in defence of their altars against the foreigner and the heretic. When it *is* let loose, the Catholic laity will make as short work of sacerdotal tyranny in Ireland as it has done in France and Italy. And in doing so it will be forced to face the old problem of the relations of Church and State. A Roman Catholic party must submit to Rome: an anti-clerical Catholic party must of necessity become an Irish Catholic party. The Holy Roman Empire, like the other Empires, has no future except as a Federation of national Catholic Churches; for Christianity can no more escape Democracy than Democracy can escape Socialism. It is noteworthy in this connection that the Anglican Catholics have played and are playing a notable part in the Socialist movement in England in opposition to the individualist Secularists of the urban proletariat; but they are quit of the preliminary dead lift that awaits the Irish Catholic. Their Church has thrown off the yoke of Rome, and is safely and permanently Anglicized. But the Catholic Church in Ireland is still Roman. Home Rule will herald the day when the Vatican will go the way of Dublin Castle, and the island of the saints assume the headship of her own Church. It may seem incredible that long after the last Orangeman shall lay down his chalk for ever, the familiar scrawl on every blank wall in the north of Ireland "To hell with the Pope!" may reappear in the south, traced by the hands of Catholics who shall have forgotten the traditional counter legend, "To hell with King William!" (of glorious, pious, and immortal memory); but it may happen so. "The island of the saints" is no idle phrase. Religious genius is one of our national products; and Ireland is no bad rock to build a Church on. Holy and beautiful is the soul of Catholic Ireland: her prayers are lovelier than the teeth and claws of Protestantism, but not so effective in dealing with the English.

English Voltaireanism

Let me familiarize the situation by shewing how closely it reproduces the English situation in its essentials. In England, as in France, the struggle between the priesthood and the laity has produced a vast body of Voltaireans. But the essential identity of the French and English movements has been obscured by the ignorance of the ordinary Englishman, who, instead of knowing the distinctive tenets of his church or sect, vaguely believes them to be the eternal truth as opposed to the damnable error of all the other denominations. He thinks of Voltaire as a French "infidel," instead of as the champion of the laity against the official theocracy of the State Church. The Nonconformist leaders of our Free Churches are all Voltaireans. The warcry of the Passive Resisters is Voltaire's warcry, *Ecrasez l'infâme*. No account need be taken of the technical difference between Voltaire's *infâme* and Dr Clifford's. One was the unreformed Roman Church of France: the other is the reformed Anglican Church; but in both cases the attack has been on a priestly tyranny and a professional monopoly. Voltaire convinced the Genevan ministers that he was the philosophic champion of their Protestant, Individualistic, Democratic Deism against the State Church of Roman Catholic France; and his heroic energy and beneficence as a philanthropist, which now only makes the list of achievements on his monument at Ferney the most impressive epitaph in Europe, then made the most earnest of the Lutheran ministers glad to claim a common inspiration with him. Unfortunately, Voltaire had an irrepressible sense of humor. He joked about Habakkuk; and jokes about Habakkuk smelt too strongly of brimstone to be tolerated by Protestants to whom the Bible was not a literature but a fetish and a talisman. And so Voltaire, in spite of the church he "erected to God," became in England the bogy-atheist of three generations of English ignoramuses, instead of the legitimate successor of Martin Luther and John Knox.

Nowadays, however, Voltaire's jokes are either forgotten or else fall flat on a world which no longer venerates Habakkuk; and his true position is becoming apparent. The fact that Voltaire was a Roman Catholic layman, educated at a Jesuit college, is the conclusive reply to the shallow people who imagine that Ireland delivered up to the Irish democracy— that is, to the Catholic laity—would be delivered up to the tyranny of the priesthood.

Suppose

Suppose, now, that the conquest of France by Henry V of England had endured, and that France in the XVIII century had been governed by an English viceroy through a Huguenot bureaucracy and a judicial bench appointed on the understanding that loyalty for them meant loyalty to England, and patriotism a willingness to die in defence of the English conquest and of the English Church, would not Voltaire in that case have been the meanest of traitors and self-seekers if he had played the game of England by joining in its campaign against his own and his country's Church? The energy he threw into the defence of Calas and Sirven would have been thrown into the defence of the Frenchmen whom the English would have called "rebels"; and he would have been forced to identify the cause of freedom and democracy with the cause of *l'infâme*. The French revolution would have been a revolution against England and English rule instead of against aristocracy and ecclesiasticism; and all the intellectual and spiritual forces in France, from Turgot to De Tocqueville, would have been burnt up in mere anti-Anglicism and nationalist dithyrambs instead of contributing to political science and broadening the thought of the world.

What would have happened in France is what has happened in Ireland; and that is why it is only the small-minded Irish, incapable of conceiving what religious freedom means to a country, who do not loathe English rule. For in Ireland England is nothing but the Pope's policeman. She imagines she is holding the Vatican cardinals at bay when she is really strangling the Voltaires, the Foxes and Penns, the Cliffords, Hortons, Campbells, Walters, and Silvester Hornes, who are to be found among the Roman Catholic laity as plentifully as among the Anglican Catholic laity in England. She gets nothing out of Ireland but infinite trouble, infinite confusion and hindrance in her own legislation, a hatred that circulates through the whole world and poisons it against her, a reproach that makes her professions of sympathy with Finland and Macedonia ridiculous and hypocritical, whilst the priest takes all the spoils, in money, in power, in pride, and in popularity.

Ireland's Real Grievance

But it is not the spoils that matter. It is the waste, the sterilization, the perversion of fruitful brain power into flatulent protest against unnecessary evil, the use of our very entrails to tie our own hands and seal our own lips in the name of our honor and patriotism. As far as money or comfort is concerned, the average Irishman has a more tolerable life—especially now that the population is so scanty—than the average Englishman. It is true that in Ireland the poor man is robbed and starved and oppressed under judicial forms which confer the imposing title of justice on a crude system of bludgeoning and perjury. But so is the Englishman. The Englishman, more docile, less dangerous, too lazy intellectually to use such political and legal power as lies within his reach, suffers more and makes less fuss about it than the Irishman. But at least he has nobody to blame but himself and his fellow countrymen. He does not doubt that if an effective majority of the English people made up their minds to alter the Constitution, as the majority of the Irish people have made up their minds to obtain Home Rule, they could alter it without having to fight an overwhelmingly powerful and rich neighboring nation, and fight, too, with ropes round their necks. He can attack any institution in his country without betraying it to foreign vengeance and foreign oppression. True, his landlord may turn him out of his cottage if he goes to a Methodist chapel instead of to the parish church. His customers may stop their orders if he votes Liberal instead of Conservative. English ladies and gentlemen who would perish sooner than shoot a fox do these things without the smallest sense of indecency and dishonor. But they cannot muzzle his intellectual leaders. The English philosopher, the English author, the English orator can attack every abuse and expose every superstition without strengthening the hands of any common enemy. In Ireland every such attack, every such exposure, is a service to England and a stab to Ireland. If you expose the tyranny and rapacity of the Church, it is an argument in favor of Protestant ascendancy. If you denounce the nepotism and jobbery of the new local authorities, you are demonstrating the unfitness of the Irish to govern themselves, and the superiority of the old oligarchical grand juries.

And there is the same pressure on the other side. The Protestant must stand by the garrison at all costs: the Unionist must wink at every bureaucratic abuse, connive at every tyranny, magnify every official blockhead, because their exposure would be a victory for the Nationalist enemy. Every Irishman is in Lancelot's position: his honor rooted in dishonor stands; and faith unfaithful keeps him falsely true.

The Curse of Nationalism

It is hardly possible for an Englishman to understand all that this implies. A conquered nation is like a man with cancer: he can think of nothing else, and is forced to place himself, to the exclusion of all better company, in the hands of quacks who profess to treat or cure cancer. The windbags of the two rival platforms are the most insufferable of all windbags. It requires neither knowledge, character, conscience, diligence in public affairs, nor any virtue, private or communal, to thump the Nationalist or Orange tub: nay, it puts a premium on the rancor or callousness that has given rise to the proverb that if you put an Irishman on a spit you can always get another Irishman to baste him. Jingo oratory in England is sickening enough to serious people: indeed one evening's mafficking in London produced a determined call for the police. Well, in Ireland all political oratory is Jingo oratory; and all political demonstrations are maffickings. English rule is such an intolerable abomination that no other subject can reach the people. Nationalism stands between Ireland and the light of the world. Nobody in Ireland of any intelligence likes Nationalism any more than a man with a broken arm likes having it set. A healthy nation is as unconscious of its nationality as a healthy man of his bones. But if you break a nation's nationality it will think of nothing else but getting it set again. It will listen to no reformer, to no philosopher, to no

preacher, until the demand of the Nationalist is granted. It will attend to
no business, however vital, except the business of unification and liberation.

That is why everything is in abeyance in Ireland pending the achievement of Home Rule. The great movements of the human spirit which
sweep in waves over Europe are stopped on the Irish coast by the English
guns of the Pigeon House Fort. Only a quaint little offshoot of English
pre-Raphaelitism called the Gaelic movement has got a footing by using
Nationalism as a stalking-horse, and popularizing itself as an attack on
the native language of the Irish people, which is most fortunately also the
native language of half the world, including England. Every election is
fought on nationalist grounds; every appointment is made on nationalist
grounds; every judge is a partisan in the nationalist conflict; every speech
is a dreary recapitulation of nationalist twaddle; every lecture is a corrup-
tion of history to flatter nationalism or defame it; every school is a recruiting station; every church is a barrack; and every Irishman is unspeakably tired of the whole miserable business, which nevertheless is,
and perforce must remain, his first business until Home Rule makes an
end of it, and sweeps the nationalist and the garrison hack together into
the dustbin.

There is indeed no greater curse to a nation than a nationalist movement, which is only the agonizing symptom of a suppressed natural function. Conquered nations lose their place in the world's march because
they can do nothing but strive to get rid of their nationalist movements
by recovering their national liberty. All demonstrations of the virtues of
a foreign government, though often conclusive, are as useless as demonstrations of the superiority of artificial teeth, glass eyes, silver windpipes,
and patent wooden legs to the natural products. Like Democracy, national self-government is not for the good of the people: it is for the satisfaction of the people. One Antonine emperor, one St Louis, one
Richelieu may be worth ten democracies in point of what is called good
government; but there is no satisfaction for the people in them. To deprive a dyspeptic of his dinner and hand it over to a man who can digest it
better is a highly logical proceeding; but it is not a sensible one. To take
the government of Ireland away from the Irish and hand it over to the
English on the ground that they can govern better would be a precisely
parallel case if the English had managed their own affairs so well as to

place their superior faculty for governing beyond question. But as the English are avowed muddlers—rather proud of it, in fact—even the logic of that case against Home Rule is not complete. Read Mr Charles Booth's account of London, Mr Rowntree's account of York, and the latest official report on Dundee, and then pretend, if you can, that Englishmen and Scotchmen have not more cause to hand over their affairs to an Irish Parliament than to clamor for another nation's cities to devastate and another people's business to mismanage.

A Natural Right

The question is not one of logic at all, but of natural right. English universities have for some time past encouraged an extremely foolish academic exercise which consists in disproving the existence of natural rights on the ground that they cannot be deduced from the principles of any known political system. If they could, they would not be natural rights but acquired ones. Acquired rights are deduced from political constitutions, but political constitutions are deduced from natural rights. When a man insists on certain liberties without the slightest regard to demonstrations that they are not for his own good, nor for the public good, nor moral, nor reasonable, nor decent, nor compatible with the existing constitution of society, then he is said to claim a natural right to that liberty. When, for instance, he insists on living, in spite of the irrefutable demonstrations of many able pessimists, from the author of the book of Ecclesiastes to Schopenhauer, that life is an evil, he is asserting a natural right to live. When he insists on a vote in order that his country may be governed according to his ignorance instead of the wisdom of the Privy Council, he is asserting a natural right to self-government. When he insists on guiding himself at twentyone by his own inexperience and folly and immaturity instead of by the experience and sagacity of his father, or the well-stored mind of his grandmother, he is asserting a natural right to independence. Even if Home Rule were as unhealthy as an Englishman's eating, as intemperate as his drinking, as filthy as his smoking, as licentious as his domesticity, as corrupt as his elections, as murderously greedy as his commerce, as cruel as his prisons, and as merciless as his streets, Ireland's claim to self-government would still be as good as England's. King James the First proved so cleverly and conclusively that the satisfaction of natural rights was incompatible with good government that his courtiers called him Solomon. We, more enlightened, call him Fool, solely because we have learnt that nations insist on being governed by their own consent—or, as they put it, by themselves and for themselves—and that they will finally upset a good government which denies them this even if the alternative be a bad government which at least creates and maintains an illusion of democracy. America, as far as one can ascertain, is much worse governed, and has a much more disgraceful political history than England under Charles I; but the American Republic is the stabler government because it starts from a formal concession of natural rights, and keeps up an illusion of safeguarding them by an elaborate machinery of democratic election. And the final reason why Ireland must have Home Rule is that she has a natural right to it.

A Warning

Finally, some words of warning to both nations. Ireland has been deliberately ruined again and again by England. Unable to compete with us industrially, she has destroyed our industries by the brute force of prohibitive taxation. She was perfectly right. That brute force was a more honorable weapon than the poverty which we used to undersell her. We lived with and as our pigs, and let loose our wares in the Englishman's market at prices which he could compete with only by living like a pig himself. Having the alternative of stopping our industry altogether, he very naturally and properly availed himself of it. We should have done the same in his place. To bear malice against him on that score is to poison our blood and weaken our constitutions with unintelligent rancor. In wrecking all the industries that were based on the poverty of our people England did us an enormous service. In omitting to do the same on her own soil, she did herself a wrong that has rotted her almost to the marrow. I hope that when Home Rule is at last achieved, one of our first legislative acts will be to fortify the subsistence of our people behind the bulwark of a standard wage, and to impose crushing import duties on every English trade that flourishes in the slum and fattens on the starvation of our unfortunate English neighbors.

THE GAELIC LEAGUE

To *The Freeman's Journal*, Dublin, 17 October 1910

Sir—Dr [S. B.] Walsh in your issue of the 10th asks where and at what time I gained that experience in Public Health administration in which I am reported to have noticed that Medical Officers of Health wax wealthy during epidemics. The reply is that I never noticed anything of the sort. In the matter of newspaper reporting I suffer from two serious disadvantages. One is that as I am a fairly rapid speaker, the reporter who does not stretch his powers to the utmost soon gets left behind. The other is that reporters almost invariably pay me the high compliment of finding me so interesting that they give themselves up recklessly to the enjoyment of listening to me and throw their duties to the winds. What I said at the Antient Concert Rooms was that the enormous superiority of the public medical officer to the private general practitioner lay in the fact that the former was judged by the vital statistics of his district, his credit, and chances of promotion falling as the death rate and sickness rates rose, whereas the income of the general practitioner varied in the opposite direction; the worse the public health, the richer the private doctor. And I added that I had myself, during an epidemic, seen the Medical Officer of Health looking more and more anxious and worried, whilst all the general practitioners on the committee were buying new clothes and visibly prospering. The reporter, too fascinated by my eloquence to keep up with the flow, just managed to get in the first part about the Medical Officer of Health and the last part about new clothes. Combining the two in his transcript, he achieved the idiotic statement which has so justly led Dr Walsh to believe that I am an imbecile. The truth is, if even one per cent. of the statements attributed to me by the press were true, I should be unfit to be at large.

May I take this opportunity of setting right another misunderstanding. This time it is not the fault of the reporter, but the fault of the general ignorance of Irish life which prevails in Dublin. The remark which I made about the artificial language propagated by the Gaelic League has been taken as applying to the Irish language as actually spoken in the

West of Ireland. In August last I asked some children on the north coast of Sligo Bay what language they spoke. Before asking the question I had found from their conversation that they spoke what is invidiously called the English language very much better than most English children of their age; they seemed to have that natural command of it which is perhaps the most tremendous weapon at present in the hands of Ireland. They informed me that they spoke Irish to their parents at home. I asked whether they could understand a stranger's Irish, meaning by a stranger a person from another county. They said they could not, and that they thought that some strangers had more Irish than they. Their third language, which they did not speak to anybody, was the Gaelic which they were taught at school. They complained of it as being very difficult to write, and when I asked them whether they preferred to write English they gave a perfect whoop of assent.

It happened that long before the Gaelic League was thought of I learnt something about Gaelic from the late James Lecky, one of its rediscoverers. It presented itself to him as a highly artificial literary exercise, comparable to V-century Latin, and having about as much to do with vernacular Irish as V-century Latin had to do with the vernacular Italian of that period, or as Trinity College Greek has to do with the Greek actually spoken today in the streets of Athens. I know that in Donegal some of our Gaelic League enthusiasts are trying hard, by setting native Irish speakers to work on their literary exercises, to produce a sort of Gaelic Esperanto which can be imposed on us as our native language; and it is possible that they may succeed so far as to convert the local dialects into some sort of standard speech, and even to produce a state of things in which a traveler, confronted with cryptic Gaelic noticeboards in all directions, may be able to ask the nearest Irish-speaking laborer what they mean without receiving a confession of hopeless ignorance. It is also possible that the Gaelic League may stimulate Englishmen to study Anglo-Saxon, and throw off the yoke of that foreign language which managed to impose itself on Shakespear as it imposed itself on Swift, and on Pitt, and on Gladstone, as on O'Connell and Parnell. And I do not doubt that an Anglo-Saxon League would do a great deal of good incidentally, as the Gaelic League has done. The Gaelic League has given most excellent advice to our countrymen, and I believe that the remarkable increase of personal self-respect and genuine patriotism, of which I have seen unmistakeable signs almost everywhere in Ireland except in Dublin, has been largely guided by that advice. But the advice was not written in Gaelic; it was written in the language of half mankind.

Along with that increase of self-respect there has arisen a new and very foolish fashion in Ireland. I have heard several Irishmen say, when the question of language was mooted, that if other nations were to have a language of their own, they did not see why Ireland should not have one. I quite expect before long to see the beginning of a movement to establish an Irish sun and moon, on the ground that the present articles are English.

Yours truly,

G. Bernard Shaw.

THE IRISH LITERARY MOVEMENT

Remarks by Shaw from the chair following a lecture by W. B. Yeats on contemporary Irish theatre, at the Adelphi Club, London, 11 March 1910. Published in *Yeats and the Theatre*, eds. Robert O'Driscoll and Lorna Reynolds (Toronto: Macmillan, 1975), from a verbatim but garbled stenographic transcription in the possession of Senator Michael Yeats; amended by the present editors.

I have very little to say; in fact, nothing. All I have to say on this subject has been said with great exactitude by Mr Yeats. What he has been saying is really, to every person who understands true poetry, a commonplace—which is the highest compliment I can pay to the lecturer. That is why he often makes a statement of great extravagance and great remoteness. But it would be a very disastrous thing if you in this audience imagined, because Mr Yeats is pronouncedly an Irishman, and because this lecture would not be delivered by Mr Gosse,[1] that Synge was a different sort of person from an Englishman, and that the problem he endeavored to solve, to bring art into existence (for poetry is only an attempt to try and get at the profoundest object of your life) . . . was at all a thing peculiar to *our* country.

It is a very significant thing that Synge began his career by wandering all over the world, and I think it probable that he did not become acutely conscious of Ireland till he got out of Ireland. *[Laughter.]* I was asked where this movement began, and I said I thought, to the best of my knowledge, it began in Bedford Park.[2] *[Laughter.]* That may not be strictly true, but what I meant was that it really exists everywhere. If you want to get an idea of the art that comes from an intense interest in life

1. Edmund Gosse was a highly respected English literary critic and librarian of the House of Lords. The lecture over which Shaw presided was the last in a series of three by Yeats on contemporary poetry and theatre, with emphasis on the accomplishments of the recently deceased J. M. Synge. William Carlos Williams, who attended the second lecture two nights earlier, remarked, "It was a very fashionable affair . . . presided over by Sir Edmund Gosse, who, it appears, hated the Irishman's guts" (Williams, *Autobiography*, 1967).

2. This was Yeats's London residence in the 1880s, when Shaw first knew him, at 3 Blenheim Road.

you have nothing to do but look at a great artist—[like] Rembrandt. That was what made him a great artist. He was not an artist of wonderful beauty. He was a man extraordinarily interested in life and all its manifestations. You will find that Bouguereau has an extreme interest in beautiful women. He tries to make their flesh look like ivory. *[Laughter.]* But if you study the paintings of Rembrandt you will find he took as much interest in old women as in young. That is always the sign of a great man. *[Laughter.]* I have always been interested in old women myself. *[Loud laughter.]* The difficulty in Ireland is that they do not want an ugly, mean, cowardly, dirty Irishman: they want an ideal Irishman just as Bouguereau wants his pretty women with skin like a visiting card.[3] *[Laughter.]*

In Ireland we still have a strong sense of religion and a strong sense of honor, things you dont meet with in England. *[Laughter.]* When I speak of religion I speak of it in a large sense. Once get a man who wants to develop life and make more of life and you have got hold of an extremely dangerous man, who will sacrifice himself, and if necessary sacrifice *you.* For the last 150 years England has been thoroughly commercialized. Perhaps it can't be helped. But since the object of commerce is to buy cheap and sell dear, and to try to "get on," and since that is entirely incompatible with religion and incompatible with honor *[laughter]*, and since you can't live without something to look for, you have got to get something from which you can get some respect for yourselves, and you get Morality! *[Laughter.]* That means, you do what everybody else does. It is different in Ireland. We have not had to supersede religion and honor by morality. I believe in this country it will some day be no longer necessary for you to do that. I believe such remnants of religion and honor as remain among you are with those who have nothing to do with morality—who do not buy and do not sell. *[Laughter.]* As far as you have got a little corner of society in which you have this—you who are living for your country and dont want to be paid so much per cent. for doing it—you have common ground of understanding with Irishmen. We may in Ireland have to go

3. Adolphe Bouguereau, a French artist popular among the Victorians for religious and mythic subjects, was noted for his ability to paint white on white. In a critical notice in *The World,* 21 July 1886, Shaw spoke of his *Spring* as a "masterpiece of ivory nakedness." Visiting cards, including Shaw's own (a set is preserved in the Shaw collection at Guelph), were printed on small rectangles of vellum.

through the same process. Then perhaps you will have religion and honor in England and we in Ireland shall have morality.

If you will do what none of you in this room have ever done, take up your Bible and read it from one end to the other *[laughter]*, you will be surprised to find that morality is not alluded to from the first page to the last, and where it is indirectly referred to it is with every opprobrium and contempt. If you will turn to the works of the tinker, [John] Bunyan, you will find when he wants to express what is most utterly damnable he describes a place called Morality, and introduces two of its leading citizens as Mr Legality and Mr Worldly Wiseman. He didnt see that by the XIX century you would all be in the town of Morality. *[Laughter.]* And that is why some of you quarrel with my play.[4] *[Laughter.]*

I do not believe the wonderful genius referred to by Mr Yeats is confined to Ireland. If you meet an artist you always find he is a monomaniac. He is born with it and must go through with it. I believe the greatest artists are the men who respond to a demand. They must have talent, if you like, but after all the really great man is always a utilitarian. I say that because I am a utilitarian myself. *[Laughter.]* I did not begin to write plays because I was inspired to do it; I began to write a play because one was asked for. I always set down myself and Lady Gregory, if she will allow me, as being persons in comparatively advanced life who found we could do something that people wanted, and we did it. *[Laughter and applause.]* I am so anxious that the peculiar impression Mr Yeats makes in coming from a strange land and a strange people should not discourage you. Perhaps it fills you with contempt! *[Laughter.]* I would like people to understand that there is just as much artistic genius in England as there is in Ireland. Now, do not, for Heaven's sake, let the moral of this evening be for you an interest in Ireland. *[Mr Yeats: "Hear, hear." Laughter.]* Ireland can take care of herself. What you have got to do is to seek your own salvation. *[Laughter and applause.]*

4. The play referred to is presumably *The Shewing-up of Blanco Posnet*, which had recently been banned by the lord chamberlain in England although successfully produced by the Irish National Theatre in Dublin in August 1909.

MY MOTTO IS IRELAND FOR ALL

Extract from a "Special Interview" on current issues, self-drafted by
Shaw for the Dublin press. Published in *The Freeman's Journal* and
in *The Evening Telegraph*, 3 October 1910.

Have your views on the Irish question, Mr Shaw, undergone any change
since the preface to *John Bull's Other Island*?

No: the preface to *John Bull's Other Island* is the final and infallible statement of the Irish question.

Have you sufficient acquaintance with Irish internal politics to have
formed an opinion on Sinn Féin or on the All-for-Ireland League?[1]

Sinn Fein I regard as an inspired title—a masterpiece. No doubt there are
four or perhaps five persons behind it—in fact, I once met a real live Sinn
Feiner, and a very nice girl she was[2]—but the title is the thing. Splendid!
But I despise All-for-Ireland. My motto is Ireland for All. Our place in the
world will depend on the quantity of work we do for it. What are our
brains for?

When are you going to write a new and up-to-date play on Ireland?

I do not intend to write an up-to-date play about Ireland. Up-to-date generally means up to the seventeenth century or thereabouts. Besides, all the
up-to-date Irish plays express the most furious detestation of Ireland. The
souls of the writers are sick of Dublin, and of all our stale brags and sentimentalities, our heroic talk, and our horrible squalor and infant mortality
and poverty. And they are quite right. Until we get rid of the Irish idea and

---

1. The All-for-Ireland League—split from the United Irish League—was
founded in Cork on 31 March 1910 by the journalist-Nationalist William O'Brien,
who called for "Conference, Conciliation, Consent" to resolve the Irish question. It
had little influence and vanished by 1918, leaving the political field to Sinn Féin. Un-
beknownst to Shaw, its full credo was: "All for Ireland, Ireland for All."

2. Mabel W. McConnell, a fellow Fabian, served Shaw as a substitute secretary
early in 1909. A fervent Irish Nationalist, she later married the Sinn Féin politician
Desmond FitzGerald.

get hold of the human idea—the true Catholic idea—we shall never be real Irishmen. We shall continue to be tired of Ireland and of ourselves, and to see our country kept up mainly because it amuses Englishmen.

What do you think—

I think that I have talked enough. If you want more come and hear me [that night] at the Antient Concert Rooms,[3] where my mother sang so often in the old days of the Amateur Musical Society. My music, which is only chin music, will not be so harmonious as hers, but you will find it stimulating and instructive. Good morning.

3. Shaw, concluding a six-week visit to Ireland, had undertaken to lecture on "The Poor Law and Destitution in Ireland" for the Irish Committee to Promote the Break-up of the Poor-law. His remarks were covered extensively in the Dublin papers on 4 October 1910.

THE IRISH PLAYERS

An "interview," written entirely by Shaw, in *The Evening Sun,*
New York, 9 December 1911

"I presume, Mr Shaw, you have heard the latest news of your Blanco Posnet in America with the Irish Players," he was asked.[1]

"No. Why? Has it failed?" Mr Shaw answered.

"Quite the contrary," he was assured.

"Oh, in that case, why should I hear about it?" he said. "Success is the usual thing in my plays; it is what I write them for. I only hear about them when something goes wrong."

"But are you not interested in the success of the Irish Players? or was that a matter of course too?"

"By no means," Mr Shaw answered. "I warned Lady Gregory that America was an extremely dangerous country to take a real Irish company to."[2]

"But why? Surely America, with its immense Irish element—"

"Rubbish; there are not half-a-dozen real Irishmen in America outside that company of actors," he exclaimed. "You dont suppose that all these Murphys and Doolans and Donovans and Farrells and Caseys and O'Connells who call themselves by romantic names like the Clan na Gael[3] and the like are Irishmen! You know the sort of people I mean. They call Ireland the Old Country."

"This time you really are not serious, Mr Shaw. You will tell me next that Mr John Devoy is not an Irishman."[4]

1. When the Abbey Theatre players toured America during the season 1911–12, Irish-Americans in half a dozen cities demonstrated against what they considered to be unflattering portrayals of the Irish people, particularly in J. M. Synge's *The Playboy of the Western World.*

2. Isabella Augusta Persse, Lady Gregory, playwright and codirector of the Abbey Theatre, accompanied the players on their American tour.

3. The American branch of the Irish Republican Brotherhood, or Fenians, founded in 1867.

4. Famous Fenian and leader of the Clan-na-Gael in New York.

"Devoy?" said Mr Shaw. "Devoy? Thats not an Irish name."

"Not an Irish name! Oh, come, Mr Shaw! Tell me that Smith is not an English name; that Roosevelt is not an American name; that Julius Caesar is not a Roman name; but not that Devoy is not an Irish name. Why, to us across the water, Devoy means Ireland," the interviewer suggested.

"It would!" said Mr Shaw compassionately. "I'm sorry for you. Theres no such name in Ireland. Theres no such name anywhere. It isnt a name. It must be de Vaux; a Frenchman who does not know how to spell his own name."

"No, Devoy. D-e-v-o-y. No mistake about it."

Mr Shaw heaved a patient sigh and became sweet-voiced.

"Listen to me," he said. "You know, dont you, that I was not brought up to be a playwright and philosopher, but to be an Irish land agent?"

"Never heard a word of it, Mr Shaw. You astonish me."

"Well, I was. I know more about Irish names than anyone outside the profession of land agency—it's a profession in Ireland—can possibly know. I have collected rents from thousands of tenants in every province in Ireland, and filled up the receipts with this hand—the hand that wrote Blanco Posnet. Such is life! Well, I tell you I never came on the name of Devoy once.

"Oh, I could not possibly have forgotten. Devlin, perhaps. Dempsey, if you like. Devenish, certainly. Dubedat, quite possibly. But Devoy— No! I know the whole country from Balbriggan where every second family is named Hamlet (Shakespear must have visited it) to Tipperary where every living soul is named Ryan, and there is not a Devoy in the place. Depend upon it, his nurse told him he was devoid of something or other—possibly of Irish blood—and he caught it up wrongly and thought she meant that his name was Devoy."

"But even then he might be Irish, Mr Shaw."

"No; he would never talk about the Clan na Gael if he were Irish. I am Irish, typically Irish. Did you ever hear me talk about the Clan na Gael? We have these Clan na Gael Irishmen in Dublin: they come over from Liverpool in the cattle boats. You know what the name means: the collectors of gold. They collect gold when they can get it—coppers when they cant. For 'Ould Ireland' of course. Shall I tell you what they did in Dublin to the Irish Players? There was a very great Irish dramatic poet, who died young, named John Synge—a real Irish name—just the sort of name the Collectors of Gold never think of.

"Well, John Synge wrote a wonderful play called The Playboy of the Western World, which is now a classic. This play was not about an Irish peculiarity, but about a universal weakness of mankind: the habit of admiring bold scoundrels. Most of the heros of history are bold scoundrels, you will notice. English and American boys read stories about Charles Peace the burglar and Ned Kelly the highwayman, and even about Teddy Roosevelt the rough rider.

"The Playboy is a young man who brags of having killed his father, and is made almost as great a hero as if he were an Italian general who had killed several thousand other people's fathers. Synge satirizes this like another Swift, but with a joyousness and a wild wealth of poetic imagery that Swift never achieved.

"Well, sir, if you please, this silly Dublin Clan na Gael, or whatever it calls itself, suddenly struck out the brilliant idea that to satirize the follies of humanity is to insult the Irish nation, because the Irish nation is, in fact, the human race and has no follies, and stands there pure and beautiful and saintly to be eternally oppressed by England and collected for by the Clan.

"There were just enough of them to fill the Abbey Theatre for a night or two to the exclusion of the real Irish people, who simply get sick when they hear this sort of balderdash talked about Ireland. Instead of listening to a great play by a great Irishman, they bawled and whistled and sang 'God Save Ireland' (not without reason, by the way), and prevented themselves from hearing a word of the performance.

"Lady Gregory and William Butler Yeats, who are really Irish, took their money in their thrifty Irish way, and waited. The Clan was soon cleaned out. It appealed for collections to keep its protest up; but little by little its resources dwindled. From occupying the whole house, it came to occupy barely half of it; and then the other half, the Irish half, began to hear scraps of the play through the noise, and found that it was so good that they wanted to hear more.

"When the Clan had dwindled a little more, the Irish nation perceived that it had a numerical as well as national advantage, and began throwing the Clan out. After a few days the whole Clan was outside, collecting for something else; and the play was being listened to as quietly and delightedly as it afterwards was throughout England. But Lady Gregory and Mr Yeats were sad. They missed the Clan's money. Good English money," added Mr Shaw reflectively, after a pause.

"Do you think there will be trouble with the Clan in New York?"

"I think there may be trouble anywhere where there are men who have lost touch with Ireland, and still keep up the old bragging and posing. You must bear in mind that Ireland is now in full reaction against them. The stage Irishman of the XIX century, generous, drunken, thriftless, with a joke always on his lips and a sentimental tear always in his eye, was highly successful as a borrower of money from Englishmen—both in Old and New England—who indulged and despised him because he flattered their sense of superiority.

"But the real Irishman of today is so ashamed of him, and so deeply repentant for having ever stooped to countenance and ape him in the darkest days of the Captivity that the Irish Players have been unable to find a single play by a young writer in which Ireland is not lashed for his follies. We no longer brazen out the shame of our subjection in idle boasting.

"Even in Dublin, that city of tedious and silly derision, where men can do nothing but sneer, they no longer sneer at other nations. In a modern Irish play the hero doesnt sing that 'Ould Ireland' is his country and his name it is Molloy; he pours forth all his bitterness on it like the prophets of old.

"The last time I saw an Irish play in Dublin, the line on which the hero made his most effective exit was 'I hate Ireland.' Even in the plays of Lady Gregory, penetrated as they are by that intense love of Ireland which is unintelligible to the many drunken blackguards with their Irish names who make their nationality an excuse for their vices and their worthlessness, there is no flattery of the Irish; she writes about the Irish as Molière wrote about the French, having a talent curiously like Molière's.

"In the plays of Mr Yeats you will find many Irish heros, but nothing like 'the broth of a boy.' Now, you can imagine the effect of all this on the American pseudo-Irish, who are still exploiting the old-stage Ireland for all it is worth and defiantly singing 'Who Fears to Speak of '98?'[5] under

5. A patriotic ballad by John Kells Ingram, praising the rebels of 1798.

the very nose of the police—that is, the New York police, who are mostly Fenians.

"Their notion of patriotism is to listen jealously for the slightest hint that Ireland is not the home of every virtue and the martyr of every oppression, and thereupon to brawl and bully or to whine and protest, according to their popularity with the bystanders. When these people hear a little real Irish sentiment from the Irish Players they will not know where they are; they will think the tour of the Irish Company is an Orange conspiracy financed by Mr Balfour."

"Have you seen what the central council of the Irish County Association of Greater Boston says about the Irish Players?"

"Yes; but please do not say I said so; it would make them insufferably conceited to know that their little literary effort had been read right through by men. You will observe that they begin by saying that they know their Ireland as children know their mothers. Not a very happy bit of rhetoric that, because children never do know their mothers; they may idolize them or fear them, as the case may be; but they dont know them.

"But can you conceive a body of Englishmen or Frenchmen or Germans publishing such silly stuff about themselves or their country? If they said such a thing in Ireland they would be laughed out of the country. They declare that they are either Irish peasants or the sons of Irish peasants. What on earth does the son of an American immigrant know about Ireland? Fancy the emigrant himself, the man who has left Ireland to stew in its own juice, talking about feeling towards Ireland as children feel towards their mothers. Of course a good many children do leave their mothers to starve; but I doubt if that was what they meant. No doubt they are peasants—a name, by the way, which they did not pick up in Ireland, where it is unknown—for they feel towards literature and art exactly as peasants do in all countries; that is, they regard them as departments of vice—of what policemen call gaiety.

"No real Irish peasant would pretend for a moment to be an authority on literature; but these fellows put down the names of all the famous playwrights they ever heard of, beginning with Shakespear, and challenge the world to—I will give you their exact words—'to single out any of their productions where all the characters without exception are vicious, depraved, or vulgar.'

"And now will you please look at the list of refined, high-minded British dramatists whom they cite as superiors of our modern Irish ones. To begin with: Wycherley! Actually Wycherley! Wycherley is purer than Synge. Congreve—their next selection—Congreve, the creator of Lady Wishfort, is the writer whose delicacy is to put Lady Gregory to shame.

"Was it kind of the editor of The Boston Post to allow these poor devils to pillory themselves in this fashion? Good heavens!" exclaimed Bernard Shaw, waving a clipping from the Post in his hand, "see how they trot out all the old rubbish. 'Noble and impulsive,' 'generous, harum-scarum, lovable characters,' 'generosity, wit, and triumphant true love'; these are the national characteristics they modestly claim as Irishmen who know Ireland as children know their mothers.

"And then, of course, the final, inevitable indecency about Irishwomen being the purest in Christendom. Irishwomen know very well what is thought of women who are not ashamed to boast of their chastity. What they must feel when men professing to be Irishmen go about the world bragging of it I leave you to imagine. It makes every decent Irishman and Irishwoman shiver with shame and disgust. Why do you stand this sort of thing in America? Why dont you pack all these fervent patriots back to Liverpool, or Glasgow, or Bermondsey, or wherever else they may have come from?"

"Well, we shall tell them your opinion of them, Mr Shaw. Are you pleased with the reception of Blanco Posnet?"

"I do not yet know how it is being received," Mr Shaw replied. "I do not mean in the theatre; it is safe enough there. But Blanco is a tract. As far as I can make out, an enormous number of young American men are Blanco Posnets. I doubt if there has ever been a country in the world's history where men were so ashamed of being decent, of being sober, of being well-spoken, of being educated, of being gentle, of being conscientious, as in America.

"The mere tyranny of fashion forces them to take oneanother into saloons and treat to drinks, to swear and fight; to speak of women only in obscene jests and religion only in blasphemies, although it is quite certain that the majority of them are doing this only on a false point of honor, and would much rather behave decently if American civilization permitted them.

"But it does not. This atmosphere of violence and drunkenness and obscenity and blasphemy is the whole of American civilization in many districts, just as it is four-fifths of modern civilization everywhere. That is what all good men have to fight; and it has to be fought by giving these men self-respect through religion. But it is now clear that the old ways of offering them religion—the cackle of Elder Daniels in my play, for example—are useless—worse than useless—because they provoke a coarser, more insolent blasphemy in derision of them.

"In Blanco Posnet I have tried another way. I have gone back to the way of the prophets to whom God was a terrible adversary, who wrestled with him and reproached him, and who yielded only when they became conscious that the will against which they were struggling was the nobler part of their own will. Elder Daniels does not like my way, naturally.

"In England, Elder Daniels is the Lord Chamberlain, and will not let the play be performed. He even persuaded Dublin Castle to try and stop it; and you will observe that the Clan na Gael instinctively takes the side of Dublin Castle; for without Dublin Castle there would be no Clan na Gael—nothing to blow up—no subscriptions. But Lady Gregory fought a routed Dublin Castle; and in America she will simply walk over the Clan na Gael unless it has the sense to understand that she is the greatest living Irishwoman, and that cultivated Americans will attach much more importance to anything she says or does than to splutterings of Bostonian sham Irish peasants who do not know the difference between Wycherley and Goldsmith and shriek in the same breath that Irishwomen are the purest in Christendom and that Lady Gregory is a disgrace to her sex."

"May I ask you one more question, Mr Shaw? You have told us who is the greatest living Irishwoman. Who is the greatest living Irishman?"

"Well, there are such a lot of them. You tell me that in America you have conceded that distinction to Mr Devoy. Mr Yeats could give you offhand the names of six men, not including himself or myself, who may possibly turn out to be the greatest of us all; for Ireland, since she purified her soul from the Clan na Gael nonsense, is producing serious men—not merely Irishmen, you understand, for an Irishman is only a parochial man after all, but men in the fullest international as well as the national sense—the wide human sense."

THE PROTESTANTS OF IRELAND

I

The Christian Globe, London, 22 February 1912

What is wanted on both sides of the channel is a little real Protestantism. This craven terror of poor old Rome—of a Pope who is less free personally than any atheist, and less powerful than the nearest surgeon—is not Protestantism; it is the cowardice that is the invariable symptom and penalty of want of faith. You have only to compare a great protestant manifesto like Houston Chamberlains's Foundations of the Nineteenth Century with the panics of Sir Edward Carson and Lord Londonderry[1] to realize how completely Ireland has been kept out of the mighty stream of modern Protestantism by her preoccupation with her unnatural political condition.

There is one force and one only that Rome cannot face, and that is Democracy. In democratic America, Irish Roman Catholics desert their Church by tens of thousands. In oligarchic Castle-ruled Ireland the bitterest enemies of the priests would die rather than desert in the face of the enemy. In France the Roman Church cannot get even common justice. In Italy the Pope is a prisoner in his own palace. In Spain priests and nuns depend on police and military protection for their personal safety. In Ireland alone the priest is powerful, thanks to the hatred, terror, faithlessness, and folly of the Protestants who stand between him and his natural enemy, Democracy.

There is only one chance for priestly tyranny under Home Rule, and that is the chance of the Protestants insisting that the Irish Parliament shall be denied the power to set the Roman house in order. The most pressing need in Ireland today is the Establishment of the Roman Catholic Church. At present the priests levy taxation without audit or responsibility, and their charges for their official services—for marriages, funer-

---

1. These were Ulster leaders. Carson, a Unionist M.P., engineered the Ulster Covenant, by which thousands of northern Irish pledged themselves to union with Great Britain and refused to recognize any Home Rule parliament.

als, &c.—would make an English farmer gasp. This taxation should be levied by the Irish Parliament, which should pay the priests and regulate the charges, besides controling ecclesiastical patronage. Factory Acts should be applied resolutely to convent workshops and the like, and the Inspector of Education should exact as high a standard from convent schools as from lay ones.

Will the Roman Church accept these conditions? If not, there is no reason to prohibit Establishment. If so, all the better. But the Orangeman will demand, with a shriek, [to know] whether he will be taxed to support the Roman Church in Ireland. There is no reason why he should not; he is already taxed to support it in Malta, and to support Mahometanism and suppress the sale of the Bible in the Soudan, not to mention still stranger things in India. All that he can reasonably claim is that, if there is to be a spiritual budget, he is entitled to his share of it. Concurrent endowment of Romans, Presbyterians, Church of Ireland, &c., is not impossible. The simplest plan, however, would be to exempt non-Catholics from the tax. Where is the difficulty?

Let us suppose that the Roman Church refuses all State interference. Continental experience proves that the interference will take place all the same. The priests cannot refuse or defy the Factory Acts of the Irish Parliament, nor expect unconditional Education grants from it. Irish priests may regard the possibility of municipal churches with municipally regulated fees as a wild dream; but the best Roman Catholic Church I ever visited was (and is) in Genoa, where the sacristan was a buttoned and braided municipal official, and the staff of officiating priests was in fact— whatever it may have been in theory—a municipal staff. If the Orangemen[2] would open their minds to these contemporary facts and practical probabilities, and clear their imaginations of thumbscrews, and stakes and faggots, and nuns on the rack, we should soon have the Irish Protestants asking the Government to make Roman Church Establishment a feature of the Home Rule Bill, and the priesthood resisting the proposal and clinging with all its might to its present irresponsible power and riches.

2. Northern Protestants in Ireland have been called Orangemen because so many of them belonged to the secret Orange Society (taking its name from William of Orange), founded in 1795 and pledged to Protestant dominance in Ulster.

Enough, then, of these drunken Ulsterics and maudlin singings of Rule Britannia. The North used to sing The Protestant Boys will Carry the Drum. It was manlier than clinging to Britannia's skirts for protection against the Bogy Man with the triple tiara.

I suppose it is useless to remind the Orange North that honor and humanity are to be found in Roman Catholic Ireland at least as conspicuously as in Belfast, and that as, though Calvin burnt Servetus, and priests have been quite as horribly persecuted as parsons, the Roman Catholics have managed to survive Protestant domination, perhaps there may be some hope for Protestants under Home Rule.

At all events, pure materialistic cowardice will not save the situation.

II

Delivered before a meeting in the Memorial Hall, London, 6 December 1912. Published in a pamphlet, *What Irish Protestants Think: Speeches on Home Rule* (London: Irish Press Agency, 1913).

I am an Irishman; my father was an Irishman, and my mother an Irishwoman; and my father and my mother were Protestants, who would have been described by a large section of their fellow countrymen in the ruder age when I was young sanguinary Protestants. Many of the duties of my mother were shared by an Irish nurse, who was a Catholic, and she never put me to bed without sprinkling me with Holy Water. What is there to laugh at in an Irish Catholic woman sprinkling with Holy Water—and you know what Holy Water meant to her—a little Protestant infant, whose parents grossly underpaid her? The fact that you can laugh at the underpayment of a poor Irishwoman shews how this open wound of the denial of our National rights is keeping us a hundred years behind the rest of the world on social and industrial questions. I shall make a few jokes for you presently, as you seem to expect them from me; but I beg you not to laugh at them until I come to them. To my mind this relation of mine to my old nurse is not a thing to be laughed at. It is a pathetic and sacred relation, and it disposes completely of the notion that between the Catholic and the Irish Protestant there be any natural animosity.

Though I have been before the British public as a political speaker for thirty years, this is the first time I have ever spoken in public on the subject of Home Rule. During that period I have taken part in more or less all the General Elections at which Home Rule was at stake. I have heard English party politicians desperately trying to excite themselves about it, and to excite their audiences about it; and I have never once heard them succeed. You may take it from me that the British electorate does not care a rap about Home Rule or Ireland. It is hard enough to induce them to take an interest in their own affairs, it is impossible to make them take an interest in ours. Why should they? They know too well that they do not govern us any more than they govern themselves. Ireland is not governed by Englishmen, but by a handful of Irishmen who exploit our country in the name of England as far as the Irish democracy will stand it.

My own personal feeling in the matter is curiously unreasonable. I will not defend it; but I will tell you what it is. My career has been in many respects a most deserving one. I have displayed all the virtues set out in Smiles's Self-Help. I have won a position of some distinction [a voice: "That was the Holy Water"]—well, many less plausible explanations are current. But the confession I have to make is that, while none of these distinctions which I have achieved by the exercise of the copybook virtues has ever given me a moment's self-complacency, the mere geographical accident of my birth, for which I deserve no credit whatever—this fact that I am an Irishman—has always filled me with a wild and inextinguishable pride. I am also proud of being a Protestant, though Protestantism is to me a great historic movement of Reformation, Aspiration, and Self-Assertion against spiritual tyrannies rather than that organization of false gentility which so often takes its name in vain in Ireland. Already at this meeting pride in Protestantism as something essentially Irish has broken out again and again. I cannot describe what I feel when English Unionists are kind enough to say, "Oh, you are in danger of being persecuted by your Roman Catholic fellow countrymen. England will protect you." I would rather be burnt at the stake by Irish Catholics than protected by Englishmen. We Protestants know perfectly well that we are quite able to take care of ourselves, thank you. I do not want to banish religion from politics, though I do want to abolish the thing miscalled religion in this controversy from the world altogether. I want to bring religion back into politics. There is nothing that revolts me in the present state of things more than the unnatural religious calm in Ireland. I do not want a peaceful Ireland in that sense. I want a turbulent Ireland. All free and healthy nations are full of the turbulence of controversy, political, religious, social: all sorts of controversy. Without it you can have no progress, no life.

In Ireland we Protestant Nationalists dare not utter a controversial word lest we should be misunderstood on the great question of national rights. I have much to say in criticism of Catholicism in Ireland; but I dare not say it lest I should be supposed to be speaking on behalf of Unionism. I have quite as much to say in criticism of Irish Protestantism; but that, too, I must not say lest I should discredit my Protestant colleagues against the day when they will have to claim their share in the self-government of Ireland—and let me say that it will be an important share; for our Catholics are far too amiable and indulgent to take care of public money as Protestants do. The Local Government Act of 1898 made a revolutionary change from the most extreme form of Oligarchy to the most extreme form of Democracy; but we Protestants are kept out of the local council because it is feared that the return of a Protestant would be a triumph for Unionism. The denial of Home Rule corrupts every election and every division in Parliament. Consider the Land Purchase Acts; to some of us they are the salvation of Ireland. To me they are its damnation—the beginning of landlordism all over again on a poorer and therefore a worse and more oppressive scale. Many thought as I did; but we all had to be unanimous in support of the Acts, because to oppose them would have been to go over to the enemy. We Irish Protestants are bound and gagged at every turn by the Union.

As to the persecution scare, I decline to give any guarantees. I am not going to say, "Please, kind English masters, if you give us Home Rule we will be good boys." We will persecute and be persecuted if we like, as the English do; we are not children: we do not offer conditions of good behavior as the price of our national rights. No nation should be called upon to make such conditions. Wherever there is a Church, that Church will persecute if it can; but the remedy for that is Democracy. We Protestants will take our chance. If you come to that, think of the chances our Catholic priesthood is taking! Look at what has happened to them in Free France! Look at what has happened to them in Rome itself! Many of them would be glad enough to be safe in the island of the saints. I am far more anxious about the future of the unfortunate English when they lose us. What will they do without us to think for them? The English are a remarkable race; but they have no commonsense. We never lose our commonsense. The English people say that if we got Home Rule we should cut each other's throats. Who has a better right to cut them? They are very glad to get us to cut the throats of their enemies. Why should we not have the same privilege among ourselves? What will prevent it? The natural resistance of the other Irishmen.

Mr Chairman, what I have said must not be taken as a reasoned case for Home Rule as a good bargain for the parties. This is not what we are here for; and it is not what the question will finally turn on. I leave such special pleading to the lawyers who are ashamed to call themselves Irishmen, though they have no objection to be called Irish officials. What I have uttered is a purposely unguarded expression of the real feelings and instincts of a Protestant Irishman.

THE THIRD HOME RULE BILL AND ULSTER

The New Statesman, London, 7 June 1913; unsigned

I

As the Second Reading of the Home Rule Bill[1] is to take place next week, and as we have not yet met a single Englishman—or, for the matter of that, an Irishman—claiming any acquaintance with the contents of the Bill, we give a brief note of its main provisions for the convenience of our readers.

If the Bill becomes an Act, Ireland will have an Upper House of forty Senators. There is no qualification insisted on. They may be crossing-sweepers if their profits run to election expenses. The first forty will be nominated by the Lord-Lieutenant. Afterwards they will be elected by the Parliamentary constituencies: Ulster electing fourteen, Leinster eleven, Munster nine, and Connaught six. They will sit for five years, and then retire together. They will not be affected by dissolutions of Parliament. By-elections will only be valid until the general quinquennial retirements. The Senate may not meddle with money Bills. The electors are to have one transferable vote.

---

1. The Third Home Rule Bill, the terms of which Shaw here describes, was introduced in April 1912 by Lord Asquith and the Liberal Party. It was bitterly opposed by Ulster leaders, notably Sir Edward Carson and Bonar Law, who wanted Ulster excluded from it. The bill passed the House of Commons in January 1913 but was defeated in the House of Lords. It was subsequently passed three times by three successive sessions of Commons, the third being on 25 May 1914, and by virtue of the Parliament Act would ordinarily now become law as soon as the king gave it the Royal Assent. Before the Royal Assent was given, though, an amending bill was introduced proposing the exclusion of Ulster; however, no action on this amendment had been taken when World War I began. The Home Rule Bill received the Royal Assent and went on the Statute Book but was accompanied by a bill suspending its operation indefinitely. Before the war ended, Home Rule—as a result of the rise of Sinn Féin—had become an archaism.

The House of Commons will consist of 164 members—two of them to be returned by Trinity College, Dublin, lest a Liberal Government should be suspected of Radical views as to University representation. Parliaments will be quinquennial. And here we come upon one of those queer aberrations with which Liberal Governments in this country are peculiarly liable to be afflicted. Thanks to Lord Courtney and his merry men, the British M.P. knows that there is in the air a fearful wild fowl called Proportional Representation, a survival from mid-Victorian times, that golden age of political and economic theorizing; and as its claims were advocated fifty years ago by John Stuart Mill many Liberals are beginning to think that there must be something in it. So, in their timorous way, they have incorporated "the single transferable vote" into their draft of Ireland's future constitution by making it applicable to the nine constituencies which return three or more members to College Green. The only real evil which the transferable vote is capable of remedying is the winning of a seat in a single or double member constituency by a candidate with a minority of votes, through the majority vote being split between two other candidates. The typical case at present is that of the elector confronted with three candidates for one seat: Brown for Unionism, Jones for Home Rule, and Robinson for Labor. The transferable vote enables him to vote for Robinson, or, if Robinson is at the bottom of the poll, then for Jones or Brown, whichever he may consider next best. But this useful application of the system does nothing to advance the mathematical theories of "Proportional Representation"; and so the transferable vote is not to be applied where it is most needed, but in only nine out of the ninetyeight constituencies created by the Act. And this in the most factious country in the world where there will be Tory candidates, Gombeen candidates, Plunkettist candidates, Labor candidates, and heaven knows how many other varieties, splitting the vote in all directions.

The Parliament Act reappears in the Home Rule Bill in a provision that, when the Senate rejects a Bill twice, the Lord-Lieutenant shall convene a joint sitting of the Senate and the House of Commons; and the resolutions of the joint sitting shall become law.

Peers are eligible for the House of Commons as well as for the Senate; but nobody can sit in both houses except a Cabinet Minister, who can sit and speak in both houses, though he can vote in one only. Acceptance of office does not vacate a seat if the Minister is only changing from one office to another. The Chiltern Hundreds not being available, members can resign. The routine of the oath, &c., is to be as in England. And the powers, privileges, and immunities of members shall not exceed those enjoyed in England. Equality is evidently making its way in the Liberal ranks.

Meanwhile, the Irish are to send fortytwo members to Westminster. And here the University member is capriciously abolished.

The supreme judicial power is to be a Judicial Committee of the Irish Privy Council. This Committee will be the final court of appeal for litigants in Ireland, and will also be the supreme court for constitutional questions. It will have its work cut out for it when it has to decide, as it probably soon will, when the Irish Parliament is acting *ultra vires* and when it is playing the game.

Exchequer business is to be controlled by the J.E.B. (Joint Exchequer Board), consisting of five members, two nominated by the British Treasury, two by the Irish Treasury, and one by the Crown. All taxes are to be collected by the British Parliament: a sagacious provision designed to checkmate Ulster if she tries to attack the Irish Parliament by a Tax Resistance League. Then the British Parliament will hand over to the Irish Parliament what is called The Transferred Sum. This sum will consist of the proceeds of the Irish taxes imposed by the Irish Parliament, the cost of the Irish services imposed by the British Parliament, and a straight tip of half a million a year for three years, which will then diminish by £50,000 a year to £200,000 a year, in consideration of which all English grants and loans are to cease. The Land Purchase guarantees drop also.

The Irish Parliament may "vary, add, reduce, or discontinue" taxes generally; but there are complicated restrictions, the general effect of which is that, whilst Ireland is bound to Free Trade with foreign States, she is not to be allowed to undercut England in excise or customs duties, or even in residential attractiveness, as far as this depends on personal taxation. Death duties cannot be imposed on the personal property of people domiciled in England. A more significant provision is meant to protect the landlords against any attempt on the part of the Irish Parliament "to expropriate the expropriators." If College Green goes ahead of St Stephen's in the matter of death duties or income tax or customs duties by more than one-tenth, the excess is to be calmly pocketed by the predominant partner. But in spite of all these restrictions the agonized suspicion of the English M.P. that the Irishman will prove too clever for him expresses itself in the glorious provision that if it should at any time appear that Ireland has been making money out of England for three years at a stretch, the J.E.B. shall report the outrage to the Lord-Lieutenant, who shall thereupon lay the report before the British and Irish Parliaments. The Irish members can then be summoned to Westminster in such numbers as will make the Irish representation equal to the English on the basis of population; and in the ecstasy of this happy reunion the financial provisions can be revised.

The Lord-Lieutenant may be a Catholic or an Atheist (which Ulster would probably prefer) or a Mahometan or a Fire Worshiper or anything that suits him. He is to serve for six years and to have £5,000 a year. This amounts to a statutory qualification of £20,000 a year private income at least; and the unhappy Viceroy will have to be pretty careful at that.

There is a special clause declaring that the assemblies and oaths of the Freemasons, though secret, are not to be deemed unlawful. Thus the Shanavest, the Whiteboy, the Ribbonman, and the Fenian of the future need only add a few masonic ceremonies to the organizing of landlord shooting and cattle driving to defy the Royal Irish Constabulary, who, by the way, will have six years' respite before they are transfered to their native rulers.

Finally, as the one way in which the Irish Parliament can control the Church of the people of Ireland, and rescue them from the despotism and pecuniary exactions of their priests, is by establishing that Church, the Bill expressly disables the Irish Parliament from any such act. It may not establish or endow any religion; may not, in effect, have any religion; but is perpetually condemned to Secularism. And so the Pope may snap his fingers at Dr Clifford after all. And nobody seems to care particularly!

Such is the Government of Ireland Act, 1912.

II

What Ulster wants requires a little more consideration than it is receiving at present. So far, we have on one side the determination that whatever Ulster wants she must go without, and on the other that whatever the three other provinces want they are not to have on any account. It would be wiser to define what Ulster wants, and then ask her whether she really wants it. Also whether the other provinces seriously object to her having it.

Of course, if Ulster wants the *status quo* she cannot have it. We are not going to begin another century of Nationalist controversy because Ulster has nothing more intelligent and mannerly to say than "We wont have it." The rest of Ireland says, "We will have it"; and there is nothing practical to be discussed except how far Ulster can be left out of the arrangement.

The worst difficulties of the situation are the result of the gross moral cowardice and vote-serving of the cultivated classes both in England and Ireland. They have allowed the children of Ulster to be brought up without remonstrance or rebuke in that blasphemous irreligion which consists in believing that all those who worship by a ritual different to that used by the child's parents are abhorred of God, and will, on their death, be burned throughout eternity in a literal hell of burning brimstone. If an Ulster Protestant child expressed the smallest skepticism as to this it would be beaten as severely as if it had done its Christian duty by asking God to bless the Pope. That is what it is taught by its parents, by its schoolmasters, by its pastors, and by a disgraceful silence which is taken as assent, and is meant to be so taken, on the part of our temporal and spiritual peers, our statesmen, our press, our learned liberal professions and, in short, all those whose plain duty it is to repudiate such abominable rubbish by every means in their power until the ignorant become aware that what they imagine to be their religion is nothing but their rancor and their share in the guilt of the crucifixion.

But for the present generation at least this mischief is irrevocably done; and we must deal with Ulster, for the purpose of the Home Rule Bill, as *in partibus infidelium*. We must also bear in mind that political opinion in Ulster is not a matter of talk and bluff, as it is in England. No English Home Ruler has the faintest intention, in any event, of throwing actual paving stones at any English Unionist. If Mr Bonar Law were to take up the mace and smite Mr Redmond with it, his followers in the House of Commons would not only be horrified and scandalized: they would be boundlessly astonished, and convinced that Mr Bonar Law had lost his senses. The Ulsterman is not like that. He is inured to violence. He has thrown stones, and been hit by them. He has battered his political opponent with fist and stick, and been battered himself in the same manner. Give him a machine gun, and he will not recoil with horror from the idea of mowing down his fellow townsmen with it; on the contrary, he will be delighted to substitute machinery for handwork; and he will not entertain a doubt that his views are completely reciprocated by the other side. He has to avenge not only the massacre of St Bartholomew and the wrongs of Maria Monk, but personal insults, injuries, and bloodlettings of quite recent date and of considerable frequency. Consequently, when he sings O God, our help in ages past, he means business. And there is a strength in his rancor which lifts it above rancor. The Ulster Protestant believes that what he calls Popery will destroy his character and make him weak and worthless. To him a Catholic is a liar, a slacker, and a slave of a priest. He may himself have all the faults of which he accuses the Catholic, and be the slave of an employer whose brazen rapacity and indifference to the interests of his workpeople no priest dare imitate; but that does not trouble him: his theme is his neighbor's failings, not his own. He fights, therefore, not only as a fanatic, but as a stern moralist. Nothing less like the bluff of political faction in England can be conceived. It is possible that the Ulsterman should be exterminated as an intolerable, unamiable, unneighborly, unsocial, unclubbable person; but as that is a job which no English Government is prepared to undertake, the alternative seems to be to comply with his demands short of exterminating all the Catholics, which, though it is what he would like, is also impracticable.

Why not, then, make the ultra-Protestant corner of Ulster an *enclave* of England, like that little *enclave* of Spain which exists, surrounded by French territory, on the north slope of the Pyrenees? There need be no difficulty in calling the County Down Downshire, and placing it exactly on the footing of Cheshire, under the English Local Government Board, the English Board of Education, and so on. The arrangement would include the advantage of an established Anglican Church. Ulster would not then be betrayed and deserted by England. She would be more English than she has ever been. She would have not only union, but identity. She would have English liberty (such as it is) instead of Castle rule. She would be getting more than she has dreamt of asking for. And her Catholics might hope at least for English security, which is more than they enjoy at present.

The advantage to the Dublin Parliament would be considerable. It would be saved from the curse of a Unionist Opposition. What that would mean may be imagined if we try to picture the present House of Commons with no Opposition except the Irish party. An Irish Parliament without a Protestant element in it would be a grave misfortune; but an Irish Parliament in which the Protestants were all Unionists would be still worse. Let Belfast send its stalwarts to Westminster instead of to College Green, and all parties will be happy.

No other solution of the Ulster difficulty is practicable. It had better be offered to Ulster. Whether Ulster, brought squarely face to face with the only workable form of what she is asking for, will like it in the concrete as much as she likes it in the abstract, remains to be seen. At all events, as she cannot have the *status quo,* nothing remains for her but either complete union or the most extreme form of Home Rule; that is, separation from both England and Ireland.

The latter would at least gratify England's undisguised anxiety to be rid of her.

A NOTE ON AGGRESSIVE NATIONALISM

The New Statesman, London, 12 July 1913

The world seems just now to have made up its mind that self-consciousness is a very undesirable thing and Nationalism a very fine thing. This is not a very intelligent conclusion; for, obviously, Nationalism is nothing but a mode of self-consciousness, and a very aggressive one at that. It is, I think, altogether to Ireland's credit that she is extremely tired of the subject of herself. Even patriotism, which in England is a drunken jollity when it is not a Jewish rhapsody, is in Ireland like the genius of Jeremiah, a burning fire shut up in the bones, a pain, a protest against shame and defeat, a morbid condition which a healthy man must shake off if he is to keep sane. If you want to bore an Irishman, play him an Irish melody, or introduce him to another Irishman. The modern Irish theatre began with the Kathleen ni Houlihan of Mr Yeats and Lady Gregory's Rising of the Moon, in which the old patriotism stirred and wrung its victims; but when the theatre thus established called on Young Ireland to write Irish plays and found a national school of drama, the immediate result was a string of plays of Irish life—and very true to life they were—in which the heroines proclaimed that they were sick of Ireland and rated their Nationalist husbands for sacrificing all the realities of life to senseless Fenian maunderings, and the heros damned Ireland up hill and down dale in the only moments of enthusiasm their grey lives left possible.

Abroad, however, it is a distinction to be an Irishman; and accordingly the Irish in England flaunt their nationality. An Englishman who had married an Irishwoman once came to me and asked me could I give him the name of any Englishman who had ever done anything. He explained that his wife declared that all England's statesmen, all her warriors, all her musical composers, all her notables of every degree were Irishmen, and that the English could not write their names until the Irish taught them. I suggested Gladstone. "She says he was an Irishman" was the reply. After this, it was clear that the man's case was desperate; so I left him to his fate.

From this you may gather that the reaction against the Nationalist variety of self-consciousness does not, unfortunately, mean a reaction against conceit, against ignorance, against insular contempt for foreigners, against bad manners and the other common human weaknesses which sometimes masquerade as patriotism. Ireland produces virulent varieties of all of them; for it is, on the whole, a mistake to suppose that we are a nation of angels. You can always find something better than a good Englishman and something worse than a bad one; but this is not so in Ireland: a bad Irishman is the vilest thing on earth, and a good one is a saint. Thackeray's Barry Lyndon is a very accurate sketch of the sort of thoroughpaced scoundrel Ireland can produce, not when she is put to it, but quite wantonly, merely for the fun of being mischievous. In point of conceit, Ireland, especially Northern Ireland, can stagger humanity. The Ulster Unionist is not a shrewd calculator who, on a careful estimate of the pressure of public opinion on any Government which should try to coerce Belfast into submission to a Dublin Parliament, concludes that he can safely bluff Home Rule out of Ulster: he really believes, as so many of the Boer farmers believed, that he can fight and conquer the British Empire, or any other empire that is not Ulster and Protestant. This is not a respectable infatuation; and if there were nothing else to be considered except the salvation of the Ulsterman's soul, it would be a positive duty for the British Empire to blow him sky high to convince him that even a Unionist God (and he believes in no other, and therefore does not really believe in God at all) has occasionally to look beyond Down and Antrim.

A new siege of Derry under a capable commander would be an invaluable corrective to the old one, as it would last about ten minutes, and end in an ignominious surrender of as much of Derry as might be left. But these military moral lessons, fashionable as they are, cost more than the souls of the regenerated (not to mention the bodies of those they kill) are worth; and it would, I think, be more sensible to make Ulster an autonomous political lunatic asylum, with Sir Edward Carson as head keeper, and an expensive fleet and a heavily fortified frontier to hold against the Pope, than to thwart its inclinations in any way. The alternative, if England would stand it, would be to make Ulster a province of England, and have the Education Acts and the Factory Acts applied in the English manner; but I doubt if Ulster would tamely submit to be identified with a country where men touch their hats to a Roman Catholic duke of Norfolk, and meet him at dinner as if he were their equal. On the whole, the notion of a Kingdom of Orangia (Ibsen invented the name in The Master

Builder) is the more amusing. When it came to paying for the frontier fortifications and the new Harland and Wolff fleet,[1] the South would smile sunnily.

What will finally settle the Ulster question, probably, is just the old-fashioned romantic Nationalism of which the South is so deadly tired. That hackneyed fisherman who saw the round towers of other days in the waves beneath him shining, pursued his not very lucrative occupation on the banks of Lough Neagh, and was no doubt an Orangeman.[2] Now it happens that the true Ulsterman is a harsh father; and his son's chief joy when he is old enough to dare to differ from his violent and bigoted parent is to profess every opinion that can defy and exasperate the old man. And, indeed, it is clear, as the world is now constituted, that prudent young men should aim at being as unlike Orangemen and as like human beings as possible, even as in the South the young men are discovering that in point of insufferableness there is not a halfpenny to choose between a Nationalist and an Orangeman. Thus, though the Protestant boys will still carry the drum, they will carry it under the green flag, and realize that the harp, the hound, and the round tower are more satisfactory to the imagination than that stupidest of decorative designs the Union Jack, which, it must be admitted, is, considered merely as a decorative design, the most resourceless of patterns. And the change can be effected without treachery to England; for if my personal recollection does not deceive me, the Gaelic League began in Bedford Park, London, W., after a prolonged incubation in Somerset House.

It is not very long since I stood on the coast of Donegal and asked two boys how many languages they had. They had three. One was English, which they spoke much better than it is ever spoken in England. The second was Irish, which they spoke with their parents. The third was a language invented by the Gaelic League, which I cannot speak (being an Irishman) but which I understand to be in its qualities comparable to a blend of Esperanto with V century Latin. Why should not Ulster adopt this strange tongue? Its very name suggests Scotland, which is what the present vernacular of the North also suggests.

1. A famous shipbuilding firm in Belfast.

2. The "hackneyed fisherman" of Lough Naigh [Neagh] appears in the second verse of Thomas Moore's "Let Erin Remember the Days of Old" (*Irish Melodies*, no. 2, 1808). He reemerges in Shaw's "On Throwing Out Dirty Water" (see p. 289).

The truth is that all the Nationalist inventions that catch on now are not Irish at all. For instance, the admirable comedies of Synge, who, having escaped from Ireland to France, drew mankind in the manner of Molière, and discreetly assured the public that this was merely the human nature of the Blasket Islands, and that, of course, civilized people never admired boastful criminals nor esteemed them according to the atrocities they pretended to commit. The Playboy's real name was Synge; and the famous libel on Ireland (and who is Ireland that she should not be libeled as other countries are by their great comedians?) was the truth about the world.

MAD DOGS IN UNIFORM

A speech delivered at a meeting in the Albert Hall, London, on 1 November 1913, to protest the sentencing of Jim Larkin, leader of the Dublin Transport Workers' strike, on a charge of seditious libel. *The Daily Herald*, London, 1 November 1913, under a banner head "London's Magnificent Rally to the Dublin Rebels." Shaw's militant speech, captioned "Bernard Shaw Hits Out" with a subhead "Mad Dogs in Uniform," so outraged the editor of *The Daily Sketch*, London, that, on 3 November, under the headline "Shaw Must Go to Gaol," the paper called for his arrest for inciting to armed revolt.

I am an old Dublin Home Ruler. . . . Being an intelligent Irishman I left Ireland at the age of twenty. I have not lived there since, and I dont intend to live there again. I am extremely glad to hear that 20,000 families in Dublin have one room to live in. In my time there was no such luxury. There were very often two families in one room, and both families took in lodgers.

It has been said before this that children are the safeguard of morality in Dublin—that if you took the children out of some of the dwellings the adults would misbehave themselves. *[Laughter.]* Dont laugh at that. It is a most appalling thing. I believe there have been people in the last few days who have given that as a reason for not allowing children to leave Dublin.[1] Ponder over that a little. Let your imagination add to that state of things the horror of a strike, the cessation of the weekly wage, and all that it means. Imagine what kind of men they must be who, seeing all this, thrust the children back into that starvation and misery.

Imagine something more horrible: a Christian priest doing that. *[Hisses.]* No! I dont ask you to hiss. I am here as a Dublin man to apologize to you for the priests of Dublin.

But the honest truth about it is that these men, although they are pious men and do a deal of good work, are ignorant and simple men with the

---

1. An attempt by the union to send strikers' children to foster homes in England for the duration of the strike of 1913 was blocked by the Catholic Church on grounds that living in Protestant homes would endanger the Catholic faith of the children.

industrial affairs of the world. I hope my words will reach them, and that they will be obliged to me for the apology I am making for them.

I hope these further words will reach them. There is something even more terrible than the horror of their individual action, and that is the horror of the great Christian Church to which they belong being made the catspaw of gentlemen like Mr Murphy.[2]

It would have been perfectly easy to make a great deal of good of this little outpouring of sympathy between the people of England and Ireland if the priests had understood that the Catholic Church is not an Irish Church but a universal Church. Understanding that, they would surely have been the first to send those children to England.

Now a word about the employers of Dublin. I am utterly ashamed for them. Mind, I dont apologize for them. Even an Englishman can employ people at decent Trade Union wages and make it pay.

The last time I was on a public platform with Mr Lansbury the Government calling itself a Liberal Government had prosecuted a Labor leader under the Mutiny Act.[3] That was bad enough. To bring yourself under the Mutiny Act you have to talk sense to a soldier. The Mutiny Act does not prevent you from talking sense to a civilian. But now we have something worse—the old law of sedition. You may take it from me that under the old Sedition Act there is no person in the room who has cheered people on the platform who could not under that Act be fined £100,000 and imprisoned for life. [Laughter.]

Any Government which will countenance such a thing as the Crown Prosecutor in Dublin charging Larkin with sedition on the ground that he said the employing class lived on profits has reached a cynical depth of absence of all shame which it is hardly possible to characterize without using improper language.

Let me warn the employing class that according to the Attorney General in Dublin every employer who makes a return that he lives by profits

2. William Martin Murphy, proprietor of *The Irish Independent*, Dublin, was management's chief spokesman during the strike.

3. George Lansbury, a lifetime Socialist, was editor of *The Daily Herald*, London, 1913–22. The public platform they shared, on 3 April 1912, was a demonstration in the London Opera House protesting against the government's prosecution of several Syndicalists, including Labor leader Tom Mann, for speeches made with reference to the employment of the military in trade disputes.

is guilty of sedition. We must make up our minds with regard to working class and industrial questions that we must have law and order.

What do I mean by law and order? I mean this, that when it comes—as it is inevitable in all civilized communities that it must come—to the employment of physical force, that physical force shall only be applied by responsible men under the direct guidance of an officer responsible to a Minister in Parliament.

If you once let loose your physical force without careful supervision and order you may as well let loose in the streets a parcel of mad dogs as a parcel of policemen. It has been the practice, ever since the modern police were established, in difficulties with the working class to let loose the police and tell them to go and do their worst to the people. Now, if you put the policeman on the footing of a mad dog, it can only end in one way—that all respectable men will have to arm themselves. *[Loud cheers. A voice: "What with?"]*

I should suggest you should arm yourselves with something that would put a decisive stop to the proceedings of the police. I hope that observation will be carefully reported. I should rather like to be prosecuted for sedition and have an opportunity of explaining to the public exactly what I mean by it.

WAKE UP, ULSTER!

The New Statesman, London, 14 March 1914; unsigned

After last Monday, all that can be said of or to Sir Edward Carson and Mr Bonar Law is that they have been and gone and done it.[1] They have engaged in a tug-of-war without remembering that the most effective move in that game is not the enemy's strongest pull, but his adroitest let-go. The oversight was unpardonable, because everybody knew beforehand that Mr Asquith had made up his mind to let go. And now Sir Edward and his leader (from behind) are sitting forlorn in the mud with the rope in their hands and little else to do except hang themselves with it. For they are now cut off from Ulster as completely as they are cut off from Waterford.

It serves them right, because they have allowed their followers to take a position which no sane statesman should countenance for a moment and no Government can meet with any other argument than a ruthless artillery fire. The case was put plainly enough by Sir Horace Plunkett.[2] He told us, with the utmost publicity and without a breath of contradiction, that the Orangemen do not regard the Catholics of Ireland more respectfully than all men regard gorillas; that is, as an inferior and mischievous species, incapable of public functions of any sort. Less respectfully, in fact; for men do not believe that gorillas will be eternally damned; and that belief concerning Catholics is one of the joys of the Orange mind as depicted by Sir Horace.

1. During the debates over the Third Home Rule Bill, a compromise offer allowing the temporary exclusion for six years of those Ulster counties that wished to be exempt was made by Lord Asquith to the Ulster leaders Sir Edward Carson and Bonar Law. Carson and Law rejected the offer, preferring instead to fight for the permanent exclusion of Ulster from Home Rule. They lost their fight, however, and the bill was passed on 25 May 1914, though it never actually became operative.

2. Plunkett was a distinguished Irish agricultural reformer, founder of the Co-operative movement in Ireland, and personal friend of Shaw.

Now, it was the clear duty of the leaders on both sides, especially the Ulster side, to declare at once that such an attitude could not be tolerated; that it is politically a criminal attitude and humanly an abominable attitude, and that if it be really Ulster's attitude (as it certainly is the attitude of the baser sort of Ulsterman), then it is the duty, not only of the Government, but of Christendom and humanity, to wipe Ulster out of existence. If Sir Edward Carson feels anything less than this about it, he is unfit for public life. If Mr Redmond accepts it as a fact, he should organize the South as Sir Edward has organized the North for its own protection against the black flag.

As a matter of fact, Sir Edward Carson does not think that Daniel O'Connell was a gorilla or Father Mathew[3] a moral dwarf; and, apart from the temporary excitements produced by political oratory, rancorous bigotry is no more general in Ulster than anywhere else. When the Ulstermen realize that their Impossibilist pose will not only forfeit the sympathy of all kindly folk, but put the electorate out of patience with their inconsiderate and uppish folly, they will begin to protest that they do not claim a monopoly of virtue. They will even remember that it is no worse to sit with Mr T. P. O'Connor as the representative of the Scotland division of Liverpool (as full of Irish Catholics as Orangemen believe hell to be) at Westminster than to sit with him at College Green as an Irish representative.

Further, they will begin to realize that if there is to be an Irish Parliament—and Sir Edward and his Unionist leaders have thrown up the sponge as to that—nothing worse could happen to Ulster than to let the Nationalists have six years' start of them in it. Sir Edward was quite right in his despairing cry on Monday, when he realized where Mr Asquith had landed him, that if Ulster is not to come in for six years Ulster must never come in at all. Suppose Mr Asquith, as a result of a little more pressure, should say: "Very well; *dont* come in at all." Then Ulster will be forced to face the plain issue that we predicted in these columns when we first dealt with the question. Will Ulster be a province of England, or will she come to her senses and make up her mind that, since Home Rule is inevitable,

3. Theobald Mathew, Irish priest and temperance reformer, was famous for his success in getting thousands to sign temperance pledges.

she will take care to secure a front seat in that arrangement with her money, her brains, and her boasted moral backbone?

It is incredible that any inhabitant of Ulster capable of grasping the political situation should accept the alternative of exclusion which Sir Edward and Mr Bonar Law are forcing on her and which Englishmen think quite good enough for her. To be left out as a result of a solemn covenant to insist on being left in is a pretty feeble result of so much arming and drilling and singing of terrifying hymns. The sooner the sensible Ulstermen realize the pit which has been digged for them by the silly fanatics who are too busy chalking up "No Surrender!" and "To Hell with the Pope!" on the walls of Derry to notice how English statesmen, to whom Ulster is merely a nuisance, are disposing of their destinies for generations to come, the better for the Protestant North all over the world.

IRELAND AND THE FIRST WORLD WAR

On 26 November 1914 Shaw wired to George Russell: "I want to write a strong letter urging the claims of the French Republic to Irish support so as to stop if possible all this silly pro-German slosh which is making mischief and doing no good. . . . Am I the best person to do it? What does Plunkett think?" Russell replied: "You [are the] best man. Plunkett agrees." Shaw's letter appeared in *The Freeman's Journal*, Dublin, 30 November 1914.

Sir,—Those who have read the extracts from certain Irish papers which, as quoted in the London Times and in Parliament, are being used to induce the Censor to muzzle the Irish Nationalist Press and to rekindle anti-Irish feeling in England, will, I think, agree with me that it is time to speak pretty plainly to the editors of these papers, not as to the effect of their utterances in England, as to which they may not feel deeply concerned, but on the honor of Ireland and of the national cause.

It is said that there is no such thing as gratitude in politics. If so, Ireland is absolved from all obligations to the French Republic. But if there is no such thing as political gratitude, there can be no such thing as political resentment. You cannot consistently fill your paper with the old injuries we have suffered from England, and refuse to remember the old championship, hospitality, and armed support we have received from France. Now, at this moment the Irishman who declares himself the friend of Potsdam declares himself the enemy of France.[1] And if there is one institution on earth that has stronger claims to the implacable political hostility of every extreme Democrat or Republican in the world than Dublin Castle, that institution is Potsdam. I am at this moment one of the best abused men in England because I, an Irishman, have criticized pretty candidly the manner in which the British diplomatists played their hand

---

1. The declaration of war was preceded by a meeting at Potsdam on 15 July 1914, at which Germany assured Austria of her support against Serbia and Russia, following the assassination of Austrian archduke Franz Ferdinand on 28 June. France was then drawn into the alignment on the side of Serbia-Russia, and subsequently England also, because of a "gentleman's agreement" negotiated with the French by the British foreign minister, Sir Edward Grey.

against both the German diplomatists and the British nation; but I have also insisted that the British nation is not responsible for what was done behind its back by the diplomatists. The English people never meddled in the matter—never, indeed, had a chance of meddling in it—until Sir Edward Grey asked them whether they could stand by and see France "bombarded and battered." And it was to that appeal they rose.

Well, if the English are willing to stand by their old enemy, is Ireland going to turn its back on its old friend? If Fontenoy is to be fought over again,[2] as seems likely enough, will the Irish Brigade betray its old comrades, the French, for the sake of Prussia? We fought for France when she was a military tyranny, as dangerous to freedom as Potsdam is now. Are we going to fight against her now that she is a Republic, and shares with America (whom she helped to her freedom) the honor of being the hope of Republicans all the world over? Even if France had not tried to help us as she helped America by sending us an army which we were unable to save from capture and defeat, it would still be a monstrous act for Ireland to throw her weight against France out of mere spite against England.

We must get rid of the tyranny of England from our minds now that at last the Act is passed that promises us an escape from her political tyranny. In this war she has only a corner share, with little to gain or lose. It is France that is holding the West against Potsdam and all that Potsdam means to western liberty; and it is French soil, on which so many famous Irishmen found a refuge from British tyranny, that is being drenched with French blood in our defence. The holiest shrines and most glorious monuments of the Catholic Church are in the charge of France, and make her cities places of pilgrimages. Is Catholic Ireland going to exult in seeing them battered with Prussian cannon, though there is no Englishman within miles of them. I have traveled through France when the name of England was hated there (in the Fashoda days), and a rigid politeness was the best I could hope for when I reached a hotel and asked to be put up for the night. The magic phrase, "Je suis Irlandais," turned all that hard stiffness into genial welcome. How am I, or any other Irishman, ever to look a Frenchman in the face again if we hound on Prussia to destroy

2. Fontenoy, a village in Belgium, was the scene of a battle in 1745 during the War of the Austrian Succession, when a brigade composed entirely of Irishmen fought heroically for France.

France in this war? No; our side is the side of France, and the Irishman who forgets it, forgets the history of his country.

I may as well confess frankly that I have an axe to grind in making this appeal. Though I have no sort of antipathy to the Germans, I regard it as a matter of cardinal importance to Western democratic civilization, and to all the most hopeful elements in the revival of real National life in Ireland, that the Prussian military machine should shatter itself to pieces on the resistance of French Republicans, and of Irishmen who have broken the domination of a similar machine in their own country. The ideal thing would be an Irish Brigade joining the French army direct, and eclipsing the London Scottish and Kitchener's army by their valor and discipline. But, as there are practical difficulties of language and organization in the way of this course, I have made a strong appeal to the War Office to do away with the silly and useless oaths and tests which stick in the throats of Irish recruits, and to set free the attesting officers for really useful service. Probably the War Office will not have sense enough to comply; but, at all events, those Irishmen who will not swear allegiance to the King need not swear it to the Kaiser. If they will not join the French army as volunteers, or the British army as regulars, they can, nonetheless, understand that the one thing they must not do if they are good Irishmen is to join the Germans or help the Germans against the French.

I have also a prejudice to gratify. I can get on well enough with an Englishman, with a Scotchman, with a Prussian, or a Russian, or a Frenchman, or an Italian, or even—though I am an Irishman myself—with another Irishman (sometimes). What I cannot stand, on any terms, is a man whose nationality is negative, instead of positive—the anti-Englishman, the anti-Irishman, and the Yankee who calls himself an American Gael, and tells you stories of how his grandfather was evicted from his happy home in the Bog of Allen, with the result, first, that you dont believe him; and second, that you wish his grandfather had been buried in the bog and his grandchildren with him. The anti-Englishman is making himself and his country ridiculous just at present by declaring for Germany on the ground that Germany is anti-English; and throwing himself into the conflict on the side of the Turks because the Turks are against the Church of England. And, of course, the anti-Irishmen immediately begin to scream for suppression of the Irish papers and the driving of what they call sedition underground, the only place where it can do any harm. I invite the Irish papers to write sedition as between England and Ireland until they are black in the face and their opponents red in the gills, if it amuses them; but as between the Irish and the French, as between the Irish cause and the cause of Western democracy, they must not come down on the side of the Turk and the Prussian militarist autocracy.

I make this appeal because it is hopeless to expect the British War Office or the British Government to see the situation from the Irish point of view. They keep scolding us for not attending instantly to the needs of "Our Country and our King," meaning thereby their country and the Kaiser's cousin. When we fail to respond with enthusiasm, they are amazed at our depravity and ask whether they are to understand that we seriously mean that we are rebels against the British Empire. We reply instinctively: "To Hades with the British Empire," not that we object particularly to the British Empire, which is useful to us in a variety of ways, but because it is beyond human patience to be lectured by pompous noodles.

That is why I ask to be allowed to intervene and do the thing in my own way, with all possible apologies to the anti-Irish, and to the delightful Parliamentary Man from Shropshire, who, in khaki clad, sees more peril to England in the "Irish Volunteer" than in a thousand Zeppelins, or even in the commonsense of yours truly,

G. Bernard Shaw.

IN BEHALF OF AN IRISH PACIFIST

Letter to Mrs. Francis Sheehy Skeffington, in *The Freeman's Journal*, Dublin,
16 June 1915

Dear Mrs Sheehy Skeffington,

I have naturally been interested in your husband's case, and have carefully read, not only the newspaper accounts of the proceedings before the magistrate, but the transcript of the speech [by Sheehy Skeffington from the dock] which you have sent me.[1] I have also noticed the references that have been made in Parliament and elsewhere in England to the contrast between the Government's treatment of Mr Sheehy Skeffington and the complete immunity with which Lord Northcliffe[2] not only endeavored to stop voluntary recruiting by refusing to insert the War Office appeals for recruits, but actually—with the same object, that of bringing about conscription—published a long letter from the Bishop of Pretoria,[3] conveying the impression, not only to the English, but to the German public that the British army in Flanders is outwearied, outnumbered, and must presently fall a prey to its enemies unless conscription was at once resorted to. Now, it is clear that if Mr Sheehy Skeffington deserves six months for his speech in Beresford-place, which would not have reached a thousand

1. Francis Sheehy Skeffington had, since his undergraduate days at University College, Dublin, been known as an iconoclast. Woman suffragist, vegetarian, and pacifist, he had been arrested and found guilty, under the Defence of the Realm Act, of making a pacifist speech in Dublin. Less than a year later, while watching the Easter Rebellion, he was arrested, detained without charge, and then shot by order of a British officer, Capt. J. C. Bowen-Colthurst. A subsequent board of inquiry and court-martial found the officer guilty of murder but insane. Skeffington's widow was offered an indemnity by the British government, which Shaw urged her to be sensible and accept, but she refused.

2. Alfred Harmsworth, Lord Northcliffe, was publisher of *The Daily Mail* and *The Times*, London.

3. The Rt. Rev. Michael Bolton Furse, Bishop of Pretoria, had published a letter, "The Nation Under Orders," in *The Times* on 25 May 1915, calling for conscription in preference to voluntary recruiting. The letter was reprinted by *The Times* as a pamphlet on 1 June.

people but for the prosecution, Lord Northcliffe must deserve somewhere about sixty years. I can only congratulate him under the circumstances on being still at large.

However, there is nothing to be done. The Defence of the Realm Act abolishes all liberty in Great Britain and Ireland except such as the authorities may choose to leave us. Even if the powers given by the Act were insufficient the Government could act arbitrarily without the least risk as there is no remedy for such arbitrariness except a revolution. It may be within your recollection that before the Act was amended it did not give the Government power to put German spies to death. Nevertheless, they shot one and amended the Act afterwards. Therefore, if they should decide for any reason to hang your husband, you will not have any practical remedy. Protests are quite useless. The Opposition in the House of Commons will not oppose. The press will not defend public liberties. England is thoroughly intimidated by Germany as far as her civilians are concerned; and sentences of six months hard labor are being dealt out here for the most trivial oversights and the most innocent suppressions in complying with registration regulations.

Under these circumstances I think your husband made a very grave mistake in putting his head into the lion's mouth as he did. Something can be done with a tyrannical Government; nothing can be done with a terrified Government, and a cowed people.

As for me, personally I should only make matters worse by interfering, even if I had an effective means of doing so. As it happens, I am not afraid of the Germans, and have very little patience with the Englishmen who are. If they cannot win at the present odds without putting Mr Sheehy Skeffington in prison for depleting the British army to the extent of half-a-dozen men or so, they deserve to be beaten. Unfortunately, this confidence of mine sends the British alarmist into ecstasies of fright. They commonly allude to me as a pro-German, and if they knew I sympathize with your husband they would declare that nothing but his imprisonment for life could save England. I can fight stupidity, but no one can fight cowardice.

Yours faithfully,
G. Bernard Shaw.

TOURING IN IRELAND

The Car, London, 5 April 1916. A variant text, reproduced below, was published in *Collier's Magazine*, New York, 10 June 1916.

In Ireland a protuberance like Primrose Hill, or, at most, Hindhead, looks like a mountain haunted by giants. You may be fresh from surmounting every pass in the Tyrol, but when you are faced by a trumpery lane through the Kerry mountains, you are filled with vague terrors: it seems dangerous to venture in and impossible to get out, even if you do not meet another car on a track that looks a tight fit for one. In Galway, south of the bay, you find stone fields instead of grass ones, and in those fields cattle gravely crop the granite and seem to thrive on it. You travel on roads that are far more like the waves of the sea than the famous billowy pavement of St Mark's in Venice.

In the north there are no stone fields, but you come to a common green one with a little stagnant pool in the corner, and from that magic pool you are amazed to see a rush of waters through a narrow, deep, sinuous ditch, which ditch is the mighty Shannon emerging from the underworld. Rivers in Ireland duck like porpoises and then come to the surface and charge along it for a space and duck again. If you are afraid to penetrate a country so full of marvels, you can stay in a hotel in Dublin and yet be within half an hour's drive by car of moors as wild as you have often traveled many hundreds of miles from London to reach in the remotest parts of Scotland, and of coast scenery after which most English "seaside resorts" will seem mere dust heaps on the banks of a dirty canal. On the west coast you can struggle for an hour and a half up an endless succession of mountain brows, each of which looks like the top until you get there and see the next one towering above you; and when you are at last exhausted and filled with a conviction that you are enchanted and doomed to climb there forever, you suddenly recoil from a sheer drop of two thousand feet to the Atlantic, with nothing but salt water between you and America. You can watch affrightedly a bull's mouth of which the grinders are black, merciless rocks and the boiling spittle Atlantic rollers. You can make strange voyages to uncanny islands which carry to its highest the curious power of Ireland to disturb and excite the human imagination; and if one of these voyages leads you in an open boat through seven or eight miles of ocean waves and tide races to Skellig Michael,[1] no experience that the conventional tourist travel can bring you will stick in your memory so strangely; for Skellig Michael is not after the fashion of this world.

To the unfortunate man who has to live in Ireland all these things are only part of the daily horror of his lot. But to the English or American tourist, whose retreat is secured, and who only screws himself up for the moment to peep in at these wonders as he screws himself up to take a flight in an aeroplane, there is no place like Ireland. You do the most commonplace and safe things with a sense of adventure and a doubt whether you will come out of them alive. And you always do come out of them alive. Even if you have no imagination, and simply like pretty scenery, you can have in Ireland all the color of the Mediterranean coast without its hard brilliance and absence of mystery and distance, and all the veiling atmosphere and fairy sunset of the land of mountain and flood without its darkness and harshness. Only you must avoid places which describe themselves as "The Irish Biarritz." If you dont, you will be astonished to see men consenting to spend a second day in them when they have every convenience for drowning themselves.

Irish roads are not so good as English roads, but rather better than French ones. When they are not rolled, and the stones lie loose in the lanes, get off the road on to the rocks when your car begins to refuse. In Ireland you must clear your mind from the cockney illusion that an artificial road is the only surface a car will travel on.

Another novel driving experience is to rush a little slope not thirty yards long nor steeper than one in twelve, and when you have just reached the brow flying, find the road, with your car on it, sink blissfully down as into a feather bed laid on a foundation of sponge. That is bog. The road is "a trifle soft." You get over that as best you can, usually at an ignominious crawl, dodging about in search of hard bits. Or you may come to a splendid stretch of perfectly straight, flat road with a good

---

1. Literally, "Michael's Rock." An enormous mass of precipitous rock rising out of the sea eight miles off the coast of County Kerry, containing the remains of an early Christian monastic settlement. See "Shaw Speaks to His Native City" (p. 334).

white surface, and let your car go all out on it until you find it bounding up and tossing the car as in a blanket. That means the road is a mere peat pontoon floating on a bog. As they say, it is "springy."

Hotels in Ireland are like hotels everywhere, very various. Inland hotels of moderate pretensions in all countries are now apt to be bad within fifty miles of the capital, because the commercial travelers, whose custom keeps such hotels up to the mark, prefer to push for home when they are as near it as that. Ireland is no exception to this rule. The custom of the motorist does not alter it, for he too makes for Dublin or Kingstown or Bray from outside the fifty-mile radius. Otherwise I consider the ordinary inland country-town hotels less depressing in Ireland than in England. If there is a castle in the town, and if the assize judge has to be entertained occasionally, you often find well-trained maids and a tradition of serving "the quality" which makes the motorist who is able to play up to that conception of him much more comfortable than an experienced tourist expects to be in an out-of-the-way place. But the main stand-by of the tourist in Ireland is the fishing hotel.

Ireland is one of the great fishing countries of the world: the Shannon, which comes down the middle of it, is a string of lakes rather than a river; and I have known Irishmen who would starve rather than eat salmon, because they had once had to eat it every day for three months. Consequently, if you are a sensible person, and can get on with a moderately tidy bachelor sort of accommodation, and enjoy breakfasts of ham and eggs and tea, lunches of mutton chops, and dinners of plain joints, you will find that these hotels will suit you extremely well. But avoid Irish clear soups. They still believe in Ireland that soup means water in which bones have been boiled; and unless your taste is sepulchral you will not like it.

Of course, if you want to dine in evening dress confronted with a bediamonded wife and flanked by daughters in the very latest, if you demand six-course dinners, and feel injured if you have to open a door for yourself, or if "Boots" occasionally gives up brown leather as a bad job, then you will be unhappy in Ireland; for just in proportion to the efforts made by an Irish hotel to meet your views is it sure to be a bad one. Ireland cannot afford that game, and would not know how to play it if she could; for an Irish gentleman is passing rich with two or three thousand dollars a year. Of course, there are exceptions. The golfing hotels like

Rosapenna in Donegal and Lahinch in Clare, the Killarney hotels, the hotels at Parknasilla and Waterville in Kerry, and, generally, the first-class hotels are like first-class hotels anywhere else: in fact, that is the only complaint one makes of them. But no experienced tourist wants to be reassured about these. It is the cheaper stopping places that matter; and after a large experience of Continental touring I cannot recall, at worst, any experience at an Irish hotel more disagreeable than I have had to endure on quite main lines of travel in France and Italy, to say nothing of Britain.

Irish people in Ireland do not play up to English romantic illusions concerning them, as they are apt to do in England when they want to make themselves popular or to borrow money. There may still be a tradition among Irish carmen plying between Bray and the show places in the County Wicklow that they should entertain English tourists with impersonations of Myles na Coppaleen and Micky Free,[2] just as there may possibly be a tradition among Venetian gondoliers that they should recite Tasso to the compatriots of Lord Byron. I do not know: the carmen never try it on me, because I am an Irishman. All such performances are pure humbug and the anecdotes are learned and repeated without sense.

Irish people are, like most country people, civil and kindly when they are treated with due respect. But anyone who, under the influence of the stage Irishman and the early novels of Lever, treats a tour in Ireland as a lark, and the people as farce actors who may be addressed as Pat and Biddy, will have about as much success as if he were to paint his nose red and interrupt a sermon in Westminster Abbey by addressing music-hall patter to the dean. Also there are certain bustling nuances of manner which are popular in a busy place like England because they save time and ceremony, but which strike an Irishman as too peremptory and too familiar, and are resented accordingly. You need be no more ceremonious in word or gesture than in England; but your attitude had better be the Latin attitude which you have learned in Italy and France, and not the Saxon attitude learned in England and Bavaria. It is as well to know, by the way, that there are no Celts in Ireland and never have been, though there are many Iberians. The only European nation where the typical native is also a typical Celt is Prussia.

2. Colorful fictional characters; the first appears in Gerald Griffin's *The Collegians* (1829), the second in Charles Lever's *Charles O'Malley* (1841).

As an illustration of the sort of police activity which is peculiar to Ireland, I will give an experience of my own. One evening in the south of Donegal it was getting dark rapidly, and, after being repeatedly disappointed of finding our destination round the next corner, as tired people will expect, we had at last grown desperate and settled down to drive another twenty miles as fast as the road would let us before the light failed altogether. The result was that we came suddenly round a bend and over a bridge right into the middle of the tiny town before we supposed ourselves to be within five miles of it. The whole population had assembled in the open for evening gossip, and we dashed through them at a speed considerably in excess of the ten-mile limit. They scattered in all directions, and a magnificent black retriever charged us like a wolf, barking frantically. My chauffeur, who was driving, made a perilous swerve and just saved the dog by a miracle of dexterity. Then we drew up at the porch of the hotel, and I looked anxiously back at the crowd, hoping it did not include a member of the R.I.C.[3] Alas, it did, and he was a stern-faced man whose deliberate stalk in our direction could have only one object. The crowd, which had taken our rush with the utmost good-humor, did not gather to witness our discomfiture as a city crowd would have done. It listened, but pretended not to, as a matter of good breeding. The inspector inspected us up and down until we shrank into mere guilty worms. He then addressed my chauffeur in these memorable words: "What sort of a man are you? Here you come into a village where there's a brute of a dog that has nearly ate two childer, and is the curse and terror of this countryside, and when you get a square chance of killing him you twist your car out of the way and nearly upset it. What sort of a man are you at all?"

My own opinion is that any Briton who does not need at least a fortnight in Ireland once a year to freshen him up has not really been doing his duty.

3. Royal Irish Constabulary.

IRISH NONSENSE ABOUT IRELAND

New York Times, 9 April 1916

There has come into my hands, from a quarter it was not meant to reach, a certain address To the Men and Women of the Irish Race in America, which is so typical of the stuff which gives its title to this article that I feel moved, in the interests of my unfortunate countrymen in Ireland, to offer America a piece of my mind concerning it. As an Irishman I have been familiar with Irish patriotic rhetoric all my life. Personally I have had no use for it, because I always wanted to get things done and not to let myself go for the satisfaction of my temper and the encouragement of my already excessive national self-conceit. I have seen it going out of fashion with the greatest relief.

When something like an Irish national theatre was established in Abbey-street, Dublin, and a genuine Irish drama began to germinate, I enjoyed the new Irish plays because the heros always brought down the house by declaring that they were sick of Ireland, by expressing an almost savage boredom at the expense of the old patriots who were usually the fools of the piece when they were not the villains, and, generally, by damning the romantic Old Ireland up hill and down dale in the most exhilarating fashion. And though this might easily have become as tiresome and insincere a trick as the most obsolete claptrap of the stage Irishmen who, obliged to confess that they have never been in Ireland, call themselves American Gaels, yet it was for the moment a notable step in advance; and it has finally straightened itself out in such admirable essays on modern Ireland as that recently put forward by a genuine Irishman of genius, St John Ervine, in the guise of a biography of Sir Edward Carson, to whom about half-a-dozen lines are allotted in the course of the substantial little volume.

The first comment provoked by the appeal "to the men and women of the Irish race in America" is that, though it is dated 1916, there is no internal evidence that it was not written in 1860 (as indeed most of it was) except the inevitable allusions to the present war. In point of learning nothing and forgetting nothing these fellow patriots of mine leave the Bourbons nowhere. Their belief that the Irish race not only takes with it to America the ideas of Athlone, but invincibly maintains in its new home not only its Irish nationality but its Irish ignorance, its Irish parochial narrowness, its Irish sectarianism, and its Irish conviction that the Irish are the salt of the earth and that all other races are comparatively barbarous, degraded, sordid, irreligious, ungenerous, tyrannical, and treacherous, and that this inferiority is essentially and disgustingly marked in the case of "the English race," shines ridiculously through every paragraph in their manifesto.

Ireland is to be freed from the horrible contamination of association with England by complete political separation from her. "Ireland looks forward with hope and confidence to the complete breakdown of British misrule in Ireland as the certain outcome of the present war." "Success for England would mean only additional heavy burdens for Ireland and a renewal of strength to her age-long oppressor and tyrant." Finally, there is an appeal to America to maintain the principles of—among other illustrious Americans—Abraham Lincoln! As Lincoln is the most famous Unionist known to history, the Separatist patriots could hardly have made a more unfortunate selection of a name to conjure with.

Now, as against all this, I venture to ask the Americans of Irish race, and even those Americans who have to blush for less glorious origins, to keep a firm grip of the following facts:

It is now half a century since the most populous and productive States of North America, compared to the least of which Ireland is only a cabbage garden, and a barren one at that, renounced all idea of independence and isolation and fought for compulsory combination with all the other States across the whole continent more desperately than the many Irish soldiers engaged in the conflict had ever fought for separation. During that half-century no small nation has been able to maintain its independence singlehanded: it has had to depend either on express guarantees from the Great Powers (that is, the combinations) or on the intense jealousy between those Powers.

In the present war the attack of a huge army of men of different races, speaking half-a-dozen different languages and estranged by memories of fierce feuds and persecutions and tyrannies, but combined under the leadership of the Central Empires, made short work of national pride, of the spirit of independence, and of bitter memories of old hostilities in England, France, and Russia. These three ancient enemies, any of whom could have swallowed Ireland more easily than Ireland could swallow her own Blasket Islands, had to pocket their nationalism and defend themselves by a combination of the British fleet, the French army, and the Russian steamroller. And even when these immense combinations were in the field one of them was glad to buy the help of moribund Turkey and immature little Bulgaria, and the other to offer Italy, in defiance of all nationalist principles, a lodgment in Dalmatia if she would come to the rescue.

In the face of these towering facts that blot out the heavens with smoke and pile the earth of Europe with dead I invite America to contemplate the spectacle of a few manifesto-writing stalwarts from the decimated population of a tiny green island at the back of Godspeed, claiming its national right to confront the world with its own army, its own fleet, its own tariff, and its own language, which not five per cent. of its population could speak or read or write even if they wanted to. Unless the American climate has the power of totally destroying the intelligence of the Irish race its members will see that, if Ireland were cut loose from the British fleet and army tomorrow, she would have to make a present of herself the day after to the United States, or France, or Germany, or any big Power that would condescend to accept her: England for preference.

Now, let me not be supposed to have any lack of sympathy for the very natural desire of the Irish, expressed by "the clarion voice of the Bishop of Limerick," to keep out of this war if possible. If I were an Irish bishop I should certainly tell my flock to till their fields and serve God in peace instead of slaughtering Germans who also ought to be tilling their fields and serving God in peace. If I were the Pope I should order every combatant in Europe, Asia Minor, and Africa to lay down his arms instantly on pain of excommunication. I should offer the Kaiser his choice between coming to Canossa and coming to hell; and I should not hold out the least hope to the President of the French Republic or the Kings of England and Italy that they had any greater claim in the eye of heaven to a verdict of justifiable homicide than the Kaiser.

But does any sane Irishman hope to persuade an American, of Irish or other race, that the French people were any less desirous to keep out of the trenches than the Irish? Is the Catholic of Bavaria any less entangled in the net of war than the Catholic of Connaught? On the contrary, he is entangled much more; for he is not, like the Connaught Catholic, exempt from conscription. The English volunteer is a volunteer no longer: he is a pressed man; and if he has rushed to the colors more eagerly than the Irishman it is because the industrial slavery he endured was so much worse than any that the Irish peasant suffers, and the places he lives in so much uglier and more revolting to human instincts than the poorest Irish cabins that still survive the activities of the Irish Local Government Board, that the billet in St Albans or on Salisbury Plain, and the trip to Flanders were an adventure as welcome to him as the separation allowance was to his wife, and—sometimes—the separation itself to both of them.

But you cannot knock into the head of the machine-made Irish patriot that either the grievances or the virtues of Ireland is to be found in other countries as well. There have been occasions on which English trade unionists have sent money to help French, Belgian, and other foreign workers in their strife for a living wage. Irish patriots send nothing but demands for unlimited sympathy, unlimited admiration, and unlimited Post Office orders. The money that Ireland has accepted from America without shame, and without perceptible gratitude, both in domestic remittances and political subscriptions, is incalculable.

We are the champion mendicants of the world; and when we at last provoke the inevitable hint that Ireland, like other countries, is expected to be at least self-supporting, not to say self-respecting, we shall rise up and denounce our benefactors as the parricidal exterminators of the Irish race. We have never seen the other side of any Irish question: to this day the protective duties by which England ruined our manufactures are denounced as an act of pure malignity, and the old notice "No Irish need apply" as an explosion of racial hatred, although every other working class in the west of Europe is educated enough to know that men willing, as we Irish are, to take the jobs of other men at wages against which a pig would revolt are the enemies, not merely of the English, but of the human race.

And now we are told—as if it were something to be proud of—that "the heart of Ireland is not changed." It does not occur to the gentlemen who have made this announcement, which is fortunately not true, that in that case the sooner it is changed the better. "Deprived as Ireland is by the

Defence of the Realm Act of the right to express any national opinion" is the beginning of their depressing declaration. Pray, is England any the less deprived of the rights of her people by this reckless act? Has anything happened in Ireland since the war began, whether in suppressions of papers, arbitrary arrests, excessive sentences without trial, even secret executions, that can be compared for a moment to the abuses of the act that have occurred in England? And can such abuses be restrained in any other way in either country than by the peoples of the two countries making common cause against them instead of, as this silly document does, accusing "the English" of guile, calumny, falsehood, cant, and what not, taunting them with the very defeats the English papers try to minimize by such headlines as Heroic Stand by the Dublin Fusiliers. The cry that England's Difficulty is Ireland's Opportunity is raised in the old senseless, spiteful way as a recommendation to stab England in the back when she is fighting someone else and to kick her when she is down, instead of in the intelligent and large-minded modern way which sees in England's difficulty the opportunity of shewing her what a friendly alliance with Ireland can do for her in return for the indispensable things it can do for Ireland.

In short, the war is a convincing demonstration of the futility of the notion that the Irish and English peoples are natural enemies. They are, on the contrary, natural allies. The whole case for Home Rule stands on that truth, and the case against it, on the contrary, falsehood. If we are natural enemies England must either hold us down or be herself held down by us. If we are natural allies there is no more ground for denying self-government to us than to Australia. There is, of course, what the Germans call the Class War always with us; but that is a bond of union between the workers of all nations and not a division. If the two countries were separate, the first care of Irish statesmen would be to fasten as many tentacles as possible on Great Britain by pooling the wider public services of the two countries, especially the military and naval services, which would crush Ireland today if they were a separate establishment. That is why it is part of the Home Rule bargain that the English army and fleet shall also be the Irish army and fleet. There may come a time when international law may be so well established that a small nation may be as safe by itself as a small man already is in the streets of a civilized capital. But that time can come only through renunciation of all the poisonous international hatreds of which the Irish hatred of England is a relic. There may even come a time when some development of the arts of self-defence, which already enable ten properly equipped and trained men to hold their own against a thousand savages, may enable ten wise men to hold their own against a thousand fools. But that time has not come yet; and if it ever does it will be a bad job for the Irish patriot if he is still parroting his dreary litany to St Patrick and Robert Emmet[1] and the Manchester martyrs[2] to be delivered from the wicked English.

As matters now stand this war is just as much Ireland's business as England's or France's. A mere victory for British navalism over Prussian militarism might be as great a misfortune as a victory for Prussian militarism over British navalism. But a victory of Western Democracy and Republicanism over Hohenzollernism and Hapsburgocracy, or a stalemate with the Prussian and Austrian legions held up hopeless by French and Irish republican soldiers, even shoulder to shoulder with Britons who think that they never, never, never will be slaves because they have never been anything else, would be a triumph for the principles that have made the United States the most important political combination in the world, and, through the United States, made the Home Rule movement possible in Ireland.

I am under no illusions as to the extent to which modern nominal democracy and republicanism are still leavened by the old tyrannies and the old intolerances. I have declared in season and out that the task before us is not so much the sweeping out of the last monarchs as the herculean labor of making Democracy democratic and Republicanism republican. It was by devoting my political life to the solution of that problem that I learned to see mere romantic nationalism in its essential obsolescence and triviality. There is such a thing as Irish freedom, just as there is such a thing as Cork butter. But it was by studying foreign butter and tracing its excellence to its source in foreign co-operation that Sir Horace Plunkett

1. Robert Emmet was the leader of an abortive attempt in 1803 to seize Dublin Castle and hold the lord-lieutenant hostage. His speech from the dock, before he was hanged, has given him immortality in Ireland.

2. Three Fenian revolutionaries named William Allen, Michael Larkin, and William O'Brien were executed in Manchester in 1867 because, in their efforts to rescue two Fenian prisoners from a police van, they killed a police sergeant. The executions produced a wave of resentment in Ireland.

and George Russell,[3] the only two noted Irishmen who have done anything fundamental for Ireland in my time, have kept Cork butter sweet.
And it is from England and America that the Irish will have to learn what
freedom really means.

Ireland as a nation cannot keep out of the present conflict except on the
plea of utter insignificance. It has yet to be seen whether America will
succeed in keeping out of it. Be that as it may, the Irishman who suggests
that the right side for any Western democratic nation to take is the Prussian side must find some better argument than that the Prussian side happens to be the anti-English side. I hope in a second article[4] to make it clear
to the Germans of America (since I can hardly reach the Germans of
Germany) why it is that I do not take their side in this war, though they
have taken my side very handsomely in my long conflict with Philistinism
and barbarism. But if, as I have shewn, the choice of sides does not now
depend on national considerations, still less does it depend on personal
ones. My present purpose is to shew that the Irishmen who can see only
Ireland and England, and see even them only as parties to a feud, can give
no counsel worth attending to in this business.

Ireland, without the least regard to its squabble with England, must
group itself in a combination of which the real centre is Western republicanism and democratic internationalism. The present appeal against this
combination to America would be stupid even if Ireland's interest and
traditions were those of Frederick the Great. But as Irish patriotism is by
tradition republican, the appeal is quite beyond patience. The Irish patriot may demand in desperation whether he is to fight shoulder to shoulder with the English Unionists and Russian autocrats against the enemies
of his "age-long oppressors"; but the reply is inexorably Yes. Adversity
makes us acquainted with strange bedfellows. The Tsar, when this war
came upon him, must have exclaimed to M. Sazonov, "Good heavens! do
you mean to tell me that I, an absolute Emperor and a Romanoff, am to
fight against my imperial cousins the Hapsburgs and the Hohenzollerns,
who stand with me as the representatives of the principle of monarchy in
Europe, on the side of this rabble of French and Irish republicans, this

3. George Russell, Irish poet, painter, and agrarian journalist, wrote under the
pseudonym A.E.
4. "The German Case against Germany," *New York Times*, 16 April 1916.

gang of Serbian regicides, this brace of Kings who are so completely in the hands of Parliaments of middle-class lawyers that their own subjects call them india-rubber stamps!" If the Tsar has to swallow that, even an Irish patriot must not be surprised at not having it all his own way. He must therefore console himself by considering that, in the words of a deservedly celebrated Irish dramatic poet,

Fate drives us all to find our chiefest good
In what we can, and not in what we would.[5]

5. The "deservedly celebrated Irish dramatic poet" was Shaw. The lines are Cashel Byron's, in act 3 of *The Admirable Bashville* (1901).

NEGLECTED MORALS OF THE IRISH RISING

The New Statesman, London, 6 May 1916

One. Be very careful what political doctrine you preach. You may be taken at your word in the most unexpected directions.

I wonder how many of those who have made such a resounding propaganda of Sinn Fein for small nationalities for twenty months past have died heroically for their principles in the burning ruins of the General Post Office in Sackville-street![1] Will Punch give us a cartoon of Mr Connolly, in the pose of the King of the Belgians, telling his conqueror that at least he has not lost his soul by his desperate fight for the independence of his country against a foe ten times his size? Probably not; and yet the parallel is curiously close in everything but the scale of the devastation and the number of deaths. It may become still closer, if the Government gives way to any clamor for frightfulness from the people who were so shocked by it when von Bissing was its exponent.[2]

Two. Do not give way to an intemperate admiration of patriotism, or make an inconsiderate use of the word Traitor.

No wise man now uses the word Traitor at all. He who fights for the independence of his country may be an ignorant and disastrous fool, but he is not a traitor and will never be regarded as one by his fellow countrymen. All the slain men and women of the Sinn Fein Volunteers fought

1. The insurrection known as the Easter Rising took place on 24 April 1916, when detachments of the Irish Citizen Army, under James Connolly, and of the Irish Volunteers, under Padraic Pearse, occupied the General Post Office in Sackville (now O'Connell) Street and other strategic buildings in Dublin. After a week of heavy fighting, the insurgents surrendered; more than one hundred of them were immediately given death sentences by military courts-martial. But after the executions of Pearse, Connolly, and twelve other leaders, between 3 and 12 May, the remaining death sentences were commuted to penal servitude for various terms. When he wrote "Neglected Morals of the Irish Rising," Shaw was unaware of the death sentences and of the executions that had already been carried out.

2. Moritz Ferdinand von Bissing, the German general in command of occupied Belgium, instituted the practice of reprisals against the civil populace for acts of violence against the German military regime.

and died for their country as sincerely as any soldier in Flanders has fought or died for his. Their contempt for pro-British pacifists, like myself, was as fiercely genuine as the contempt of our conscriptionists and military authorities for Mr Clifford Allen.[3] As a Republican forlorn hope, their ideal cannot be insulted without insulting our ally France and our friend America; and by the time the whole world has become Republican and Romance has covered their graves with its flowers, the last of the Irish rebellions will be a stock subject of British heroic verse.

Three. Do not rashly assume that every building destroyed by an enemy is a palatial masterpiece of architecture.

It is greatly to be regretted that so very little of Dublin has been demolished. The General Post Office was a monument, fortunately not imperishable, of how extremely dull XVIII century pseudo-classic architecture can be. Its demolition does not matter. What does matter is that all the Liffey slums have not been demolished. Their death and disease rates have every year provided waste, destruction, crime, drink, and avoidable homicide on a scale which makes the fusillades of the Sinn Feiners and the looting of their camp-followers hardly worth turning the head to notice. It was from these slums that the auxiliaries poured forth for whose thefts and outrages the Volunteers will be held responsible, though their guilt lies at all our doors. Let us grieve, not over the fragment of Dublin city that is knocked down, but over at least three-quarters of what has been preserved. How I wish I had been in command of the British artillery on that fatal field! How I should have improved my native city!

Four. To delay overdue legislation for the sake of a quiet life may make more trouble than it saves.

Had Home Rule been in operation, not only would both the Sinn Fein and the Ulster Volunteers have been technically traitors (both are on precisely the same footing as to that), but the Irish Parliament would have introduced compulsory military service to get rid of them, if it had found itself too weak to prevent such armed forces being raised.

Five. Do not forget that a rising may be induced in England and Scotland at any moment by the same means.

If the party which openly aims at the destruction of British Trade Unionism were to fabricate and circulate an elaborate military plan of

3. Allen, general manager of *The Daily Citizen*, London, was imprisoned during World War I as a conscientious objector.

campaign for seizing all the Trade Union offices, cordoning the mining villages and unionist quarters, and capturing the secretaries, the result, though it would be called a series of local riots and not a rebellion, would cost more lives and burn more buildings than the Dublin affair. That was the trick by which the Dublin rising was precipitated. I have a copy of the fabricated document which Mr T. W. Russell has repudiated on behalf of the Castle.[4] I have a copy of a letter which Mr Sheehy Skeffington vainly tried to induce the London press to publish, warning us that Sinn Feiners believed that there was a Castle-cum-Carsonite plot to disarm them and seize their quarters, and that there was the gravest danger of a defensive-offensive movement.[5] Whoever forged the document was a clever scoundrel; but clever scoundrels have never been lacking in Ireland, where unless this particular scoundrel is detected and dealt with accordingly, it will never be believed that the document was not genuine. Can England confide so absolutely in the stupidity of her scoundrels or the virtue of her clever men as to feel safe from a similar ruse and a similar result?

Six. If you wish men to be good citizens, you must teach them to be good citizens.

Whose fault is the dense ignorance and romantic folly which made these unfortunate Sinn Feiners mistake a piece of hopeless mischief for a patriotic stroke for freedom such as Shelley sang and Byron took arms

4. The "fabricated document," headed *Secret Orders Issued to Military Officers,* ostensibly a government order for the roundup of nationalist leaders and the suppression of nationalist organizations, was circulated for the purpose of creating in the populace a sympathetic attitude to the projected insurrection. The document was actually in the handwriting of Joseph Plunkett, one of the leaders subsequently executed for his part in the rising. The English government in Dublin Castle immediately repudiated the "orders" as a forgery. The texts of this document and of Sheehy Skeffington's letter of warning were published adjacent to Shaw's article in *The New Statesman.*

5. Sheehy Skeffington had written to Shaw from Dublin on 7 April 1916, enclosing a copy of the letter of warning, which he had sent to several London newspapers: "I think it quite likely that none of them will publish it; so I am sending you a copy for your personal information, that you may understand how critical the position is here. It will require all the efforts of all men of goodwill to avert bloodshed in Ireland; and perhaps you, having the ear of the press, may be able to intervene effectively" (hitherto unpublished letter in the Shaw archive, British Library, London, by permission of Owen Sheehy Skeffington, 1961).

for? Were they taught citizenship in their schools? Were their votes bought with anything but balderdash? Granted that their heads, like their newspapers, were stuffed with ultra-insular patriotic conceit, is this a time at which England can with any countenance throw a stone at them on that score? Has not the glorification of patriotism, of reckless defiance, of superior numbers and resources, of readiness to kill and be killed for the old flag, of implacable hatred of the enemy and the invader, of the sacred rights of small nations to self-government and freedom, been thundered at them for more than a year by British writers who talk and feel as if England were still the England of Alfred, and Socialism, the only alternative to Sinn Fein, were sedition and blasphemy? Is it not a little unreasonable of us to clamor for the blood of men who have simply taken us at our word and competed for our hero-worship with the Belgians and the Serbians, who have also devoted their Sackville-streets to fire and slaughter in a struggle at impossible odds with giant empires?

I can speak my mind freely on this matter, for I have attacked the romantic Separatism of Ireland with every device of invective and irony and dialectic at my command. As it happens, my last onslaught on Sinn Fein reached Ireland, through the columns of The Irish Times, two days before the insurrection. It was too late; and, in any case, the Volunteers had plenty of assurances from the most vociferous English patriots that I am not a person to be attended to. But exasperating as the mischief and folly and ignorance of the rising are to my practical sense, I must not deny, now that it is crushed, that these men were patriotic according to their own lights, brave according to our lights, public in their aims, and honorable in their Republican political ideal. I notice, also, that the newspapers which describe them as personally contemptible contradict their correspondents by pictures which exhibit them as well-set-up, soldierly men.

What is to be done with them? As to many, the answer is simple: bury them. But what about the others—the prisoners of war? It would be hardly decent to ask them to take the oath of allegiance to the English King. They are Republicans. But the notion that they are any fonder of the Protestant monarchy of Prussia is nonsense. Why not make a present of them to Joffre, with a hint that his right wing is the safest place for them? He needs good Republicans, and France knows of old the value of an Irish Brigade.

THE EASTER WEEK EXECUTIONS

To *The Daily News*, London, 10 May 1916

Sir,—You say that "so far as the leaders are concerned no voice has been raised in this country against the infliction of the punishment which has so speedily overtaken them."[1] As the Government shot the prisoners first and told the public about it afterwards, there was no opportunity for effective protest. But it must not be assumed that those who merely shrugged their shoulders when it was useless to remonstrate accept for one moment the view that what happened was the execution of a gang of criminals.

My own view—which I should not intrude on you had you not concluded that it does not exist—is that the men who were shot in cold blood after their capture or surrender were prisoners of war, and that it was, therefore, entirely incorrect to slaughter them. The relation of Ireland to Dublin Castle is in this respect precisely that of the Balkan States to Turkey, of Belgium or the city of Lille to the Kaiser, and of the United States to Great Britain.

Until Dublin Castle is superseded by a National Parliament and Ireland voluntarily incorporated with the British Empire, as Canada, Australasia, and South Africa have been incorporated, an Irishman resorting to arms to achieve the independence of his country is doing only what Englishmen will do if it be their misfortune to be invaded and conquered by the Germans in the course of the present war.

Further, such an Irishman is as much in order morally in accepting assistance from the Germans in his struggle with England as England is in accepting the assistance of Russia in her struggle with Germany. The fact that he knows that his enemies will not respect his rights if they catch him, and that he must therefore fight with a rope round his neck, increases his risk, but adds in the same measure to his glory in the eyes of

---

1. When Shaw wrote this communication, twelve of the insurgents had already been executed. Two more, including James Connolly, were to be shot on 12 May. The remaining ninety-seven death sentences were commuted to sentences of penal servitude.

his compatriots and of the disinterested admirers of patriotism throughout the world.

It is absolutely impossible to slaughter a man in this position without
making him a martyr and a hero, even though the day before the rising he
may have been only a minor poet. The shot Irishmen will now take their
places beside Emmet and the Manchester martyrs in Ireland, and beside
the heros of Poland and Serbia and Belgium in Europe; and nothing in
heaven or on earth can prevent it.

I do not propose to argue the question: it does not admit of argument.
The military authorities and the British Government must have known
that they were canonizing their prisoners. But they said in their anger:
"We dont care: we will shoot them; we feel that way." Similarly the Irish
will reply: "We knew you would: you always do; we simply tell you more
or less politely how *we* feel about it."

Perhaps I had better add that I am not a Sinn Feiner, and that since
those utterances of mine which provoked the American Gaels to mob my
plays some years ago to the very eve of the present rising I used all my
influence and literary power to discredit the Sinn Fein ideal, and in particular to insist on the duty of Ireland to throw herself with all her force
on the side of the French Republic against the Hohenzollern and Hapsburg monarchies. But I remain an Irishman, and am bound to contradict
any implication that I can regard as a traitor any Irishman taken in a fight
for Irish independence against the British Government, which was a fair
fight in everything except the enormous odds my countrymen had to
face.

I may add that I think it hard that Mr [Augustine] Birrell, an Englishman, should be sacrificed on the tombs of the fallen Sinn Feiners. Mr
Birrell and Sir Matthew Nathan[2] did what they could with their hands tied
by the Army commands and Sir Edward Carson. Obviously the one
thing that could have made Ireland safe from an outbreak of civil war was
the impartial disarmament of the civil population, as in the sixties during
the Fenian scare. Failing that, it has been the merest chance that the outbreak occurred in Dublin, and was headed by Sinn Fein, provoked by a
bogus Castle plot. A Popish plot, equally ingeniously simulated, might

2. The chief secretary and undersecretary for Ireland, respectively, at the time of
the Easter Rising.

have produced the same result in Belfast, headed by the Ulster Volunteers. A convincing announcement of the abandonment of Home Rule would set the National Volunteers shooting tomorrow. Why were they not all disarmed? Because the government was afraid of Sir Edward Carson and "the Mutineers of the Curragh,"[3] and to attempt to disarm one side without disarming the other would have been an act of open war on Irish Nationalism. The only alternative was to introduce compulsory military service, and send all the volunteers to Mesopotamia or Flanders; but this again could have been done by a national Parliament only, and the Government had postponed that. Under such circumstances, if George Washington had been Chief Secretary for Ireland, and Cavour or Carnot Under-Secretary, they could have done nothing but try their utmost to preserve goodhumor, and hope that nobody would throw a match into the gunpowder.

And this, it seems, is exactly what they very wisely did. But it should not be forgotten that all Governments of the Dublin Castle type are really in the hands of their police and permanent officials, who do very much as they please because they cannot be disowned or "turned down" in the face of the democratic enemy. Mr Birrell, like the Kaiser or the Tsar, had not the sort of control that President Wilson or Mr Asquith enjoys. All autocracies are shams as to real public power. Ireland is governed by police inspectors, gombeen men, and priests, not by Secretaries of State.

At all events, if Mr Birrell and Sir Matthew insist on their assailants explaining exactly what they should and could have done that they did not do, I shall be greatly surprised if either their critics or the gentlemen who are undertaking to replace them will venture to answer them.

G. Bernard Shaw.

3. In March 1914, sixty British officers at the Curragh military camp in County Kildare resigned their commissions in protest of the probability—as they saw it—of troops being used against Ulster Unionists who objected to Home Rule. Their resignations were not accepted, and the government assured them that it had no intention of deploying troops in Ulster for such a purpose.

ROGER CASEMENT

I

Prefatory note to *A Discarded Defence of Roger Casement*, privately printed by Clement Shorter (London, 1922), limited to 25 copies

The following document explains itself to anyone who knows that Sir Roger Casement, an Irish patriot who had served with distinction in the British Consular Service, and been knighted for it, took advantage of the war of 1914–18 to seek the assistance of Germany in an attempt to achieve the independence of Ireland. He was conveyed to Ireland in a German submarine, and was immediately captured by the British forces there, taken to London, tried for high treason, and executed on the scaffold.

Casement's personal ill luck in being so promptly captured gave an air of shallow futility to his enterprize which it did not deserve. His scheme was precisely what might have been expected from an educated professional diplomatist. He had proposed it in some clever and well-written papers published by him in America, which were not noticed or criticized in England because British journalists do not understand enough of diplomacy or know enough of history to be able to tackle such documents. Casement knew that the only chance of independence for a small and militarily impotent nation among the Great Powers was to be guaranteed by them, like Belgium or Greece, either as a Buffer State or because its annexation by any one of them would upset the Balance of Power and provoke war with the others. He believed, as seemed likely enough for some time, that Germany was going to win; and in that case an obvious step would be the detachment of Ireland from England as a hostile independent State under German protection in England's gate, just as, now that the fortune of war has taken the opposite turn, an independent Poland and a detached Silesia are set up on Germany's eastern frontier. Any trained diplomatist would have speculated in this way. Indeed, he could not have speculated in any other way, because there was no other possible move on the diplomatic board.

I did not know Casement personally, but I had read his proposals and understood his scheme. I did not support it, not in the least because there was any treason in it for me or any other Irishman, but because, first, I had taken the side of England against German Junkerism strongly from the beginning; second, I did not believe Germany was going to win; and, third, the so-called independence of Belgium and Greece seemed to me the most dangerous and expensive kind of political servitude, much less eligible than the position Ireland would be in, if, as I believed possible, she could obtain the position of being in the British Commonwealth on exactly the same terms as England, or even better. But Casement was entitled to his contrary opinion; and I did my best to prevent him being hanged, just as any Englishman would, I presume, have done his best to save any other Englishman from being hanged by the Irish Republican Army, however much he might differ from him as to English policy.

Unfortunately, there was nothing between Casement and the scaffold except the jury at the trial. I thought that if he claimed to be treated at worst as a prisoner of war captured in the prosecution of a perfectly legitimate enterprize for the liberation of his country from a foreign yoke, there might be a Tom Broadbent[1] or two on the jury to secure a disagreement. The difficulty was to induce him to take my advice instead of that of the lawyers, whose routine was certain to hang him. I did not succeed. At the instance of his devoted friend and cousin, Miss Gertrude Bannister, who, by the way, was actually dismissed from the educational post which she had held without reproach for seventeen years because she visited him in prison, I put down on paper a scheme for his defence, and drafted a speech to be made from the dock, not, of course, necessarily in my words, but in whatever paraphrase came most naturally to the accused.

It was no use. Casement liked the speech, but failed to take in the plan of defence, or to see why Counsel should not, or rather would not, plead it. He consented, fatally, to allow Counsel to put up the usual sham defence of denial. Of course it was knocked to pieces with contemptuous ease by Counsel for the Crown (the present Lord Birkenhead); and when the Lord Chief Justice had solemnly complimented Casement's counsel on having done everything for his client that human forensic skill could

1. Tom Broadbent is a character in Shaw's play *John Bull's Other Island*.

achieve, the verdict of Guilty was duly delivered. Then, if you please, the virtually dead man got up and made his speech. A couple of members of the jury were, I am told, good enough to say that if they had heard it before the verdict they would have dissented. But that possibility, on which I had banked, had been averted by the best available legal advice, and Casement was duly hanged, and was no doubt duly avenged many times over in the guerilla warfare that followed.

The draft I made for him was preserved, and came finally into the hands of Mr Clement Shorter. He has printed a few copies privately for his friends; and at his request I have written this explanation of what Casement was driving at, and how I came to advise him as to his trial. I am bound to add it was Mrs Parry's (then Miss Bannister's) devotion that forced my sympathy into action; for Casement, who did not know me, had not invited me to interfere; and I should hardly have done so spontaneously.

There is no harm in adding now that the British Government, being determined to execute Casement, could have put itself in order from his own point of view by treating him as a spy. But this would have implied a recognition of the Irish as a nation at war. It would also have required a moment's thought, the last thing any modern Government seems capable of.

II

Shaw's discarded defense of Roger Casement,
drafted in 1916, and first published in 1922

REX *v.* CASEMENT

Suggestions as to the line the defence may take.

1. The Counsel may take the case out of the prisoner's hand, and contend that he is insane and incapable of pleading.
2. Counsel may go through the usual routine of minimizing the evidence, cross-examining the witnesses, keeping the Crown within strict technical bounds, bringing out any sympathetic aspects of the prisoner's conduct and making a strong bid for sympathy and clemency by dwelling on his services in the Putumayo affair.

3. The prisoner may admit all the facts relied on by the Crown, defend his conduct as an Irish Nationalist, and claim to be held as a prisoner of war, not as a traitor. This defence and claim could be put forward by Counsel, or by the prisoner himself, if he is capable of it.

No. 1 admits of no discussion. The Court would no doubt require medical evidence.

No. 2 could not possibly affect the verdict; and the appeal for clemency would present the prisoner in an attitude of humiliation which would have a chilling effect on romantic public opinion, which is the only sort of public opinion from which the prisoner has anything to hope. However eloquently Counsel might glorify the prisoner's past, the Lord Chief Justice could, and of course would, smudge the picture out by a few sentences describing the worst side of the Dublin catastrophe.

No. 3 is the best course for the prisoner. In weighing it the prisoner should bear constantly in mind that no credible denial of the facts on which the indictment is based is possible; that no legal ingenuity can reduce or exclude enough of the evidence, and no browbeating discredit the Crown case sufficiently to open even the very narrowest door of escape for the prisoner; and that the very desperation of the case is the sole element of strength in his position, as he cannot possibly make his case worse and may make it better by an extreme and daring frontal attack on the position of the Crown. But it is to be observed that it would be so difficult to induce Counsel either to advise such an attack or to undertake it with the necessary wholeheartedness—not to mention that its novelty would leave the Counsel almost at the disadvantage of an amateur in point of experience—that its adoption would probably involve the conduct by the prisoner of his own defence.

In this he would have the advantage of much greater latitude than Counsel could take, and of a certain degree of conscientious guidance from the Bench.

The Lord Chief Justice would probably snub a barrister taking a line startling enough to seem unprofessional; and as the barrister has to consider his future, whilst the prisoner, having lost all, has nothing to lose and everything to gain, the best the barrister could do for his client would be to advise him to conduct his own case if he has had sufficient public experience to address the Court without positive collapse.

The line taken by the prisoner would be as follows. First, that his plea of Not Guilty must not be taken as implying any denial of the essential facts relied on by the Crown, but simply a denial that any guilt attaches to them except the guilt that attaches under the higher law of God to all who draw the sword against their fellows even for their country: a guilt which attaches to all present in the Court equally with the prisoner himself. That he heartily wishes that the Court might have been spared the tedium of calling witnesses to prove facts which he did not dispute, was in no way ashamed of, and was quite willing to add to and amplify if the Attorney-General cared to call him as chief witness for the Crown on the facts. As far as the facts are concerned, he embraces the Crown case, instead of repudiating it. He had made up his mind (query: after the shelving of the Home Rule Act?) that his country ought to achieve her independence of English rule by force of arms. He had hoped that in a very humble way he might do for his country what Garibaldi had been honored in England for doing for his country. The Court might smile at his vanity now that he had failed, but the Court knew that nations were not freed by personal modesty any more than by personal vanity; and a nation which could not produce a Garibaldi had to be content with Casements, and the Casements must do their best. It was no more possible in his opinion for Ireland to free herself without foreign alliances than it had been possible for Italy to free herself without the help of France, or than France, Britain, and Russia could now withstand the Central Empires singlehanded. He therefore very naturally and properly sought to obtain, and to a certain extent did obtain, the assistance of the German Empire in his enterprize. He had no apology whatever to make for that: it was his plain duty to his country.

The prisoner might proceed in the following terms:

I must observe, however, that I had to negotiate with Germany under limitations. I had to accept German help in the form in which Germany chose to give it, because I had little to offer and beggars cannot be choosers. And I did not want German troops in Ireland. I have just the same objection to a German occupation of Ireland that this Court has to a Russian, French, or Italian occupation of England, however friendly. I did not want to have any soldiers in Ireland, except Irish soldiers. What I wanted from Germany was money, munitions, and Irish soldiers, and this was all I accepted. The German authorities collected their Irish prisoners and invited me to persuade them to take part in my enterprize. I did my best. I need hardly say I did not ask any English soldier to fight against his own country: I know how to respect other people's nationality because I know how to respect my own.

It is not necessary for me to trouble the Court with particulars of the assistance I received from Germany over and above this access to the Irish prisoners. Its extent can be estimated with sufficient accuracy from the Crown case; and all I have to say is that, such as it was, I am duly grateful for it.

An attempt has been made to prejudice me on the ground that I was formerly in the pay of the British Empire, that I was knighted for my services to it, and that in acknowledging that honor at the hands of the King I expressed myself in the manner customary among gentlemen on such occasions. I am quite unable to follow the logic of the Attorney-General on these points. The right honorable and learned gentleman must in the earlier stages of his career have often found himself in the pay of clients whom he may at any moment be called upon to prosecute. And if that occurs—if it has not already occurred—his former client may re-proach him very bitterly for biting the hand that fed him, and may even go so far as to call him a traitor. But surely the right honorable gentleman will reply very properly that he received no fee that he had not hand-somely earned. That is my answer too. Englishmen have rendered great services to Germany and been paid for them with German money. En-glishmen have received civilities from the German court, and have ac-knowledged them in terms suitable to the social relations between them and the German Emperor. Will the Attorney-General or anyone else contend that these Englishmen are now traitors to Germany because they are now making war on her, or admit that the Germans would be justified in inflicting the legal penalties of treachery on any English prisoner to whom they could trace payment of German money for services rendered to Germany?

Well, my position is even stronger than theirs; for no Englishman has been compelled to render services to Germany by exclusion from other markets, whereas I was not allowed to exercise the abilities I possessed in the service of my country otherwise than through a public service com-mon to it and England. I am glad of that now, because the fact that I served England well enough to have my services publicly acknowledged and specially rewarded shews that I have no quarrel with England except the political quarrel which England respects and applauds in Italy, Poland, Belgium, and, in short, in every country except those conquered and denationalized by England herself. If the King were to offer me any further mark of his appreciation today, I should not, as the Attorney-General seems to think I ought, strike a melodramatic attitude and exclaim, "Tyrant, I spurn your effort to corrupt me!" I should express myself very much as the Attorney-General no doubt expressed himself when he was enrolled with me in the order of Knighthood, or as he perhaps expressed himself when he was introduced to the Kaiser during his last visit to London.

I now come to the general considerations on which I claim to be found not guilty on the indictment, and transferred to a place of detention for prisoners of war.

Almost all the disasters and difficulties that have made the relations of Ireland with England so mischievous to both countries have arisen from the failure of England to understand that Ireland is not a province of England but a nation, and to negotiate with her on that assumption. If you persist in treating me as an Englishman, you bind yourself thereby to hang me as a traitor before the eyes of the world. Now as a simple matter of fact, I am neither an Englishman nor a traitor: I am an Irishman, captured in a fair attempt to achieve the independence of my country; and you can no more deprive me of the honors of that position, or destroy the effects of my effort, than the abominable cruelties inflicted six hundred years ago on William Wallace in this city, when he met a precisely similar indictment with a precisely similar reply, have prevented that brave and honorable Scot from becoming the national hero of his country. It may seem to some of you gentlemen of the jury that if I ought not to be hanged for being a patriot, I ought to be hanged for being a fool. I will not plead that if men are to be hanged for errors of judgment in politics, we should have such a mortality in England and Ireland that hardly one of us would be left to hang the other. But I may ask you if you nevertheless lean to that opinion in my case, whether my attempt, desperate as it seems, has been after all so disastrous a failure. I am not trying to shirk the British scaffold: it is the altar on which the Irish saints have been canonized for centuries; but I confess I shrink a little from the pillory in which the public opinion of the world places men who, with the best intentions, can do nothing but mischief to the cause they embrace. But I do not think I shall occupy that pillory. Will you understand me when I say that those three days of splendid fighting against desperate odds in the streets of Dublin have given back Ireland her self-respect. We were beaten, indeed never had a dog's chance of victory; but you also were beaten in a no less rash and desperate enterprize in Gallipoli. Are you ashamed of it? Did your hearts burn any the less—did your faith in the valor of your race flag and falter because you were at last driven into the sea by the Turks? Well, what you feel about the fight in Gallipoli, Irishmen feel all over the world about the fight in Dublin. Even if it had had no further consequences— even if it had not sent your Prime Minister, who shelved the Home Rule Act as if it had been a negligible parish by-law, scuttling to Dublin and forced The Times to say at last that Dublin Castle is no longer possible, I should still glory in that feat of arms.

And now, gentlemen, you may hang me if you like. I will not even add "and be damned to you," because I feel no more ill-will to you than I did in the days when you were glad enough to claim my public work as the work of an English Consul. You have no immediate vengeance to fear: it cannot be said that you dare not kill me as it may be said that the Turks dare not kill General Townshend,[2] much as Turks of the baser sort might relish the spectacle of his impalement. I hope that my countrymen, what- ever happens, will not waste their energy and degrade their souls with idle dreams of vengeance, even if the fortune of war should make it pos- sible for them to give effect to them. My neck is at your mercy if it amuses you to break it: my honor and my reputation are beyond your reach. The Lord Chief Justice will presently tell you—I could anticipate the inevi- table summing up for you if I doubted his ability to express it far more weightily than I—he will tell you, as he must, that legally I am a traitor. But history will not on that account absolve you from the most sacred duty of a jury: the duty of standing on the side of right, truth, and justice between all honest laymen and that part of the law that was made against their own consent to destroy them. The question for you is not whether I have broken this law or that, nor whether what I have done comes under this or that legal classification. The question for you is whether I am

2. Major-General Sir Charles Townshend surrendered to the Turks on 29 April 1916, after his army had been besieged at Kut al Amara in Iraq.

guilty or not guilty; and if you allow any judicial direction to distract you from that issue, you will betray not only me, your political enemy, but every man alive who has nothing but a jury between him and the worst that the dead letter of unjust laws can do to him.

I hope that I have spoken here today as you would desire to hear an Englishman speak in a German Court if your country shared the fate of mine. I ask for no mercy, no pardon, no pity. I sincerely and humbly beg your pardon if at any moment during this trial my inextinguishable pride in being an Irishman and my exultation in the bravery and devotion of my countrymen has betrayed me into any exhibition of vanity or arrogance. Of any trace of malice I know I am entirely free, for I feel none and shall feel none whatever the upshot may be. Gentlemen, I have done my duty: now it is your turn.

III

Petition for Casement drafted by Shaw in 1916, reproduced from the original draft now in the National Library of Ireland. In a letter to Clement Shorter, on 5 August 1916, Shaw stated that he did not sign this or any other petition for Casement "because my name might have frightened off some of the more useful signatures."

To the Right Honorable H. H. Asquith, K.C., M.P., Prime Minister.

Sir,—We, the undersigned, beg leave to place before you certain considerations affecting the case of Roger David Casement, now under sentence of death for high treason. Our object is to shew reason why the sentence of Court should not be executed.

We will not occupy your time with matters as well known to you as to ourselves, and on which your judgment cannot be challenged, such, for example, as the conspicuous public services of the condemned man and so forth. We address ourselves solely to points on which you may desire information as to the state of public opinion.

We assume that the penalty for high treason is peculiar in criminal law inasmuch as it depends for its sanction not on the general principle of the sacredness of law, but on its effect on the public peace. The conclusion is arrived at in every case by balancing the deterrent effect of carrying out the sentence against the conciliatory effect of remitting it. Recent events in South Africa have accustomed the public to this view. We therefore need trouble you with no apology for treating the decision as one of expediency only.

In our opinion, Casement had not, up to the time of his trial, any serious hold on the Irish people. His Nationalist writings were circulated in America, not in Ireland. His political projects, being those of an educated diplomatist, were too technical to be understood by such groups as the Republican Brotherhood and the irreconcilable section of Sinn Fein. We are confident that if during your recent visit to Ireland you inquired what Casement was driving at you would not have received a single well-informed reply. You certainly did not find him a national hero; and we venture to assume that you do not wish him to become a national hero.

There is, however, one infallible way in which that can be done; and that way is to hang him. His trial and sentence have already raised his status in Nationalist Ireland; but it lacks the final consecration of death. We urge you very strongly not to effect that consecration. In the position of Mr Arthur Lynch and General De Wet,[3] Casement will be harmless, disabled by his own failure. On a British scaffold he will do endless mischief. The contrast between ruthless severity in his case, and conspicuous leniency—not to mention impunity—in others, will provide an overwhelming argument and illustration to the propagandists of hatred and revenge, whilst the halo which surrounds the national martyr will make a national faith of his beliefs and a gospel of his writings.

As against this nothing can be claimed except that other rebels may be intimidated. But the likelihood is all the other way. The Irish movement is not a solid phalanx of irreconcilables. The Casementites and Fenians were a negligible minority of it until the Rebellion. If, though still a minority, they are no longer negligible, it is precisely because of the policy of intimidation, of "giving Ireland a lesson," attempted by General Maxwell.[4] The swing of the pendulum, not only in Ireland but in the neutral

3. The positions of Arthur Lynch, Nationalist M.P. and Irish expatriate journalist, and Christian R. De Wet, Boer general and statesman, were similar to Casement's because both were tried for treason for having joined the Boer cause. Instead of being executed, however, they were given prison sentences.

4. Sir John Maxwell, commander of British military forces in Ireland during the 1916 insurrection, evoked widespread disapproval, particularly in the United States, by his summary execution of the Irish insurgents.

countries which are interested in Ireland, was immediate and unmistakeable. But it has not been decisive. The Nationalist movement is still reasonable; and a friendly settlement is easy, provided no more executions take place. Even the crude notion that England owes Ireland a life for Mr [Sheehy] Skeffington's had better be respected.

You will observe that in putting the case thus before you, we have deprived ourselves of the support of those who see in the specific proposals of Casement a real hope for Irish independence, and who must therefore, within the limits imposed by common humanity, desire the strenuous impulse which would be given to his authority and influence by his death in an English prison as an Irish patriot. But you will hardly attach the less weight on that account to our urgent representation, which is prompted by a sincere desire for an unembittered settlement of the question which has occupied so large a share of the labors of your administration.

We are, Sir,

Your obedient Servants.

IV

Shaw's letter, "Shall Roger Casement Hang?"—rejected by *The Times*, London—was published in *The Manchester Guardian*, 22 July 1916, and reprinted in the *New York American*, 13 August 1916.

Sir,—As several English newspapers have answered the above question vehemently in the affirmative, may I, as an Irishman, be allowed to balance their judgment by a reminder of certain considerations, easily overlooked in England, which seem glaringly obvious in Ireland.

First let me say that I have no sentimental appeal to make. Casement (he is no longer technically Sir Roger: but I really cannot bring myself to throw Mister in his teeth at such a moment) has lived his life not without distinction. His estimate of the relative values of the political rights of his country as he conceives them and of the integrity of his neck may be more Irish than English (though I hope I have no right to say so); but at any rate he has staked his life and lost, and cannot with any sort of dignity ask, or allow anyone else to ask on his behalf, for sentimental privilege. There need be no hesitation to carry out the sentence if it should appear, on reflection, a sensible one. Indeed, with a view to extricating the discussion completely from the sentimental vein, I will go so far as to confess that there is a great deal to be said for hanging all public men at the age of fifty-two, though under such a regulation I should myself have perished eight years ago. Were it in force throughout Europe, the condition of the world at present would be much more prosperous.

I presume I may count on a general agreement that Casement's treatment should not be exceptional. This is important, because it happens that his case is not an isolated one just now. There are several traitors in the public eye at present. At the head of them stands Christian De Wet. If De Wet is spared and Casement hanged, the unavoidable conclusion will be that Casement will be hanged, not because he is a traitor, but because he is an Irishman. We have also a group of unconvicted, and indeed unprosecuted, traitors whose action helped very powerfully to convince Germany that she might attack France without incurring our active hostility. As all these gentlemen belong to the same political party, their impunity, if Casement be executed, will lead to the still closer conclusion that his real offence is not merely that of being an Irishman but of being a nationalist Irishman. I see no way of getting round this. If it was proper to reprieve De Wet, whose case was a very flagrant one, Casement cannot be executed except on the assumption that Casement is a more hateful person than De Wet; and there is no other apparent ground for this discrimination than the fact that Casement is an Irishman and De Wet a Boer. Now this is clearly a consideration that should not weight the scales of justice. It may represent a fierce feeling which, though neither general nor civilized, is real and natural; but its gratification in the exercise of the Royal prerogative would make all the difference between an execution and a political assassination.

Sir Harry Poland and Sir Homewood Crawford are obviously right in claiming that Casement's trial was conducted in a manner which was, if anything, unduly indulgent to the accused, though Sir Homewood might perhaps have found a more tactful precedent than the case of Wainewright the murderer. Nevertheless, the real case was not put before the Court at all. The Crown, sure of its verdict, contented itself with a perfunctory police-court charge. The defence, after manufacturing a legal point to provide technical ground for an appeal, put up the sort of excuse usual in criminal cases: that is, the excuse of a pickpocket. Accused, having—very unwisely in my opinion—allowed his case to be pleaded for him instead of pleading it himself, could not very well repudiate the defence he had thus brought on himself: he could only ignore it. It was then too late. But there is no reason why the real case should not be stated now. It is fully set forth in Casement's recent writings published in America. No one dares publish them here, apparently, though the works of Treitschke and Mr Houston Chamberlain, under cover of derisory titles and prefaces that deceive no sensible reader, circulate freely.

Casement's contention is simple enough. He does not pretend that Ireland can be a Power. But Belgium is not a Power. Greece is not a Power. They exist politically because it suits the Powers to maintain them as "buffer States" or "open doors." Casement, like Sir Edward Grey and all the professional diplomatists, knows that the sore point in the British position for the rest of the world is our command of the sea. He argued that, if Britain is ever defeated, the victor's first care will be to abolish our power of blockade, and he suggested that the most obvious and effectual means of doing this would be to establish an independent kingdom of Ireland, guaranteed as an open door by the non-British Powers. So far, his views are on record. I infer that he regarded a victory by the Central Empires in the present war as probable enough to justify him in opening negotiations with the German Government with a view to the eventuality he had forecast.

Now, this was a perfectly legitimate political speculation. An Irishman cannot reasonably be deterred from entertaining it, and even acting on it, by any loyalty which he yet owes to the British Empire. My own objection to it, for instance, is expressed by pointing to the predicament of Belgium and Greece, and asking whether that sort of independence is really preferable to the integration of Australia or Bavaria, with adequate modern units of defensive force. It seems to me an obsolete speculation, but it implies no moral delinquency.

On the question of allegiance, Casement was equally explicit. He pointed out that five centuries of Turkish rule in the Balkans had not, in the opinion of the British nation, abrogated the right of every Serbian to strike for independence, and he concluded quite logically that the same period of British rule could not abrogate the right of every Irishman to do the same. In England we are still so strongly of that opinion so far as Serbia is concerned that we have not allowed an event which could be paralleled in these islands only by the assassination of the Prince of Wales in the streets of Dublin to shake our adherence to, and our support by armed force of, this principle of nationality. It seems to me that Casement is here quite unanswerable. In any case, the word traitor as applied to a rebel has always been a mere vituperation from the days of Wallace to those of Sir Edward Carson and Sir Frederick Smith,[5] and in my opinion it should be disused in this sense by intelligent men. Certainly, no one outside Great Britain will have any desire to apply it, even for vituperative purposes, to Casement.

Public opinion seems to be influenced to some extent by the notion that because Casement received money for his work from the British Empire, and earned it with such distinction that he became personally famous and was knighted for it, and expressed himself as gentlemen do on such occasions, he is in the odious position of having bitten the hand that fed him. To the people who take this view I put my own case. I have been employed by Germany as a playwright for many years, and by the Austrian Emperor in the great theatre in Vienna which is part of his household. I have received thousands of pounds for my services. I was recognized in this way when the English theatres were contemptuously closed to me. I was compelled to produce my last important play *[Pygmalion]* in Berlin in order that it might not be prejudiced by the carefully telegraphed abuse of the English press. Am I to understand that it is therefore my duty to fight for Germany and Austria, and that, in taking advantage of the international reputation which I unquestionably owe to Germany more than to any other country to make the first statement of the case against her which could have convinced anybody outside England, I was biting the hand of the venerable Franz Josef, whose bread I had eaten? I cannot admit it for a moment. I hope I have not been ungrateful. I have refused to join in the popular game of throwing mud at the Germans, and I have said nothing against them that I did not say when many of our most ardent patriots were lighting illuminations and raising triumphal arches to welcome the Kaiser in London. But to Germany's attack on France I remain a conscientious objector, and I must take my side accordingly. Clearly, Casement may claim precisely the same right to take his side according to his convictions, all the more because his former services prove that he does so without malice.

5. Sir Frederick Smith, who later became the first Earl of Birkenhead, was attorney-general and the prosecutor of Casement.

The reasonable conclusion is that Casement should be treated as a prisoner of war. I believe this is the view that will be taken in the neutral countries, whose good opinion is much more important to us than the satisfaction of our resentment. In Ireland he will be regarded as a national hero if he is executed, and quite possibly a spy if he is not. For that reason it may well be that he would object very strongly to my attempt to prevent his canonization. But Ireland has enough heros and martyrs already, and if England has not by this time had enough of manufacturing them in fits of temper experience is thrown away on her, and she will continue to be governed, as she is at present to so great an extent unconsciously, by Casement's countrymen.

Yours, &c.,

G. Bernard Shaw.

V

Shaw's eleventh-hour appeal for Casement, who was hanged
at Pentonville Prison, London, on 3 August, was published
in *The Daily News*, London, 2 August 1916.

Sir,—May I point out that the case of Captain Fryatt[6] adds greatly to the weight of Mr Nevinson's appeal for Casement's reprieve on the ground that his execution would not have the support of neutral public opinion? It will be remembered that before Easter, following the visit of Colonel House[7] to this country, American sympathy with the allies had reached a point at which the active intervention of the United States on our side did not seem at all unlikely. General Maxwell unfortunately made an end of that possibility for the time.

But the extraordinary luck which never seems to desert England has ordained that the Lusitanicide Germans should again select just the wrong moment (for themselves) to produce a new revulsion in our favor by shooting, on technical grounds, a man whom all the rest of the world regards as a prisoner of war. The sensation is reinforced by the reports

6. Charles Algernon Fryatt, merchant captain, was captured, tried, and executed on 27 July 1916 by the Germans because he had attempted to ram and sink a German submarine that had surfaced and signalled him to stop.

7. Colonel Edward M. House visited Europe in 1916 and talked with rulers and statesmen as the personal representative of President Woodrow Wilson.

of the deportations of the citizens of Lille for forced labor in Germany. General Maxwell is eclipsed.

Is it wise to thrust him into the middle of the stage again by executing Casement? Everyone abroad, and all the sensible people at home, know that the temper and spirit in which the German military authorities shot Captain Fryatt is not peculiar to Germany and that we can retain the sympathy, not only of the democratic neutrals of the west of Europe and of America, but even of our own allies, whose attachment we have to turn into something better than cupboard love, by convincing them that this temper and spirit, though it exists here, is not the controling and characteristic factor in British policy.

We have now a priceless opportunity of placing a reprieve of Casement in the sharpest contrast to the execution of Captain Fryatt. If we miss it, and miss it in cold blood, we must not expect America or France or any other country to draw that distinction between the merciful and magnanimous Briton and the cruel and ruthless Hun, which most of us, I hope, would like to see realized in deeds as well as in printer's ink.

Yours, &c.,

G. Bernard Shaw.

VI

To *The Irish Press*, Dublin, 11 February 1937

Sir,—Dr. Maloney's book entitled The Forged Casement Diaries[8] is probably making a very superfluous addition to the bad blood still existing between England and Ireland. As bad blood between near neighbors does nobody any good, may I point out that there was no forgery in the business and no villainy. I remember the circumstances quite well; and I had some personal acquaintance with the late Lord Birkenhead, who, as

---

8. Dr. W. J. Maloney is one of a number of writers who challenged the English government's claim, made during and after Casement's trial, that he was a homosexual. The evidence supporting the charge was contained in Casement's diaries, seized at the time of his arrest but not made public until 1959. As the title of the book indicates, Maloney believed that the erotic passages in Casement's diaries were forged by the English authorities to discredit him and thus prevent him from becoming a martyred hero in the eyes of his countrymen. These passages are now generally believed to have been written, like the rest of the diaries, by Casement.

Attorney-General, was prosecutor at the trial, and Admiral Sir Reginald Hall, who exhibited the documents pretty freely at the Admiralty.

Now, I cannot imagine either of these gentlemen as the villains they would certainly have been had they known that the documents found among Casement's belongings were memoranda of Putamayan cases made by Casement in the famous campaign against horrible atrocities in that region as Britannic consul there. Galloper Smith Birkenhead was hated as the boldest and most unscrupulous political reactionary of his day; and as Casement's prosecutor he was in the predicament of having notoriously committed the very offence with which Casement was charged, that of levying arms against the Crown. And he was not in the least put out by it. Later on he stepped brazenly and cynically down from the woolsack into the City. He drank shamelessly. Yet he was an irresistibly likeable man. I never met anyone who knew him personally who disliked him, and I found it impossible to dislike him myself.

As to Admiral Hall, there is no evidence in his record and no suggestion in his personality that he is a melodramatic villain. That these two men were capable of committing a diabolical fraud on public opinion to secure the conviction of a distinguished public servant of their own class, whose pardon would not have done them the smallest harm, is too improbable to be believed without overwhelming proof.

There is, as far as I can see, no proof. The trial occurred at a time when the writings of Sigmund Freud had made psychopathy grotesquely fashionable. Everybody was expected to have a secret history unfit for publication except in the consulting rooms of the psychoanalyst. If it had been announced that among the papers of Queen Victoria a diary had been found revealing that her severe respectability masked the daydreams of a Messalina, it would have been received with eager credulity and without the least reprobation by the intelligentsia. It was in that atmosphere that Casement was accused of keeping a psychopathic diary; and though innocents like Alfred Noyes and Redmond were shocked, the rest of us were easily credulous; but we associated no general depravity with psychopathic eccentricities; and we were determined not to be put off by it in our efforts to obtain a pardon. The Putumayo explanation never occurred to us.

Why, then, should it have occurred to those who wanted to have Casement hanged? Smith, who apparently did not want to have him hanged, proved his complete sincerity, as Dr. Maloney's book reveals, by characteristically disregarding his obligations as Crown Counsel and advising the defence to plead insanity and use the documents to prove their plea. This seems to me to settle the question of Smith's good faith and good nature. He made no use of the documents in court. And as the members of the Cabinet and the civil and military services chiefs were no cleverer, to put it moderately, than F. E., it is reasonable to suppose that they also believed the current misinterpretation of the documents. For they did not invent the documents. The documents existed and were authentic. What were they to think of them?

As to the notion that a British Cabinet is capable of an organized conspiracy in which every member knows all that his colleagues know and all that their departments are doing, Mr Lloyd George's memoirs have made an end of that. No Cabinet Minister seems to have known what his own department was doing, much less what his colleagues knew; and the war would have gone to pieces had not Mr Lloyd George been made dictator. Mr Yeats calls on Mr Alfred Noyes to repudiate a forgery;[9] but, I repeat, there was no forgery; the documents were there, and Casement was dead long before the clue he gave to their real nature was followed up and the truth brought to light. Then there was nothing to be done officially, for as the Government had made no use of them at the trial, there was nothing for them to withdraw.

Nevertheless, as the supposed diary had been busily gossiped about and exhibited to discredit the petitions for clemency which were being rained

---

9. William Butler Yeats's ballad "Roger Casement" appeared in *The Irish Press* on 2 February 1937 under an epigraph that read: "After reading *The Forged Casement Diaries* by Dr. Maloney." In the poem Yeats called upon Alfred Noyes and others to add their voices to Dr. Maloney's in defending Casement. As a result of a letter from Noyes to the same newspaper, Yeats wrote to *The Irish Press* on 13 February, accepting Noyes's "explanation" and submitting a revised text of the poem in which Noyes's name was now omitted. An interesting aftermath of the incident is contained in Yeats's letter of 18 February 1937 to Dorothy Wellesley, in which he writes: "I told you that my Casement ballad came out in De Valera's paper some three weeks ago—it has stirred up no end of a commotion. Shaw has written a long, rambling, vegetarian, sexless letter, disturbed by my causing 'bad blood' between the nations; and strange to say Alfred Noyes has done what I asked him in the ballad—spoken 'his bit in public' in a noble letter" (*The Letters of W. B. Yeats*, ed. Allan Wade, London: Hart-Davis, 1954).

on the Prime Minister [Asquith] at the time, and Casement's high reputation is still befouled by a slander with which not only his relatives but the whole Irish nation are deeply concerned, some opportunity should be taken by a responsible British Minister to declare that the Government has no documents in its possession which reflect on Casement's personal character, and that all rumors to the contrary were based on a misunderstanding which has since been cleared up.

A question in the House of Commons could elicit this easily enough, but only on condition that the declaration could not be mistaken for an admission of the guilt of deliberate forgery and international calumny. If Casement is to be used by the enemies of England as another stick to beat her with, it will be impossible for England to do him justice. If his case is reasonably and frankly put, there should be no difficulty in obtaining the only reparation that is now possible and now a long time overdue.

Yours, &c.,

G. Bernard Shaw.

VII

To *The Irish Press*, Dublin, 15 March 1937

Sir,—I see that a legend is growing up to the effect that I was one of those to whom the Casement documents were exhibited. I was not. Two intimate friends of mine, one of them a noted editor and the other a distinguished public servant, were shewn some sheets of what they took to be an imaginary autobiography or diary which Casement had amused himself by writing. It was not supposed to be a record of fact, but simply evidence that Casement had a depraved imagination, and was therefore unworthy of the sympathy that was expressing itself in petitions for his reprieve. I did not ask for any details: the word "masochism" used by one of my informants was sufficient indication of the nature of the papers. I did not learn until many years after that an eminent lawyer who had seen the documents had made the remark—taking the authenticity of the handwriting for granted—that there was nothing to shew that the pages were part of a diary. No doubt, he knew too well what unpleasant stuff has to be written for use in the courts.

But this explanation was not guessed at the time, especially by those who, like myself, did not know Casement personally. I never met him.

And I must repeat that it only confuses the issue and makes reparation difficult to contend that the Cabinet did not misinterpret the documents as credulously as most of Casement's own partisans. As nobody now has any interest in maintaining the misinterpretation, the Government should either make amends by an assurance that it has no documents of Casement that do not admit of an innocent explanation, or else allow them to be examined by a representative commission of inquiry.

I do not agree with the view that the question is of no importance because Casement is a hero in Ireland and that opinion elsewhere does not matter. Ireland is not quite so unimportant as that. If a rehabilitation is due it should be made, as many people, in Ireland as well as in England, still believe that there was something wrong about Casement, and they may as well be disabused.

Yours, &c.,

G. Bernard Shaw.

BROGUE-SHOCK

The Nation, London, 24 March 1917

I wonder whether even Mr Maurice Hewlett could write a version of the recent Home Rule debate[1] in which the unfortunate English people would appear pitiable rather than ridiculous. In his Hodgiad, the finest and indeed the only readable epic English literature has produced in these days, he shews the Englishman, incapable of knowing his own mind, helplessly bullied and overridden by Dane, by Norman, by everyone with the necessary bumptiousness and some little mental clarity. He omitted one canto: the canto of the last and most humiliating bullying of the doomed race by the Protestant Irish—my own people. When I see Mr Lloyd George on his knees to my fellow Dubliners, Sir Edward Carson and Lord Northcliffe, protesting that he would never presume to coerce Ulster as he means to coerce the comparatively negligible and contemptible Central Empires; when this abject assurance has no sooner been heard with difficulty through his tears than Mr Redmond, with a terrible frown, throws the whole Commons into a twittering panic by walking majestically out of the House with his party in procession behind him; when the appeals of Mr Ginnell and Mr Healy,[2] themselves Irish, to the House not to allow itself to be frightened by playacting, fail utterly to stem the rout, I realize as I never did before what a mistake I have made in trying all my life to argue and amuse the English out of their follies instead of simply kicking them. Beyond a doubt, we Irish are the governing race in these islands; and I am not sure that the transfer of the seat of government from Westminster to Belfast or Dublin would not be the most natural solution

1. After the 1916 insurrection the English government, impelled by the international situation and by the necessity of placating American opinion, resumed Parliamentary discussion of Home Rule. The issue was one of getting Sir Edward Carson to accept Ulster's inclusion in Home Rule or John Redmond to agree to Ulster's exclusion.

2. Irish members of Parliament. Laurence Ginnell was one of the founders of the Irish Literary Society and author of a book on Brehon law. Timothy Michael Healy later became first governor-general of the Irish Free State.

148 → THE MATTER WITH IRELAND

of the problem. There would never be a Home Rule movement in England.

The end of the debate was that Mr Asquith appealed to the Overseas Dominions to come and help his bewildered and scared countrymen out of their predicament, and the Prime Minister[3] snatched at the suggestion like a drowning man.

That is England all over: fighting millions of the most elaborately equipped and organized soldiers in Europe with gigantic strength and unconquerable obstinacy, and jumping up on her chair with shrieks of terror when a mouse squeaks at her with an Irish brogue. What a people!

Fortunately, there are benevolent Irishmen who hate to see even Englishmen frightened and confused; and I am one of them. Besides, I do not believe that frightened and confused men can solve the Irish problem, and I conclude that those Irishmen who are frightening and confusing them are not all quite clear on the subject themselves. May I offer my services in an explanatory capacity?

The British Empire consists of several States flying the British flag and defended by the British fleet, but otherwise differing widely in their laws and institutions. The only one which is governed without the slightest regard to the character and views of the inhabitants is England. In the others the people are more or less consulted, the opposite extreme to England being reached in Ireland, where governmental action is never based on commonsense, political science, or on anything except some empirical and mostly fantastic estimate of the Irish species.

Hitherto it has been assumed without question that all units of the Empire must be geographical: that Bombay must belong to the Indian system, Dundee to the Scottish system, Belfast to the Irish system, and London to the English system. This, however, is no more a necessity of the case than that Gibraltar should belong to the Spanish system. It is quite conceivable that London, observing that the best-trained and most competent governing body in the Empire is the Indian Civil Service, might desire to be regarded as a part of British India; that Galway might attach itself to Canada, Dundee to Australia, and Oxford University to the

3. David Lloyd George became prime minister of a coalition government in December 1916.

Straits Settlements. This would not involve the disruption of the Empire: on the contrary, it would lead to a healthy competition among its Governments, culminating in the survival of the fittest. Probably Westminster would be left without a single constituent at an early stage; but the Empire would get on quite well without it.

The first step in this new mode of development has been provoked by the Home Rule Act. A new system being proposed for Ireland, Belfast repudiates it, and claims to be attached to England. It is hard to see what reasonable objection can be advanced to this, provided the rest of Ireland be allowed to distribute itself over the Empire in the same fashion. The entire Irish question might be disposed of in this way. Ulster would, on second thoughts, probably attach itself to Egypt or India, which are garrison States. The other provinces would join the Overseas Dominions. The Giant's Causeway, the Blaskets, Tory, Arran, and Dalkey could become Solomon Islands; and England could at last govern herself in her own way without having to think about Ireland instead of about herself. It sounds too good to be true; but there is nothing impossible or extravagant about it; and if Sir Edward Carson does not mean this, I am at a loss to understand what he does mean; for he, as a lawyer, clearly cannot mean that Belfast should be made the Holy City of the British Empire, with privileges denied to London itself.

Now that we are quite clear about the scope of the Ulster proposal, the sooner it is carefully debated on its merits in the House the better.

It may be that the House will decide against it, and maintain the geographical unit. One rather awkward consideration against it is that there would be two parties to each transfer, and they might not always agree. Ulster, in her determination never to desert Mr Micawber, has taken his welcome for granted; but it lacks confirmation. What is to happen if Parliament decides that Ireland, within her girdle of salt water, must remain one and indivisible?

Parliament will not maintain the *status quo*, because Parliament is afraid of Mr Redmond. Parliament will not coerce Ulster, because Parliament is afraid of Sir Edward Carson. Well, Parliament can do its duty all the same. The Home Rule Bill can still be enacted for all Ireland, and its administration left to the Irish Parliament. This will release 60,000 troops for service at the front. Ulster with her volunteers will be left face to face with Leinster, Munster, and Connaught with *their* volunteers.[4] If Ulster risks the politically suicidal step of allowing the South to get ahead of the North in the new Irish Parliament, instead of at once sending a resolute and capable Protestant representation to it, the Irish Parliament will be no more disabled than the British Parliament is now by the abstention of Count Plunkett. It will save the Ulster salaries. If, when it proceeds to collect the taxes it finds that its writ will not run in Belfast, it will not be the first time that the King's writ has not run in a rebellious Irish district. The situation may be left to develop its own inconveniences. The Irish Parliament will not be in a position to coerce Ulster by distraint warrant, bailiff, policeman, and soldier. It cannot, without unutterable infamy, call in English soldiers to coerce Irish rebels: it was through that error that Ireland lost her independence. And England can hardly send soldiers to act as mutineers. Ulster will not be coerced, but she will be outlawed; and though she can set up an outlawed Government as a mutinied crew sets up a captain, she will find her position so unsatisfactory that she will have sooner or later either to accept Home Rule, or else to conquer both Ireland and England and the rest of the British Empire, and forcibly restore the Union.

It is possible that the Nationalists might take the position taken by the Republican party in the United States of America fifty years ago, and attempt to maintain the unity of Ireland by force. In that case there would be civil war in Ireland. Well, civil war is one of the privileges of a nation. The British Government is pledged not to interfere, because it is pledged not to coerce Ulster; and it could not interfere without coercing Ulster, as the law would be on the Nationalist side. It could only look on and sell ammunition to both sides impartially, in the hope that they would exterminate oneanother. Mankind still longs for that consummation; but it has never happened, and is too much to hope for.

I doubt, myself, whether it would come to civil war. I do not deprecate that method; for if hatred, calumny, and terror have so possessed men

4. The Ulster Volunteers were organized in 1912 under Sir James Craig's leadership and pledged to resist any attempts to impose Home Rule upon Ulster. A year later the Irish Volunteers were organized in Dublin to protect the south against threats from the north. Both volunteer organizations smuggled arms into the country in defiance of the law.

that they cannot live in peace as other nations do, they had better fight it out and get rid of their bad blood that way. The British fleet could keep the ring with no greater preoccupation with the Irish coast than is necessary at present. The combatants would be receiving a practical military training for subsequent service in defence of the Empire, to which both sides are attached by the hard fact that neither of them can afford to do without it except by attaching themselves to some other Empire not so easily bullied, and unable to detect the terrifying brogue.

But it not unfrequently happens that when two men quarrel, and are held back by the bystanders, their pugnacity and animosity reach a pitch that convinces everyone that it would be simple murder to let them go: yet, if nevertheless released, they suddenly begin arguing with oneanother instead of falling to fisticuffs. When the recent fighting began, Sir Edward Carson was as shocked as Mr Redmond; and all Ireland, instead of flying to arms, responded so very prudently that if England had not supplied a sensational bombardment and a Reign of Terror to impress the imagination of the world with the heroism of the patriots and the magnitude of their blow for independence, the lesson of the event would have been that neither of the political parties meant business as far as fighting was concerned, though the Larkinite proletarians and the poets did.

The moral is very simple. A Government that lets itself be rattled will never solve the Irish or any other problem. A Government that goes ahead on the plain constitutional lines that are understood throughout the Empire and the world will have no difficulty; though a Government that treats the enforcement of an Act of Parliament as something not to be thought of if it annoys anybody will bring both Parliament and itself into such utter contempt that its own tenure of office will never be worth two days' purchase. If the earth shied from its orbit every time it met a wasp in its course round the sun, the wasps would be flattered, but the universe would go to smash. It is needless to consult the Colonial Premiers on a point so obvious. I can give their reply beforehand. It would be: "Why not go right ahead? You have an Act with three general elections behind it. You are dealing with a depopulated little island, the entire fighting force of which, even if it were solid instead of divided, the British lion can squelch with one slash of his tail without turning his head from his scrap with the centre of Europe; and the Colonies will support him if he is doing the straightforward thing. Where is the difficulty?

If the Government nervously replies that there is Lord Lansdowne, the Colonial Premiers will ask, with Colonial emphasis, who the Hades is Lord Lansdowne?[5] If it pleads Sir Edward Carson and Lord Northcliffe, they will ask whether the British Isles are governed by Parliament or by Dublin barristers and newspaper proprietors. They may even go so far as to ask whether the Prime Minister is a statesman who knows his business and his plain duty, or a victim of brogue-shock whom anyone can scare by pretending to throw a brick at him.

I do not see any difficulty in the matter myself. If the British Parliament cannot go like a steamroller over Sinn Fein and Ulster and Carmelite-street, the sooner it tells the Imperial Conference that it has not character enough to govern the British Empire, and asks Germany to appoint a commission to undertake the management of these islands for a suitable consideration, the better.

5. Henry Charles Lansdowne, Unionist leader in the House of Lords, in 1917 published the sensational Lansdowne Letter, which questioned Britain's war aims and urged peace overtures to Germany.

HOW TO SETTLE THE IRISH QUESTION

In November 1917 Shaw was invited by Ralph D. Blumenfeld, editor of *The Daily Express*, to contribute an article on Ireland. As the *Express*, owned by Lord Beaverbrook—then Sir Max Aitken, M.P.—was, from the Fabian Socialist point of view, editorially in the enemy camp, Shaw rejected the offer with alacrity and a certain degree of contempt. Undismayed, Blumenfeld repeated his offer to open his columns to Shaw, in a letter on 7 November 1917:

> "I am grateful to you for your frankness. Your castigation is not so crushing as to prevent me from repeating my invitation. I am quite certain that you do not read the *Daily Express*, or you would, at least, have a different opinion as to my views on Ireland. It may surprise you to know that I have given the subject considerable thought and that my alarm at the situation has caused me to treat the subject, even in the despised columns of the *Daily Express*, without party bias, and from the larger point of view.
>
> "I was not at all disposed to lark when I asked you seriously to go to Ireland or, again, when I invited you to write your views. Nor do I intend to poke fun at any suggestion that you care to make. Seriously, this question is too big for foolery, and if you and I can hammer it out between us—you will laugh at this bizarre partnership—we shall have done well of the world.
>
> "In the columns of the *Daily Express* you preach to a new audience. You are quite wrong in labelling my clientele as a 'mob.' It is most responsive—and again you may laugh—but I can assure you that it is intelligent; and effective in its conclusions. In the *Daily Chronicle* you will be preaching to the converted. Why not have a try at missionary work? I'll give you the run of my columns in a serious attempt to reach a solution of the problem. It may not do anything of the sort but, at least, it will be a contribution to the literature of the Eternal subject" (letter published for the first time herein, courtesy of the Blumenfeld family).

Recognizing Blumenfeld's sincerity and the validity of his argument, Shaw instantly set to work to draft a sequel to his *Common Sense about the War*. Under the title *How to Settle the Irish Question*, it appeared in *The Daily Express*, London, and was syndicated in several Irish newspapers on 27–29 November 1917. A month later the work was issued in Dublin and London as a pamphlet. It was also serialized in the *New York American* on 23 and 30 December 1917 and on 6 and 13 January 1918.

Introductory Note

This series of articles, written by me at the suggestion of the London Daily Express, was published simultaneously in London and Dublin, Cork and Belfast on 27, 28, and 29 November last: a moment chosen in view of the critical stage the deliberations of the Irish Convention were then believed to have reached.[1]

My qualification for dealing with the subject is that though I am an Irishman of the Protestant landlord variety, I have not lived in Ireland since I left it in 1876, and that though I have since then been occupied almost continually with the problems of modern political science, I have studied them from the point of view of white civilization as a whole, having no constituency to conciliate and no social ambition to further; for it has been my fortune to secure by my artistic activities a public position infinitely preferable to any that political life or office has to offer. I can, without compromising that position, say things that no party politician dares say, and that even those politicians whose public spirit is above party can hardly say without too much offence to the factions they are striving to reconcile.

1. In May 1917 the government of Lloyd George attempted to resolve the differences between northern and southern Irish leaders by suggesting a convention of all Irish parties to work out a solution to Home Rule. Participants were to be selected from local government bodies, political parties, churches, and labor unions, and the government was to nominate fifteen eminent Irishmen from public life. But Sinn Féin, which was rapidly evolving into a political party and had already won two by-elections against Redmondite candidates, refused to participate on the ground that it would thereby be conceding Ireland's right to complete independence. Shaw wished to be one of the fifteen government nominees and wrote Lord Haldane on 12 July 1917: "It is perfectly clear that I ought to be in the business, not only by pre-eminent celebrity but because I am the only public person who has committed himself to the only possible solution: to wit, federation of the four home kingdoms. . . . I am prepared to demand a nomination" (unpublished letter in the National Library of Scotland, Edinburgh). He was not nominated, however, and he had to content himself with going to Dublin while the Convention was in session in the autumn of 1917, staying with his friend Horace Plunkett, who was chairman of the Convention and presumably exposed to Shaw's persuasive arguments. The Convention sat for eight months and voted 52 to 19 for an Irish parliament with authority over all Ireland. No action was ever taken by the government to implement the Convention's recommendation.

Thus I am not only disinterested, but disengaged. This is not altogether my own fault. Believing that I might be of some service on the Convention, I conceived it to be my public duty to take steps to have it suggested to the Government and to the Convention itself that I should be nominated or co-opted as a member. By doing so I brought the British Government and the Irish Convention nearer to unanimity than was supposed possible at the time. Fortunately for me, as it turned out when secrecy was imposed on the Convention, I was left free when the officially accredited representatives of Irish opinion were muzzled. That was not the intention; but it has been the effect. I mention this circumstance because I want to make it clear that I do not enjoy the confidence of the Government or of any party in the Convention. My articles were not concerted with any individual or group, nor read before they were in print by anyone except in the course of newspaper business. I had discussed the question carefully, in my capacity as chairman of a committee of the Fabian Society called The Empire Reconstruction Committee, with English and Australian students of the Empire problem. Without such critical discussion I should have nothing but my personal notions to put forward, and this work would be an impertinence. But my Fabian colleagues are as completely out of Irish party politics as I am myself. I represent nobody on the Convention, though I have valued friends on it. I represent nobody in Parliament or in the Government (this is nowadays not always the same thing). I am only the spokesman of Common Sense, and of the experience already gained in the integration of distinct nations with distinct creeds into a single Power.

In the course of my occasional visits to Ireland and conversations with Irishmen interested in the national question, I had noticed that two considerations which were quite familiar to me were new to them. The first, bearing on the fiscal problem, was the enormous part which socialization of the rents of land, capital, and personal ability, as part of the now irresistible European movement for Redistribution of Income, must play in all but the most provisional and perfunctory schemes of public finance. The other was the final demonstration by the present war of the hollowness of the national independences and neutralities which are set up, not by the internal strength of a nation's position, but by the interested guarantees of foreign Powers. For obvious reasons, it is almost impossible for popular statesmen to be frank on this subject; but diplomatists know perfectly well that a great Power guarantees the independence of a small nation only to acquire control of its foreign policy without responsibility. Many English people are furiously angry with me for giving away this open secret because of its bearing on the case of Belgium. But as it is the sole really convincing reply to Casement's plan of a German-Irish alliance, I am not prepared to allow numbers of patriotic young Irishmen to involve themselves in treasonable intrigues merely to gratify the taste of patriotic old Englishmen for virtuous indignation.

For the rest I have no novelty to offer except the presentation of the Irish problem in something like reasonable proportion to the rest of the world's business.

I

The task of the Irish Convention is to reconcile three parties, all of whom have impressed their views on the Irish people by a long and sensational propaganda. The three are the Home Rule or Parnellite party in the House of Commons, the Ulster or Carsonite party, and Sinn Fein. The first, having been hammered and worn down into opportunism by long Parliamentary experience, will accept any settlement that may enable them to come to their constituents as the saviors of their country and the restorers of the Irish National Parliament in College Green. Old Parliamentary hands care little for the quality of a settlement provided it will pass on the platform and at the polling-booth.

The other two, Ulster and Sinn Fein, are the hard nuts to crack. It is quite hopeless to expect that Sir Horace Plunkett can reconcile them by inducing either to accept the views of the other. But if a solution can be found which reduces them both to absurdity, then Sinn Fein may embrace it because it shews up Ulster, and Ulster may tolerate it because it makes Sinn Fein ridiculous. And therein lies the hope of the Convention; for, as the Ulster talk and the Sinn Fein talk are both mostly baby talk, any sane solution must have this double effect. It only remains to find such a solution, and to make a propaganda of it sufficient to convince the Parliamentary Opportunists that it has acquired enough backing from public opinion to make it possible for a candidate to advocate it without losing votes.

I shall therefore begin by demonstrating to the entire satisfaction of Ulster that the Sinn Feiners are idiots. I shall then demonstrate to the satisfaction of Sinn Fein that the Ulster Impossibilists are idiots. Having thus ingratiated myself with both parties, I shall venture upon a few incidental references to the interests of England and of the rest of the Empire in the question. Finally, I shall propound the solution.

Sinn Fein means We Ourselves: a disgraceful and obsolete sentiment, horribly anti-Catholic, and acutely ridiculous in the presence of a crisis which has shewn that even the richest and most powerful countries, twenty times as populous as Ireland and more than a hundred times as spacious, have been unable to stand by themselves, and have been glad to accept the support of their bitterest traditional enemies.

Sinn Fein has an extremely high opinion of the Irish people: that is, of itself. It has an inborn sense of superiority to all who have had the misfortune to be born in other countries, which I share, quite irrationally. It is hardly too much to say that Ireland is the Malvolio of the nations, "sick of self-love," and that Sinn Fein's delight is to propagate this morose malady. Some of the results are dangerous, others only ridiculous. The dangerous result is the arming and drilling of young countrymen so stupendously ignorant of the magnitude and resources of the Great Powers that they speak and read of "striking a decisive blow at England" without suspecting that England or any other Western European Power, except, perhaps, the principality of Monaco, could wipe them off the face of the earth from the water or the air without setting foot on Irish soil. They are quite capable of attacking a police station with all the seriousness of the Germans attacking Verdun or Sir Douglas Haig investing the Flanders ridges. They actually put up a stunning fight in Dublin in Easter 1916, and were so clumsily and barbarously tackled that they are able to point to the walls and portico and statues of their stronghold, the General Post Office, standing unscathed in the midst of acres of devastation, as a proof that the British artillery cannot hit a haystack at pointblank range.

Fed on dreams and Irish air, they are subject to an agonizing desire to die for Ireland which makes it quite impossible to keep them in order by the police methods customary in free countries. To them the war against England has the medieval double quality of being a holy war and a chivalrous romance at the same time; they not only carry the flag of Freedom but wear the colors of the Dark Rosaleen: a Dulcinea proof against all disillusion. Baton charges and silly police court prosecutions of Boy Scouts for illegal drilling produce as much effect on them as briars and bee stings on a bear. Forbidden to wear uniform or carry arms, they formed a column three miles long, fully equipped and armed, and gave an impressive funeral to Thomas Ashe,[2] whose body lay in state under their guard at the Dublin Guildhall, with the British army hiding in the cellars.

Dublin Castle says: "This is intolerable. Let us provoke them to fight and then annihilate them." It provokes them accordingly, and finds that it has not the heart to finish the program. Theoretically, the Castle should furnish every police station in Ireland with a couple of machine guns, and replace the batons by Mills bombs. It should exhibit these weapons in practice every week at public gardens and drills. It should shew the constabulary co-operating with aeroplanes and the two co-operating with the local sanitary authority in demolishing a slum occasionally. But practically it does none of these things, perhaps because it dares trust nobody, not even the Royal Irish Constabulary, who are more Irish than royal, and perhaps because it is even more hopelessly out of date than the Sinn Feiners themselves, and still thinks of a revolt as an assembly of pikes at the rising of the moon, to be put down by bayonet and Brown Bess, with plenty of informing and hanging to follow. However that may be, the Sinn Feiners have not the least idea of what they are up against, and see nothing extravagant in the notion that less than a million adult males, without artillery, ships, or planes, could bring the British Empire to its knees in a conflict of blood and iron. This is the dangerous (to themselves) side of their Sinn Fein.

Now for the ridiculous side. They propose that the Irish question should be settled by "The Peace Conference." By this they mean that when the quarrel between the Central and Ottoman Empires on the one side, and the United States of America, the British Empire, the French Republic, Italy, Japan, &c. &c. &c., on the other, comes to be settled, the plenipotentiaries of these Powers, at the magic words, "Gentlemen, IRELAND!" will rise reverently, sing God Save Ireland, and postpone all their business until they have redressed the wrongs of Rosaleen. A wise Irishman might well pray that his country may have the happiness to be forgotten when the lions divide their prey; one hardly wants the unfortunate island to be flung like a bone to a half-satisfied dog, as Cyprus was at

2. Thomas Ashe, one of the leaders in the Easter Rising, went on a hunger strike in Mountjoy prison and died on 17 August 1917 as a result of forcible feeding.

the Berlin Conference. Sinn Fein is not troubled with any such modest misgivings. It really does think that the world consists of Ireland and a few subordinate continents.

Now let us turn from the megalomaniac delusions of Sinn Fein to its practical aspirations. First, there is the Casement scheme. Casement was no ignorant countryside dreamer: he was a traveler and an official diplomatist. His plan, which has been for a long time in print in America, was that Ireland should bank on a German victory when the great war came. Germany's main object would be to break Britain's command of the sea; and he suggested that the most effective step in that direction would be to make Ireland an independent State right in the fairway of England's maritime commerce.

This was a perfectly legitimate political speculation; and it may still, in spite of the revolution made in the sea problem by the submarines, recommend itself to Germany in the event of her coming out of the war in a position to demand such a change. It rushes into the head of Sinn Fein as air rushes into a vacuum. Before the war there was something to be said for it in Ireland, for there was then some excuse for the popular belief that the treaties by which Great Powers, for their own purposes, guarantee the independence of little States as buffers and the like are something more than scraps of paper. That is to say, the independence of Belgium and Greece seemed worth having then. Does anyone think it worth having now?

Surely, of all sorts of dependence, the most abjectly wretched is that in which a minor State is helplessly dependent on a powerful neighbor, who accepts no responsibility for her and shares nothing with her, but makes her soil the no-man's-land between two frontiers hostile when war breaks out. If the English had a pennyworth of political sagacity instead of being, as they are, incorrigible Sinn Feiners almost to the last man, they would long ago have brought the Irish Separatists to their senses by threatening them with independence. It is as plain as the stars in heaven that if England tried to cast Ireland off, it would be necessary for Ireland, if she could, to make war on England, as Lincoln made war on Jefferson Davis, to maintain the Union. Yet here are these two sets of fools: one repudiating an invaluable alliance in the name of freedom, and the other insisting on conferring the boon by force in the guise of conquest. How Irish on the part of the English! How English on the part of the Irish!

Sinn Fein has one other pseudo-practical cry: Fiscal Autonomy. And if Sinn Fein does not think better of it, Sinn Fein will get what it is inconsiderately demanding. For here again it is quite clear that England has everything to gain and Ireland everything to lose by separate banking accounts. It means shilling telegrams for Ireland and ninepenny ones for England, with postage rates to correspond. It means grants-in-aid to all the English counties for housing, education, public health, roads, and railways, out of the colossal fund of British rent nationalized by supertaxation, and nothing for the Irish counties. It means rent and taxes collected in Ireland and spent in munition-making in England.

When Blücher saw London he said, "What a city to loot!" That is how I, as an Irish Socialist, feel about London and her ground rents. Sinn Fein wants to protect London from me, and thinks that in doing so it will be protecting Dublin. *Sancta simplicitas!* The beggar refuses to pool with the millionaire; and the millionaire, terrified, calls for horse, foot, and artillery to force the beggar to rifle his pockets. When people ask me what Sinn Fein means, I reply that it is Irish for John Bull.

Well may Ulster ask, "Are these Sinn Feiners to be allowed to rule us?" Deeply may Ulster feel that in me, the Protestant Shaw, she has found an inspired spokesman. But wait a bit. In my next section I shall put Ulster's brains on my dissecting table. And then my momentary popularity in Belfast will wane.

II

It is in the power of the Westminster Parliament to reestablish the Irish National Parliament in Dublin and place Ulster in the position of having either to accept the government of that Parliament or undertake a rebellion which would be a rebellion against England and the Empire no less than against Ireland. This does not trouble Ulster much: she is fully as rebellious as any other province. What is more, she could carry such a rebellion through if only her front remained united. The Speaker's writ would not run in Antrim if Antrim were solid on the point of treating it as a scrap of paper. All the rest of Ireland could not coerce a united Ulster, and to repeat the original sin that delivered Ireland into England's hand by calling in English soldiers to coerce Irishmen would be morally impossible.

There is quite as much fight in Ulster as in Sinn Fein, though Ulster repudiates the national flag, and classes the Dark Rosaleen with the Virgin Mary as an idol. It does not want to die for Ireland: on the contrary, it believes that those who die for Ireland go straight to hell; but it wants to send them there and have the island all to itself. "No surrender" is burnt so deep into its brain that it still chalks that dogged phrase upon the walls as if it were only yesterday that the bows of the Mountjoy burst the boom, and the hosts of King James scattered and left Derry starving but victorious.[3] Ulster children still repeat the derisive doggerel, "Sleether slaughter, holy wather"; and the adults are as determined as ever that "the Protestant boys shall carry the drum."

As a Protestant myself (and a little to spare), I am highly susceptible to the spirit these war cries express; and though I know that King William is as dead as Bloody Mary, and that if it should turn out rather unexpectedly that the old Ulster brimstone hell actually exists, all the thoroughgoing Protestants of Ulster will most assuredly spend eternity in it for usurping the divine judgment seat, yet if it comes to a fight between the North and South, I will back Ulster to at least deadlock any military force that Catholic Ireland can bring against her.

A united Ulster could hold the Protestant counties against a Dublin Parliament and form an independent State like the little republic of Andorra. It could not, of course, force Ulster members on the English Parliament. It could not do the thing by halves: it would have to cut the London painter as completely as the Dublin one. But it could absolutely ignore and boycott College Green, and beat Home Rule by Homer Rule, if I may put it that way. And in its consciousness of this lies the strength of its "We wont have it" and the Cromwellian force of its rendering of "O God, our help in ages past."

But there is the If to be got over. *If* Ulster were united! Now, Sir John Lonsdale has no misgivings on that score; he has told us that on this question he and his poorest laborer will stand shoulder to shoulder to the death. He has no prevision of what very cold shoulders they would be when the situation began to develop.

3. The siege of Derry city by the troops of the deposed King James II in 1689 was raised when a squadron of ships successfully passed over a boom erected across the river Foyle and brought supplies and reinforcements to the besieged.

For Sir John Lonsdale, speaking authentically with the voice of Protestant Ulster, never was more mistaken in his life than he is about that solidarity of his with his poorest laborer. He is obsessed with an illusion as gross as the megalomaniac illusions of Sinn Fein, and so is his poorest laborer; hence their present agreement. They have a penny-dreadful vision of an Irish Parliament establishing the Inquisition, massacring the Protestant infants, condemning all the maids of Ulster to the doom of Maria Monk, inviting the Pope to transfer the Vatican to Maynooth, exempting the priests from the jurisdiction of the civil courts, making mixed marriages illegal, reviving the penal laws[4] with the boot on the other leg, and crushing the shipyards of Belfast by huge import duties on steel, raw materials, and everything English, whilst dispensing unheard-of bounties to farmers, graziers, dairymen, and convent workshops.

Now, no doubt, if an Irish Parliament behaved in this insane manner, Ulster would be solid against it. So would the rest of Ireland. That is why no Irish Parliament would behave so even if it wanted to. For a long time it would be mortally afraid to touch the religious question at all; and when at last it was driven to do so by the abuses which the irresponsible power and wealth of the Roman Catholic Church have produced (it is really far more tyrannical than the Established Church of England, just because it is not State-established and State-regulated, as every national Church ought to be, and is indeed not even national), its operations would be exactly like those of all the other jealous secular Governments in Europe: that is, they would consist of curtailments of the power of the clergy, reduction of fees for masses and for birth, death, and marriage services, inspection and regulation of school and convent workshops, State selection of bishops, and an interference with the multiplication of religious houses which might go the length even of suppression.

The notion that a democratically constituted modern secular authority ever has used or will use its power to increase the power of its rival, the Church, or even refrain for long from disabling if not actually plundering the Church, is, to say the least, extremely unhistorical. As to the shipbuilding industry, if Belfast ever loses it, it will be because the great gan-

4. Anti-Catholic measures, known as popery laws, were enacted in Ireland in the late seventeenth and eighteenth centuries. They were eventually replaced by various Relief Acts beginning in 1778 and culminating in the Catholic Emancipation Act of 1829.

tries will have flown to the Atlantic coast, which, when St George's Channel and the Straits of Dover are tunneled and bridged by aeroplanes, will be the extreme west coast of the Eurasian continent. Its magnificent natural harborages will tempt shipbuilding capital from all over the world, beginning, let us hope for the honor of Protestant enterprize, with Belfast. Harland and Wolff, if they are not hopelessly extinct volcanos, must have already surveyed all the great Irish Atlantic bays, from Blacksod and Killary to Kenmare and Bantry, with a view to these imminent possibilities.

In opposition to the Sinn Fein cry of Fiscal Autonomy, Ulster raises the cry of Fiscal Unity. It is just as inconsiderate a folly as the other; there can be neither fiscal unity nor fiscal autonomy between Ireland and Britain. What both parties are thinking about is the old tariff war between England and Ireland, put a stop to by Adam Smith and William Pitt. Ireland's imagination is still in the XVIII century when it is not in the XVII. The danger now is not that this war will be revived by Home Rule, but that, Home Rule or no Home Rule, Irish industries may be involved in tariff wars between England and the Great Powers, in which the interests of Ireland will be as little considered as those of the Blasket Islands.

Ireland needs fiscal autonomy enough to keep herself out of these wars, and fiscal unity enough to prevent Birmingham and Lancashire from trying to capture the industries of Belfast. What the Cork Chamber of Commerce calls Fiscal Autonomy is quite compatible with all the Fiscal Unity Belfast need demand. Ulster should study the Tariff Reform movement in England before shouting any rash ultimatum. That movement was a very simple one. The manufacturing midlands in England wanted to manufacture everything that was used in England, and demanded a tariff to keep foreign goods out. The coast towns of England, being maritime carriers, wanted everything used in England manufactured abroad, and everything made in England sent abroad to pay for it. That, and not the principles of Free Trade, which nobody in the country understood or cared about (except Mr Balfour, who was forced by his party to go back on them), was what defeated the Tariff Reform League.

Now, Belfast is a coast town and a dockyard, as overwhelmingly interested in Free Trade as Portsmouth or Southampton. Its demand for fiscal unity with the English midlands, now biding their time for another and possibly successful attempt, is suicidal imbecility. What it needs is free trade with the other island, and a free hand to maintain free trade with the rest of the world whether the other island discards it or not. One would think that so obvious a point could not have escaped a moderately intelligent hen, much less a community that prides itself on its hardheadedness as Ulster does. That is what comes of thinking about King William and his ally the Pope when you should be thinking about Mr Hewins and Mr Austen Chamberlain.[5]

But when Ulster comes to her senses on the tariff question, her solidarity will still be unimpaired, for here Sir John Lonsdale's interest is also that of his poorest laborer. All Ulster's power of ignoring the Irish and defying the English Parliament rests, as we have seen, on this solidarity, and it is clearly not the fiscal question that will break the united front. What will break it with ridiculous ease and suddenness is something that neither Ulster nor Sinn Fein foresees, because it is something that is hardly half a century old: to wit, Socialism in Parliament.

When Parnell began his agitation, the notion that men working for weekly wages could become Cabinet Ministers, that Labor parties should not only exist in British Parliaments, but hold office there, that Socialist leaders in office, even at the head of Governments, should become too common throughout Europe to be worth mentioning: all this would then have seemed the maddest moonshine. It is now commonplace contemporary fact. Yet it seems still as incredible and unnatural to the Ulster Protestant as the story of Noah's ark and the adventure of Jonah seem plausible and natural enough to be of the essence of religious truth.

But Ulster's incredulity, which it usually calls its faith, cannot keep Labor and Socialism out of an Irish Parliament. And at the first breath of Socialism the solidarity of Ulster will vanish like the mirage it is. The Ulster employers could say, no doubt, "We shall not put up an Ulster Protestant to contest a seat in this Parliament of rebels, and our workmen will see that no Catholic does it, so there will be no election." But what about a Labor candidate, with his Fabian pamphlets and his labor mani-

5. William A. Hewins was an economist, a Unionist M.P., and secretary to the Tariff Reform Commission. Austen Chamberlain, eldest son of Joseph Chamberlain, held financial posts in the governments of Salisbury, Balfour, and Asquith. He had recently resigned as Secretary of State for India.

festos, and his Whitley report,[6] and his eight-hours day, and his minimum wage, and his denunciation of profiteering, and his skilful irritant touch on all the open sores: the continual nibbling at the piece-work rate, the sweating, the victimization, the unemployment, the slum death rates, and so forth, culminating in the glad news that the Ulster seats can be won for Labor without a blow, as the employers are sulking against Home Rule and allowing their "hands" a walk-over at the polls?

Is it not clear that the Ulster boycott of the Irish Parliament would break down at the very first glimpse of the possibility of this, and that the employers would rush to contest all the seats, and, if they won them, would be only too glad to combine in the Irish Parliament with the Catholic farmers of the South to curb the pretensions of the industrial proletariat?

Thus Ulster's "We wont have it" turns out, the moment it is confronted with the realities of modern life instead of the grudges and bigotries of 1689, to be the idlest of petulances. Without violating a single letter of Mr Lloyd George's pledge that Ulster shall never be coerced, the Irish Parliament will assimilate Belfast as easily as a whale assimilates a pteropod. The dream of passive resistance is as impracticable as that irresistible blow which the Sinn Fein Volunteers think they can strike at the British Empire. Ulster cannot prevent the Westminster Parliament setting up an Irish Parliament; and the moment an Irish Parliament comes into existence the Irish Protestants cannot allow the Irish Catholics to get five minutes start of them in it. So much for the Lonsdale boycott!

Some Ulster diehards will not flinch from this demonstration. They will say: "What you have convinced us of is that we must not be content with passive resistance: we must make war on the South; and we will." To which I reply, simply, "You wont. You cant afford to. Look at your figures. There is more money in Irish butter and cattle than in Irish ships and textiles. And if you did, all you could achieve would be Protestant Home Rule, with all the rest of Ireland to hold down, and all the rest of the Empire against you. No doubt you are as ready to take on that job as Sinn Fein is to conquer England. But how many sane Ulster men will you carry with you in that crackbrained enterprize?"

6. The Whitley report was issued by a committee founded to study relations between labor and management, chaired by John Henry Whitley, Liberal M.P.

When the Sultan of Zanzibar ordered the admiral of his second-hand penny steamboat to go out and sink the British fleet, and the poor devil actually went, the British sailors cheered him. There is always something exhilarating in the infatuation of a heroic ignoramus. No doubt Ireland, North and South, teems with Zanzibari courage. Sir Edward Carson had not a jot more sense than Connolly and President Pearse. Before the war he had the consolation of believing that the little handful of officers who then commanded the British army would refuse to fight against Ulster. They are a pretty big handful now. Both North and South, by lifting up a finger, could find experienced officers enough to lead all the volunteers that Ireland could produce, if they were fools enough to think that the Irish question can be settled today as it was when the English king was beaten at the Boyne by the Dutch king and the Pope.

Thus we see that the Ulster variety of Sinn Fein, like the southern one, has not a leg to stand on. But of the two, Ulster is far more in the grip of modern industrial civilization than the other provinces. Agricultural Ireland, with Sir Horace Plunkett and the Irish Agricultural Organization Society to teach it, is actually building a new co-operative civilization for itself out of the resources of the Irish soil and climate, whilst Belfast remains up to its neck in the old XIX century form of industry that is dependent for its materials, as for its credit and cash nexus, on the international capitalist civilization of which it is a part.

Mr George Russell could make out a serious case for a self-sufficient South with his Irish Homestead as its trade paper. Sir John Lonsdale could not make out the shadow of a case for the power of Ulster to say "We wont have it" to any industrial group on earth, in England or out of it, unless the "we" means "you and I." It is this very dependence that makes Ulster cling to the Union and dread separation.

Well, there is not going to be any separation. On the contrary, there is going to be much more union than ever there was before. That will become apparent in the next section, when I will give the obvious solution of the problem. Being obvious, it will not be new. It will indeed be older than Parnellism. But when it was new, it was too good to be true. And bigger places than Ireland had to come first. It will be none the worse for us now that it has been tried on the kangaroo.

III

Even more important than the setting up of an Irish Parliament is the abolition of the now hopelessly obsolete institution at Westminster that calls itself an imperial Parliament, and is neither imperial nor national nor English nor Scottish nor Irish, neither flesh nor fowl nor good red herring. It was hopelessly beaten by its work in the old days of *laisserfaire*, when it was believed that the secret of government is not to govern. Today, when it has been discovered that the secret of government is to let nothing alone, it has been reduced to absurdity; and the country is being governed partly by the major-generals, and partly by bodies unknown to the Constitution.

There is only one Dublin Castle in Ireland: there are a dozen in England. When is that wretched country going to insist on enjoying Irish liberty? Sir Horace Plunkett has not to demand Home Rule for Ireland: he has to offer it to England, to Scotland, and even to Wales, if Wales cares for it. At present the four nations are supposed to be governed by an Anglo-Scottish-Irish-Welsh Parliament, in which the Irish, though representing only one-tenth of the population of the whole and less than a third of the area, has more than a sixth of the membership, holds the balance of power, and occupies so much of the time of the House that its business seems to consist mainly of Irish legislation and the discussion of Irish grievances, though Ireland is in every way a happier and freer country to live in than England.

The Irish members also interfere extensively in English and Scottish business, but are so successful in keeping Ireland out of British arrangements that until very lately Irish clocks did not keep the same time as English ones. Irish laborers and small cultivators live in cottages built for them out of public funds, whilst English navvies and skilled workers in the building trade pay half-a-crown a week for half a bed in a room containing six or eight inmates, and are fortunate if they can find even this accommodation within two miles of their job. Irish farmers buy their land cheaply on English security, whilst Englishmen can hardly obtain even allotments at exorbitant prices. The English laborer is forced into the trenches to fight for Ireland; the Irish laborer pleases himself as to whether he joins the army or not. Any nation less sheepish than the English would have cut the cable long ago and insisted on having a Parliament of its own for its own affairs.

Therefore Ireland must force English Home Rule on England as a measure of common humanity and good political sense. Scotland will not refuse a Scottish Parliament, and Wales can have a Welsh one if she likes. But Ireland will not let England go quite free: the British military forces are too valuable an asset; and Ireland has too much to gain, as we have seen, by pooling services and pooling rent with the other island. Besides, England, left to herself, would go to the devil politically, and her fate would involve the others. There must, therefore, be a Federal Parliament in addition to the national Parliament; and in this Federal Parliament of the British Isles, Ireland will retain her representation, and probably continue to occupy more than her share of attention.

But she will have a further representation. The Empire (for convenience' sake I use that offensive and inaccurate term) will be held together by a Conference, which will be a new experiment in democracy, forced on us by the fact that the Dominions will not stand the imposition on them of a central body with legislative or coercive powers of any sort. This Conference will be a representative body, and its business will be to consider the affairs of the Empire as a whole, and to recommend necessary simultaneous measures to the Federal Parliaments. It must consist of representative statesmen from all the federations concerned. Some of the British federation's representatives will be Irish statesmen. Ireland will thus have her national Parliament, her representation in the Federal Parliament, and her voices in the Imperial Conference.

The Irishmen who want anything less than this are clearly Separatist; and, I repeat, separation is out of the question, as it would leave England with as strong a hold over Ireland as over Belgium, whilst Ireland would have no hold over England at all.

From the moment the word "Convention" was mentioned, it was clear to those who knew the history of such conventions that the federal solution was inevitable. The British North America Act was the outcome of the Quebec Convention. The Australian Commonwealth was the outcome of the Sydney Convention. When the Irish talk of "Dominion Home Rule" they seldom know very accurately what Dominion Home Rule is, because neither in the Canadian, Australian, or New Zealand federations, nor in the Union of South Africa, is there anything like the ridiculous Home Rule Bill on which Parnell and the Irish Parliamentary party wasted thirty years [in] ignoble squabbling, only to find, when it came to the point, that Ireland wants national self-government and not a grudged latchkey given with an intimation that the door will be bolted at half-past ten every night. What is meant by "Dominion Home Rule" is, roughly, that Ireland is to be like Canada and Australia and South Africa, and not like Egypt and India. And this means a federation of the British Islands.

Later on, the Eastern Empire will have to be dealt with; and whoever cannot see the importance of having the Irish question settled on lines which will make the Western Empire as homogeneous as possible politically is not much of a statesman.

This solution sweeps Catholic Sinn Fein and Ulster Sinn Fein into the same dustbin. The childish parochialism of "We Ourselves" and "We wont have it" becomes ridiculous when Ireland is seen in its relation to the political system of which it forms a part. It is no use pretending that what is good enough for England, for Scotland, for Quebec, for Ontario, for New South Wales is not good enough for Ireland. Ireland sulking in a corner by herself is nothing; Ireland with her finger in every pie will gather more than her share of plums.

One result will be that Ireland will cease to be Republican. Being a Republican myself, I think this a pity; but it is impossible to ignore the steady resistance of the Dominions to the substitution of any stronger link than the Crown for the Britannic Alliance (as the Fabian Society calls the Empire). The explanation is plain enough. The "Crowned Republic," which is the hollowest of journalistic phrases in England, is a reality in Australia, in South Africa, and in Canada. There the career is open to male political ambition and female social ambition as completely as in any republic, which is very far from being the case in London. And the control of the King is negligible, whereas that of a President might be formidable. Now, this is precisely the state of things that will be produced in Ireland by Federal Home Rule. We are thus within easy distance of the time when England, seething with Republicanism, will have the Crown firmly held down on her writhing brows by all the other members of the Britannic Alliance, headed vociferously by Ireland.

General Smuts has voiced for us the cry of the Empire overseas: No Imperial Federation, and no Republicanism. Let Mr de Valera take counsel accordingly.[7] It may be the fate of America, with France and Russia, to impose the discrowned republic on Ireland and the other crowned republics as Mr Wilson has so bluntly threatened to impose it on Germany; but Ireland will certainly not impose it on England, nor even want to when she is restored to normal political health by Federal Home Rule.

Sir Horace Plunkett, then, must draft his Bill to establish Federal Home Rule not only in Ireland, but in England and Scotland as well. It will not be necessary to consult England—nobody ever does consult her about her own business—she will swallow it as she has swallowed Dora and the bureaucratic autocracy of the new departments. Scotland will not object—the days when no Scot leaving his country to make his career ever took a return ticket are passing—Scotland will acquiesce. The danger is not that the scheme will be rejected, but that the new national Parliaments may be weakened, and the Federal Parliament, the London Parliament, unduly exalted by an excessive provincialism.

Dreamy Ulster, steeped in its glorious, pious, and immortal memories,[8] has not noticed that there is a far stronger case for giving separate provincial legislatures to the industrial north and the residential south of England than for doing as much for the north and south of Ireland. It is now many years since Mr H. G. Wells woke up the Fabian Society to the fact that the units of local government in England are too small, and their boundaries (often passing down the middle of a main city thoroughfare) absurdly obsolete. If the Fabians found it necessary to propose a heptarchy for public local industrial organization, it will be easy to trump up a case for two English Parliaments. But if statesmen who would magnify

7. Éamon de Valera, the predominant political figure of modern Ireland, was born in New York but brought up in Ireland. He took part in the Easter Rising of 1916 but escaped execution, unlike the other leaders of the Rising, presumably because of his American citizenship. In 1919 he was elected president of the first Dáil, or parliament, which immediately was proscribed. In 1926, after the establishment of the Irish Free State and the ensuing Irish Civil War he founded a political party, Fianna Fáil, and in 1927 was elected to the Free State Dáil. He became *taoiseach*, or prime minister, with Fianna Fáil's victory in 1932. For the next twenty-seven years, with the exception of the years between 1948 and 1951 and those between 1954 and 1957, when he was out of office, he dominated the political life of Ireland. In 1959 he resigned as *taoiseach* and was elected to the presidency of Ireland for two terms, 1959 to 1973. He died in 1975.

8. Shaw is echoing the Ulsterman's traditional toast to William III.

the central power are allowed to confuse national with local government, and by a multiplication of provincial Parliaments reduce these Parliaments to the level of county councils, the Bill will be wasted as far as the satisfaction of national sentiment is concerned.

Both in England and Ireland the present system of local government by counties will have to develop into local government by industrial watersheds, so to speak; but as the divisions of these will certainly not follow the divisions of the existing provinces, provincial parliaments, or even provincial councils, [it] would become a serious obstacle to the scientific reorganization of local government which will soon become inevitable. There would be ten times more sense in making two separate Irish Parliaments for agricultural Ireland and city Ireland (say Belfast, Cork, and Dublin) than for making one Parliament for Antrim and another for Donegal.

If England were to split herself into north and south, the harm would not be very great, as there is no national question involved, and the division would be in no sense a secession; besides, either half would still contain about five times as many people as the whole of Ireland. But in Ireland no national division is possible. The internal model there must be the Union of South Africa, not the federations of Australia and British North America. Even the South African provincial councils would have to be very cautiously adopted in Ireland, where national homogeneity must be absolutely unbroken unless the old troubles are to begin all over again.

Neither this nor any other scheme is compatible with that Intransigence which is only a cloak for the Anarchism which makes crude peoples afraid to be governed at all, and which is responsible for most of the miseries of England. Parliamentary self-government is not liberty, but a means by which capable men with character enough to use it, courage enough to face the inevitable risks of majority rule, and sense enough to see that the alternative of minority or foreign rule is still more risky, can secure what liberty is possible to individuals in civilized society under that tyranny of nature and daily need against which no political constitutions can avail.

Whether the Irish have that capacity, that character, that courage, that commonsense will be tested at the Convention. In all communities the lack of it is betrayed by one infallible sign, and that is the demand for security. Let the Irish factions remember that they cannot have liberty and security together any more than the English ones. The men of Devonshire, being in a minority in England, must take their chance of the English Parliament passing a law that all persons speaking with the Devonshire accent instead of the Oxford affectation shall have their noses cut off. The members of the Countess of Huntingdon's persuasion [Methodism] must risk the establishment of the Mahometan faith, and the Roman Catholics must risk the revival of the Elizabethan persecutions.

If they were not willing to face these risks they would simply be unfit for free institutions, and have to be placed under tutelage as "non-adult." And if Ulster Protestants are not prepared to take the risks of Parliamentary government, then what they need politically is neither Home Rule nor Union, but a sufficiency of paternally managed orphan asylums. For the Union offers them far less security than Home Rule. The Catholics have been able to force the Westminster Parliament to desert them. They are in an insignificant minority there in members; and as to their wealth and commercial enterprize, do they really believe that the monstrous cities in which Birmingham and Wolverhampton—nay, Lancashire and Cheshire—are swallowed together as mere parishes can see Belfast without the aid of a magnifying glass?

In Ireland Belfast is formidable: in England Belfasts are six a penny, though the doughty Scot (probably of Ulster parentage) whose comment on London was, "Peebles for me!" is cherished in England as a legendary figure with affectionate admiration, which, however, butters no parsnips. If Ulster is not fit for self-government, it may as well be tyrannized over by the Pope as by Dublin Castle. In fact, the hand of the Pope is heavier on it at this moment than the hand of the Castle. It will never beat the Pope except by means of an Irish Parliament, and it will not beat him that way if it is cowardly enough to tie the hands of the Irish Parliament in respect of religion. Nothing in the Home Rule Bill condemns it more conclusively than the faithless and insulting clause that attempts to shut out religious organization from the competence of the miserable Committee-with-a-Reference which it offers as an organ of national government. By all means let us have that part of the Australian Clause 116 which forbids the setting up of religious tests, the imposing of religious observances, or the prohibition of the free exercise of any religion, but not that part of it which condemned Australia to teach her children nothing but the materialistic doctrine of the Secularist sect, and forbade her to establish her religions.

Sinn Fein must also face the risks of the glorious enterprize of political liberty. If it makes conditions with liberty by refusing it except on condition of fiscal autonomy and the like, it will get government without liberty, and serve it right! In federating with the Britannic Alliance it will have to give the Alliance certain guarantees in return for the power and consequence it will have as a member. But if it begins asking for guarantees from the Alliance that national self-government will not hurt it, it will justify the Scottish officer who said to me impatiently the other day, "Oh, let us give the wretched place its independence, and make it a foreign Power. Then we can conquer it and treat it as a conquered country, and have no more nonsense about it." That Scot was a man after my own heart, and I hope Sinn Fein will have the gumption to applaud him.

When France faced England and all Europe with the flag of liberty, and beat them, it was not with the cry of "Security, security, and still more security," but "Audacity, audacity, and still more audacity." When Germany lost her nerve, and, instead of taking her chance with Western democracy, wanted security, she plunged herself and dragged the rest of Europe into the black slavery of war, and destroyed even the common securities of life and property which are practicable for civilized nations. And if we lose the war it will be through the terrors of those who would lose the substance of victory in a feeble snatch at the shadow of security.

Liberty is not a shelter for weaklings and children: it is an adventure for the brave and strong; and if any Irishmen can be found to disgrace their country by clamoring for security, I exhort the Convention not to coddle them with conciliation, but to brace them with wholesome contempt.

It remains only for the Convention secretariat to draft the Bill. All they need is a pair of scissors, a pot of paste, a set of copies of the British North America Act, 1867, the Commonwealth Constitution Act, 1900, and the South Africa Act, 1909, with a few special clauses which the Convention must by this time be able to draft with full knowledge of the political, fiscal, and industrial considerations which demand specifically Irish handling and conciliation. Then strike out the colonial names and figures and replace them with Irish ones, and the thing is done. The expenses can be covered by selling the existing copies of the Home Rule Bill as wastepaper.

THE NEW NATION

The Irish Times, Dublin, on 19 December 1917, published a letter and a set
of memorial verses by George Russell (A.E.), under the caption "The
New Nation," in which he averred that Ireland was not, as commonly
described, a nation of Celts and Saxons, but a new nation whose "ancient
Celtic character" had been profoundly changed by the influence of other
cultures—Norman, Dane, and Saxon. It was a hopeless dream, he argued,
"that the ancient Celtic character could absorb the new elements, become
dominant once more, and be itself unchanged. It is equally hopeless to
dream the Celtic elements could be eliminated. We are a new people,
and not the past, but the future is to justify this new nationality."

Shaw's response was published in *The Irish Times*,
Dublin, on 24 December 1917.

Sir,—I wonder would it help the noble-minded and eloquent appeal of
"A.E." if I were to betray a secret known, so far, to expert ethnologists
only? I hardly dare; but Christmas and "A.E.'s" verses give me courage—so here goes!

There are no Celts in Ireland. There never were. Now the murder is
out!

Two thousand years ago Cato the Censor[1] defined a Celt as a person
devoted mainly to warfare and witty conversation. From that hour to the
beginning of the present century every conceivable variation and elabo-
ration of this absurd definition has been a pet amusement of romantic
pseudo-historians and patriotic poets. But at last scientific human nature
could bear it no longer; and the ethnologists rose up and said that this
short, swarthy, black-haired, tall, pale, light-haired, totally uncivilized
and highly cultivated race had gone beyond the bounds of human credulity, and that we must make up our minds once for all what we mean by a
Celt. As it then appeared that we meant nothing and did not know what
we were talking about, the matter was gone into seriously; and the Celt
was finally run down and unmasked as a man with a shortish stocky
figure, a smallish pippin-shaped head, and a stupidly energetic, anti-

---

1. Marcus Porcius Cato, also known as Cato the Elder, was a Roman politician,
orator, and influential prose writer of the second century B.C.

democratic temperament. This identification was not a matter of tradition or romance or patriotism, but of ruthless measurements. He had not come from the west, but from the east. His scanty vanguard had pushed as far west as the borders of Wales, but never crossed the Irish Sea; and his main body had stopped and settled on the Baltic. He is now known as the typical Prussian. He and the Irishman are the opposite poles of European humanity. Even the Iberian type, common in Ireland, though it contrasts so strongly with the now fashionable Anglo-Irishman, is not a bit like him.

I am not a professional ethnologist, and take the facts from the experts as I get them. But as it is clear that the Celt of romance is not merely a monster, but a mass of contradictions going beyond the possibilities even of monstrosity, and as the Prussian Celt does visibly go to and fro on the earth, armed to the teeth, I accept the fact rather than the figment, whatever the theory may be worth.

Yours, &c.,

G. Bernard Shaw.

LITERATURE IN IRELAND

A lecture delivered by Shaw in Dublin, 26 October 1918, was reported in
The Irish Times, Dublin, 28 October 1918, with partially verbatim text and
was captioned "Mr. G. Bernard Shaw and Irish Literature: His Advice
to Irishmen." It was reprinted in *Shaw: The Annual of
Bernard Shaw Studies*, vol. 18 (1998).

On Saturday evening, in the Little Theatre, 40 Upper Sackville Street,
under the auspices of the Dublin Literary Society, Mr. George Bernard
Shaw delivered a lecture on "Literature in Ireland." He said that, as a man
of letters, the last place in which he desired to appear was addressing a
literary society, if he could help it, for he knew nothing about literature.
He did not read other people's works; he had enough to do to read his
own proofsheets. But it occasionally happened that if he was writing a
critical article, and he had to quote Mr. [H. G.] Wells or some other of the
literary lights of the day, he found that it was with the greatest difficulty
that he could refrain from altering the sentences. From the moment his
hand began to copy Mr. Wells' work, he wanted to write the thing entirely
differently. He admitted that he liked his own style. The burlesque in his
plays was not nonsense. He defied any man to get more fun out of his (the
speaker's) work than he had got himself. People told him that it did not
matter what he said about anything. But there was one thing that strikes
everybody who faces modern Irish literature, and that was that Ireland
only produces literature by a sort of cross-fertilization. They had got no
Irish literature until George Moore went to Paris and began to write. In
the same way they had Synge, who had done nothing at all until he went
to Paris. And now they all go to Paris. *[Laughter.]* There was Mr. Joyce.
He gets a sort of double cross-fertilization; he goes there and gets his inspiration from Strindberg, a Swede. Mr. Joyce translates Strindberg's *Inferno*
(a description of his life in Paris) into Ireland, and he proceeds to show
that Dublin may be as much a hell to him as Paris was to Strindberg.[1]

1. Although James Joyce's *Ulysses* was not published as a book in its entirety until
1922, extended portions of it were serialized, commencing in March 1918, in *The
Little Review* (New York). Shaw had, as he informed the novel's publisher on 11 June
1921, read "several fragments" in the journal (*Shaw's Collected Letters, 1911–1925*,
1985).

"Most of your poetry about the Irish rising," said Mr. Shaw, "is not Irish at all. When you come to the literature that is represented by the Gaelic League and Sinn Fein in Ireland—and nobody knows the origin of that better than I do, for the Gaelic League was invented in Bedford Park, London—you find that there never was a more tremendous delusion than the delusion that the Gaelic League is modern Ireland. The natural effect of it is to make the Irishman absolutely self-conscious as an Irishman. That is a diseased state of mind. No healthy Irishman is in that condition. We go into all the qualities of man outside his nationality and we allege that the Irishman is a wonderful product, enormously superior to any man on the face of the earth. *[Laughter.]* We have got that idea to a particular degree, and it is all nonsense. We are an exceedingly futile and disagreeable people. Our misfortunes are all the fruit of our own character. I am continually telling Englishmen that they are entirely mistaken in admiring Irishmen, and that they have the worst qualities of all the rest of the human race. I tell my English friends that I like them better than I like my own countrymen. I regard them as grown-up children, and though occasionally some of them will kill women and children and knock down part of a town—I am sorry it was not the worst part of the town—still, I do not regard them as vindictive." *[Laughter.]*

Returning to the subject of literature, Mr. Shaw said he was convinced that there was no more Irish literature—no literature that was more Irish—than his own works. He did not mean to say that he did not admire certain qualities in the works of Mr. Moore and Mr. Joyce. Some of it sickened him. In Mr. Moore's latest work there was a lot that was not decent, and he did not see why it should have been written. He (Mr. Shaw) would write indecency if it justified itself, but Mr. Moore's indecency does not justify itself. He admired it as literature, but not as Irish literature. He did not admire the plays of Synge as Irish literature. The thing did not come out of Irish life; it came out of that life which a man learns a good deal about in Paris. The first criticism he would pass upon *The Playboy of the Western World* was that an Irish peasant would be disgusted and revolted by it. The main theme of the play exhibited the curious tendency that people have to admire crime; but that was not in the slightest degree peculiar to Ireland any more than it was to any other place. It was true of almost the entire human race.

One could get a good deal of music out of the speech of the Irish people, and Synge had got it; nevertheless, the intellectual drawing of the thing was not Irish at all. It could not have been produced by a man who had never been out of Ireland, and who did not avail of the modern methods by which people got the culture of Paris from the reading of books. The same thing was true of the literature of the modern movement. The play that idealizes Ireland is almost always a play which comes from foreign inspiration. When you come to the literature that tries to throw a glamor over Ireland, and shows her to be a delightful place, you always find that it is essentially a foreign literature, and when you come to the literature which represents Ireland to be a backward, dull place, you are unfortunately obliged to admit that it is an Irish play about Irish life. That, said Mr. Shaw, was a very serious indictment to bring against the literature of the nation, and yet he did not see his way out of it.

Criticism, especially in Dublin, took the form of derision. From his childhood he had imbibed the habit of derision. He had tried to get out of it, but he could not, quite. In spite of living in England, he found that curious cackling derision breaking out in him, and he wished that he had been born somewhere else than in Dublin. Dublin people could not quite get rid of what was a fundamental lunacy—namely, in thinking that they are Ireland. They really thought they were superior, but they had done nothing to justify it. In spite of a certain flexibility of mind, they had not justified their existence as yet.

Sometimes, when the Irishman went abroad, he became a success. In America he immediately achieves success as a policeman or a ward politician. *[Laughter.]* He [Shaw] had said that he would help recruiting,[2] because it was a magnificent way of getting Irishmen out of Ireland. *[Laughter.]* The best thing to do with an Irishman is to take him by the scruff of the neck and show him some other place, and when he came back to Ireland something might be made of him. And then every Englishman should be sent to Ireland for a certain period of his life. The climate of Ireland has such an effect upon an Englishman who spends eighteen months here that he is a changed man for the rest of his life. It would not be well for him to stay in the South of Ireland, for if he did he would lose his character altogether. *[Laughter.]* The Irishman had no opportunity of doing anything until he got out of Ireland. He advised those

2. See "War Issues for Irishmen," pp. 184–201.

who could to go over to England by the next boat, for until they did they would not have any real understanding of what Ireland is.

But he also advised them, if they have a grievance, to forget it, or at least conceal it. If they have a grievance, healthy people would say, "Serve you right." His opinion was that Ireland was too much given to making a poor mouth of it, and without sufficient reason. Up to a little time ago, he believed that the Irish had a certain religious and political genius. The Irish Convention shook that belief. The Convention should have come to a certain conclusion, and if it had the faculty of saying what it thought[,] the majority would have issued a report, and would have affirmed its opinion. But it allowed two relatively small minorities to produce a report. The consequence was that one had to admit that the Irish Convention, to that extent, was a political failure—that somehow the Irish were not taking their politics with sufficient conviction, that the winners did not take their winnings, and that they allowed their opponents to take up whatever was lying on the table. He felt sure that after the researches of Irish literary people in Gaelic literature they would go back to English authors, and read Shakespeare and Dickens, and the works of other such preposterous persons.

Mr. Bridgman moved a vote of thanks to Mr. Shaw, and Mr. Ernest Boyd,[3] in seconding the motion, remarked that Mr. Shaw had dodged the question of Irish literature. The literature he had been speaking about was not Irish, although it was written by Irishmen.

The vote of thanks was passed with acclamation.

3. Bridgman (spelled *Bridgeman* in the same day's report in *The Freeman's Journal*, Dublin) has not been identified. Ernest Boyd, astute writer, critic, journalist, and translator, eventually settled in New York.

THE CHILDREN OF THE DUBLIN SLUMS

I

The Star, London, 4 June 1918

Judge Henry Neil [of Chicago] has visited my native town of Dublin. He is very properly ashamed of the condition of the children there, and he asks me to second his appeal to America to send I forget how many thousand pairs of shoes and stockings to clothe them.

It is certainly more sensible than sending them handkerchiefs to cope with the effect of bare feet and wet flags. But my advice to America is not to send a single cent to Ireland ever again, for shoes or anything else.

Ireland is perfectly well able to feed and clothe her children if she chooses. It is a mistake to suppose that she is poor; she is only an incorrigible beggar, which is not the same thing. She persuades you that except for a corner of Ulster, where a handful of bigoted enemies of hers build ships and make linen, she is penniless. Do not believe her.

The trade of the Irish Catholic South in butter, cattle, and agriculture generally represents far more money than the shipyards and mills of Belfast. Co-operation can develop this agricultural industry by leaps and bounds: it has already done so. Ireland can afford a pair of good boots and a couple of changes of warm woolen stockings every week for every one of her children; and if she is a bad mother and prefers to leave the children barefooted and hungry whilst she is enjoying herself at hunt meetings, regattas, horse shows, and the routine of sport and fashion generally I do not see why America should encourage her.

It is true that America does the same thing, and worse: I am not forgetting the poor little slaves in the cotton mills of Carolina, on whose behalf I am prepared to solicit, not shoes and socks, but fire from heaven (serve America right if the Germans supply it!); but the moral is that if America wants to rescue children from poverty and slavery she had better look at home, and not supply another superfluous demonstration of the fact that the eyes of a fool are in the ends of the earth.

I do not want to see children fed and clothed by the hand of Charity. Let them be fed by the hand of Justice.

When an Irish gentleman with thirty pairs of trousers complains that he has not yet ordered his thirty-first, I would have Justice (quoting Shakespear, as a cultured Justice naturally would) say, "Nor shalt not, till necessity be served." People cannot be got to see that the necessity is the nation's necessity: they think it is only the child's necessity, and that its parents should look after it, the said parents having been starved in their youth out of all possibility of looking after themselves effectively, much less their children.

Baby-killing is an international crime.

The English kill their babies fifteen times as fast as the war kills men. The Germans are worse. The Italians worse again. The Russians perhaps worst of all. I dont know exactly where America comes in, but Judge Neil has let out the fact that he found America's kindness to children worse than her neglect. He makes no complaint of that kind against Dublin. There you see the straight thing—the rags and the bare feet.

The Judge says that it is the bare feet that get at an American; but I am a Dublin man and think nothing of bare feet; if you give a country girl in Ireland a pair of good boots she will carry them in her hand for miles to the fair or the market town, and then put them on to make a fine show with. What got at me when I walked about the slums of Dublin lately were the young women with the waxen faces, the scarlet patches on the cheeks, the pink lips, the shuffling, weary, almost ataxic step, representing Dublin's appalling burden of consumption. They are not the product of bare feet, but of wet feet in broken boots, of insanitary poverty generally.

When the police were driven from the streets by the week-long struggle for an Irish republic in Easter 1916, these people came out and began to pillage the shops as naturally as their neighbors a mile or so away pick up cockles on Sandymount strand. Civilization is nothing to them: they have never been civilized. Property is nothing to them: they have never had any. The priest came and drove them away as if they were flies; but the moment he passed on they came back like flies. Civilization means "Respect my life and property and I will respect yours." Slumdom means "Disregard my life and property and I will disregard yours."

Giving money is no use.

It is like people at a railway accident offering surgical instruments and splints and bandages to oneanother when there is nobody who knows how to use them. If you give shoes to a hungry child, it will eat them (through the medium of the pawnbroker) and be just as hungry next week. And the person who gives the money or the shoes, instead of feeling like a scoundrel because the children were in misery, feels saintly because he has played the generous sailor of melodrama.

Until we all acquire a sense of social honor and responsibility as strong as our present private family sense (and even that is not very strong in many of us), the children will shock that social conscience in Judge Neil.

I do not object to his shewing up Ireland, which poses as warmhearted, affectionate, impulsively generous, chivalrous, and all the rest of it. I am fed up (unlike the children) with these professions. If the United States, instead of asking its immigrants silly questions as to whether they are anarchists and the like, so as to make sure that all her foreign anarchists shall also be liars, were to refer to the statistics of infant mortality in the country or city from which the immigrant came, and send him back contemptuously if the rate were anything like so infamously high as it is in the slums of Dublin, such a step would do more to call the attention of Irishmen to the disgrace of their annual Slaughter of the Innocents than all the shoes that were ever pawned.

Charity is only a poisoned dressing on a malignant sore.

If we are callous enough and silly enough to let that easily preventible sore occur, the only remedy is the knife; and if it is too long delayed, the knife may take a triangular shape and slide in a tall wooden frame overhanging a Procrustean bed.

Starved children always revenge themselves one way or another.

II

"Postscript" in *The Daily Herald*, London, 5 December 1927

It is not invariably true that a good sermon improves with keeping. This one was written I forget how many years ago, when Judge Neil, shocked at what he saw of Dublin poverty, asked America to come to the rescue.

Why my sermon should suddenly be revived now, *à propos* of nothing, I do not know. It has moved the Daily Express to declare, in its largest type, that G.B.S. Attacks the Irish, and to heap reproaches on me, feeling no doubt that England has just surpassed anything that Irish mendacity has ever achieved. She has begged her Shakespear National Theatre from America, and got it. Any other country would have died of shame.

England exults at having imposed on Uncle Sam with her tale of deserving poverty. Stratford-on-Avon is henceforth extraterritorial: an *enclave* of the District of Columbia. Thank heaven, Ireland's national theatre, though but a little thing, is her own.

WAR ISSUES FOR IRISHMEN

In the autumn of 1915 Shaw received an appeal for assistance from Lt. Col. Matthew Nathan, then undersecretary at the Viceregal Lodge, Dublin, who was concerned about the failure of the Castle's recruitment propaganda. The trouble, said Shaw, was that the appeals were inept, since they were not appeals to Irish, but to English, patriotism. And it was ludicrous, after the bombardment of Dublin by General Maxwell to suppress the Easter rebellion, to plaster the ruins with posters asking the Irish whether they wished their homes to be wrecked as the Germans had wrecked Louvain. Shaw therefore drafted a poster text for Nathan that incorporated what he considered sane and cogent reasons for enlistment; this text, which Shaw submitted in December 1915, was apparently never put to use.

The Irish recruiting program continued to lag, and in September 1918, while vacationing at Parknasilla, County Kerry, Shaw received a fresh appeal, from Captain Stephen Gwynn, to assist Gwynn and Captain James O'Grady, M.P., in the work of the Irish Recruiting Council. He instantly drafted a lengthy "Open Letter to Colonel Arthur Lynch [M.P.]," which Gwynn arranged for Maunsel and Company to publish. Shaw received proof in October 1918, but by this time the course of the war had rendered some of his material obsolete, and to keep pace with current events he was obliged to draft a foreword, which he predated 10 November.

Maunsel rushed into print its edition of *War Issues for Irishmen*, as the volume was now called, and was ready to issue it just as the Armistice was declared. All but a handful of copies were scrapped.

A Word Going to Press

In war, when events move in earnest, they move so much faster than the brains of the fastest thinker or the pen of the fastest writer that every really well considered utterance arrives the day after the fair. They have certainly moved with a vengeance since conscription was threatened in Ireland. That threat was made in a moment of panic so acute that the British Government actually announced that it was abandoning the English harvest, and tearing its necessary cultivators from the fields regardless of consequences, to meet the military emergency created by the rout of the Fifth Army. Compared to this desperate and suicidal demand on the English nation the demand for conscription in Ireland was moderate and pardonable. Any special bitterness on our side concerning it seems to me to be inhuman. Both demands were, from the military point of view, insane: neither of them could have operated in time to save the situation. Both had to be dropped rather shamefacedly when the scare subsided. But they shew how appallingly close to the brink of utter defeat the Government believed us then to be.

That was only a few moments ago as moments are counted in this war. Yet as I write these last few hurried words before going to press the German Empire is in the dust; the Austro-Hungarian Empire is changed, as if by an enchanter's wand, into three Republics and a Revolution; the Ottoman Empire is suing for mercy on its knees; and the fact that Bulgaria is out of the war and, with Roumania, declared a Republic, is hardly worth noticing in the general political metamorphosis. The difficulty now is to persuade the Allied nations that the war is not yet over, and that the European chaos, though a necessary accompaniment of a huge transition from what we in Ireland call Castle rule to popular rule, is for the moment a danger that calls, even more urgently than the mere struggle to avoid defeat of the last four years, for the resolute unification and military organization of Western democracy. That the Hohenzollern and Hapsburg empires have fallen may fitly be received here with exultant cheers. But if you go deeper and put it that the whole centre of Europe has fallen to pieces politically, the wise man in the West will look to his arms more anxiously than before.

Still, it is a glorious day for Democracy; and it is fortunate for us that there are enough Irishmen in the Democratic army, and enough soldiers' widows and orphans in Ireland, to make it impossible for Democracy to turn a cold shoulder to us in the hour of her triumph and say, "No thanks to you Irish." But some of us are still open to that reproach. Out of five hundred thousand farmers and farmers' men in England, two hundred thousand who had never dreamt of soldiering before volunteered for service at the beginning of the war to fight for the ideals which Nationalist Ireland has professed in season and out of season. There are Irishmen who plead that we might have done equally well in proportion to our numbers if the English Ascendancy had let us. I do not like the excuse, because I do not see why we need have let the British Ascendancy hinder us; and I could tell stories of how some of the first English volunteers were received when they rushed to the colors, which would set Ireland wondering that England ever raised an army at all. But however that may be, the fact remains that we are allowing England to beat us in her contribution to the victory of Democracy, and that America, whose subsidies have kept our Nationalist party in parliamentary existence for thirty years on the understanding that we Irish are all born soldiers of freedom, is reminding us that if we are too poor to pay we are not too poor to fight, and asking us pretty emphatically which side we are on. Sinn Fein, replying through the mouth of its Congress the other day that it will "make itself felt at the Peace Conference" (whatever that may be), apparently by some mystical force inherent in doing nothing, has made itself so acutely ridiculous that it had really better elect the ex-Kaiser Grand Master of its Order, and retire with him to Dalkey Island, which he would doubtless prefer to Saint Helena as a jumping-off place for any future operations his enthusiasm for Irish liberty may suggest.

There is still time for more Irishmen to affirm their true allegiance to Democracy. They will find in the following pages no attempt to confuse that allegiance with the false allegiance which is only the bargain of Esau. And I am happy to be able to add that they will find no argument which is weakened, and some which are strengthened, by the astonishing turn which Europe has taken since my letter to Colonel Lynch was penned six weeks ago.

Ayot St Lawrence,
10 November 1918.

Parknasilla,
September 1918.

Dear Colonel Lynch,

It is extremely difficult to do any effective recruiting by written appeals in Ireland, because the British Government, instead of addressing itself to the practical problem of inducing Irish workers to enlist, seeks rather to justify its own position in the war from the point of view of the governing class, and will be content with nothing less than a demonstration that it is the duty, not only of the Irish, but of all the other nations of the earth, to take up arms in its defence. This is natural enough; and no doubt we Irish would do it ourselves if we were in the same position; but the

result is that the goods are not delivered. The reproaches hurled at
Irishmen for not rallying to the side which professes to be "making the
world safe for Democracy" hit Sweden and Spain and Holland harder
than they hit Ireland; for none of these countries have had their nationality and their right to popular government denied, as Ireland has, by the
British Empire. Accordingly, Ireland, finding herself in highly respectable company with much stronger reasons for neutrality, treats such obviously interested reproaches with derision, and maintains her neutrality.

The appeal to Ireland to ally herself with the French Republic was used
by myself and, if I mistake not, by you, early in the war; but as England is
not a republic, and in fact sentenced you to death on one occasion for
fighting, as a Republican, on behalf of a republic which was at war with
her monarch, there was no response in England except from Mr H. G.
Wells. At that moment there was the most urgent need of an Opposition
in the House of Commons which could oppose without being suspected
of Pacifism. It was obvious that only a Republican Opposition could fulfil
that condition. Yet Mr Wells's suggestion was followed by a dead silence.
Under such circumstances it was inevitable that an appeal on Republican
grounds on behalf of an alliance in which England was the principal
figure should fall flat. Its success would have been regarded in many
influential British quarters as a defeat more serious than any that was to
be feared from the Central Empires.

The appeal had therefore to be based on the profession by the Allied
Governments of those democratic and nationalist principles which may
be supposed to have a binding effect on the political consciences of
Irishmen. But was this profession credible in view of the antecedents of
the Allied Governments? Loud and unhesitating as the reply in the
affirmative is from the suspected parties and their recruiting authorities, I
cannot expect any Irishman to be convinced by them. An Empire champi-
oning the cause of nationalities is a contradiction in terms; and the British
Empire is the one in which the contradiction is grossest. Facts are too
much for so absurd a pretension; and Ireland is one of the leading facts in
the case. Even the allusions that were made so recklessly to the great
fights for liberty at the beginning of the XVII, XVIII, and XIX centuries
did not include any mention of the fact that on those occasions the victorious troops of liberty did not get the liberty they fought for. The enthusiasts who defeated Philip II, Louis XIV, and Napoleon won their vic-

tory; but they won nothing else: they returned home—those who did return—to a tyranny as oppressive as that from which they had meant to rescue the world. Common men fight and die for liberty and equality and other inspiring ideals, but it is the actual Governments of the victors that decide what effect the victory shall have on political institutions. To ask Irishmen to die for freedom is one thing: to ask them to die in order that Lords Curzon and Milner may get the upper hand of the Hohenzollern dynasty is another. It is silly to pretend that the governing classes of Europe can be unanimous in desiring to make the world safe for Democracy. There is something revolting in the democratic professions of politicians whose whole career flatly contradicts the notion that they are fighting to overthrow the social order which they have always defended, and which is in all essentials the same in the Central Empires as in their present enemies. It was evident in 1914 that on most questions which divide the interests of the man of the people, Irish or English, from those of the governing classes, the figureheads of the Allies sympathized with the Kaiser and not with the figureheads of proletarian democracy. It is still evident that their opinions and interests have not changed. They govern in the interests of the country house and the counting house, regarding labor as a source of rent for the one and profit for the other. As between King William Hohenzollern and Mr Arthur James Balfour, dominated as they both are by the economic interests and social ideas and traditions of their class, there is, from the point of view of the man who lives by labor, nothing to choose. It is not possible to believe that Mr Balfour feels otherwise on the Irish question than the Kaiser on the Polish question.

I do not see how recruits can be gained in Ireland by shirking these considerations. They are obvious to all neutral and detached nations; and Ireland is not only neutral and detached, but hostile and critical where England is concerned. Whoever is to recruit effectively in Ireland must put all these cards frankly on the table. The Irish may be persuaded to enlist, or forced into the army as slave soldiers, but they will not be humbugged into enlisting by the rhetoric of British patriotism.

It does not follow, however, that they may not be dissuaded from enlisting, and are not in fact at present being dissuaded from enlisting, by the rhetoric of Irish patriotism, or that this rhetoric is freer from humbug than the British variety. The considerations I have stated above lend themselves very easily to Sinn Fein orators who wish, for one reason or another, to keep Ireland out of the war. But the fact that the official reasons for Irish enlistment will not hold water does not prove that there are no sound reasons to justify the many thousands of Nationalist and Catholic Irishmen who have already enlisted. Sweden, Spain, and Holland may be right to keep out of the war as far as they can; and the United States may have been right in doing the same up to the point at which events proved too strong for that policy, and President Wilson drew the sword at last. That shews that the Irish nation may without dishonor remain neutral. But it does not follow that neutrality is the best policy; and if England would only appeal to Irish interests instead of trying to hypnotize Ireland into a sense of imaginary moral delinquency by claiming a "loyalty" which is regarded as treachery in Ireland, and threatening such an infamy as conscription by Dublin Castle, your recruiting campaign would move more rapidly.

It is a mistake, and in every sense of the word a vulgar one, to suppose that when we have convicted the advocates of a certain opinion of insincerity and hypocrisy, or of motives other than those they allege, we have refuted that opinion. The Christian religion, for instance, does not stand or fall with the good faith of Judas Iscariot, nor Irish Nationalism with that of Leonard MacNally[1] and the Irishmen who took the bribes of Pitt to pass the Act of Union. No cause on earth is free from partisans whose motives and character will not bear examination. It is possible to be on the better side, but not possible to be in exclusively good company. Therefore the first thing a sensible Irishman has to get out of his head is the notion that in choosing sides in the war he can be guided safely by mere reaction against the motives and character of his Allies.

This may seem a hard saying; but the truth is that this war, whatever the intentions of the European Foreign Offices and Courts may have been, has become a war of ideas and institutions, and not a war of dynastic ambitions and capitalistic market hunts. It is true that the sun in heaven is not more conspicuous than the fact that the late Nicholas II had not the

---

1. MacNally, a Dublin attorney and member of the British secret service in Ireland, served as defense attorney for Robert Emmet. His duplicity was not known until long after Emmet's trial and death.

faintest intention of making the world safe for Democracy when he mobilized against Austria, and that none of the statesmen in England and France who deliberately sought his alliance instead of that of the United States can be credited with any genuine sympathy with Democracy. But war has a way of taking very little account of the aims of the individuals who plan it. In 1871 nothing was further from the thoughts either of Bismarck or Napoleon III than to give Monarchy its death-blow in France and finally establish Republicanism in its place. Bismarck, when he made France pay what he thought a colossal indemnity, certainly did not intend to produce a ruinous financial crash in Berlin, and provide the peasants of France with a first-rate investment for the contents of their old stockings. If the Pacifists, instead of alleging in the teeth of all experience that war produces no results except its own miseries and atrocities, were to remind pugnacious statesmen that wars hardly ever produce the results they were intended to produce, and often overthrow the order they were meant to consolidate, they could make a stronger case for themselves. Any fool can make a war if chance places him in command of the army, just as any fool can open the door of a tiger's cage if he happens to inherit the key. But to control it afterwards may be beyond the powers of Alexander, Caesar, Cromwell, Peter, Catherine, Washington, Lincoln, and Napoleon all rolled into one.

Consider what the present war has done. Nicholas, aiming at a Pan-Slav empire, has been slaughtered, like a horse no longer worth his scanty food, by jailers so obscure that their names are unknown. The Kaiser, aiming at the destruction of the military prestige of the only Republic in Europe which seriously challenged the efficiency and respectability of the Hohenzollern tradition in government, has plunged all Europe to the east of him into the crudest regicidal Anarchism; brought the great North American Republic, raging and multitudinous, on his other flank, avowedly to tear him from his throne; and is fighting desperately to avoid surrendering Alsace-Lorraine to a France whose military reputation has revived to a point approaching that boasted of by the Napoleonic glory merchants of 1812. Mr Asquith and Viscount Grey, after vainly throwing Lord Haldane to the wolves, are down and out: their determination to exact a terrible price for the German devastation of Louvain ended in their own devastation of Dublin. France is wishing that she had allied herself with the devil rather than with the Tsar, and had kept her capital at home to mend her own slums instead of exporting it to Petrograd. America thought she would look on and make money; but Destiny has taken her by the throat and flung her into the war almost before the end of the presidential election in which she voted for the man who had kept her out of it so skilfully. Plenty of food here, is there not, for the derision which is Dublin's staple intellectual commodity, and which more or less infects all urban Ireland, to the great detriment of our national character, and the mean satisfaction of everything that is envious, conceited, and ignoble in our souls?

What we Irish have to consider, then, is not what the kings and their councillors and their warriors intended this war to be, but what, in the hands of that inexorable Power of whom it used to be said that "Man proposes: God disposes," it has now actually become over and above its merely horrible aspect as an insane killing match. If there is anything at stake except military prestige, and the resulting Overbalance of Power, what is it? I think we must reply that the war has become a phase of that great struggle towards equality as the sole effective guarantee of democracy and liberty which is being constantly waged against the delivery of human welfare into the custody and control of privileged persons and classes: in short, against robbery of the poor and idolatry of the rich.

Idolatry to me is something much more real than an abusive catchword of Irish Protestantism. The particular idol I want this war to knock over is a highly Protestant idol of the purest Dublin Castle brand. I do not spitefully deny that King William Hohenzollern has done his best to earn the worship he claims by a good deal of public-spirited hard work. When an Irish lady at the beginning of the war wrote a little book to shew what a horrible and unhappy place Cork would be if it were occupied by the German army, she had hardly written two chapters before she discovered that her Prussian villain was improving Cork out of all recognition in spite of her; and by the time she had reached the end of her book the villain had become a hero. I have seen a good many German towns, and they compared very favorably with most Irish towns in such respects as depend on good government and high social organization. In Ireland itself, such towns as Lismore, under the despotism of the Duke of Devonshire, are more civilized and creditably kept than towns which belong to a miscellaneous lot of little landlords or freeholders. But there is no permanence in the prosperity which depends on the character of a single man carefully brought up in a false and artificial relation to his fellow men: in short, to an idolized man. Towns should belong neither to dukes nor freeholders, but to all the people who live and work in them, subject to the general interest of the whole nation in them. For towns and nations do not die; but good dukes die and may be succeeded by bad ones; and little freeholders are too poor to keep their backyards clean, much less make a city great. Accordingly, I object to the centre of Europe, with its hundred and sixty million people, being the feudal estate of the Hohenzollern and Hapsburg families, without any guarantee that the head of either family at any moment may not be a lunatic or a scoundrel or both: indeed with a strong guarantee that he can never come quite sane out of the monstrous isolation and idolization which he has to undergo from his childhood.

These two principles, Idolatry and Democracy, were not at issue when the war began, because idolatry at its very vilest, represented by the Russian Tsardom, was the antagonist of the Kaiser, whose rule was almost democratic by comparison. As long as Nicholas could turn the scale, the professions of his Allies to represent Democracy were an insult to history and to contemporary fact. But now that the war has destroyed the Tsardom and given its place in the alliance to the great Federal Republic of North America, the situation is changed. Far from Republicanism being outnumbered and outpowered and outfinanced by its Imperial Allies, it is now the predominant partner in the Alliance. It has visibly saved the military situation for them. It will, if they are victorious through its aid, practically dictate the terms of peace; and President Wilson's oration at the tomb of Lincoln on the fourth of July last left no doubt that the American terms would not be favorable to those political institutions which England and Germany have inherited in common from Feudalism. Both America and France will be obliged, in defence of their constitutions, to insist on their victory as a victory of Republicanism over feudal Monarchy. In that case, nothing but a very strong public opinion on the democratic side from English and Scottish labor, from the Irish nation, and from the Overseas Dominions, reinforced by Italian, German, and Austrian Social-Democracy and by Jugo-Slav and Czecho-Slovak nationalism, can defeat the inevitable tendency of the reactionary elements in the Peace Conference to combine against the popular elements, even if it means combination with enemy forces and opposition to Allied ones.

That Ireland can look idly on at such a situation whilst Americans, Canadians, Australians, and South Africans are fighting as furiously as Jugo-Slavs, Czecho-Slovaks, and Poles, is not to be excused by mere soreheadedness over our relations with England. What, for instance, has Irish Labor—that is, four-fifths of the Irish people—to say to the American Federation of Labor's manifesto as to the aims of the American working-class in supporting the Allies? If Dublin Castle were wise, it would circulate that manifesto throughout the length and breadth of Ireland. But as the castle is itself a typical example of the sort of political institution that American Labor is out to destroy, it is much more likely to suppress it forcibly. American Labor, however, will not take ignorance as an excuse for our not answering. President Wilson may be open to the retort from Sinn Fein that the Feudalism he represents—the Feudalism of the beef baron and the newspaper millionaire and the steel, coal, railway, and oil trusts, in which Mr Rockefeller can do things to Colorado that Reginald Front de Bœuf dared not have done to Nottingham for fear of Robin Hood—is worse than the Junker Feudalism of Prussia; but that retort does not touch Mr [Samuel] Gompers. American Labor, knowing more about American Capitalism than Sinn Fein does or ever will, nevertheless thinks it worth its while to throw itself into this war on the side of the Allies as fiercely as British Labor, though it is traditionally anti-English and pro-Irish more unitedly than Irish Labor itself. It is not asking Irish Labor to help England: it is asking it to help Labor all over the world, and not sulk because Ireland has wrongs and grudges of her own to nurse.

This challenge from America, in which Labor accepts all the conditions of President Wilson, and adds them to a long list of demands which make any equivocation as to the thoroughgoing democracy of its spirit and aims impossible, proves that the war is now conceived by the Western peoples to whom we belong as a war of advancing world-Republicanism against Hohenzollernism fighting in its last ditch. The spirit of every nation will be judged according to the side it takes in it. It is useless for us to sneer at such a conception on the ground that the cleavage between the belligerents is not completely consistent: clean cleavages of that kind do not occur in the affairs of nations. Neither the Mikado of Japan nor the King of Italy, not to mention the Balkan kinglets, is at issue with the Kaiser as to Democracy. But it is none the less clear that the defeat of the Central Empires will be a discredit from which the social order they represent, typified in Ireland by Dublin Castle, can hardly recover; whilst the defeat of the United States and their Allies would practically convince Europe that efficiency and safety can be secured only by idolatrous Imperialism. That ought to settle the question for any Irishman who really stands for liberty.

So far it is plain that the Irish side is for once the side on which the English find themselves; and the English generals naturally want Irish soldiers because, though they do not like them, and resent the detachment and frank derision with which they regard British moral pretensions in respect of nationalities struggling to be free and so forth, they know their value as soldiers and are anxious to have an Irish element in every battalion. Why does the Irishman hold back?

Not, clearly, that he is more afraid of being killed than other people: he is actually sought for because he raises the standard of military courage in the field under the spur of his insurgent national pride, as the Irish casualties shew. Not, either, in any number of cases worth reckoning because he wants Germany to win with a view to the German terms of peace including the establishment of Ireland as an independent nation, like Belgium or Greece, under the guarantee of the victorious Central Empires. This was Roger Casement's plan; but it is too technical politically for anyone but a professional diplomatist like Casement to understand; and the ruthless exposure by the war of the utter dependence of Belgium and Greece on their ruthless guarantors, and the uselessness of the "scraps of paper" which guaranteed them, ought by this time to have set every intelligent Irishman implacably against such skull-grinning Independence as that.

The common Irishman takes a simpler view. He regards England as Ireland's enemy; and his conclusion is that England's enemies are his friends. This is natural logic; but it is bad logic. The Chinese pirate is the Englishman's enemy; but if the Irishman were on that account to depend on the friendship of the Chinese pirate, or even to refrain from very strenuously helping the Englishman to hang him, he would probably have his throat cut for his sulkiness. The Englishman and the Frenchman fight with what help they can get: Japanese, Negro, Red Indian, Pathan, Senegalese (none of them bosom friends of white men, to say the least) are good enough for them when they have a common foe to overcome. Any Irishman who will not fight for his side in the world conflict because the English are fighting on that side too has no political sense; and an Ireland composed of such men could never be free, even if the gates of freedom were open wide before her. It is a case not of refusing to help the English in a bad cause, but of refusing to take advantage of the help of the English in a good one.

Then there is the more intelligent Irishman who hopes that the war may end in the establishment of a League of Nations, and that this League may take up the Irish question and insist on Ireland having its place as a nation, and not remaining a conquered territory governed by her conqueror. America, he thinks, may have a good deal to say in the matter on behalf of Ireland. She may have more if Ireland takes a generous share in the war. But we must not deceive ourselves as to the interest the rest of the world takes in our little island and our little people. Those of us who talk and think as if, outside England, all the great federations, empires, and nations of the world were enthusiastic branches of the Gaelic League, or that they will put Irish interests before their own lightest advantage in the settlement after the war, or that they care twopence more for Ireland than they do for Poland, Finland, Bohemia, Armenia, or any of the Jugo-Slav conquests of Austria, are deceiving themselves very ridiculously. The truth is that these great European and Asiatic Powers will be hardly conscious of Ireland when the settlement comes. We are too far out of their way. We shall count for less with them in the treaty than Cyprus did in the Treaty of Berlin. We can make England feel us; and America is well aware of us; but we cannot make Europe feel us. The beginning of diplomatic wisdom with us is to realize our own insignificance outside the group of islands to which we belong.

But if we have no diplomatic importance, our sentimental importance in America and the Overseas Dominions, and our political importance within the British Islands, is considerable: it is, in fact, out of all proportion to our merits. And if Sinn Fein is to mean anything but organized national selfishness and insularity, it must take serious count of English and American sympathy. If I say that the Irish people are under very strong obligations to the English people, obligations which it would be the grossest ingratitude to deny or forget, I shall no doubt astonish those bookmade Irish patriots who are too busy reading about the Treaty of Limerick[2] and the feats of Brian Boru[3] to see anything that happens under their noses. But at least they must be dimly conscious that there was an attempt made in Dublin in the Easter of 1916 to establish an independent Irish Republic, and that one of its leaders was a noted Socialist trade unionist named James Connolly who, being captured by the British troops, was denied the right of a prisoner of war, and shot. Now, Connolly owed his position and influence as an Irish National leader to the part he had taken in organizing the great strike of the transport workers in Dublin in 1913, and the remains of his organization was the nucleus of the little army of the Irish Republican Brotherhood. That strike was sustained for many months after it would have exhausted the resources of the Irish workers had they not been aided from abroad. Where did the aid come from? From the reckless generosity of the English unions. The English workers fed, out of their own scanty wages, the Irish strikers and their families for months. I myself, with Connolly and Mr George Russell, was among the speakers at a huge meeting got up in aid of the strike by Mr James Larkin in London.[4] It was a genuine non-party meeting called by English workers and crowded by thousands of English people, who rallied to the Irish strike with unbounded enthusiasm and with as much money as they could afford, and indeed more than they would have thrown away on that doomed struggle if their heads had been as clear as their sympathies were warm. Connolly got the money by the plea that the cause of Labor was the same cause all the world over, and that as against the idler and the profiteer England and Ireland were "members one of another." We did not set up the cry of Sinn Fein then. We did not say

2. The Treaty of Limerick (1691), which concluded the fourth and final conquest of Ireland by the Williamite invasion, is considered a classic example of British betrayal because promises of religious toleration for the Roman Catholic masses—the price of surrender—were later abrogated by a Dublin parliament from which all Catholics were excluded by law.

3. Brian Boru, high king of Ireland in the late tenth and early eleventh centuries, was famous for his successful battles against the "Danes."

4. Larkin, an Irish Socialist Trade Unionist, was one of the leaders of the great Dublin strike of 1913. The meeting was held on 1 November 1913 in the Royal Albert Hall, London.

"WE OURSELVES are sufficient to ourselves: you can keep your English money and leave us to take care of ourselves." We took the money and were glad to get it and spend it. We cannot now with any decency forget Connolly and change the subject to Cromwell and General Maxwell. I have the right to remind the Irish people of this, because I was one of those who asked for the money; and I was cheered to the echo by English-men and Englishwomen for doing so. I am an Irishman; and I have not forgotten. English working-class mothers have the right to say to me: "Our sons are in the trenches, fighting for their lives and liberties and for yours; and some of your sons who took our money when they were starv-ing are leaving them to fight alone." Not a very heroic position, that, for an Irish movement which is always talking heroics.

Naturally, General Maxwell and the Unionists of the War Office, with the British and Irish Junker class generally, take particularly good care not to remind the Irish people of this obligation. They can hardly hold up Connolly as a hero after shooting him, or claim the payment of debts due to him as debts of honor. They dread that sinking of national differences in the common cause of Labor all over the world far more than they dread a German victory. They will tell you to remember Belgium, to re-member Poland, to remember Servia, to remember any place that is far enough off to have no obvious bearing on the relations between you and them; but they will not tell you to remember Dublin and Connolly. And yet it is only through Connolly and the international solidarity that Connolly stood for that the Irish worker can be made to feel that his cause and that of the English worker is a common cause, and that he is in debt to English Labor through a very recent and very big transaction. And the worst of it is that the Nationalists and Sinn Feiners are as guilty of this ungrateful suppression as their Unionist opponents, and as blind to the fact that the Irish workers by themselves are negligible, though in combi-nation with European and American Labor they are part of the only force that can finally make an end of all the empires and turn them into com-monwealths of free nations.

Let me turn now from the broad unselfish view to the narrow and inter-ested one; for it is useless to pretend that lads brought up as so many of ours have been, drudging for mean wages on small farms in petty par-ishes, can be expected to reason like statesmen or to feel obliged to repay benefits that came directly only to workers in cities they never set foot in.

To them you must say that, horrible as this war is, it has raised millions of men and their families from a condition not far above savagery to comparative civilization. A trench is a safer place than a Dublin slum; and the men in it are well fed, well clothed, and certain that, whatever the Germans may do to them, at least their own commanders are keenly interested in the preservation of their lives and the maintenance of their health and strength, which is more than can be said of their employers at home. Their wives get a separation allowance; and the children are considered and allowed for too. The huge sums of money that this costs are taken largely from the incomes of rich landlords and capitalists who have to give up one pound out of every three they possess to feed, clothe, and equip the soldier, and keep his wife at home. The wonder is that any man chooses to live in a slum or drudge as a laborer on a farm when he can get into the army. But at least, some of them will say, you do not get blown to bits by high-explosive shells in a slum. Unfortunately, you do. Bombs are raining on civilian slums, farmhouses, and cottages every day in this war; and the rain gets heavier from week to week. If the slums of Ireland have escaped so far, it is only because the slums of England are nearer to the German lines; and the day is not far distant when, if the war goes on, the soldier in his bombproof dug-out will be safer from shells than the slum dweller in his wretched room. The aeroplane and the torpedo are making short work of the safety of the civilian in war.

Then take the case of the lad on the farm. He knows nothing of the world: his only taste of adventure is pretending to be a soldier by doing a little precarious drilling which teaches him nothing of real modern warfare, though it may easily tempt him to throw away his life in a hopeless rising of men fed on dreams against men armed with tanks and aeroplanes. His wages would be spat at by a dock laborer in a British port; and the farmer keeps them down by employing his own sons as laborers for a few shillings pocket money. He is under everyone's thumb; yet he is afraid of military discipline, which, severe as it is, yet has limits beyond which the soldier is reasonably free, and even unreasonably free, whereas a laborer is never free at all. The laborer is never sure of his food from week to week; but in military service he never has to think about this: food, lodging, and clothing are provided for him as certainly as they are for a general, in return for a round of duties which, though the slightest neglect or slackness in performing them is fiercely punished, are, taking one year with another, neither as heavy nor as wearing as the never-ending jobs of an agricultural laborer. In many branches of the service, such as the air force and artillery, there is valuable mechanical training to be had; and even the physical training of the ordinary infantry soldier pulls the country lad together and smartens him up, besides forcing him to do things that must be done promptly and to make up his mind instead of mooning. Traveling and the sight of foreign countries and contact with foreign peoples, which form an essential and expensive part of the education of a gentleman, can be obtained by an Irish country lad in no other way than through military service. Now that the service is compulsory in England the soldier finds himself in ordinary respectable company, often better than he has ever been in before. I am not playing the tricks of the recruiting sergeant and trying to persuade Irish lads that a soldier's life is all beer and skittles. If it has opportunities and advantages, it has also dangers and hardships which are inevitable; and it has injustices and cruelties which are all the harder to bear as they are mostly stupid and mischievous relics of the days when soldiers were the dregs of the population. But if an Irish agricultural laborer compares the soldier's condition, not with a condition of ideal happiness and freedom, but with his own, he will think twice before missing such a chance as the war offers him of seeing a little more of the world than the half-dozen fields and the village public-house which now imprison him. When one considers what the daily life of four out of every five young Irishmen is, one wonders that more laborers do not jump at the chance the new army offers them.

At this I must leave it. Let me just sum up the case as it presents itself to me.

1. Though almost all the official arguments used at the beginning of the war to persuade Irishmen to join the army prove on candid examination to be claptraps, yet their exposure, tempting as it is to anti-British journalists and orators, does not affect the real case for recruiting. The Irishman still has to decide his attitude towards the war exactly as any American, Frenchman, Italian, or Britisher has. If there are as good reasons for Ireland taking her share in the war as for Portugal, she cannot excuse herself for holding back by pleading that the recruiting authorities give her bad ones, or that Portugal is not held down as a conquered territory by Spain.

2. The Irish workers have no grievance against the English workers.

There are actually more Home Rulers in England than in Ireland; and the organized workers of England have not only endorsed the Irish national cause as a matter of course, but have handsomely subsidized Irish Labor in its struggle for better conditions of life in Dublin. In both countries, as in all commercial countries today, there is a struggle between the propertied classes and the working classes; and for the workers of Ireland to quarrel with those of England in the interests of the Hohenzollern and Hapsburg dynasties would be as dangerous a mistake as a division between the English and French or the French and Italian workers, who have sunk all their national differences and traditional enmities in the common cause of Democracy.

You will notice that I have said no word about that conscientious objection to war as war which is nevertheless a powerful factor in the situation. I myself, like that very typical Irishman the Duke of Wellington, have a conscientious objection to war so strong and deep that I do a most painful violence to my nature and conscience whenever I am compelled, as I am now, to accept war as a necessity of which we must make the best by acquitting ourselves like brave and astute warriors and statesmen rather than Christians. Nowhere is this conscientious objection to war more general and more deeply felt than in the army. If my own acquaintance with the men now actually fighting is at all typical, I must conclude that at least ninetynine per cent. of the men agree with the conqueror of Napoleon that war is so dreadful a calamity that only half-witted men would engage in it, or countenance it, if any honorable alternative were possible. I can respect no Christian pope or priest who ceases during war to press the question, "Sirs, ye are brothers: wherefore do ye wrong one to another?" I will even say that if we Irish were indeed a nation of saints, and had never drawn the sword in our own or in any other cause, nor glorified the Irish soldiers who have, on one side or the other, maintained our boasted military prestige from Fontenoy to Gallipoli, then we might claim the benefit of the Act, and say, "The Irish do not fight." As it is, I am afraid all Europe would laugh at such a plea. I therefore rule that consideration out, as one to which we can make no moral pretension.

What we *can* plead is that as, like the Americans, we did not make the war, and are free of the guilt of bringing such a calamity on mankind, and as we can take part in it only on what we conceive to be the side of political emancipation in spite of our intense preoccupation with our own acute national problem, we shall be acting with complete national disinterestedness in the spirit of men with a duty to the world as well as to ourselves. Unless Dublin Castle has hopelessly broken our spirits and limited our horizon, the Irish soldier will carry the burden which war throws on the conscience of every sane man all the more lightly because he will be able to say honestly, "At least we had nothing to gain by it that the whole world did not share; and we did not hesitate to risk our lives for the national liberty of men who had denied national liberty to us." The Irishmen who have been fighting since 1914 can already say this. Can the rest hope to be able to say anything more honorable to Ireland?

Faithfully,

G. Bernard Shaw.

SIR EDWARD CARSON'S OTHER ISLAND

In an interview in *National News*, London, on 13 October 1918, Sir
Edward Carson gave as his reason for opposing Home Rule that he could not
understand how separation from Great Britain could be anything but disastrous,
both for the United Kingdom and for Ireland itself. He suggested that, in
order to bring about a united, contented, and prosperous Ireland, a cabinet in
Dublin should be formed to advise the Irish executive upon the economic
development of the country and so divert people's minds from internal
agitation to economic effort. Shaw's reply appeared in
The Daily News, London, 14 October 1918.

This interview is unintentionally funny. It is plain from Sir Edward
Carson's first answer—the all-important one—that the Irish question is
to him what it is to a child saying its lessons out of Little Arthur's History
of England, that is, a question of whether Ireland and England are to be
separate, independent, foreign kingdoms, or exactly what they are at
present. His answer has no sense on any other basis, and it is on this childish assumption that he has organized armed rebellion and sought the assistance of Germany, with the effect of destroying the authority and prestige of Parliamentary institutions in England, and convincing the Kaiser
that the British Empire, confronted with a civil war in Ulster, would not
fight. What can one say but Sancta Simplicitas!

Home Rule for Ireland is not Separation: it is the alternative to Separation. The advocates of Separation fiercely oppose the Home Rule party,
and, like Sir Edward Carson, raise armed forces to defy the British Parliament. They say of Home Rule exactly what Sir Edward Carson says,
"We wont have it."

Sir Edward Carson cannot conceive two Parliaments in what he calls
"the heart of the Empire" without social, financial, and economic disas-
ter, constant friction, and ultimate secession. He does not know that the
constant friction generated by the attempt to govern the British Empire
from London has long since been relieved by the creation of several Parliaments in British North America, several Parliaments in Australasia, and a
Parliament in South Africa, and that this war has proved that these Parlia-

ments and their constituencies have rallied enthusiastically to the Empire in its day of need, whilst Ireland, Egypt, and India are thorns in its side, and ironical contradictions to its professions of democratic good faith.

Please remark that Sir Edward Carson's ignorance as to the political constitution of the Empire he champions is not an affectation, like his innocence as to the question about the sexual morality imposed by the Irish priesthood. No statesman would compromise himself by an exhibition of political ignorance before the American public if he really knew any better. Sir Edward knows just one thing more than the apprentices who shut the gates of Derry against James II; and that is that the United States have separated themselves (no doubt—in his opinion— temporarily, regrettably, and rebelliously) from Great Britain. And he cannot draw the moral even of that.

In the end, as might be expected, Sir Edward Carson turns out to be a Home Ruler. Like Sir Horace Plunkett, he wants an Irish Cabinet to advise the Irish executive and to frame schemes for the British Parliament. But how on earth is he to have an Irish Cabinet without an Irish Parliament? And why should he swallow the one and strain at the other? It is like demanding an Irish king whilst insisting on an English beadle. Let Sir Edward think out his scheme for five minutes with competent expert advice, and he will see that his Irish Cabinet—not, observe, an Ulster Cabinet, but an *Irish* Cabinet—will land him in a far more complete scheme of Home Rule than the wretched makeshifts of Gladstone or Mr Asquith.

The only solution of the Irish question that will bear examination for half an hour is the American one: that is, the federation of the three nations (four, if you count the Welsh), with Ireland in it on the same terms as England and Scotland. England suffers severely from the lack of Home Rule and of an English Parliament. So does Scotland; and, what is more, Scotland knows it. All three nations suffer from the fact that their common Parliament, which is neither Irish, English, nor Scotch, is nobody's Parliament. It is too much cumbered with local business and local representatives to attend to its Imperial business, and too much distracted by the consequences of its neglect of its Imperial business to attend to its local business. It pretends to understand both and understands neither. It is pompous, windy, ignorant, despised, and *found out*. What Dickens knew about it fifty years ago the world knows now.

Sir Edward will sit in an Irish Parliament yet, if only for the generosity and public spirit with which he refrained from exploiting the rising of Easter 1916 for party purposes in Parliament. But I hope he will take a course at the London School of Economics and Political Science first. What is good enough for Westminster will not be good enough for College Green.

THE DOMINION LEAGUE

I

Extract from a hitherto unpublished letter to G. K. Chesterton, 9 June 1919

[Horace] Plunkett wants me to take up his new organization[1] just being founded; but they want to convert me to the ideas they got from me and call them Dominion Home Rule. I am a Federalist (of the three kingdoms) and want Ireland to be in the British Combine on exactly the same terms as England is in it, and not as a demd dominion; but though they all agree with me, they have picked up this catchword of Dominion Home Rule and will listen to nothing else. What is wanted is a demand for English Home Rule; for England, having no English parliament, suffers severely for want of Home Rule, and through the confusion of her national consciousness by imperial vain glory, whilst Ireland is maintained in a blaze of martyrdom and a transport of megalomania by her wrongs, to which she instinctively clings, knowing subconsciously that if they are redressed she becomes an uninteresting island like Wight or Man, a St Helena without a Napoleon.

If you would start a Home Rule for England movement with a book shewing up Yeats's Ireland as Archer shewed up Tagore's India [*India and the Future*, 1917], you would be a public benefactor. . . .

II

To *The Irish Statesman*, Dublin, 30 August 1919

Sir,—Every successive number of your paper confirms and reinforces my conviction that the way to help Ireland is not to propose solutions but to draft a Bill. Solutions are easily swallowed; but they are not a bone-building diet. The Dominion League every week conciliates Peter by

1. The Dominion League, formally known as the Irish Dominion Party, was founded by Sir Horace Plunkett in 1919 as "a moderate party" designed to break the Irish deadlock. Its organ was *The Irish Statesman*, Dublin, sponsored by Plunkett with the financial backing of Dr. James Ashe. The Dominion League received a fair amount of support in Ireland and in August 1920 held an Irish Peace Conference in Dublin, with about six hundred representatives from all of Ireland. Its resolutions were presented to Dublin Castle, where they received scant attention.

offending Paul, and when Paul remonstrates, it conciliates him by offending Peter. It is at last getting carried to lengths which must shock the moderation of Sinn Fein and revolt the nationalism of Sir Edward Carson. Let me state the program as it stands at present:

1. The League is anti-Republican.

2. The League is anti-Federalist.

3. The League is anti–Sinn Fein.

4. The League is anti-Ulster.

5. The League is anti–Home Rule.

6. The League is implacably opposed to Self-Government in England.

7. The League repudiates the doctrine of Natural Rights as expressed in the American Declaration of Independence.

8. The League insists that the Irish Question is *sui generis* and does not exist in England, Scotland, Wales, or any other of the outlandish wastes of the non-Irish earth, the Irish being by implication a Chosen Race and Peculiar People.

9. The League proposes to provide for the military security of Ireland by buying England an annuity to look after it, and washing her own hands of it forever.

10. The League denies Ireland's right to be represented in any Parliament which controls Ireland jointly with the other island.

11. The League nevertheless demands that Ireland shall be represented in whatever Council, Conference, or Parliament of the Empire may be set up.

12. The League is consequently Imperial-Federationist.

13. The League demands that Ireland shall have the status of a Dominion in the British Commonwealth.

14. The League nevertheless demands that Ireland shall have the status of a nation in the League of Nations.

15. The League nevertheless denies the right of Ireland to detach herself as a separate nation from England.

16. And the League hopes that everybody is satisfied now.

Unfortunately, nobody is satisfied except on the point that Ireland has lost her sense of humor. There is no use going on like this. All the sane men in the country agree with Sir Horace Plunkett that it is the Centre, and not the marginal Impossibilism, that must formulate the demands of Ireland. All the wise men would rather be associated with Sir Horace than with any other leading figure in Irish politics. But how can the Centre be organized by a body with such a program and basis as I have reduced to black and white above? I am a Republican, and have been so ever since I was old enough to understand the word. I am excluded not only on that account simply, but because I deny that Republicanism is a specifically Irish question. I am a Federalist, seeing in Federal Commonwealths the only alternatives to Empires. And on that account also I am excluded. I insist strongly on the representation of Ireland, or rather the access of Irishmen, to the supernational Federal organs which must deal with foreign policy *(Welt-politik)*, high finance, and international trade. And that rules me out. I face the fact that the Dominion status, which secures the virtual independence of Canada, Australasia, and South Africa, would have no such effect in Ireland any more than it would have in Yorkshire or the Isle of Wight. And the Dominion League cannot swallow that.

I do not believe in the success of any Centre party which cannot assimilate men with all or any of my views. It is useless to urge that a little goodwill is all that is needed to unite the country. If you come to that, a little goodwill is all that is needed to throw Sir Edward Carson into the arms of Mr de Valera. Nobody expects his neighbor to vote with him out of goodwill. A Centre party ought to be founded by a group of men of all opinions except the rigidly Conservative-Unionist opinion which, being fixed and published, does not need any further expression and does not seek discussion. Its organizers should follow the precedent of the Convention (which is also the normal order of public meeting on the Continent) as to the first stage of their proceedings: that is, talk all round the subject without being tied by resolutions. But they should not, like the Convention, be free to run away from their work when they are tired of talking, leaving the chairman to save their face by pretending, with his well-known literary charm and skill, that they have arrived at a conclusion when they have flatly refused to do anything of the sort. They should pledge themselves to sit until they have produced a draft Bill. That Bill would be the answer to the English complaint that we were asked what we wanted, and couldnt or wouldnt say. It would be the program of the Centre party, which, until the Bill existed, should have no program. It would be a Dominion Bill, a Federal Bill, a Nationalist Bill, an Internationalist Bill, a Sinn Fein Bill, and an Ulster Bill. And it would also be a sort of Bill that could never have come out of these sections separately; in short, an Irish Bill. The end of that would be that it would be an English Bill too.

I cannot pursue the matter further without an unreasonable demand on your space. My main object is to open the eyes of the Dominion League to the fact that its present procedure is taking it further and further away from the aim, with which it started, of combining all the elements between the two Impossibilist extremes of that Irish insularity which is probably a characteristic British trait conferred on us by the Plantations.

Yours truly,

G. Bernard Shaw.

WANTED: A STRONG GOVERNMENT

The Irish Statesman, Dublin, 11 October 1919;
New York American, 7 December 1919

All the regular old Unionists tell you that what Ireland wants is a few years of strong resolute government.[1] They are perfectly right. Why they should limit their prescription to a few years, as if Ireland might thereafter be abandoned to anarchy or to feeble irresolute government, I do not know; and probably they do not either; but there can be no mistake about the present need. Ireland actually wants strong and resolute government parliamentarily, and will stand much more of it than the English, who are all at heart anarchists, and will put up with the utmost evil that human nature can bear if the only remedy be good government. The Irish are not like that: they understand law and like it. One can see it in their litigiousness. A quite considerable little country town in England will get on quite well with one lawyer visiting it twice a week. A town of half its size in Ireland will support six solicitors in flourishing practice. We can stand Brehon law,[2] Roman law, Canon law, and any other law we can discover or invent, all piled on top of oneanother: the more the merrier. We join orders and chain ourselves with vows for the sake of a little

1. As a result of the general election of December 1918, seventy-three Sinn Féin candidates, pledged to the Republic, were elected to Parliament. Of the 105 Irish seats at Westminster, the Irish Party managed to retain only seven of the eighty-three seats it had had in 1914. The party of Parnell was dead. Instead of going to Westminster, however, the elected Sinn Féin members (minus thirty-six of their members still in English prisons) assembled in Dublin in January 1919, organized themselves into Dáil Eireann (the Assembly of Ireland), and declared themselves the governing body of "the Republic established in Easter Week." The British government immediately declared Dáil Eireann illegal, and the organization went underground. From this date until July 1921, Ireland lived virtually under martial law. The Anglo-Irish War, as it is known in Ireland, was a period of ambushes, raids, and acts of terrorism.

2. Brehon law, the laws of ancient Ireland, are so called after the *breithecamh,* or judge, who administered them. Transcripts, made mostly in the fourteenth century, of fragments of the Brehon laws still exist. They were effective in Ireland as early as the third century and as late as the seventeenth century.

more regulation. Our objection to being chastized by England with whips is probably at root that it prevents us from chastizing ourselves with scorpions.

We may therefore agree with the old Unionists with great heartiness in their advocacy of resolute government and plenty of it. How is it to be brought to pass?

Everyone who is not an idiot will admit, to begin with, that no Government can be strong, or indeed govern at all, without the consent and cooperation of the governed. Laws are enforced, not by the police, but by the citizens who call the police when the law is broken. If the citizens connive at breaches of the law and shield the lawbreaker instead of denouncing him, it is all up with the Government. The executive may refuse to admit checkmate for a time. If it has sufficient manpower at its disposal it can bring about a state of things in which out of every five persons in the country one is a spy, one a policeman, and two are soldiers. If it has sufficient money it can put the whole population in prison and support them there. But that is not governing: it is mere coercion, destructive to production, incompatible with prosperity, ruinous alike to the coercer and the coerced. It cannot settle the country, develop the country, secure property and person in the country, satisfy the country, or, in short, achieve any of the ends of government. This is so obvious that the advocacy of such coercion by sane men will be taken as evidence of a design to ruin the country, and a very stupid one when the circumstances are such as to make it impossible for even a Cromwell to go through with the process.

A Government, then, can govern just as much as the people will allow it to govern, and not a bit more. It may have troops and tanks and aeroplanes and Mills bombs enough to wipe out the whole population, but govern them it cannot. When the man who disobeys its orders and slays its officers to avoid arrest can depend on his neighbors not to denounce him, and is assured by his spiritual adviser that he is justified in resisting, even to that extremity, the authorities can proclaim districts, can shoot and bludgeon and arrest and imprison those whom they can catch redhanded; but they cannot keep the peace: they can only break it; and as to constructive measures, the mere suggestion is laughable. In a word, such a Government is miserably weak, irritable, mischievous, and perpetually at its wits' ends. Its strength is as useless to it as the strength of a bull in an arena: it can gore a horse here, toss a picador there, and even kill the matador if he attacks before it is tired out; but it is never for a moment master of the situation; and the end, however long it may be delayed, is foredoomed.

All this sounds like an extract from The Child's Guide to Knowledge and I apologize to the universe for offering it to grown-up people as if they did not know it already. But our Unionists do not seem to know it; and the poor English whom they bully so scandalously are afraid to say it. The Castle clings to a feeble plausibility given to its impotence by the fact that civilized men know that they must keep a certain minimum of order spontaneously if business is to be carried on at all; so that common thieves are still denounced to the police though rebels are not. When a rebel is by chance caught out by the authorities, the laugh is undeniably on their side: the prisoner may put on his hat and "refuse to recognize the Court"; but as the Court can immediately knock his hat off and handcuff and browbeat and imprison and ruin him, its triumph is very real and his defiance depressingly Platonic. But what about the man they have not caught, and will never catch—the man who has a gun and has used it, who is known to everyone in the town except to the police and military as an active rebel, the man who remains at large and trusted by the infatuated British garrison because the citizens are on his side? The Castle loves the old saying that the Irish conspirator is a figure of farce; and that criticism is quite true if it be confined to the Simon Tappertits who form secret brotherhoods and leagues, take oaths, drink out of a skull if one can be found, and perhaps send a bullet through a policeman under the impression that they are dealing a deadly blow at the British Empire. Such conspirators are found everywhere among romantic *poseurs*. Simon Tappertit was an Englishman; and I have known men who held monthly meetings of Leagues of the Proletariats of the World, three or four strong, throughout the years when England's prosperity was said by Gladstone to be increasing by leaps and bounds, with Presidents, minute books, registers of tyrants to be exterminated (after the taste of Madame Defarge), and all complete. The number of branches of The International formed in France in the 1860s by the police agents of Napoleon III must have filled the Castle with envy; and the climaxes, when every police agent threw off his wig and, seizing the other police agent, declaimed "I am Hawkshaw the detective,"[3] must have been thrilling. These conspiracies of playboys may win promotion for their promoters, and perhaps make Castle officials feel clever, but they are only child's play: the really formidable conspiracy is the conspiracy of the whole nation, acting spontaneously without brotherhoods or oaths or indictable evidence of any kind.

Such a conspiracy seems to be as completely realized in Ireland at present as it ever can be within the limits of political possibility. The Government calls our attention to ten Sinn Feiners in handcuffs, and cries melodramatically, "Beware!" We call their attention to a million Sinn Feiners not in handcuffs nor likely to be, and cry, less impressively but more sensibly, "Get out!"

It is a situation not good for business, to say the least. No man with a business scheme in hand feels sure either that Sinn Fein will let him carry it out, or, if he squares Sinn Fein, that the military authorities will let him carry it out. Business schemes cannot easily be hidden either from the police or the people; and they can be both proclaimed and boycotted. He who attempts to do anything out of the beaten track is as likely as not to be suspected by the Castle of being a Sinn Feiner and by Sinn Fein of being "an exterminator of the Irish race." What are the business men of Ireland going to do about it? They need law and order, security for reasonably established expectation, free markets, free transit, normal neighborliness. The Castle Government is utterly unable to give these things to them. Sinn Fein chuckles over their uncertainty. The Castle does not understand their position, being too gentlemanly to have any knowledge of business. Things are going from bad to worse; yet the business men do not wake up: political Ireland is a sort of flaming corona with an eclipsed centre. It seems silly, does it not?

Will our Chambers of Commerce be good enough to think it over from the strictly business point of view? If they are satisfied, there is nothing more to be said as far as they are concerned. If not, had they not better make themselves felt a little?

3. Character in Tom Taylor's play *The Ticket-of-Leave May* (1863).

WHY DEVOLUTION WILL NOT DO

I

The Irish Statesman, Dublin, 25 October 1919

There is at first sight something to be said for the blessed word Devolution.[1] In the London House of Commons, when you want to do anything, you must persuade the lymphatic majority that you are not doing it. And if, as is more often the case, you want to avoid doing anything, you must persuade the mercurial minority that you are doing it. Thus, when it at last became evident to the more intelligent Unionists that Home Rule was inevitable, they had to find a plausible disguise for it. As a measure of satisfaction for Irish national sentiment it would have provoked the Unionists to die in the last ditch (in the persons of their agents and of the Royal Irish Constabulary and its military auxiliaries) sooner than vote for it. But as a measure of relief for an overworked British Parliament it could be presented as an obligation of our common humanity. Surely such minor but time-consuming duties as the administration of the islands off the British coast could be shifted from the Atlas shoulders of the British Government by bringing Ireland into line with the Isle of Man and the Channel Islands, and thus "devolving" her affairs upon local bodies. After all, Sherky Island in the Kenmare River is governed, not from Westminster, but by its king, whose bodyguard, consisting of a single vigilant and energetic bull, repels invasion and maintains order much more effectively than the multitudinous battalions on the mainland, with their tanks and aeroplanes and gas bombs and machine guns. Why not, then, call Home Rule Devolution, and move the second reading in an affecting speech shewing that Devolution, far from being the repudiation

---

1. *Devolution* was the name given to the scheme for the administration of Ireland as enunciated by the Irish Reform Association in 1903. It meant the devolving of Irish affairs upon local bodies—a degree of local freedom—without changing the fundamental relationship between Ireland and England. The policy was revived by Prime Minister Tony Blair and now establishes local parliaments with limited power in Scotland, Wales, and Northern Ireland.

of the Union, is its inevitable consummation as a Union of Hearts? The Nationalists would vote for it because it was Home Rule; the Unionists would vote for it because it wasnt; and the British public would applaud it as statesmanlike, the popular British conception of sensible statesmanship being Humbug All Round. This seems so simple and conciliatory and satisfactory to all parties that I feel bound to explain why, when some of the most amiable and intelligent Unionists said, "Surely here is the solution of the Irish question," I had to sing sadly, "Not there, not there, my child."

What the Irish want is the freedom of their country. Now, you cannot make either a country or an individual free by making out a list of things they are to be allowed to do. The list would take fifty years to think out, five to copy out, and five hundred to debate in Parliament item by item. And even then it would be absurdly incomplete, as it would be concerned with every conceivably possible human activity, and nobody could remember half of them. The thing simply cannot be done. What can be done is to make out a list of the things that free men are always willing to agree not to do for the sake of living in a stable society where their persons and properties are safe, and of the things they are always willing to do at their common expense to enforce and administer the arrangement.

Such an agreement establishes freedom, not by binding its signatories to do certain specified things, and not to do certain other specified things, but by leaving them free to do everything else they please. It is to secure order and peace for the exercise of this general freedom that they accept the limitations set up by the agreement; and they are so jealous of their freedom that they never put half the things into it that ought to be there. That is why every Irishman and every Englishman is today free to do several things for which in an intelligently organized community he would be deservedly hanged. There are crimes, and very serious ones, which nobody will consent to penalize, because everybody hopes to commit them.

That, however, is not my present point, which is that the question whether a man is free or not turns, not on the number of laws, positive or negative, which he has to obey, but on his sphere of action outside these laws. If he may not do anything except what the law expressly authorizes or enjoins, then he is a slave, no matter how generous the code may be. If he may do everything except what the law expressly forbids him to do, he is free, no matter how Draconian the code may be. His residual rights, not his legal obligations or disabilities, are the test. The children who have to run to their parents for leave when they want to do anything are not free. "Mother, may we go out?" "What do you want to go out for?" "Only to see the Lord-Lieutenant, mother." "Certainly not. Stay at home and learn your lessons." "Well, may Tim and Con go out, mother?" "What do they want to go out for?" "To throw stones at the police barrack, mother." "They may, darling; and you may go with them." "Oh, thank you, dear mother. Come on, Tim. Con, dont forget your catapult." That is a slave dialogue. The free child goes out without asking leave, and cheers Lord French or throws stones at the police barrack just as it pleases. Usually it does both.

If the definition of freedom is now quite clear, it will be seen that it is easier to enslave a nation politically than to enslave an individual person-ally. It is virtually impossible to prevent a living person from doing any-thing without a permit: even the child and the henpecked husband of whom the neighbors say that they hardly dare to breathe and cannot call their souls their own, could not survive if they never acted without or-ders. But it is quite easy to enslave a legislative body, and through it the nation for which it legislates. Poynings's law (which was levelled at the garrison, by the way, and not at the aborigines) enslaved the Irish Parlia-ment by forbidding it to do anything without the leave of the British Crown.[2]

When the enfranchisement of the Dominions began with Canada, the question on which freedom depends—namely, which party is to have the residual powers—was hardly raised. Those were early days for democ-racy, and the residual powers were left technically to England. But when the turn of Australasia came, the tide of democracy was at the floor. Half of North America had broken loose from the British Crown and achieved its independence. This had been followed by the French Revolution, and by a series of Reform Acts in London which had reversed the assump-tions on which the Canadian settlement had proceeded. Australasia de-manded the residual powers, and obtained them. And it has made a stag-

---

2. Sir Edward Poynings, lord-deputy of Ireland, convoked a parliament that passed Poynings's law in 1494, stipulating that no law could be valid in Ireland until it had received the approval of the king of England and the council.

gering use of them by introducing a mass of Labor legislation which could not possibly have been authorized from London, where such activities were still undreamt of. Canada quietly and unconsciously assumed residual powers. If any constitutional lawyer said to any Canadian premier that Canada had no power to pass such and such a measure, the premier had only to ask, "What will happen to us if we nevertheless pass it?" The lawyer had to reply that nothing would happen except that the measure would become law, and that England would take it lying down rather than provoke Canada to declare her independence or join the United States. Thus Canada was able to attack English industries by hostile tariffs, quite as vigorously as England had attacked Irish industries, without fear of being reminded that England could retaliate presently by insisting on Canada keeping within her devolved powers.

But if Ireland were misled by the cry of Dominion Home Rule into accepting a settlement on the original Canadian lines instead of on the Australasian ones, England could and certainly would play the very deuce with her by declaring any Irish measure *ultra vires* unless there were a clause covering it in the Home Rule Act.

The bearing of this on Devolution is now, I hope, apparent. To a nation seeking its freedom Devolution means no more than "Good doggie! you may carry my stick." It leaves all the residual powers with England, and puts upon Ireland the burden of such legislative jobs as the London House of Commons is too busy or too lazy or too stupid to find time for. It is rather like profit-sharing in the industrial world: an ingenious method of making the worker sweat himself to save his employer trouble. It would be as great a relief to the London Parliament as the engagement of a valet is to an old-fashioned gentleman who has hitherto brushed his own clothes. But to Ireland it would be an affirmation of her slavery and an aggravation of it by putting upon her the drudgery of government without the freedom to govern herself as she pleases. It would unload part of England's job on to Ireland without making it Ireland's job. And Ireland's inevitable reply is, "We wont have it." For, regarded merely as a cue for the band, that formula suits The Wearing of the Green quite as well as O God, our help in ages past.

If we are to remain in the British Commonwealth voluntarily, we will remain on exactly the same terms as England. First, we must be free as England is free: that is, we shall order our national life in our own way to our own taste over the whole range of it that is not touched by our treaty with the Commonwealth. That treaty will bind us, as it will bind England and the Dominions, to do certain specified things, to refrain from doing certain other specified things, and to accept a certain specified division of labor in public work between the States of the Commonwealth in matters affecting the whole organism. Outside that contract our relation to England will be that of France to England or the United States to Switzerland: that is, the relation of one grown-up man to another. What it will be inside the contract will depend on the covenants; but it will be like the relation established by the Australian contract as distinguished from that established by the original Canadian contract in respect of the residual powers.

And so, Devolution, goodbye. Please dont call again.

II

The Irish Statesman, Dublin, 15 November 1919

Lord Brassey and the other gentlemen whose pastime it is to settle the Irish question in the correspondence column of The Times have a way of calling their notions Federal Devolution. The result is that clearheaded persons like myself, who will have nothing to do with Devolution, and are strong Federalists, find ourselves misunderstood. When we shew up Devolution we are supposed to be exploding Federalism. When we advocate Federalism we are supposed to be accepting Devolution. Let me try to dispel this confusion.

There are at present two alternatives to Federalism. One is Sinn Fein: the other is Devolution. If Ireland is fated to become that hapless thing, a modern independent Republic without any fighting weight, all questions of Federation or Devolution drop; and Ireland's only rock and refuge is the League of Nations, which at present exists only in the form of an Imperialist Trust with England as an influential director and preferential creditor, and Ireland nowhere. That is what Sinn Fein is heading for. Consequently, between the non-Separatists and Sinn Fein there need be no discussion of Federalism or Devolution. Sinn Fein offers a clear alternative to both, and we must take it or leave it. The Dominion League leaves it.

I have already demonstrated, as fully as I know how to, that devolution is irreconcilable with nationality. If there is to be any devolution among free nations, it must be devolution from the circumference to the centre, from the federated to the federation, and not vice versa. England can, if she likes, establish by force a branch of the English Parliament in Dublin, and even call it an Irish Parliament in official documents, but no intelligent and sincere Nationalist will be taken in by that. For thirtyfive years English Liberals have been desperately trying to work up public interest at elections on devolution embodied in Home Rule bills; and it is significant that they complain that in drawing up these bills they have never had any assistance from Irish members. I have never met an Irishman whose enthusiasm for a Home Rule bill survived his reading of it: the whole agitation, as far as anyone became really agitated, was based on national sentiment in the abstract and on the fact that nobody ever read the bills. They raised no more question of federation than the County Government Acts which established County Councils. The London County Council is a bigger thing than any Irish authority limited to expressly devolved powers could possibly be.

But if Ireland is to enter the British Commonwealth as a self-determining nation not less independent than Australasia and not less responsible than England, the question of federation arises at once very sharply. The more complete our permanent national emancipation, the more important become the nature and terms of our permanent international contract. If we are not to let England go, and let Scotland go, and let Australasia and Canada and South Africa go, we must make up our minds as to the nature of the partnership. If it is not to be a federation, what is it to be?

It cannot be too often repeated that Ireland cannot shirk the question of her relations with England, as the overseas communities have shirked it. As these communities stand, they have all the independence of separate republics, and all the stability and protection of Imperial provinces. Their independence is guaranteed by their power to cut the painter when they please. How little power of that kind Ireland has may be estimated from her attempt at a War of Independence in 1916, which Irishmen have been heard to call the Easter Rebellion, though the Englishman Gilbert Chesterton scrupulously calls it a Rising. It lasted a week, and hardly extended beyond the sixpenny cab radius. Ireland could not procure for her soldiers even the privileges of prisoners of war: their officers were shot in cold blood, and the rank-and-file imprisoned as common criminals. It is true that the British Government dares not bombard Belfast even on the most humiliating provocation; but then Belfast does not want to cut the painter: it uses it as a leash to hold the British bulldog. If Belfast were to assert Ireland's independence instead of merely asserting its own, it would be bombarded as ruthlessly as Dublin was.

Let us therefore not deceive ourselves. England never asks for what she can take, nor argues with an adversary whom she can coerce. Much may be said for her method: it saves time. Force is an excellent remedy when you have enough of it; and there is still much truth in Cromwell's remark that, when dealing with the Irish, stone dead hath no fellow. Any man who tries to ignore the fact that there is no spot in Ireland that is not within seaplane flight of the British fleet will not succeed as an Irish diplomatist.

This does not mean that in the game with England Ireland has no trumps in her hand, or even that England has the ace. The ace is the public opinion of the world, especially the English-speaking world. The Irish speak more English than the English, and speak it more fluently, more persuasively when they have a good case, and more abusively when they have a bad one. In this matter England has really no case at all, and does not carry even her own public opinion with her. For example, the committee of Englishmen that was formed in London to save Casement, though it failed, was a more important one than could have been formed in Dublin. If Casement had taken sensible advice instead of legal advice he would probably have been alive today; for the jury declared that they would have disagreed if they had heard before the verdict the speech that Casement made after it. Lawyers know how to defend pickpockets; but they only know how to hang patriots. Casement took their advice, and was duly hanged; but half-a-dozen separate and influential English petitions from different sections of English opinion were sent to Mr Asquith to reprieve him. I have sometimes, as a public speaker, lost patience with the ridiculous way in which English crowds will cheer every allusion to the wrongs of Ireland instead of attending to their own.

If this occurs in England among Englishmen without a drop of Irish blood in their veins, the state of public feeling in the Empire overseas and in the United States may be imagined. Not that the pro-Irish and ex-Irish English, Scots, Canadians, Australasians, and South Africans, much less the Americans, are going to die for Ireland, or even to quarrel seriously with England on her account alone. But the English proletariat, as the railway strike [1919] shewed, are deeply disaffected to the English Government. There is a distinct Republican Separatist party in South Africa, a good deal of the same sentiment in Australasia, and a whole Catholic province in Canada. The Americans and the English are bound together at present by the ties of war, and by that sort of cousinly love which expresses itself in private by foaming at the mouth. However sentimental, romantic, and unreal the indignant sympathy of all these people with us may be, they find Ireland a very knobby stick to beat the British governing-class dog with; and that is why England is uneasy enough to desire some solution that will put the stick into her own hand, and why, if we conciliate public opinion throughout the world, she will be driven finally to put it into our hand and make it worth our while to use it on her side.

Now, the only way in which we can conciliate public opinion abroad or consolidate it at home is by making ourselves thoroughly intelligible to it. At best even the most enthusiastic pro-Irish foreigners and colonials and Americans complain that they cannot make out what we want, and that we do not seem to know ourselves. Take our present subject of Federalism. When I tell an Irishman that I am a Federalist he immediately assures me that he quite agrees with me, but that no other Irishman will hear of it. In this conceit of uniqueness we all denounce Federalism loudly and piously. But imagine the effect in the United States, where nobody can even conceive of any alternative to separation but federation! Australia is a federal commonwealth; so is Canada. To them it seems ridiculous that the British Islands should not be organized as the Dominions. They regard a man who demands Dominion Home Rule and denounces Federalism as an idiot clamoring for teetotal whisky. They do not see what more freedom Dublin need desire than Melbourne or Montreal. Lord Grey, who has gone to America to conciliate public opinion there by assuring the Americans that Mr Lloyd George is going to do the right thing by Ireland, and that the only obstacle to a settlement is the unreasonableness of the Irish themselves, will have the cheapest of jobs if he is able to describe the proposals of Mr Walter Long's committee as proposals to federate, and then cites repudiations of Federalism by all the Irish parties. He will say: "You see, what is good enough for the United States is not good enough for Ireland. What was good enough for Washington and Hamilton and Jefferson is not good enough for Dillon[3] and de Valera. What would you have us do with such people, you who bathed your country in its own blood for three years sooner than allow any of your States to break the federal bond?" And this will be entirely convincing, except to those Americans who are still Separatists both for Ireland and South Carolina. But their support will cut no ice for us.

The moment we accept a partnership at all we must insist that it be a federal partnership, because it is the only one that does not obliterate the individuality of the nation that enters into it. The real reason why we jib at it, and why the British Government jibs at it, is that it finally involves Home Rule for England too; and the English governing classes, though prepared to leave Ireland to stew in its own juice if they must (that is how they regard it), have the most strenuous objection to allow the English people to govern themselves. English peers and the cadets of their families, and even their womenfolk, will haul trunks about for railway passengers and boast that they have made ten shillings in tips in one morning, in a frantic and ridiculous attempt to break an English railway strike. They would not carry an Irishman's suitcase half a yard at Westland-row or Kingsbridge, even for a tip of five shillings a yard, to prevent Mr de Valera being crowned by the Pope in St Patrick's Cathedral. They tolerate an English Parliament only because it is neither English, Scotch, Irish, nor Imperial, and yet, having the work of all four on its hands, necessarily muddles a tenth of it and neglects the rest. Sooner or later, in spite of their teeth, there must be established at least three National Parliaments in the British Islands, with, in addition, a Federal Parliament for joint affairs in which Ireland will be duly represented, and in which a career will be open to Irishmen gifted with that larger political genius which finds its proper scope in world politics.

And now comes the question, need Ireland wait until the English realize this necessity and remodel their constitution? By no means. It is our business to demand a National Parliament and a Federal Parliament in which we are represented; but we want the National Parliament first.

3. John Dillon (1851–1927), M.P., was an Irish Nationalist politician. See also p. 255, note 3.

When we have got it we shall ask where is the Federal Parliament, which is to manage the joint affairs of the two islands. When the English innocently point to the existing London Parliament we shall exclaim: "What! This old thing! This discredited anomaly and absurdity that our veteran Nationalist members stood on its muddled head for thirty years! Youre joking." Nonetheless, we shall send our representatives to it until it suddenly dawns on the English electorate that Ireland is sailing ahead of them because the Irish have a National Parliament and the English havnt. For there is one point on which the Englishman is superior to the Irishman. If an Englishman calls an Irishman a fool, the Irishman flames into a rage (being the most selfsatisfied snob on God's earth) and knocks the Englishman down if he can, or reviles him if he cannot. But if an Irishman calls an Englishman a fool, the Englishman goes away sorrowfully and says to himself: "God forgive me; so I am. That Irish beast was right. Something must be done." And then we can tell him what to do.

But in the meantime please remember that those of us who are neither Separatists nor Unionists are either Federalists or mere anti-nationalist devoluters. I repeat for the hundredth time, if we stay voluntarily in the British Empire, we stay in it on the same terms as England or the commonwealth overseas. And that means federation. Not Imperial federation, which the commonwealths overseas will not hear of, for very good reasons which are valid for us also, but federation by geographical groups, with a central organ developed from what is now called the Imperial Conference. It will have a permanent staff, and as much authority as it can get without any coercive power.

Before the English came to India, the self-governing villages there had a rule that laws must be debated until nobody cried No to them. But they also had a rule that persons who kept on crying No to everything should be removed from the meeting with the utmost possible violence. Ireland professes a high opinion of the wisdom of the East. There is clearly an opportunity here for giving effect to her admiration. The next man who cries No when somebody says Federalism should be very closely watched. He is probably a man who says No to everything. The effective remedy is the Indian one.

III

To *The Irish Statesman*, Dublin, 22 November 1919

Sir,—I have purposely refrained from answering your correspondent "X" until the publication of my article [of 15 November] should have enlightened him as to my attitude on the federal question.

For the rest, he seems to me to have occupied a column of your space by taking a matter which I had left quite clear in its bearing on the Irish question, and confusing it for the sake of contradicting me. "X" is textually accurate in his statements of the law and history of the Canadian and Australian Federations; and, if he likes, I am, say, textually elliptical; but the net result is that "X's" accurate statements leave the reader addled as to what the whole business is about, whereas my elliptical statements left him clear as to the meaning of residuary powers and the importance of the Australian precedent in their bearing on the Irish national question.

In Professor Egerton's Federations and Unions in the British Empire, on page 92, we are told that "Australia followed the example of the United States and not that of Canada in making the States [meaning the Australian States] and not the Commonwealth Parliament the holder of the residuary powers not specifically allotted to either authority." Now my point was and is that when the Federation of Ireland with the British island is constituted, the precedent of Australia and not of Canada must be followed: that is, instead of the Federation devolving certain specified powers on the Irish Parliament and retaining the unspecified residue, the Irish Parliament shall have all the powers which it shall not expressly hand over to the Federation.

If I had wanted to muddle up this position instead of making it so clear that he who ran might read, I could have made a parade of my technical and historical knowledge. I could, for instance, have warned the reader not to confuse the relations between the States and the Federations in Australia and Canada with the relations between the Federations and the Crown; that is, with England. But, as it happened, I wanted him to identify them because for the purposes of the present situation they can be treated as identical. Or again, had I remembered how many unemployed schoolmasters there are about, I could have saved my face by a historical rigmarole shewing how the conclusions of the Quebec Conference of 1864 gave "prodigious satisfaction" in London, whereas the conclusions of the Adelaide-Sydney-Melbourne Conference of 1897–98 were vigorously kicked against on behalf of the supremacy of the Judicial Committee of the Privy Council, the Imperialist attitude thus identifying itself with the local Centralist attitude. Canada, amazing as it seems, has actually a Poynings's Law by which the Dominion Executive can disallow provincial Acts of Parliament. Australia can alter its constitution by Referendum. Such Australian powers were denounced by Imperialists as preliminaries to separation, whilst the Canadian limitations were approved because they fortified the denationalized central organ which was most directly under the thumb of the Crown. These two facts shew how important is the distinction between the Canadian settlement and the Australian one in view of the certainty that both settlements will be referred to for precedents when Ireland is federated.

For the sake of simplicity and intelligibility to Irish readers I foreshortened the case so as to reduce it to its essentials. The result was, I think, that the readers of The Irish Statesman understood, and understood rightly, the nature of residuary rights, the distinction between Canadian and Australian Home Rule, and the importance of claiming the Australian variety for Ireland. The result of "X's" interference is that the same readers do not now know whether they are standing on their heads or their heels, but have a vague impression that the Canadian Federation is more democratic than the Australian, and that there can be no question of residuary powers as between London and Dublin, but only as between Dublin and Belfast, Cork or Galway, superposed on a quite sharp impression that I am a plausible and dangerous impostor, ludicrously ignorant of law and history and hopelessly wrong as to facts, contrasted with "X" as a man of infinite learning, a consummate lawyer and an omniscient historian. And when they have read this letter, they will conclude that there is a pair of us, and that the Irish question is one that no man can understand. I am sometimes tempted to think that Treitschke was right, and that the Irish and the Poles are impossible people politically, destined to be ruled forever by nations who want to get things done, and not merely to quarrel over them.

In my article last week I tried to clear up that confusion between Devolution and Federation of which "X" rightly complained. I fully expect to find a letter from him next week occupied half in disparaging me, and half in making that confusion worse confounded.

I call on "X," if he is a genuine patriot, to go to bed and stay there until the Irish question is settled.

> Yours, &c.,
> G. Bernard Shaw.

IV

To *The Daily News*, London, 7 January 1920

Sir,—In your issue of the 5th, your special correspondent in Dublin announces that "wide publicity has been given to an article on present-day Ireland by Mr Bernard Shaw, published in the New York American, in which he strongly condemns Federal Devolution as an inadequate solution of the Irish problem."

May I call the attention of your special correspondent to the existence of The Irish Statesman, a weekly review published in Dublin as the organ of Sir Horace Plunkett's Dominion League? The article he quotes appeared in that review some months ago. Not the slightest notice of it was taken in the English press, by your correspondent or anyone else. But now that (as I have just ascertained) some enterprizing pirate has sold it as a novelty to the New York American, which no doubt believed it was dealing with me, it is quoted under a sensational headline as a contribution by me to a hostile newspaper.

In the same way, the preface to my Heartbreak House, published here months ago and extensively reviewed, has been flaming all over the British press for the past week as an article contributed by me to Die Neue Freie Presse of Vienna behind England's back for the comfort and support of her enemies.

In future, when I wish to impress English public opinion, I shall take care to send my views to foreign newspapers. It seems waste of time to address this unhappy nation in its own language.

Allow me to add that I did not attack Federal Devolution. I am a Federalist, and therefore an anti-devolutionist. Federal Devolution is a contradiction in terms, and its vogue shews that its advocates understand neither federation nor devolution.

Since the article was published, Dublin Castle and its party have managed to change the situation in Ireland so much for the worse that nothing is now worth considering except the alternatives of a Reign of Terror in the Amritsar manner—or rather of two conflicting reigns of terror carried on by the Castle and the neo-Invincibles—and the election of a Constituent Assembly to define Irish self-determination.

Yours, &c.,

G. Bernard Shaw.

HOW IRELAND IMPRESSED MR CHESTERTON

Review of G. K. Chesterton's *Irish Impressions*.
The Irish Statesman, Dublin, 22 November 1919

These Irish impressions are not, as the title-page states, impressions by Mr Chesterton. They are impressions by Ireland on Mr Chesterton. I am tempted to recommend the book in which he has recorded them as a proof that an Englishman is a much pleasanter, jollier, kindlier human variety than an Irishman; and though I am checked by the reflection that all Englishmen are unfortunately not like Mr Chesterton, and that he describes himself as a blend of Scotch, French, and Suffolk Dumpling, still the net result is the sort of man that England can produce when she is doing her best. Like all such Englishmen he is a thoroughgoing Irish patriot, and will not hear of romantic Ireland being dead and gone. It exists still for him; and he holds us in an esteem which would make us blush if so conceited a nation knew how to blush, for we are very far from deserving it. Our vices are so obvious that they have troubled him, though they have not estranged him. Of Dublin he tells us faithfully that though the inhabitants can dream, they cannot sleep, having all the irritability of insomnia and all the meanness and jealousy of perpetual wideawakeness, and that they slander oneanother with an abominable ungenerousness. In Belfast he is staggered into laughter and horror at the mad pride and wicked selfishness of the purse-proud commercial Irish Calvinist; and if he had traveled south instead of north, he would have discovered that the kindlier life and thought of Catholic Ireland does not save it from the infatuate and deadly-sinful conviction that it lives in a world of its natural inferiors. Mr Chesterton is too kind, and too sensible of his position as an honored guest in Ireland, to put it quite so bluntly; but I am an Irishman and need not mince matters. I know what he means, and that he has said too little instead of too much. I am not implying that he has been insincere, or that he has stooped for a moment to blarney; but when I recall those few impish but deadly-well-aimed pages in Joan and Peter, in which

Mr H. G. Wells described that stone corridor from Donnybrook to Stillorgan which in England would be an open country road; reduced some of the heros of the 1916 rising to the dimensions of mischievous boys with catapults; and exposed the facile derision of Dublin as the ill-natured incontinence so much of it really is, I feel how enormously friendly Mr Chesterton has been, even though he has spoken a more terrible word than any that fell from Mr Wells, by frankly and gravely saying that he found every fine quality in Dublin except charity. If he could have said that he had found nothing else, we could have held up our heads before him.

Mr Chesterton begins with a *fantasia* on Browning's theme, the Statue and the Bust. The statue is George II in Stephen's Green, and the bust is Mangan.[1] It is, like all Mr Chesterton's *fantasias*, a very pretty one; but it is foreign to Dublin. It presents the brazen George as an insult to our nationality. I ask Mr Chesterton to consider this a little more curiously. Human feeling is not rooted in mere politics. The fact that the man on the horse was meant to represent a foreign tyrant has no effect on the Dublin child—and it is as a little child that the Dubliner first sees George prancing in the eye of heaven. Lives there the child, Irish or English, who does not rejoice in a gigantic toy soldier, with horse and sword all complete, or who does not recoil in terror and loathing from that unnatural thing, a black metal head with the face of a schoolmaster and no body? Equestrian statues are always romances to those who are brought up in their shadow, however infamous the name on the pedestal. It is usually in Latin; and anyhow, who knows or cares more about George II than that he risked his own skin in his battles; that the Irish brigade licked him at Fontenoy; and that he made a joke good enough to be made again by Abraham Lincoln? The only equestrian statue that has ever excited political feeling in Dublin is King William in College Green, who was not a German but a Dutchman, and was the Pope's ally to boot; and, curiously enough, the Irish Protestants have succeeded in making William so amusing that the most rabid Nationalists cannot feel really angry with him and the only attempt to blow up his statue was the work of the Prot-

1. James Clarence Mangan (1803–1849), Irish poet, is considered a precursor of the Irish Literary Revival because of his full translations and adaptations of traditional Irish themes in such poems as "Dark Rosaleen," "The Woman of Three Cows," and "A Vision of Connaught in the XIIIth Century."

estant students of Trinity College, Dublin. Could Mr Chesterton take even the Kaiser seriously if he had heard him from childhood described as "glorious, pious and immortal," and seen him daily in the costume of Julius Caesar on a horse engaged in demonstrating with his legs the geometrical heresy that two sides of a triangle are together equal to the third? No: in spite of Macaulay, William's glory will fade, and his piety become incomprehensible; but his immortality is assured as long as one stone of Dublin stands on another.

Besides, did not Mr Chesterton notice that Dublin is a perfect museum of Georgian art, especially the art of domestic architecture; so that you can find streets upon streets in which the hall doors, the fanlights, the steps, and the placing of the windows fascinate observant English connoisseurs like the walls of a picture gallery? Any attempt to disparage Georgian art in Dublin must be sternly silenced by shouts of "No Politics."

There is one other passage in which Mr Chesterton seems to write not only as an English stranger, but as one of our conquerors. It is perhaps the most surprising passage in the whole book. He speaks of "a horrible whisper which can scarcely now be stilled," of something "still too hideous to be easily believed." And what is this evil which blackens the sun for Mr Chesterton? Nothing but this, that "it is said, with a dreadful plausibility, that the Unionists were deliberately trying to prevent a large Irish recruitment, which would certainly have meant reconciliation and reform. In plain words, it is said that they were *willing to be traitors to England* if they could only still be tyrants to Ireland." But bless your eyes, Mr Chesterton, why not? The Belfast Unionists cannot be "traitors to England" simply because they are not Englishmen. Do you suppose that the use they make of the British army and the British fleet and the British Castle and the British Treasury and all the other weapons of the ascendancy is to serve England's ends, or that the intense scorn and self-righteousness, which you yourself felt to be infernal as it shews itself towards their own ragged townsmen no less than towards their Catholic fellow countrymen, changes to disinterested devotion when they turn their eyes to England? As far as they have any historical sense and self-denying fanaticism at all, their heros are Gustavus Adolphus, William III, and Frederick the Great. King George, not having been born in Belfast, and having often shaken hands openly with black Papists, is to them nothing but a recreant Defender of the Faith, a mere English Ritualist who has no true Orange respect for his coronation oath. A readiness to kick the English crown into the Boyne on the slightest tolerance of the Pope is the first test of a good Orangeman. England's loyalty to Ulster they understand; but Ulster's loyalty to England! God help your innocence, Gilbert Chesterton!

However, let me confess that in what I have just said, I am, for educational purposes, dealing with what Mr Chesterton says rather than [with] what he means. He is not really thinking of loyalty to England, but of loyalty to Christendom, as he conceives it. He has a theory of the war which in Ireland will seem to be little more than a bee in his bonnet. To that I should say that it is and it is not. I think Mr Chesterton is right in his generalization that in the war, though it was quite patently planned on both sides as an old-fashioned struggle for the Overbalance of Power, yet a triumph for the Hohenzollerns would have been a triumph for Dublin Castle and all that Dublin Castle stands for, a triumph of matter over spirit, of fact over faith, of despair over hope, of Caliban over Prospero. I myself took Mr Chesterton's line almost exactly in the matter of Irish recruiting, and it may interest him to know that I was baffled by the determination of the authorities not only to stop recruiting by going the wrong way about it, but to stop every attempt to go the right way about it. My stifled appeals[2] were in part almost paraphrases of Mr Chesterton. But I cannot agree with him that the materialistic side of the Renaissance began in Berlin, or that Machiavelli was a Pomeranian grenadier. The utmost any Irishman can concede to an English guest is that the English governing classes are no worse than the Prussian governing classes; and even this civility can hardly be justified except on the ground that both were as unscrupulous, as aggressive, and as—shall we say?—acquisitive as their opportunities made possible. Belfast is in a position to say to Mr Chesterton, "You want to hate the Germans? Look at home. And go down on your knees and pray that both German and Briton may escape justice and be saved by mercy." I cannot understand how a man of Mr

---

2. In addition to its apparent failure to make use of Shaw's recruiting-poster text (see p. 184, editors' note), Dublin Castle had, by quiet pressure, obliged the Abbey Theatre to cancel its proposed production of Shaw's recruitment play, *O'Flaherty V.C.*

Chesterton's moral genius can mistake the filthy rags of anti-German righteousness for good sense, much less for a philosophy of European history.

This queer anti-Prussian, anti-Semitic, pseudo-historical theory is oddly mixed up with an economic Utopia which Mr Chesterton and Mr Belloc call the Distributive State. To me, who have a rival Utopia, it seems to consist of a pound of trite sense, and several tons of the most dangerous error and the most frightful nonsense. The pound of sense is that every man shall have his own vine and his own fig tree and that none shall make him afraid. The error is that proprietorship is good for the soul. And the nonsense is that a decent civilization could be made by a hoard of small proprietors each squatting jealously on his own dunghill. I have often told Mr Chesterton that he would not believe all this if he were an Irishman. And now he has at last visited Ireland, and come back apparently without having exchanged a word with a peasant proprietor or with a priest. When at last he came up against his hobby, the Catholic Church, for which he has done everything except join it, he does not appear to have noticed it. He did find himself in a road with a big property in a neglected state on one side and several little properties well looked after (probably by co-operators) on the other. And he exclaims, "I told you so." He assumes that the minds of the little proprietors are so well culti-vated as their acres; but he does not seem to have put this assumption to the test of any personal intercourse with them. On that road he may have met, and I have no doubt did meet, certain men in black coats and clerical collars who had absolutely no property at all: men who, when the British Government paid them for acting as chaplains in the trenches, endorsed the cheque without taking the trouble to look at the amount, handed it over to the treasurer of their order, and never gave it another thought. To these destitute and miserable slaves—for such they must be if there is anything in Chesterbelloquacity—Mr Chesterton might in charity have addressed a few exhortations, in the manner of Tennyson's northern farmer, to save their souls by acquiring a little property. He could have easily called out the nearest peasant proprietor to give the unpropertied man an object lesson in the magic of property in its effect on the mind and character. But perhaps he tried, and the peasant would not come. There is nothing like peasant property for teaching people to keep themselves *to* themselves. If the peasant had come, it might have proved that his prosperity was due to his having allowed the I.A.O.S.[3] to corrupt his Robinson Crusoic independence of his neighbors. The I.A.O.S., I may inform Mr Chesterton (though I suspect him of knowing it), is an order of pestilent fellows who preach that it is the greatest possible mistake to own your own threshing machine, or your own churn, or your own horse, or your own steam engine. In my opinion it is a still greater mistake to own your own land, and the worst mistake of all to own your own soul. Anyhow, it is a historical fact beyond all question that England ruined Ireland and India by destroying the character and wrecking the happiness of their villagers, and that the precise method by which she did it was the substitution of private for communal property in land. The truth is, private property in the earth is contrary to commonsense and incompatible with human nature.

But all this affects only the first two little chapters of Mr Chesterton's book. The rest is delightful, deep, and spiritually nutritious. Some of it is better fun than any Irishman could make: for example, the story of the Unionist who was shot by the British troops, and Mr Chesterton's moralizing thereon. With a turn of the hand this extraordinarily skilful literary virtuoso, pretending all the time to be nothing but a carelessly jolly Englishman, misquotes Mr Yeats to shew that he can paraphrase him in as exquisite Irish English as Lady Gregory's, and makes us laugh, in the characteristic Irish manner, at some barbarous calamity that would make sane men grieve. He is enormously robust and exquisitely subtle (like Handel), as funny as a harlequinade and as serious as an epic, and doing it all with an immense goodhumor which prevents his prodigious cleverness from ever wearying or tiring you, and makes him a model guest because he is such a perfect host. The world is not half thankful enough for Chesterton; and I hope Ireland will not be among the ingrates; for no Irishman alive or dead has ever served her better and more faithfully with the pen than he.

3. The Irish Agricultural Organisation Society was founded in 1894 by Sir Horace Plunkett to develop a system of co-operative marketing for the Irish farmers and to improve the state of agriculture generally.

SOCIALISM AND IRELAND

A lecture delivered before the Fabian Society, 28 November 1919.
Supplement to *The New Commonwealth*, London, 12 December 1919

I have been now, I think, for thirtyfive years an assiduous speaker on all sorts of platforms in this country. I have spoken on almost every political subject under the sun. I am an Irishman and yet I find myself here speaking on the subject of Ireland for the first time in my life. Can you account for that? I am what you call a patriotic Irishman. I have an absolute conviction that in having been born in Ireland I enjoyed a very great privilege and honor. I pity all the rest of the world who happened to be born anywhere else. I take care to live in England, and on the whole I think I like Englishmen better than Irishmen. But I recognize that an Irishman is a grown-up person; I do not consider an Englishman that. I cannot. Part of his charm for me is that he is not grown-up; that he is a child in many ways intellectually. I like him all the better for that, just as you like children, but I tell you frankly that that is my attitude, and you may have noticed, those of you who have seen something of my platform work and occasionally read some of my writings, that that tone of encouraging and lecturing the English people occasionally does turn up. There, however, is another reason. I suppose if I had been an Englishman I should have lectured on Ireland and on Macedonia, in fact, on every place under the sun except England. Yet I am not quite sure about it, because the reason that one avoids Ireland as a subject is that it is an extraordinarily dull subject.

The Irish question is really, from the point of view of political science, quite the dullest question that there is on the face of the earth. The case of Ireland is certainly an urgent case, but it is an urgent case just exactly as a case of wife-beating is an urgent case. It is important that the wife-beating should be stopped; it is certain that the woman is suffering a good deal; it is possible she may be killed, and therefore it may be urgently necessary to take some means of putting a stop to it. But wife-beating is not in itself an interesting occupation. It does not present any kind of problem to the man with the genuinely active intellect. You know exactly what is the matter; what the remedy is. The whole thing is obvious; there is nothing to study in it, there is nothing to be said. That is exactly the case with Ireland. Everybody knows quite well what is the matter with Ireland, and everybody knows that if the grievance was removed, if Ireland was made self-governing and became free, it would be all right. But that is not very interesting. Everybody knows it, there is nothing to be said about it, and the reason that nevertheless there is a good deal of talk about Ireland is that people have a certain crude taste for suffering. They interest themselves in Ireland just as they interest themselves in the Chamber of Horrors at Madame Tussaud's. It is rather like the case of Christianity. You find that what is called Christian Europe never does anything that Christ told it to do; never concerns itself about Christ's teaching. It is enormously interested in Christ because of the fact that he was put to a very cruel death. He was crucified. Ireland has been crucified for centuries, and that is the whole secret of the interest that there is in it. And people are not conscious of the nature of the interest. They feel the sensation of the suffering; their sympathies are moved by it; their sensational faculty is roused by it; and I am afraid the result is when they see a lecture on Ireland advertized they pay money under the impression that they are going to hear something interesting. But they are not. As a matter of fact, I shall have for this evening, at any rate, to be comparatively dull, and allow you to draw the moral of my dulness.

There is, of course, another thing which makes me always shy of subjects like Ireland, that is to say, of subjects of suffering. The course of my political activities has led me across a great many victims of tyranny in my life, and I have learned to beware of them. Victims always let you down if you take up their cause, unless you take it up in a purely abstract way. I remember quite in the early days of my Socialistic career there were certain unpleasant things that happened in Barcelona, and in the prison fortress near Barcelona there was a celebrated case called the case of the Spanish Anarchists, and a certain sensation was made by the fact that some of those anarchists were horribly tortured in that prison. Three of the men who were tortured came to this country in order to see whether they could not work up some sympathy here for their Socialist comrades, and it fell to my lot and that of my friend Mr Henry Salt, who is the Secretary of the Humanitarian League, to go and interview these three men who had been horribly tortured. Salt, naturally, being humanitarian, did not like the task, and I, being a sensitive sort of person, did not like it either. However, we made an appointment, and as the Movement at that time was not able to command halls like this, we made the appointment in the open air, opposite Apsley House, Piccadilly. I remember one fine summer day Salt and myself walking through the Park, very much troubled; we imagined the men we were going to meet. We could see those dark-haired Spaniards, their white faces, and the traces of torture, and we felt we would have to be as sympathetic as possible. We came out of the Green Park, crossed to Apsley House, and saw three robust, jolly, florid men, with sandy hair, roaring with laughter. We looked inquiringly to see what they were laughing at, and they all simultaneously took off their hats, advanced, and announced themselves as the tortured anarchists. Well, there was nothing more to be said. Part of the business that Salt and I met them on was to make arrangements for their appearance at a public meeting to engage the sympathies of the British public, and at the first glance one perceived it was not the slightest use. Practically, I should have had to go down to the theatre, hire three actors and get them properly made up as tortured Spaniards, with dark wigs, and that would have been our only chance. But, you see, that was only one of many experiences. It is a mistake to suppose that men or women who have suffered very much are interesting on that account. If that were so it might be worth while to suffer. But the fact of the matter is people are worse for it. Michael Davitt was an interesting man; he would have been more interesting if he had not spent seven years in prison.[1] I have met with Russian women who spent twenty years in prison for teaching children to read and write. One sympathized and felt indignation; nonetheless that did not make the woman herself any more interesting; it made her less interesting, because to be shut up for twenty years in a prison cell instead of being out in the world getting experience does not make you an interesting person.

That is the last reason I shall trouble you with for avoiding the suffering of Ireland. Ireland's sufferings do not make her more interesting, they

1. Michael Davitt, Irish nationalist, served seven years of a fifteen-year sentence for importing firearms into Ireland. He was chiefly famous for having founded the Land League in 1879. His autobiographical book, *Leaves from a Prison Diary*, was reviewed anonymously by Shaw in *Time*, London, February 1885.

make her less so. If you compare the tremendous progress that has been made in certain material aspects and certain developments and changes of social life in America, in Japan, in Germany, in Italy, for example, during the XIX century, or that part of it we can remember, those changes make them more interesting. You see that those countries are developing; every time you visit them there is something new there. You see what modern culture and civilization is; it is constantly alive and constantly changing. If you go to any of them the country has that particular interest for you.

One of the advantages that I have as a student of history from having been born in Ireland is that I was literally born in the XVII century; that is to say, my father's house from the snuffers on the drawing room table to the sanitation in the yard was just precisely the sort of house that Samuel Pepys lived in. There was perhaps one difference, the house was lighted with coal gas, which was then rather a novelty, but except for these gas lights the life there was exactly the XVII century life, and it is so very largely still. If you go from here to Ireland you get back into the XVII and XVIII century atmosphere. You find a curious ease of life. It is a country of easy living and easy dying, and it is sometimes a very healthy thing to get back into that sort of atmosphere. The people being poor, and not expecting oneanother to be rich, they have a good deal of time for thinking and a good deal of time for talking. Let me give you a curious example of that. I was lately in Ireland and was talking to a man whose condition might strike you, from my first description, as that of a very miserable man. He possessed nothing; he had no money; he had no house belonging to himself. He was dressed in a costume which he was not allowed to choose for himself, a sort of uniform. When I met him somebody had given him a little money to take a holiday with. He had no property whatever of his own. If I had handed him a cheque for £100—which I did not do—he would not have looked at the amount of money on the check; he would have seen how I had spelt his name, endorsed the cheque, and handed it over to somebody else, that is to say, to the principal of his order. He belonged to a religious order and I, although a Socialist, still had a commercial feeling, surely this is a terrible thing for a man to be absolutely without property of any kind. I asked him what it felt like. "Oh, well," he said, "of course, I havnt a care in the world. I havnt to think about anything." What he meant was he hadnt to think about the things that Englishmen are always worrying about from one end of their lives to the other, their clothes, their houses, their respectability, and the things that fill up an Englishman's life so much that he has not time to think of anything else. This man had plenty of time to think of other things. I said, "Are there any drawbacks to this condition in which you live?" He said: "Yes, there is a drawback; this kind of life does develop one's individuality to an extraordinary degree. The fact of the matter is there is not a single man over the age of thirtyfive in my order who is not a perfectly hopeless crank!"

I invite your consideration, because you see that although this man belonged to a religious order, and had taken vows of poverty, he was very comfortable in consequence. Most of the population of Ireland, not having taken any vows at all of the kind, nevertheless might just as well have taken them, because on the whole they are terribly poor people, and, as I repeat, are living in the old XVII century way, which is comparatively an easy way. Therefore, they have a very considerable vivacity of interest and a strongly-developed individuality, and one consequence of that is that if you take an English town and an Irish town—a small country town of about equal size—you will discover that in the English town all the lawyers' work that is done there can be done by a solicitor visiting the town for three hours in one day of the week. A town of exactly similar size in Ireland will keep six solicitors in flourishing practice. If there is any young gentleman here who is beginning a legal career and finds getting on is rather slow in this country, he has nothing to do but go to Ireland and he will find as much business as he can possibly transact.

Now I am purposely rubbing into you this existence of people who have got a certain ease of life and a very highly developed individuality and plenty of intellectual activity which they very largely use in, let us call it, litigiousness. They are extremely fond of the law, as I pointed out, because I should mention that just exactly as you see in the town six solicitors in flourishing practice, if you go on to the church you will see a notice on the church door: "Absolution for the crime of perjury is reserved to the Bishop." The two things are connected intimately.

You will find later on in my lecture that all this has a very considerable bearing on the future of the two countries, and has had a considerable bearing on them in the past, but for the moment I want to point out to you that this perfect development of individuality, all this cleverness, has got nothing to bite on in this XVII century country except the national griev-

ance. They all feel that the first thing to be done is to get rid of that grievance, to make their country a free and self-governing country, and for the
rest they have to employ their restless intellects on concerns—I do not
want to say on dreams—but really on a sort of restless intellectual discussion of matters that only concern themselves. It does not succeed in making them interesting to other people. If you pay a visit to Ireland, you are
taken at first by all that extremely rapid, very clever kind of gabble; they
talk and tell stories and are amusing for a while, but after a little time you
discover the interest does not really sustain itself; you only discover it is in
many ways an easy and pleasant country to live in. Many parts of it are
extremely beautiful. Even parts not beautiful have a peculiar charm you
get nowhere else, a sort of legendary charm. A mountain which is 1,000
ft. high in Ireland looks 5,000 ft. high. In climbing the mountain, when
you get three-quarters of the way to the top you get frightened and believe you are lost. There are all sorts of curious things, and round the
coast there are places of extraordinary beauty and barrenness. You will
see later on what are the consequences of Ireland being a country of
clever people, and also a country which in many ways is a country of
great amenities for the purposes of living, because among them I must
include a climate which makes it possible for a man to dispense with a
great deal of the coal he has to burn here, and a great deal of the clothes
he has to wear. You can live more cheaply comfort for comfort—or
rather discomfort for discomfort—in Ireland than in England.

You will see that a country like this is not ripe for Socialism. It is still
very largely an agricultural country, and as an agricultural country it has
suffered during the XIX century all the extremities of landlordism at its
very worst. In England a landlord is expected to build barns for his tenants; to make improvements of various kinds; if he lets a farm he is supposed more or less to equip it as a farm before he lets it. The Irish landlord never did anything of the kind. The Irish landlord simply took his
rack-rent[2] and the tenant had to do everything. No matter how many improvements the tenant left those were taken by the landlord. There is cultivated land which you may see in Ireland; you will see it on the coast of

2. In general the term *rack-rent* means any excessive or extortionate rent, but in
Ireland it described a practice on the part of landlords of raising the rent of any
tenant who increased the productivity of his land, thereby penalizing rather than
rewarding hard work.

Galway Bay: stone fields—literally field on field with walls between them to give them the air of a field, and they are all stone, and the hill in the background has a solid cap of stone. You stare at it in amazement; you discover there are cattle apparently browsing on the stone, and goats. How they manage to get a living you cannot understand, but they do. It has often happened in Ireland some unfortunate man has gone and cleared away the stones from a place of this kind with his own hand and turned it into a little holding. The moment he had done that the landlord came down and charged him rent, and if he could not afford it he turned him out and got somebody else who could. The ground was always rack-rented. The highest rent payable was got. The rent had reference to the very utmost the tenant could pay. The result was the cultivator of the land was really forced, according to his lights, to cultivate it to the very utmost extent he was capable of, compelled to employ labor on it, to do his very best, and even then the landlord only left him the barest and most miserable living. Bear that fact in mind, because a good deal hangs on it.

At about the year 1870 England began to have rather a bad conscience about Ireland, and by the time we came to the beginning of the century, about the year 1900, I think you would have found throughout Ireland a disposition to believe that, although England had ill-treated Ireland very horribly in the past, nevertheless for the thirty years or so before that she had been honestly, in her own stupid way, trying to atone for the past, and to improve matters in Ireland. I need hardly tell you that at the present moment any idea of that kind has completely and utterly disappeared. Nevertheless, it may be within your recollection that, as I say, at the beginning of the century that was a very prevalent opinion. Now, how had the English dealt with the Land question? Had they made an advance in the direction of Socialism? No. They did the thing in the very stupidest possible way. They bought all the landlords out, with English money; they took some of it from Ireland to begin with, I admit, but still it was done very largely with English money. They bought all the land from the landlords and then gave that back to the actual cultivators, to the tenants; gave them opportunities of buying their own holdings and on very easy terms compared to any terms they had ever experienced before. They were to pay over the purchase money mainly by instalments spread over a number of years. The landlords were given land stock at a respectable percentage, and then England felt: Now we have settled the Irish question. Of course, they had only pushed the Land question in Ireland about a century back from the prospect of settlement.[3]

Why do I call this an extraordinarily stupid settlement? If it had been an intelligent one England would have bought the land of Ireland, but instead of throwing it back unconditionally to the cultivators, and leaving them with the screw of the landlord, which used to make them cultivate the land, taken off, and with their standard of livelihood degraded to the utmost possible point humanity could bear; instead of doing that, which was a crime, they would have given them the land conditionally. They would have said: We will give you the land, but we will require from every man who has so much land a certain annual product, and he must produce that. The rent we put upon him shall be on a sliding scale, that is to say, the rent will go up as his product goes down, in such a way that if he does not cultivate the land to the utmost extent he will lose his land. They did not do that. The consequences, of course, were inevitable. Instead of cultivating their land to the utmost, and raising their standard of living, living more expensively, these people cultivated the land to about three-quarters or even less of the extent to which it could be cultivated, and simply went on living in their own bare way, except that they were able to live it with a great deal of leisure. They liked a good talk and they got a good talk. They used not to have the good talk before, because they were always slaving for the landlord, but they took it out in talk instead of taking it out in the English way in product. If they had been forced to work the whole time they would have become as stupid as the English, probably, but would have lived very much better, and on the whole they would have raised the level of civilization.

But that was the way the thing was done, in that hopeless, thoughtless way that everything is done in this country. The Socialists remonstrated. Many of the Irish members at that time were quite well instructed in the Land question. They were Henry Georgites. They knew this was no so-

---

3. The land problem in Ireland was dealt with by two great land acts, one identified with Gladstone in 1881 and the other with George Wyndham in 1903. The first established the three F's—Fair Rent, Fixity of Tenure, and Free Sale—which amounted in effect to joint ownership by landlord and tenant. The second act, as Shaw described, abolished dual ownership by instituting a system of voluntary purchase by the tenant, with the government paying the landlord an amount equal to the difference between the terms offered by the tenant and those demanded by the landlord.

lution of the Land question. They knew it was simply beginning land-lordism over again. I myself am an Irish landlord, and I can quite well remember once being in Ireland and suddenly getting an idea, I will go and see my estate. It flashed on me I was in the neighborhood of it, and accordingly I went and saw the gentleman who really looked after the estate, my agent [William Fitzmaurice of Carlow Town]. He introduced me to his son, a young man about twenty at that time. I was naturally interested. I said, "What are you going to make of your son?" "Oh, land agent, of course." "A land agent?" I said. "Surely that is all over. The landlords are all gone?" "Oh, no," he said, "not at all; it will be all right presently. Meantime, I get a percentage from the Government for collect-ing the instalment of the purchase money, and so on, and the old estates are coming together again." I took occasion traveling about the country a little to speak to people when visiting some old place or other; some guide or farmer would talk to me, would tell me about "land grabbing," as they called it. They said: Fellows come here and stand a lot of beer and make themselves popular. Then, of course, a good many of these people have got land and they dont know how to manage it. They sell it to anybody who comes along. These fellows come and buy and buy, and the old pro-cess is beginning again. The estates are getting re-integrated, and if mat-ters go on as they are at present it is only a question of time when you will have all the old landlordism, but with a new set of landlords. But the landlord is always the same sort of person, and his relations with his ten-ants always really the same thing. And that is your Land Purchase scheme. That is how the thing exists at the present time in Ireland, and, as you see, instead of its being anything like an advance towards Socialism it has developed back again to the business of the big estates. Even that may not be a very bad thing for the country at large, because you will very likely get a larger yield out of the large estates when they have drifted into the hands of more capable men for a time. At least it will be a better state of things than a number of small holdings in the hands of compara-tively incompetent men.

Now, the industrial problem in Ireland is not really different from the industrial problem anywhere else. In Belfast you have great shipyards and factories, you have the capitalist system in full swing. The people are extremely poor; the sweating is very bad, but there is nothing new in that. That exists in England. It exists everywhere. Therefore, the solution of that problem is not one which is in any special sense an Irish solution. What is peculiar, of course, are the political conditions of Ireland at the present time, and they are very distinctly different to the political conditions in England. You have in Ireland a police force which is larger than any other police force in the world relatively to the population. If you take policemen per head of population there is a larger police force in Ireland than anywhere else in the world, although Ireland is, politics apart, a comparatively crimeless country. In order to protect these policemen you have an army of 60,000 men. The lot of the police and the soldiers is not a very pleasant one. For instance, in an Irish town there are a number of these soldiers stationed; they naturally have a very dull time. They are unpopular; they are hated. They are the British army. You know what a soldier's life is, it is pretty dull even in Ireland. The soldier wants to go out for a walk occasionally; he wants to go out with a girl. The only girls he can go with are Irish girls. If an Irish girl, in many Irish towns now, takes a walk with an English soldier her own countryfolk spit in her face. Under these circumstances, the young lady does not take a walk with an English soldier, and if she does it is very unpleasant for the English soldier, because he is called upon as a man of honor to fight the gentleman who spits in the face of the lady he is with, and as the gentleman who does it is practically supported by the whole of the town it is an unpleasant job for the soldier. He is apt, under those circumstances, to become a bit of a misogamist. He takes his walks in solitude.

I will give you another incident which will illustrate what goes on. A man wrote to me the other day about some theatrical business. He mentioned incidentally that he wanted to do some theatrical touring in Ireland. He explained to me he had been taking round a concert party in Ireland, and he sang a patriotic song. He was immediately seized and sentenced to two years' hard labor. They kept him in prison for nine or ten months until his health had completely broken down. In the meantime his wife had tried to keep the concert party going, but it was invariably attacked by practically bayonet and baton charges. When the concerts could not be put a stop to by milder means they were stopped in that way. He came out with his health broken, and tried to get on again. But it was no use. In anything of a musical nature it was immediately assumed he was going to sing this patriotic song again, and the 60,000 soldiers and large police force, all equipped with the resources of civilization developed in the Great War—they have got aeroplanes, tanks, and everything of the kind—were all brought to bear. This sort of thing is continually going on.

Now, a country in these circumstances is not governed at all. You cannot govern a country in that way. Ireland is a country which really does, from the character of the people, require a strong Government. The Irish have a strong sense of law and they like a strong Government. They can understand law better than many other nations, and they would bear a more comprehensive code of laws probably than any other nation in Europe, and yet there is virtually no law at all. The reason of that is that no Government can possibly be strong without the consent of the people, without the support of the people. The way a Government enforces its authority is through the police, but how do the police enforce its authority? They can enforce its authority in this country not because of the policeman really, but because of the citizen who will always call the policeman when the law is broken. That is the real condition through which you can have authority in a country. The moment you produce a state of things in which the citizen will not call the policeman then your police are no use at all. The only disobediences to the law which can be put down are those disobediences which a policeman happens actually to witness himself, but the policeman may be standing there in the street and the law may be broken in every single house in the street, and that is a very common state of things in Ireland at the present time, if you call breaches of the law conspiracies of one kind or another against the Government. Here, if in every house people began to commit crimes, somebody would throw up a window and call the police, and the crimes would be stopped. But in Ireland nobody will call the police, nobody will give away another Irishman to the policeman, and the result is you have a miserably weak Government, and you always have had it as long as you have had that system of coercion. Here you have every sort of liberty trampled on. You have people in a state of the most furious hatred of this country; all these petty persecutions, annoyances, these flingings of men into jail, putting down newspapers, charging political meetings with bayonet and baton charges have produced a condition of the most furious revolt against the British Government, and, of course, you have the governing class in this country quite deliberately and unmistakeably going on with that in order to provoke revolts against them which will enable them to say it is impossible to give Ireland self-government. It is not concealed by the people who are absolutely determined to maintain the existing state, the rule of Dublin Castle.

Well, now, in such a political milieu as that, with all that going on, what is the remedy which our Coalition Government is likely to apply? To the best of my information they find themselves in what is almost an impossibility of coming to any agreement as to the settlement of the question at all. Nevertheless, Mr Lloyd George thinks he has got a House of Commons which will pass anything he introduces, and he has very good warrant for that belief. Therefore, I believe what is contemplated at the present time is the establishment of two Parliaments in Ireland, one for Ulster—I dont know whether for the six counties only or the whole of Ulster[4]—and another for the South of Ireland; and, those two Parliaments being established, they are to try whether they cannot in some way or other manage to evolve a council of some kind which will be virtually a Parliament for the whole of Ireland. That is as far as they have got at present, and, as far as my information goes, that is what is being contemplated. I do not quite see these two Parliaments. In the first place, I suppose, if such a state of things as that was established, the Ulster Parliament would immediately organize its own army and proceed to the conquest of the whole of Ireland. Already you will see in Ireland orders given to Sir Edward Carson's forces in Cork and Southern towns in view of the conquest of Cork by Belfast; and since in the speech which was delivered from the chair some question was raised as to whether Belfast was an Irish town, let me tell you it is about the most Irish town in Ireland. Nothing can be more intensely Irish than Orange. In fact, it is almost agreed today that the south of Ireland is not as Irish as Belfast. Do not make any mistake about this. Just go and tell a Belfast man he is not an Irishman; tell him he is an Englishman and he will probably knock you down. That is about the last thing he is prepared to stand. Unfortunately, what misleads you is the fact that, in addition to those quite harmless XVII century relics I told you of at the beginning, there is another XVII century condition which prevails in Ireland, and that is there are wars of religion; they still go on.

4. Present-day Ulster—the result of the partition in 1922—comprises only six of the nine counties that make up the traditional Ulster.

Take this business of trying to settle the Irish question. The two Parliaments is a solution which will not be accepted for one moment either by the North or the South. They wont want to make it work. I have suggested that Ulster, under the leadership of Carson, would probably proceed to the conquest of the South. There is no doubt whatever what the South would say. The Southern Parliament would immediately declare itself an independent republic. And possibly a good many people who propose that solution are quite aware it will happen and want it to happen, because there are many people like a certain Scotch officer who once said to me: "I would not have all this nonsense about Home Rule. I would give Ireland complete freedom at once, then we could reconquer her and make an end of the business."

What is the real solution of the mere political question, as far as I have been able to work it out, must be begun in England. England, after all, suffers a great deal more from the want of Home Rule in direct political ways than Ireland does. There is no English Parliament. There is a Parliament which is neither an Imperial Parliament nor a Federal Parliament, neither an Irish, Scottish, nor English Parliament. It tries to do all sorts of jobs and the result is the work of England is not done by its Parliament. What England wants extremely badly is an English Parliament for English affairs, to get Irish, Scottish, and Imperial affairs taken off the shoulders of that Parliament by a higher body, which I do not think will be an imperial body but which clearly ought to be a federal body. I am convinced the proper solution is the federation of the two islands.

There is, of course, always the alternative in Irish minds which now fills them, of complete independence. I am not fond of that solution because I have seen far too much of this wonderful independence, of the independence of Belgium and of Greece during the last war. That is not the sort of independence that has any particular fascination for me. On the whole I would rather incorporate myself on honorable terms with some larger and more powerful unit, and I have always said that I think Ireland ought to remain in the British Commonwealth, but on exactly the same terms that England or Scotland remains in it. My business is to try and rouse the English to the degree to which they suffer by the want of an English Parliament; then I look forward to the fact that you will get practically—I dont like to use the term Dominion Home Rule because it is ambiguous, but still I do not suppose Ireland is going to wait, but if you put Ireland more or less into the position that Australia and Canada are in, roughly speaking, you will make a beginning. If you did that I believe the logic of events would very speedily compel federation. Of course, you cannot put Ireland virtually in the position of Australasia and Canada for this reason, that Australasia and Canada are by nature and geography really independent. Canada could cut the painter tomorrow if we oppressed her; if any attempt were made to treat Canada as Ireland is being treated, with anything like a tenth of the tyranny imposed on Ireland at present, Canada would have several alternatives. It could, for instance, offer to join the United States. If the United States said: No, thank you, we dont want to be embroiled with England, you had better set up independently for yourselves, Canada could immediately set up as an independent republic, and as an independent republic in North America it would have the protection of the Monroe Doctrine just as completely as if it were part of the United States. Also, if Australia were determined to cut loose it would be very difficult to prevent her doing so. Ireland is not in that position. Ireland is too close. She has no way really of detaching herself from England. It is not to her interest to have a separate defence system. It is strategically impossible for England to allow her any genuine independence in that way, and therefore she must remain in very much closer relations with the Mother Island than Canada and Australia, and the solution is the federation of these particular islands.

I do not want to elaborate that. I want to come to what is perhaps the most important part of my lecture, and that is this: What is it that has produced all this political chaos that I have been describing in Ireland? Why is it that Ireland is still in the XVII century? What has happened to Ireland? Why has this always been going on, at least within the modern period of history? The reason is the reason I gave at the earlier part of my lecture. Ireland is an easy and a cheap country to live in. Irish labor is cheap, is frightfully industrious. It is perfectly horrible the way the Irishman works. You never get an Englishman to do it. He is also very docile. With any sort of decent treatment the Irish are a people who have a sort of tribal habit of making the nearest person in command their chieftain. Furthermore, there is a great deal of intellectual vivacity in Ireland, a great development of men's individuality, and the combination of these conditions has invariably produced this result, that the moment England let Ireland alone and gave her a chance she began instantly to develop industrially to such an extent that under the capitalist competitive system England began to discover Ireland was taking her markets away from her. Accordingly, you find whereas up to the time of the Restoration in the XVII century—you may say it is roughly true that up to that time there was no legislation, no industrial or financial legislation for Ireland that was different from the legislation imposed on England—the legislation applied to both countries alike; there was no grievance in that way, but as the capitalist system began to develop from the Restoration onwards, there was a long series of Acts of Parliament by which England was deliberately destroying the growing industries of Ireland, and it was an inevitable thing, having the power to do it, that she should do so, because it really was a question of the Irish taking away the industries of the English farmer, and, accordingly, the English capitalists and employers and the workmen themselves objected to have the bread taken out of their mouths. In short, Ireland is a sort of Western China. You know the horror we have of the Chinese because of their industry and virtue and hard work. Under the capitalist system, where men have to compete with oneanother instead of helping oneanother to live, where they are all snatching bread out of oneanother's mouths, we have found white men cannot stand up against the competition of the Chinaman, therefore he is excluded from Australia and from the western coasts of America. In just the same way the English have had to practically suppress the Irish. There has been a continual series of uprisings and flourishings of Irish industries and a continual throwing of them back by legislation deliberately aimed at the destruction of Irish life. Therefore, Ireland has been compulsorily and by force of arms, by the bludgeon and the bayonet, deliberately kept back in the XVII century.

Home Rule is not going to cure this. Supposing, for instance, you settle the question. Supposing our plan, the Fabian Federal plan, succeeds. What then? Then Ireland will begin to go ahead. Then what will the alternatives be? You will find the first alternative will be that England, having set Ireland free and made it prosperous, may then deliberately go and reconquer and destroy and suppress it again. Remember that that is not a new thing; that has happened before. Remember that in the XVIII century Ireland really did get a sort of independent Irish Parliament, and at that time, just before the Great War, Ireland suddenly sprang into great prosperity. The result was the Act of Union and the deliberate suppres-

sion and destruction of the prosperity that had arisen in Ireland under the
Irish Parliament. History sometimes repeats itself. In transactions of that
kind English history does repeat itself very often, and I am afraid if you
are not careful it will repeat itself once too often. But I have to face that
first alternative. The whole thing is brought off beautifully; Ireland gets
self-government, begins to prosper. England discovers Irish capitalists
and labor are taking away orders and work from English firms, and the
cry will be raised again that protective legislation shall be introduced.
Remember, at this present moment you are preventing Ireland from trad-
ing with any foreign country. Ireland is not allowed to send any goods
anywhere except through England. That is the existing law. It is only a
specimen of what is going on. If you do that out of jealousy of Irish
industry, you wont be made into different human beings by Home Rule,
but Home Rule will make the Irish into a different set of human beings to
the extent that it will make them much more successful and dangerous
competitors with your commerce. Therefore, you may go and destroy
Ireland again. The only question is whether the public opinion of the
world will allow you to do that. Ireland cannot prevent you. You can destroy Ireland from one end to the other without landing a single Englishman on her shores. You can get your fleet, your seaplanes, your 600-lb.
bombs, and all that sort of thing, and you can do it without running any
risk, and, as I say, there is only the Ireland beyond the seas, the Irish in
America and Australia, who too have their sympathies. You have your
position in the world to consider, and they may disapprove, but it is a
question whether they would go to war with England in order to disapprove. I state that as an alternative.

The second alternative—I am going to give you three—would be an
immense immigration in Ireland. Ireland, as you know, has been emptied
by emigration and is being emptied by ten per cent. of the population
every year. The tide may turn the other way. Capitalists, discovering everything that I have been telling you about Ireland, cheap labor, intelligent management, a very pleasant place to live in, an easy climate, and so
on, may say: Let us go to Ireland. There are magnificent harbors all along
the West Coast. You can put up miles of docks and shipbuilding yards
right on the Atlantic. Any amount of opening for commerce. Therefore,
I hold out the prospect to you of an emptying England and a filling-up
Ireland. A delightful place to live in, a climate that makes your brains

more flexible, the end of the matter being England will remain as a sort of Siberia, a place with a hard climate relatively, where probably Ireland will become the centre of the whole Western Empire, and you will send your convicts to live in England, make it a convict settlement like Siberia, all undesirable characters sent back to live in the fog. It is not altogether a joke. Things of that kind have happened in the history of the world before. At the same time, there is the alternative of suppression, and there is a third alternative—that alternative, ladies and gentlemen, is Socialism.

THE REIGN OF TERROR

The Irish Statesman, Dublin, 3 January 1920

The British Occupation of Ireland has just produced an attempt to assassinate the Viceroy; and it is not the Occupation's fault, but Lord French's luck (on which I cordially and unreservedly congratulate him), that the attempt failed.[1] The incident is no more surprising than an outbreak of smallpox would be in a district where the Public Health Authority had not only neglected its duties, but sedulously introduced and enforced a series of anti-sanitary measures. When such incidents used to occur in Russia before any considerable investments of French or British capital had taken place there, the English newspapers, notably The Times, used simply to ask the Tsardom what it expected if it suppressed every popular liberty. If men are treated in certain ways, some of them will retaliate by assassination as certainly as they will get drunk if sufficient rum is poured down their throats.

The mischief of political coercion in a body like the British Empire is that the coercion cannot be organized so as to stop short of the extreme provocation at which bombs and pistols come up just as turnips and scarlet runners will when they are duly sown. The present case is an example of this. The Castle had gone pretty far; but still there was no reason in Ireland why Lord French should have been shot at last week in particular. The pot was seething, but it was not boiling over. Unfortunately, something occurred which was quite beyond the Castle's control. That something was the disclosure of the proceedings of General Dyer at Amritsar in India.[2] General Dyer [banned] an Indian Nationalist meeting. The inhabitants disregarded the proclamation and held the meeting. General Dyer saw that if he took this defiance lying down, he should look like a

1. On 19 December 1919, members of the Irish Republican Army attempted to assassinate Lord French, lord-lieutenant of Ireland, at Ashtown, a few miles outside Dublin. Lord French escaped without injury, but one of his assailants was shot dead.

2. An inquiry at Lahore in November 1919, at which General Reginald Dyer testified to the extreme repressive measures he had taken at Amritsar, resulted in his being ordered to resign his command.

fool. He does not seem to have foreseen what he looks like now, after asserting himself very effectually. He went to the meeting with a force of magazine rifles, and poured ten minutes' rapid fire into the crowd. This operation was a complete success. The meeting was broken up, and five hundred Indians will never disregard a proclamation again, unless indeed they defy the summons of the last trumpet. The wounded were not succored by their conquerors. The General, whose logic is sound and precise, remarked that "there were hospitals," and that it was for the civil authorities to clear away the *débris* of the meeting.

I must admit that there was nothing incorrect in this military operation. It is the business of the military to kill people who will not obey the Government. In ordering his troops to "shoot good and strong," General Dyer's conduct was entirely dutiful and proper to his profession, though his grammar was deplorable. Had he hesitated to shoot, the Government would have fallen into derision and contempt.

But that was not all. There was a certain street in which an offence had been committed, and along this street General Dyer insisted that all Indians should crawl on their hands and knees. Now, this was not a military operation. The fact that it was done by a military officer no more constitutes it one than the hamstringing of an Indian would be a surgical operation if it were done by a doctor. There is nothing in the military code about denying to men the upright posture which distinguishes men from beasts. There is nothing in any civil code legalizing such a penalty. It is a deliberate insult to humanity: a proclamation that its victim is a lower creature, of an inferior and servile species, without rights, without honor, existing only by the sufferance of those who have the power to impose such humiliation on him before the whole world.

This, and not the ten minutes' rapid fire (which is at least a thing that honorable men do to honorable men in war), made every citizen of the world who valued liberty and human dignity see red. It revolted England. What effect must it have had in Ireland, where every man knows that General Dyer's next command may be where General Maxwell's was in Easter 1916, and that there is no military distinction between the Nationalist Indian and the Nationalist Irishman? Dublin Castle did not foresee that, and could not have prevented it in any case. The temperature arranged for by the Castle was under 112; but the news from Amritsar sent it up fifty degrees, and the result was that Lord French, safe enough a week before, found himself under fire again at closer quarters than at Ypres.

It is idle to deal with a situation of this kind by platitudinous expressions of horror at the wickedness of assassination. This is not merely because it is so like Joseph Surface talking to Lady Teazle about his honor. It is because it evades the question really at issue. It is [to] the honor of The Times that it no longer suspects the leaders of the Irish nation of complicity in this attempted murder as it suspected and accused Parnell of complicity in the murder of Lord Frederick Cavendish. The Unionists of both islands may well exult in the blow the assassins have dealt to Mr de Valera no less than to Sir Horace Plunkett. They have missed their enemy and hit their friends, as the manner of desperados and fanatics is. And yet, though all the Nationalists in Ireland would hang them for being fools as heartily as the Unionists would hang them for being rebels and murderers, they are quite likely to get off scot free, because there is no Irish Government to which they can be denounced by the Nationalists, and no likelihood of the Unionists knowing where to put a finger on them. The Government can do nothing but offer a reward and a pardon; but can it protect an informer? No doubt there are Irishmen who would accept either or both if they could do so safely; but the precedent of James Carey is not encouraging.[3]

What, then, is the reasonable majority to do? Nothing, as far as I can see, except organize secret tribunals, after the manner of the Ku Klux Klan or the Ribbon Lodges, to deal with their own desperados. And if such a thing were done, these secret tribunals would very soon abuse the irresponsibility of their secrecy and become a worse evil than the disease they were founded to remedy. Sinn Fein could offer Lord French a bodyguard pledged to share all his risks from bullet and bomb; but would he accept it? *Could* he accept it without making the King ridiculous? There is absolutely no remedy except the cessation of the present political relations between the two countries, which are simply criminal relations, incapable of breeding anything outside their own kind.

3. James Carey was one of the Invincibles, an extremist organization responsible for the murder of the chief secretary and the undersecretary of Ireland in the Phoenix Park, Dublin, on 6 May 1882. Carey tried to save himself by turning queen's evidence on his accomplices, but he was murdered in revenge by an Invincible aboard a ship bound for Cape Town.

Meanwhile, we must all, at heavy disadvantages, do what we can to stop explosions of mere blind hatred. Assassination will not temper despotism: it will exasperate it and make it provoke more assassination, imprisoning Ireland in a vicious circle which is also an odious one. And it will make certain mischievous acts of a less sensational sort seem harmless by comparison. For instance, just before the news about Lord French came to London, The Times had made it known that Tuam was boycotting Belfast commercially. Nothing more stupid could be conceived: England's policy of destroying German trade and cutting the throats of her best continental customers is wisdom and common sense in comparison. In making Belfast independent of Tuam by forcing her to sell her goods elsewhere (probably in England) Tuam is deliberately working for the partition of Ireland. Spite is a bad counselor; and if Ireland loses her temper Ireland is lost. But who will listen to a lecture to Tuam when there are assassinations to be discussed?

I must add that as I write this I am by no means clear as to what has actually happened. The accounts in the English papers range from a pitched battle in which thirty men attacked a vanguard which was led by Lord French and presently reinforced by a main body brought up at the double and badly winded in the process, and a waylaying by a squad of bombers who fled and left one of their number slain on the field. By the time this [article] appears no doubt the matter will be clearer; but I have not hesitated to assume that the incident was an attempt to assassinate the Viceroy, simply because the conditions at present imposed upon Ireland always do produce such calamities.

THE BETRAYAL OF ULSTER

The Irish Statesman, Dublin, 10 January 1920

England has gone too far this time.[1] She has done what I thought impossible. She has rallied me to the side of Ulster. Now I suppose I shall be shot; but I cannot help that. Am I not a Protestant to the very marrow of my bones? Is not Carson my fellow townsman? Are not the men of Ulster my countrymen? Am I to stand by and see them betrayed by a Welshman, and mocked by his English congregation? No: my blood boils: I feel like Fenimore Cooper's Jacobite admiral who stood off from the battle until he saw his countryman's ship caught between two French broadsides, and thereupon cast the Pretender to the devil and came to the rescue with all his cannon thundering. Not for forty thousand de Valeras will

---

1. In December 1919, while Ireland was living virtually under martial law, Lloyd George announced a bill for the "better government of Ireland." It provided home rule and a local parliament for twenty-six "southern" counties and, at the same time, home rule and a separate local parliament for six counties of Ulster. Northern leaders, opposed to home rule in any form, were reluctant to accept it because partition not only would dilute their connection with England but might also leave Ulster exposed to coercion from the south. However, pressure from the government of Lloyd George—Shaw's "little wizard"—forced their acceptance; and the bill, which received its first reading in February, became law on 23 December 1920 and was actually brought into force on 19 April 1921. As a result of a general election in the north in May 1921, an Ulster parliament was elected and, shortly thereafter, functioned within the limited powers assigned to it by the Partition Act. In the south, however, Sinn Féin announced that the ostensible objectives of the election being held under British writ were to be ignored and that candidates so elected would constitute the elected assembly of the Republic of Ireland. As a result, 124 Sinn Féin and four Unionist candidates, the latter representing Dublin University, were returned unopposed. Ireland was thus partitioned on 22 June 1921. Two days later Lloyd George opened negotiations with Éamon de Valera to end the Anglo-Irish War. Hostilities ceased three months later, and the terms of the treaty, agreed to by representatives of Dáil Eireann and the English government in December 1921, made final the partition of Ireland. The Ulster parliament lasted until 1972, when Westminster took direct control of Ulster. See p. xix.

I see any Protestant Irishman under the feet of Lloyd George or a million such.

Does Ireland owe nothing to the Lord Chancellor [Frederick E. Smith, Lord Birkenhead]? Only the other day England broke out into one of her schoolboy riots. In London a brave and respectable American gentleman was dragged from a public meeting by a mob of educated English aspirants to one of the liberal professions. They all but broke his back; they destroyed one of his eyes; they carried him to and fro like a Guy Fawkes through the main streets of the West-end in broad daylight, and finally left him in a hospital, injured and half blinded for life. If anything so horrible, lawless, and cowardly had happened in Dublin or Cork, it would have produced—and justified—a Draconian Coercion Act. In England they thought it rather a lark. Because the victim, with heroic Christianity, did not reproach them, they told him cheerfully that he was a good sport. Because President Wilson, for some inscrutable reason, did not demand the dismissal of the chief of police and the payment of half-a-million dollars to Mr Johnson as compensation, they remained jovially unconscious of having misbehaved themselves.[2] The chief of the Paris police had to go, and Clemenceau to apologize, when one of the retinue of the German envoys—a red-handed alien enemy—was assaulted without serious consequences. But in England, an ally, in the very highest effusion of the alliance, an elderly man, a public man, a man conspicuous for the courage of his convictions, was left as unprotected in the streets of the capital as he would have been in a Balkan vilayet during a Turkish raid.

On these occasions it is always an Irishman who has to point out to the English that civilized people do not do such things. Parnell used to have to do it; and when he died Mr Dillon succeeded to that thankless duty.[3]

2. William Eugene Johnson, American temperance advocate (known as "Pussy-foot" Johnson because of his quiet efficiency in enforcing temperance legislation as a federal agent), attempted to convert other countries to temperance. While delivering an address in London in 1919, he was heckled and abused by students who threw missiles at him. As a result, he lost the sight of his right eye.

3. After the split in the Irish Party created by the Parnell scandal, in which John Dillon declared against Parnell, Dillon became leader of the anti-Parnellite wing of the party. He later succeeded John Redmond as leader of the reunited party. The party itself was extinguished by Sinn Féin in December 1918.

On this occasion the Lord Chancellor did it. He is not an Irishman; but as everybody believes that he is because he is more Orange than Belfast, he saved the honor of Ireland, which would otherwise have seemed to be as much amused by the incident, and as unconscious of its being any worse than the wall game at Eton, as our incorrigibly jejune neighbors.

And this is the man whom Mr Lloyd George and Mr Walter Long[4] and the rest of them have befooled!

For just consider. Ulster demanded a pledge that Ulster should not be coerced if it broke the law.[5] Now, what would an Irish statesman, or any other civilized statesman in the world except an English statesman, have said to such an anarchic demand? He would have bombarded Belfast as soon as a battleship or an aeroplane could have been got within range; and he would have bombarded Cork, Greenock, and Portsmouth next day, just to demonstrate impartially that there was still a power in the land that could maintain law there. Even Richard the Third, not a morbidly public-spirited politician, could ask on occasion:

Is the chair empty? Is the sword unswayed?
Is the king dead? The empire unpossessed?[6]

but to a British Prime Minister it seemed the most natural thing in the world to trade off his most sacred charge against a few votes in the House. Besides, when a Prime Minister is also a Welshman and "a little wizard," may he not give assurances to Macbeth Carson with a private conviction that when the time comes he can keep the word of promise to the ear and break it to the hope?[7]

We cannot deny that the wizard has succeeded. He has not coerced Ulster: he has offered her self-determination. She is to have a Parliament all

4. Walter Long, colonial secretary in the cabinet of Lloyd George and later first lord of the admiralty, was British cabinet adviser on Irish affairs.

5. The resistance of Ulster to the Third Home Rule Bill, under the leadership of Sir Edward Carson and Lord Birkenhead, almost turned into an open rebellion.

6. Shakespeare, *Richard III*, 4.5.470–71.

7. This may be precisely what happened. The existence of at least one private pledge made by Lloyd George to Sir Edward Carson was revealed by Carson on 29 September 1920, when he claimed that Lloyd George had promised him in 1916 that partition would be permanent and that the boundaries would remain inviolable. When Lloyd George denied having given such a pledge, Carson issued to the press the letter containing Lloyd George's pledge.

to herself, and is to decide her own destiny. How simple! How just! How generous! What more could Ulster ask? What less could she accept? Three cheers for Lloyd George!

And yet, could Sir Edward Carson and Lord Birkenhead have been put more completely in the cart if the British Government had made Ireland a present to the Pope? What is Ulster to do with her self-determination? One-eyed people are full of surmises as to what the southern Parliament will do, prophesying, with assumed confidence, that it will declare the Republic. Nobody thinks of poor Ulster, who is in a far more difficult position. For the first act of her Parliament must be to re-unite her with England. That goes without saying. But the difficulty will begin earlier. Can she consistently elect a separate Ulster Parliament at all? Is she not bound by all her vows and covenants to boycott this abomination of a Home Rule Parliament: nay, of two Home Rule Parliaments? And yet if she does, Labor will jump the claim.

Is it any wonder that Sir Edward Carson sat glum and refused to give any assurances to the perfidious Welshman who, with an air of solving the problem for him, was putting him into the worst hole of his career? As to Lord Birkenhead, no more will he raise the cry, "Gallop apace, ye fiery-footed steeds,"[8] to the defence of the Union: he is asking himself what the deuce he is to do when the Ulster Parliament declares that it never will desert Mr Micawber. The South *may* boycott the election. It *may* accept it and declare the Republic. But the wretched North *must* both boycott the election and hold it, and then declare the Union with every likelihood that England will say, "No, thank you: we are well rid of your bullying, and mean to remain so." And what is the prospect then? A derelict Ulster in a state of total political dissolution. This is the reward of loyalty to the British Crown. This is how Welshmen keep their words. The Protestant North, that yesterday made footballs of British Cabinets, and spat defiant treason in the teeth of British Ministers, will be kingless, kaiserless, countryless, and yet apparently so indulged and privileged and kept faith with that her wrath will win no more sympathy than the wrath of a millionaire over his income-tax assessment.

I do not see how Sir Edward Carson can now hesitate as to his course. He has been betrayed in the most unbearable of all forms of betrayal: that

---

8. Shakespeare, *Romeo and Juliet*, 3.2.1.

of being humbugged. He must oppose the Government scheme on the general ground that it is a scheme of self-damnation disguised as self-determination, and on the particular ground of the reservation of Customs and Excise, which leaves the Lagan at the mercy of the Clyde. He must then join Sir Horace Plunkett, his natural Protestant ally, in demanding an Irish Constituent Assembly in which North and South can come to an understanding, and Ireland substitute self-determination for Welsh electioneering. Nothing else except mere coercion has the ghost of a chance now.

In the meantime, would it be possible for Mr Lloyd George to hold his unlucky tongue? His impulses to conciliate are so closely followed by panics in which he threatens and insults that they do far more harm than good. He poses as Jefferson Davis to please the Disruptionists. He sees Sir Edward Carson scowl, and instantly he poses as Lincoln to please the Unionists. Ten lines in the Daily Mail, and he will pose as Metternich: ten more in the Manchester Guardian, and he will pose as Lenin. Why does he not visit America, and learn the cult of the man who can look his fellow man (or newspaper) in the eye, and tell him to go to hell?

PARTITION OF IRELAND: A FORECAST

To *The Irish Times*, Dublin, 1 December 1920

Sir,—Sir Edward Carson's acceptance of Home Rule, as finally affirmed in his letter to Lord Birkenhead, was foretold by me when Sir Edward was prepared to die in the last ditch declaring that "We wont have it." It is dangerous to repeat a prophetic success of that sort, but I do not hesitate to foretell here and now that we shall yet see Sir Edward calling on every Protestant in Ireland, and indeed on every landholder, Protestant or Catholic, Royalist or Republican, Covenanter or Sinn Feiner, to rally for a struggle to the death against Partition. That will not be a more complete *volte face* than the one he has already made, and it is just as inevitable and as easy to foresee.

In Ireland, as elsewhere, the social strains set up by the opposition of pecuniary interests between property and proletarian Labor finally determine the political divisions, however the strains set up by Nationalist and Unionist sentiment may cut across them. When Ulster has segregated itself from the South, Ulster Capital will discover that it has segregated itself from its natural proprietary allies, the Southern farmers, and compelled itself to fight organized Labor, at the greatest possible disadvantage, in the field where the industrial proletariat is concentrated in overwhelming electoral force. Sir Edward Carson has admitted in Parliament that Labor can win every seat in Ulster if it likes. Why, then, have the Ulster employers accepted the Bill? Partly because, as I warned them, their old intention of simply ignoring any Home Rule Act that might be passed collapsed the moment they realized that the only effect would be that Labor would jump the claim and have a walkover at the Ulster polls; but chiefly (my argument being too unfamiliar for most of them to take in) because they had a blind dread that an All-Ireland Parliament would tax Ulster commerce to death. To escape that they have placed themselves politically at the mercy of their own employees, who have every conceivable motive for not only raising wages and shortening hours of labor by trade union action, but also for imposing further factory legislation, and providing unemployment insurance, education, housing, school meals, slum abolitions, electric light, trams, parks, bands, and a dozen other municipal services yet undreamt of, with the cost provided by grants-in-aid, and thus thrown on excess profits, unearned incomes, and all the other sources at which property is vulnerable to socialist schemes of rating and taxation. Against such schemes the ancient incantations in the names of the Pope and King William are powerless.

When this in turn is realized, the second *volte face* will take place, and in due time be announced by Sir Edward Carson to the Rupert of the Covenant [Lord Birkenhead]. Everywhere in Europe now the industrial employers are holding Socialism off in spite of the growing urban Labor party by getting their backs against the immense and almost immovable conservative mass of the peasant proprietors. In Ireland that mass is composed mainly of Sinn Fein farmers, who, though perfectly ready to kick the King's crown into the Shannon, may be depended on not to budge an inch when they are threatened by their laborers with high rates, high wages, and field legislation. Partition will mean, when the situation develops, an XVIII century individualist Southern Ireland, with the farmers' profits maximized by the co-operation taught by Sir Horace Plunkett, side by side with a Bolshevist Ulster, with the dictatorship of the proletariat made much less reasonable by democracy and electoral ignorance than the intelligent despotism of trained professional thinkers and students of political science like Lenin, Trotsky, and Krassin.

It is, therefore, for the wage-workers of Ulster to demand and support Partition, and for the landlords, capitalists, employers, and luxury-tradesmen to call on Sir Edward to declare that they will [not] suffer their beloved country to be rent in twain; that Ireland's watchword must be, "United we stand, divided we fall"; that all Irishmen are brothers; that Romanism and Anglicanism are mere superficial variants of the same Catholic faith; and that the true unity of Unionism is the unity of the Parliament of Ireland, one and indivisible.

I do not suppose that your readers will believe this until it actually happens, any more than they believed my previous forecast until it was fulfilled, by which time they had forgotten that I made it. Still, I think it is worth recording, as there may be an intelligent person here and there capable of being convinced by it. We are sufficiently embittered and perplexed by old antagonisms without the added horror of believing them to be irreconcilable when, in fact, they are bound to dissolve presently under pressure of circumstances.

May I add a word as to the complete change in the military possibilities of Ireland, and of all other relatively small and poor countries, which the War Office and Marshal Foch have evidently impressed on the Prime Minister and on Mr Winston Churchill with terrifying effect, Ireland being now described by Mr Churchill with perfect seriousness as "a fearful danger" to the British Empire? This change has been produced by the war, which has proved that the most formidable armaments are not now those costly battleships and big battalions which rich and populous countries only can afford, but cheap submarines and aeroplanes, cheaper bombs and floating mines, still cheaper poison gases, and, cheapest of all, infected—and, consequently, infectious—microbes. These things unquestionably do make small communities far more dangerous to large ones than they were ten years ago. But they are not a reason for subjugating small communities, because it is part of their danger that they elude mere subjugation, and can be removed only by extermination. They also make large communities quite horribly dangerous; for example, France is enormously more dangerous to England than Ireland is, and a war of extermination waged between France and England in pursuit of the illusion of security would exterminate civilization. There is one remedy, and one only; and that remedy is conscience. I recommend it to the consideration of the next person in Ireland, to whichever side he may belong, who feels tempted by the devil to commit murder.

Yours, &c.,
G. Bernard Shaw.

THE BRITISH OFFER

The Daily News, London, 6 September 1921

Mr Lloyd George and his Cabinet have at last set themselves right with public opinion, both in England and abroad, on the Irish question. They have made an offer which is considered handsome not only by themselves but by their foreign critics. And by doing so they have put Mr de Valera in a very difficult position.[1]

He cannot refuse without being given up as an Impossibilist both by the Centre party in his own country and by the rest of the world. He cannot accept without throwing over the Irish Republican Army, which has brought the Government to its knees by an application of military force, which has forced it to choose between the surrender its present offer implies and such a ruthless and crushing employment of all its powers of destruction as it dare not venture on without a vigorous public opinion behind it.

Just as women, though physically weaker than men, can and often do get their way by being so violent that the men must either yield or take the poker and abandon all chivalry, so the I.R.A. [Irish Republican Army] has beaten the Castle and its forces to a point at which the Irish gentry can no longer bear the military terror in which they are held. Yet there is so much popular sympathy even in England with the Irish cause that the British lion would be hissed intolerably if he uttered the old roar, made the old spring, and let his terrible teeth and claws rip.

It is necessary to emphasize this situation. The public has never been told, because nobody in Ireland dare tell it, how complete the Irish victory has been. Sir Hamar Greenwood's myrmidons assure him from time

---

1. The Anglo-Irish Treaty deliberations, which began in London on 11 October 1921 and lasted for seven weeks, were preceded by a series of negotiations—and one meeting—between de Valera and Lloyd George that attempted to establish a common ground for discussion. De Valera indicated that he would settle for nothing less than Irish independence, which Lloyd George seemed willing to grant, but de Valera balked at allowing England to retain military bases and the right to conscript in Ireland.

to time that there are no complaints in the districts they have just patroled.[2] Mr Lloyd George, learning that his warriors have shot a woman who was unlucky enough to be nursing her child by the roadside when they were passing on a joyride, triumphantly declares that he has got murder by the throat. It is all nonsense. What he calls murder has got Ireland by the throat; and when her country gentlemen are asked in military fashion whether they have any complaints they, like experienced Army privates, know better than to make them. They do not want to have their houses burnt. They do not want to figure in a military execution. The terror is as complete in the fringe of parks and mansions round Dublin as in Cork and Kerry. In short, the offer of the British Government is not a burst of repentant magnanimity, but a forced capitulation, submitted to after Sir Hamar Greenwood has done his utmost in the way of crude reprisal, and got the worst of it.

Naturally, the I.R.A. is flushed with success. Most of its members, innocent as they are of the great world beyond the Irish countryside, really think that Sir Hamar Greenwood's worst was England's best, and that they can force an unconditional surrender just as they forced an unprecedented capitulation. They mistake the Black and Tans whom Mr Lloyd George contemptuously let loose on them for the British army, navy, and air force. They know that the authorities left unfortunate policemen to be shot down and bombed and burned out for want of the wireless installations which could have brought a couple of battleplanes to raise the siege and scatter and destroy the besiegers within half an hour, and they take these authorities as samples of the Haigs and Rawlinsons who held up the German armies in Flanders, and who will take the job of smashing the I.R.A. in hand when the English Government gains moral support enough to employ all its military resources in earnest.

Let me assume that Mr de Valera, whom I have not the privilege of knowing personally, understands the world of highly-developed capitalism and Imperialism in which Mr Lloyd George is living, and that he is well aware that England can crush Ireland more completely than she has ever crushed her before if she can once get the necessary popular sanction for the appalling ferocity with which the operation will have to be con-

2. Sir Hamar Greenwood was chief secretary for Ireland from 1920 to 1922 and thus was responsible for military operations against the Irish Republican Army.

ducted. In that case he is between the devil and the deep sea. He must either sacrifice Ireland by refusing the offer and bringing down the avalanche, or sacrifice himself by accepting it; for the I.R.A. will not hesitate to burn his house, and execute him into the bargain, if it conceives him as having sold his country. In such a ticklish situation he is bound to temporize. The notion that it was possible for him to embrace the offer with a cry of "Oh, Mr Lloyd George—or may I call you David?—how magnanimous of you! Thank you a thousand times," could only occur to people who do not know the facts, or to those Englishmen who are transported with their own generosity, very much as a man might be who, having beaten his wife savagely for years, had made her a present of five shillings and promised never to beat her any more unless she was very provoking.

Mere temporizing, however, will not help matters; the longer Mr de Valera evades answering without stating a positive case, in terms, not of XVIII century idealism, but of realist politics, the more will public opinion rally to the view of the matter so sensibly stated by General Smuts. For, though it would be ridiculous, after Sir Hamar Greenwood's performances as a modern Alva, to give the Government any credit for the generosity it is now exploiting, that generosity exists in the character of the common people. They do not know that the offer was a forced offer. They judge it on its merits, not on the motives of its framers; and if it be unreasonably rejected, their generosity will be wounded, and the chorus of "Let us be kind to Ireland" may change its tune and its words, and become a chorus of "Serve Ireland right."

What, then, is to be said for Mr de Valera's insistence on complete independence for Ireland, or, as it will be called in the United States, Secession, a parallel which Mr Lloyd George has been quick to exploit? Well, to begin with, the homogeneity on which Mr Lloyd George is insisting is not a social but a military homogeneity. He makes it clear every time he speaks that he is only too willing to leave Ireland to go to the devil in her own way (I think that is the spirit of it) provided only England retains the island as a military base and a recruiting ground. The chronic panic of militarist Imperialism has obsessed him. But this happens to be precisely the point on which Mr de Valera's objection has the strongest human appeal. For what is the next military enterprize to which Mr Lloyd George has expressly committed himself? Nothing less than a conflict with the United States for the command of the seas.

Now, it is hardly conceivable that the United States will voluntarily suffer any other single Power to command the seas after the appalling demonstration of what that command meant in the last war. The race of naval armaments between England and the States has already started, and unless the old Balance of Power diplomacy is abandoned, the result will be the same as that of the race of naval armaments with Germany which began twenty years ago. And what sign is there of any such abandonment? At the Foreign Office, to Amurath an Amurath succeeds: Lord Curzon, though not more dangerous than Lord Grey (because that would be impossible) is hardly less so. To such diplomatists the difference between their dear friend Japan and their dear friend the United States is only the difference between Codlin and Short;[3] and Mr Lloyd George's effusive propaganda of gratitude to Japan (which hardly went beyond its own obvious interests as the United States did) suggests that in his opinion Codlin's the friend, not Short. Therefore the insistence on the military union between Ireland and England means practically that Ireland must take the side of England in the war with America for the command of the seas for which the British Prime Minister is heading.

Now, this would be an act of unnatural ingratitude and self-slaughter on the part of Ireland. For the last thirty years the cause of Irish Nationalism has lived on American money and American sympathy. The huge flood of Irish emigration has always been emigrative to America. There are probably more families named Conolly and Larkin, Murphy and O'Reilly, Ryan and O'Toole in North America than in Ireland. Can America seriously blame Mr de Valera for refusing to consent to Ireland being committed to a war with her?

The English people do not see this point because they are innocent of any intention to sink the American fleet, and will go on believing that the British Government is equally innocent until they are stampeded into war by the usual methods, and the American President succeeds to the horns and tail of the ex-Kaiser. And the leaders of opinion will take care not to enlighten them, because a good understanding with America is as impor-

3. Characters in Charles Dickens's *The Old Curiosity Shop*.

tant as a good understanding with Germany used to be when General French was officially reconnoitring in Belgium and the two rival fleets were preparing for Der Tag. But the leaders of opinion in America value the strategic importance of Ireland from the other end of the battlefield. It is clearly their business to back Mr de Valera against Mr Lloyd George.

Let no one imagine, however, that in the event of a British war, with America or any other Power, Ireland could enjoy neutrality. Even if Ireland were an independent neutral State, England would necessarily treat her exactly as she treated Greece in the late war, and as Germany treated Belgium. And according to the morals of war, she would be quite right. Galway is not more sacred than Salonika, nor Dalkey Island than Eubea. Ireland could do nothing but protest, as King Constantine protested; but at any rate her hands would be guiltless of American blood. It may be said that she could fight the violators of her neutrality, as Belgium did. But the fate of Belgium made an end of that heroic pedantry. Greece took it lying down, as Ireland would have to take it. Still, there would be all the difference in the world between being unable to help America and actively attacking her in her hour of peril.

It is only fair to observe here that America would not be able to respect Irish neutrality in a war with England any more than England would. But in the race for Ireland England would win, the course being so much shorter. If the campaign were a land campaign on the east side of the Atlantic, Ireland would be the cockpit of the struggle, just as Flanders has been the cockpit of the old struggles for the balance of power in Europe. The moment this situation is grasped, Mr de Valera's apparent Impossibilism changes its aspect completely. His demand for freedom for Ireland to keep out of England's Imperialist enterprizes becomes the plainest commonsense. Whether it is obtainable or not is another matter.

Thus Mr de Valera has two trumps—first, the threatened war with America; second, the power of the I.R.A. to force England to horrifying extremities as the price of victory. The two hang together. If Mr de Valera can convince public opinion that his demand for military independence and the right to neutrality in the war with America, which Mr Lloyd George will, as I demonstrated in these columns, make inevitable if he persists in his Security First policy, then the coercion of Ireland may lead to Mr Lloyd George's defeat at the next ensuing General Election, which is perhaps the only sort of catastrophe a hardened Parliamentary leader can appreciate.

Then there are the Dominions to be considered. They are monarchist because the Crown, without interfering with them, enables them to escape a much more despotic President who probably would interfere with them; but this very practical view does not imply any sentiment of devotion to the throne among the masses who have no hope of obtaining titles. To them, as far as they think about the question at all, the Crown is a convenient anachronism. And the loyalty of Canada and Australia, in the event of an alliance between England and Japan ending in a war with America, would be so strained that I hardly dare discuss what might happen. That is another ace in Mr de Valera's hand.

The bearing of the military question on the case of Ulster has also to be considered. If Ireland were independent it would be very difficult for her to take sides in a war between the United States and the British Empire, because the South would want to support America and the North England. Neutrality would be the most plausible solution, and it would be a possible one, because Ireland is not, like Canada and Australia, overshadowed by Japan.

Meanwhile, sympathy is all-important to both sides at present. If Mr de Valera cannot get it, he will have to allow himself to be defeated by the Irish Centre, which agrees with General Smuts, and may be roused from its present futility by the popularity of the Offer to revolt against the military tyranny of the Left and accept it. But if he can look beyond Ireland and play the world game, he may yet get support enough to compel Mr Lloyd George to enlarge the offer. More than that cannot be said at present.

I must add for the benefit of those who would like to know what allowance they should make for my personal bias in the above statement that Home Rule for England is my hobby.

THE IRISH CRISIS

New York American, 25 December 1921;
The Manchester Guardian, 27 December 1921

No decision has been reached by Dail Eireann as I write these lines; but that does not matter: whether it ratifies the agreement or not, Ireland will have to govern herself in future, which means that her troubles are beginning, not ending.[1] If Mr Lloyd George unsheathes the sword which he flourished in the face of the Irish plenipotentiaries on their last evening together before dinner, he will be fighting for the agreement and not for Dublin Castle. If President de Valera repeats the achievement of Washington, he will only stiffen Ireland's job by a navy and a few other things. In either case the Castle falls; the garrison goes; and Ireland is governed by an Irish Parliament, into which the Ulster capitalists will be driven by the Ulster proletariat; for without the support of the agricultural interest, always inveterately on the side of private property, urban Capitalism cannot hold its own anywhere in the world. The Dail debate is really a storm in a teacup; but Ireland has a wonderful power of magnifying herself and her affairs in the eyes of the world. An Irish mountain eleven hundred feet high looks so much higher than Mount Everest (and haunted into the

---

1. The Anglo-Irish Treaty, signed by representatives of Lloyd George's government and Dáil Eireann on 6 December 1921, granted Ireland a degree of independence similar to that of Canada, Australia, New Zealand, and South Africa. But Ireland had to accept a governor-general, take an oath of association with the British Commonwealth, and grant Great Britain the right to retain naval facilities in Irish harbors. Ulster had one month in which to decide whether to continue under its own parliament established by the Partition Act in April or throw in its lot with the new Irish state. After acrimonious debate, Dáil Eireann ratified the treaty on 7 January 1922 by a vote of 64 to 57, opposition to ratification being led by de Valera. Ulster immediately opted out, and in December 1925 the boundary separating six counties of Ulster from the rest of Ireland was drawn by a boundary commission. The name of the new Irish state—Saorstat Eireann, or Free State—was changed by the constitution of 1937 to Éire, and again in 1948 to the Republic of Ireland. It is referred to colloquially as "Southern Ireland," but it includes in fact the most northerly part of the island.

bargain) that you are afraid to go up it. And an Irish altercation between Mr Griffith[2] and President de Valera seems big with the doom of empires, though its upshot will not even settle the question of the agreement.

Some of the difficulties have been wantonly manufactured just because men like to annoy each other. Take the oath of allegiance, for example. In 1628 Oliver Cromwell took the oath of allegiance to Charles I, and in 1753 George Washington took it to George III. Perhaps some spiritualist will consult these monarchs as to its value. It is difficult to keep one's temper when the affairs of the world are held up by such trifling. All these oaths and tests should be thrown into their proper receptacle, which is the dustbin of history.

But that, again, does not greatly matter; for any practical statesman will, under duress, swallow a dozen oaths to get his hand on the driving wheel. If he refuses, it is because he either doubts his ability to drive or has his reasons for waiting. It is never the oath that stops him. Unfortunately, practical statesmen are scarce in Ireland; and the sentimental patriots are the slaves of fixed ideas and phrases which they have not examined. Such words as "The Republic," "Independence," and "The Memory of the Dead" can bring a lump into the throat of most Irishmen; but really modern political problems cannot be solved by lumps in the throat. The attempt has always ended in the problem being aggravated instead of solved, and the lump being corrected by the external application of a noose. Let us examine these appeals to the thyroid scientifically.

"The Memory of the Dead" may be dismissed at once because there are so many dead on both sides that if we are to be bound by the ideas they died for we shall never get on at all. The Irish Republican Army has taken good care that Mr Lloyd George has a good many dead men to go back on, and be denounced by the British Imperialists accordingly; and if he stands for the living whilst the Irish stand for the dead, then God help Ireland! If the dead are to have a say, what about the dead prophet [Jesus] who told us to let the dead bury their dead? A prophet nearer home, St Terence MacSwiney the Martyr,[3] left us some very sacred canons of conduct as to choosing the public servants of Ireland. I venture to prophesy

2. Arthur Griffith, who became the first president of the Irish Free State, had been the leader of the Irish delegation that signed the Anglo-Irish Treaty.

3. MacSwiney was lord mayor of Cork and died in Brixton Prison in 1920 after a hunger strike.

that St Terence will turn in his grave when the spoils of Ireland's victory come to be divided up. So much for that popular claptrap.

Then, "The Republic." What is *the* Republic? Is it the Republic of San Salvador or Andorra? Or of the United States of America? Or of France, with its sixtyfive per cent. of subjugated aliens? Or the Irish Republic of Pearse and de Valera? Obviously not a bit of it. *The* Republic, the idea for which the best men have striven in all ages, is the *civitas Dei*, from which no man can be excluded because he is English. I repeat, there are more Republicans in England today than in Ireland, and a severance between them and the Republicans of Ireland may or may not be expedient on other grounds; but it is anti-Republican. It would force thousands of Irishmen to go through a repulsive mummery of becoming "naturalized Englishmen" simply because the world will not work nowadays in na-tion-tight compartments. The Republican ideal is not to detach your country from its neighbors as much as possible, but, on the contrary, to establish as much organic connection with them as is compatible with their full and free activities in cleaning their own doorsteps.

Independence is a fine shibboleth for a slave, but the moment he is free he discovers that we are members one of another, and that independence is an egocentric dream. England calls herself independent, but why has she been afraid to let Ireland go until she was forced to? Admittedly be-cause she is so dependent on Ireland. She has tried to plunder Germany, only to find that she is dependent on Germany. She has helped to ruin Russia, only to find her streets filled with millions of starving Englishmen clamoring to be allowed to work for Russia in order to live.

Look at it from the Irish end. How can Ireland be independent of En-gland? In a war England would march into Ireland with as little cer-emony as she marched into Belgium and Greece. Cut off the Anglo-Irish trade, and both parties will presently find out, by the slackness of their belts, how dependent they are one on another. Why, the proposed evacu-ation of Ireland by the British army has already produced Eirephil pro-tests on the ground that Ireland will lose the six millions a year spent by these open-handed warriors, mainly in her public-houses!

The truth is, Ireland independent is Ireland as conceived by Arran is-landers, and by villagers on the mainland who are just as insular. They might as well live in Juan Fernandez, which did once have an independent population whose realm there was none to dispute. Ireland is not like that, and never will be. It is, for its size, a centre of extraordinary activity, intellectual and practical. It is quite possible that it may yet become the predominant partner in the connection with Britain. It is as certain as anything human can be that it will never be independent of the European complex. Such independence is for savages, not for supercivilized communities like the Irish. The English resist civilization with remarkable stubbornness: they still confront it as reluctant barbarians. But the Irish, no: you have only to glance at the Book of Kells to realize that their danger lies the other way—in a civilization pushed to effeteness. What is the matter with President de Valera sometimes is that he is subtle to the point at which subtlety, face to face with the cheerful barbarism of Westminster, produces all the effects of stupidity.

It seemed clear when the negotiations began that Mr de Valera could not without hauling down his flag accept any proposal that Mr Lloyd George could conceivably make, and that it must be accepted over his head by the Irish Centre party. Only, there was apparently no Irish Centre party. Sir Horace Plunkett made a desperate effort to invent one and call it the Dominion League. But the futility of the Irish gentry, despairing of the Castle and disaffected to Sinn Fein, beat him, as it had beaten him in the Convention. The Republican President stood [pat] and carried the country with him. It was to have been deluged in blood (as at present) in consequence, but was not (as at present it will not be). Instead, Mr de Valera had the great success of extorting a new offer, going far beyond the former one. So good is it, in fact, that a party in favor of jumping at it develops this time in the Republican ranks; and Mr Griffith and Mr Collins, taking up the rôle of Sir Horace Plunkett, pass from the extreme right (the extreme left from the English point of view) to the moderate centre. They are for acceptance.

And Mr de Valera still holds out. The question is, Will he succeed again in extorting a higher bid? It is not quite impossible; the form of oath he proposes is obviously very much better, if only as a piece of literature (and it has no other real value), than Mr Lloyd George's; and there are several matters left unsettled which might well be settled now rather than left to the fierce debate which will take place when the Act comes to be drafted and discussed. Note that Mr de Valera has abandoned the impossibilist position, and will swallow the Throne and the connection with the

Association of Nations, *ci-devant* Empire, if he can get what he thinks Ireland can command.

To understand the strength of his former position and the comparative weakness of his present one it is necessary to grasp the fact that Ireland has made a revolutionary discovery. She has found out how to make a successful rebellion. The secret is not to rebel at all, but to imitate the lady in Mrs Stetson's poem who vanquished a prejudice, after many unsuccessful efforts, by walking through it as if it wasnt there.[4] Do not advocate a republic; simply assume a republic, appoint its administration and its Parliament, and carry on. If you are interfered with by ill-disposed persons, appoint your police and army, and defend your extant republic. Very simple, like Relativity and all the other great discoveries. And the measure of its success is the difference between Mr Gladstone's Home Rule Bill and Mr Lloyd George's articles of capitulation. It has settled the Irish question; and it will settle the Egyptian question and the Indian question.

But it is only practicable by a united nation. And the Irish nation, hitherto solid behind its President, has split on this last bid of Mr Lloyd George's. What we are now waiting to see is whether this split will sweep Mr de Valera away for the moment or leave him strong enough to have one more try for Mr Lloyd George's really highest bid. That is all there is in it now.

Meanwhile, there is no reason to fuss about the upshot of the Dail debate. The promised deluge of blood will not flow on this side of the General Election. The Irish will take as much as they can get, and Mr Lloyd George will give as much as he can spare. He is at the disadvantage of being in a hurry. Ireland has been in her present plight so long that she can bear it a little longer. And so we can look forward to tomorrow's newspapers without losing our sleep.

4. Charlotte Perkins Stetson, "An Obstacle," in *In This Our World* (London: Unwin, 1895).

THE EVE OF CIVIL WAR[1]

Reply to a request for an opinion on the Irish situation, written in Dublin on the eve of Shaw's return to London. *The Irish Times*, Dublin, 21 August 1922

Well, what can anyone say that has not been said already until people are so tired of it that the words have lost all meaning? If you ask me what on earth Mr de Valera and Mr Erskine Childers[2] are driving at—what they think they are doing, as the English say—I can only say that I dont know. And that is the weakness of their position. From the moment when the elections went against them so completely that the members they were allowed to return by arrangement could not pretend to any representative character, they had either to accept the popular verdict and set to work to convert the Irish people to their views or to choose between the two other courses open to them. One was to subdue the country by armed force, British fashion, and coerce it to become an independent little republic,

1. The debates in Dáil Eireann over ratification of the Anglo-Irish Treaty—which Shaw had optimistically called a "storm in a teacup"—actually proved to be a prelude to civil war in Ireland. Formally the debates centered upon the oath of association, but the real issue was partition. Arthur Griffith and Michael Collins, who had been members of the Irish delegation that negotiated the treaty, argued for acceptance and were supported by a narrow majority. Éamon de Valera led the minority opposition. The civil war commenced when a majority section of the Irish Republican Army refused to submit to the authority of the Free State government. When a contingent of IRA men under Rory O'Connor took possession of a public building in Dublin in June 1922 and began to commandeer lorries for a sortie into Belfast, where skirmishes had taken place between Protestants and Catholic Nationalists, Michael Collins as commander in chief of the Irish Free State Army was forced to bombard O'Connor's "headquarters." The civil war ended ten months later.

2. Erskine Childers, son of a distinguished English father and an Irish mother, was educated at Cambridge and served as junior clerk in the House of Commons for fifteen years before becoming involved in the republican movement in Ireland. He served as special adviser to the Irish treaty delegation but, as a member of Dáil Eireann, stood with de Valera in opposition to ratification of the treaty. During the civil war he was captured by Free State forces and executed on 24 November 1922 in Dublin. Outside Ireland he is known chiefly for his authorship of a classic thriller, *The Riddle of the Sands*.

whether it liked it or not. The other was to take to the mountains and live more or less merrily by brigandage in the manner of Robin Hood.

What has happened is that Mr de Valera and Mr Childers have attempted the first alternative, but having no war chest and apparently no program beyond calling Ireland a republic, they have been forced to tell their troops on payday that they must live on the country, which means in practice that the leaders are to be republicans contending for a principle and their troops are to be brigands.

This is an impossible situation. No community can tolerate brigandage, even when it is goodnatured brigandage. The existing brigandage is not goodnatured; and Ireland is obviously on the point of losing its temper savagely with Robin Hood, Alan-a-dale, Friar Tuck, and the rest of them. When the explosion comes, General Collins will be able to let himself go in earnest, and the difficulty of the overcrowded jails and of the disbanded irregular who takes to the road again the moment the troops have passed on will be solved, because there will be no prisoners; the strain will be on the cemeteries.

General Collins beat Sir Hamar Greenwood at the wrecking game because he had the people behind him. What chance against him has Mr de Valera without military aptitude or any of Sir Hamar Greenwood's enormous material resources? Of course he can enjoy the luxury of dying for Ireland after doing Ireland all the damage he can. What matter if for Ireland dear we fall[3] is still the idiot's battle song. The idiocy is sanctified by the memories of a time when there was really nothing to be done for Irish freedom but to die for it; but the time has now come for Irishmen to learn to live for their country. Instead of which, they start runaway engines down the lines, blow up bridges, burn homesteads and factories, and gain nothing by it except such amusements as making my train from Waterford to Rosslare several hours late. Ireland would be just as free at this moment if I had arrived punctually. You see, the cause of Ireland is al-

3. Misquotation by Shaw. The correct reading should be: "Oh, what matter, when for Erin dear we fall," from the verse "God Save Ireland" and set to the popular melody best known as "Tramp, tramp, tramp, the boys are marching," written by the Fenian poet Timothy D. Sullivan in commemoration of the Manchester Martyrs. First published in Young Ireland's *The Nation*, 7 December 1867, it became the unofficial national anthem for the next few decades.

ways dogged by the ridicule which we have such a fatal gift of provoking, and such a futile gift of expressing.

I suppose it will have to be settled, as usual, by another massacre of Irishmen by Irishmen. If Mr de Valera had any political genius he might avert it. But with the strongest sentimental bias in his favor I cannot persuade myself that he has any political faculty at all. He has literary talent and that very dangerous plaything, an amorphous ideal; but ever since Arthur Griffith and Michael Collins left him behind when the Treaty was to be negotiated with Mr Lloyd George, and he himself consented to be left behind, it has been evident that all three were agreed that political negotiation is not his job.

I have a friendly personal regard for Mr Erskine Childers; but like all genuine Englishmen, he is a born anarchist, and will smash heaven and earth to have his own way unless there is a policeman standing over him.

I am returning to England because I can do no good here, and because the postage is a halfpenny cheaper. I was a Republican before Mr de Valera was born, and could never bring myself to take any interest in Parnell because he seemed to me a whole epoch behind his time. I objected to the old relations between England and Ireland as I object to the present ones, because they were not half intimate enough.

I am a Supernationalist and a Socialist; and all I have to say to an Irish carpenter (for instance) is that as long as he hates an English carpenter he will be a slave, no matter what flag he flies. I cannot stand the stale romance that passes for politics in Ireland. I cannot imagine why people bother so much about us: I am sure we dont deserve it. Look at Russia: now there is a really interesting country politically. The bottom has fallen out of the centre of Europe, and England is on the brink of the abyss. But what matter if for Ireland dear we fall! It is too silly: I must hurry back to London. The lunatics there are comparatively harmless.

ON THE DEATH OF MICHAEL COLLINS[1]

A letter to Michael Collins's sister Johanna, in John Lavery's *The Life of a
Painter* (London: Cassell, 1940). The Shaws had dined with Collins at Horace
Plunkett's home in Kilteragh on 19 August 1922; the letter was written
from London on 24 August, three days after Shaw had left Ireland.

Dear Miss Collins

Dont let them make you miserable about it: how could a born soldier
die better than at the victorious end of a good fight, falling to the shot of
another Irishman—a damned fool, but all the same an Irishman who
thought he was fighting for Ireland—"a Roman to a Roman"?

I met Michael for the first and last time on Saturday last, and am very
glad I did. I rejoice in his memory, and will not be so disloyal to it as to
snivel over his valiant death.

So tear up your mourning and hang up your brightest colors in his
honor; and let us all praise God that he had not to die in a snuffy bed of a
trumpery cough, weakened by age, and saddened by the disappointments
that would have attended his work had he lived.

Sincerely,

Bernard Shaw.

1. Michael Collins, one of the most attractive of the Irish revolutionary figures,
succeeded Arthur Griffith (who died on 12 August 1922) as head of the new government of the Irish Free State. While inspecting military installations in his native
County Cork, he was killed on 22 August when his party was ambushed by republican irreconcilables at Bealnablath, on the road between Skibbereen and Cork city.

HOW TO RESTORE ORDER IN IRELAND

New York American, 5–7 March 1923; *The New Leader*, London, 16 March 1923

Some little time since[,] I was sounded as to whether I would, if invited, accept service on the Senate of the Irish Free State.[1] I replied that I would consider it if the seat of the Irish Government were transferred to London.

This was not a joke. It was the only answer any sane man could be expected to give at that moment. But, as such, it was a reduction to absurdity of Irish Nationalism.

Ireland is now called a Free State, but the problem of how to make Ireland a country fit for civilized men to live in has not been solved. Its freedom may be gauged by the fact that no newspaper is allowed to criticize the Government, and that its military authorities are empowered to take any citizen into barracks and shoot him without keeping any record of the event or being answerable for it in any effective way. In spite of these despotic measures, reinforced by savage, unauthorized floggings by the soldiery, armed young men and boys raid shops, seize bicycles and motor cars on the high roads, burn mansions, wreck railway tracks and bridges and trains, throw bombs about and keep up fusillades in the streets of the cities, kidnap senators and officials, and blow up their offices and houses, and behave generally as if they were in an enemy country with no Government, no police, and a population of imbecile cowards.

More amazing still, if the people attempt to defend themselves they are punished for it by the authorities. If, when a boy with a revolver enters

1. The civil war in Ireland was still in progress at the time Shaw was writing. Six weeks later, however, Éamon de Valera ordered all Republican commands to cease aggressive action, and the war ended. Meanwhile, the constitution of the Free State government, which came into being on 6 December 1922, provided for the establishment of a bicameral legislature based on the British model of a Lords and Commons. The Dáil was to be an elective and representative body, but the senate was to consist of sixty nominated senators, thirty of them chosen to give a voice to minorities and to the cultural and intellectual aspects of the nation's life. Among those who accepted nominations were W. B. Yeats and Oliver St. John Gogarty. Among those who declined nominations were George Russell and Shaw.

the shop of a respectable grocer and proceeds to loot it, the respectable grocer produces a gun, the result is that either the marauder shoots first and kills him, or he shoots the marauder, in which case he is himself executed by the Government for the crime of having arms in his possession. If he calls on his neighbors to assist him they do not stir, because they too are disarmed and intimidated both by the Government troops and the Irish Republican Army, to which the marauding boy claims to belong. Thus the main body of industrious and orderly citizens, the only body that can possibly restore order in Ireland, is paralyzed and exhibits to the world, and especially to the English (who always had their doubts as to whether the Irish were capable of self-government), a most contemptible spectacle. A Dublin man said the other day, with the true Dublin laugh at whatever makes more civilized capitals cry, "For seven hundred years we have been the first flower of the earth, and first gem of the sea; and now, bedad, we are found out." I myself find that whereas my Irish nationality was formerly a valuable asset to me in England, I am now expected to apologize for it by men with wooly heads [blacks] or number six noses [Jews]. The Irishman, once a hero *ex officio* in the romantic imagination of the West, is now the hopeless political imbecile and personal scalawag described by Treitschke when he lumped the Irish and the Poles together as fit for nothing better than Imperial tutelage under Nordic or Latin rule.

All this, however, is mere romance. The Irishman is just as capable of civilization as the German or the Englishman. Order has been restored in Belfast, and can be restored in Dublin. But its restoration by professional policemen backed by military force will cost more than it is worth. The experience of South America has shewn that when an empire breaks up, it leaves behind it in each of its fragments a *bourgeoisie* and an industrial proletariat brought up to depend wholly on the Imperial police and soldiery for the security of their lives and property. They are unaccustomed to the possession and use of weapons, or to the organization of their physical force in any militant way, such activities having been suppressed sternly as treason to the empire. When the Imperial police and army are withdrawn these pacific citizens suddenly find that their lives and property are at the mercy, not only of the militant idealists who have defeated the empire, but of the materialist adventurers who are of opinion, like Froissart's knights, that "to rob and pill is a good life." Thus the best-intentioned active spirits are combined with the worst in a proportion which steadily changes as the atrocities of the worst disgust and drive out the best. During that process they disagree among themselves, and form factions which fight for the mastery of the country, living on it in the military sense meanwhile, and marking their successes and defeats by changing Presidents and shooting the discarded one, the *bourgeoisie* and their employees meanwhile submitting to the looting and shooting as to the act of God, just as they submit to earthquakes or hurricanes or bad harvests, without raising a hand to defend themselves.

This is what is happening in Ireland; and the case of South America shews that there is nothing to prevent it going on for the next hundred years (if the natural resources of Ireland will bear the damage for so long) unless appropriate measures are taken to cope with it.

What are these appropriate measures? They are fairly obvious. First, register the whole population, as the British Government did in 1915 under pressure of the war. I still possess my certificate of registration, giving my rural district, name, address, and profession. If I happened to be in a distant English village or town in which any looting or shooting was in progress I could be called on to stand and deliver my registration card; and if I could not give a satisfactory account of my presence so far from home, I could be presumed to be one of the shooters and looters, and dealt with accordingly.

Every citizen should receive, on registration, not only his card, but a gun (in the general American sense) and a supply of ammunition. He should be warned that if he were found at any time without that weapon, loaded and ready to his hand, he would be arrested and charged with having unlawfully disposed of it. If he cleared himself from that, he would still be heavily fined for neglect of duty. Further, it should be impressed on him that if, on receiving an official alarm by whistle, bell, maroon, or what not, or on hearing shots or cries for help or sounds of disturbance in the streets, he did not at once sally from his house, weapon in hand, by night or day, to co-operate with his neighbors in shooting down all rioters and incendiaries, and arresting all persons whose registration cards proved them to be strangers, he would be liable to be shot for cowardice and desertion.

The state of things produced in this way would be that which exists spontaneously in all pioneering settlements. Even in a considerable city like Johannesburg today, a commotion of any sort does not mean that rioters disturb the peace whilst the orderly citizens cower indoors until the noise ceases. Every man turns out and takes a hand on one side or the other, and the most formidable insurrections are speedily and ruthlessly suppressed. Then why, it may be asked, does not the same thing occur spontaneously in Ireland, or in South America? Simply, I repeat, because the pioneers have never been dependent on an Imperial bureaucracy for the protection of their persons and property: they have carried their lives in their hands and their pistols loaded. The enormous gulf which lies between the peaceful habits of a respectable tradesman under the British or Spanish Empire and such an act as killing a human being does not exist for the pioneer; consequently, when it is necessary for the *ci-devant* Imperial citizen to do his own police work, he must be armed and instructed and disciplined for the purpose.

When an Imperial bureaucracy is driven by some emergency to make use of him in this way, it invites him to volunteer as a special constable; and this, under English conditions, has always proved sufficient to reinforce the official police if he is given a club and a badge and a position to watch; for he is at most only an auxiliary to a powerful professional police force with an irresistible army behind it. Take away that police force and that army and you will have to give him something more lethal than a club, and substitute compulsory and general service for casual volunteering. But the principle is the same: what is needed in Ireland is that every man of military age should be made a special constable and registered, equipped, and badged accordingly.

The first objection to this is the old Imperial objection. It gives the people power not only to defend themselves against marauders, but to upset the Government. The Irish Free State has enlisted and equipped a good many men who have presently taken their equipment away with them to join the Republican army. But a Government that will not take this risk cannot pretend to be a genuine national Government. If the main body of orderly Irish civilians want an independent Republic the sooner they establish it the better. Nothing but the return of the British army and the Royal Irish Constabulary can in the long run prevent them; and England has said so decisively that she is not going back in that way, that a senator whose house had just been shot up exclaimed, "England has betrayed us again." If any Irishman desires the return of the British garrison, his only chance is to foment another European war, in which event England will reoccupy Ireland almost automatically.

But it is pretty clear from the result of the elections that most Irish citizens see their profit in their additional citizenship of the British Commonwealth, just as most South-Afrikanders, Australasians, and Canadians do. That they also want peace and order is only another way of saying that they are not lunatics. At all events they must have their way, whichever direction it takes: for they and they alone can save Ireland from the systematic military devastation and casual sabotage which are destroying her civilization. I am aware that the Free State Government declares that it has all but crushed its opponents by the action of its troops alone; but after waiting six months for some proof of this I find that no man's house is insurable nor his life safe even in Dublin and its suburbs, and that Free State Senators and Cabinet Ministers are as much "on the run" from the Republican forces as the Republicans are from the Free State forces. Clearly Ireland cannot live much longer on assurances that "we have cleared the County Clare" or on the shooting of hostages. What is the use of shooting hostages? Has Ireland already forgotten the late Lord Clanricarde and his famous saying: "If you think you can intimidate me by shooting my agent, you are very much mistaken"? The Republicans for whose exploits Mr Erskine Childers was shot probably take the Clanricarde view, precisely. Reprisals are a game at which the worst wins, and hostage slaughter is flat murder, and will never be felt by the conscience of mankind, however war-seared, to be anything better.

Further, it is ridiculous to shoot a man because he is a Republican. It is also an insult to America. But to shoot a man who comes to burn your house, loot your shop, kidnap you, or kill you, is simply good sense; and your neighbors will help if the Government will trust them with the means.

I am quite aware that the prospect of being called out to do deeds congenial only to cinematographic cowboys and bushrangers will fill the peaceful shopkeepers of Ireland with dismay, and will not be welcome even to the comparatively hardy farmers. But what is the alternative? Just that the Government must restore order by a military force which a British general with experience of guerilla warfare estimates at 75,000 soldiers. Their keep will cost a million a month, without counting munitions. The first result will be a national debt, with heavy taxation to pay the interest, which, as it seems unlikely that the money can be raised in Ireland, and the most obvious lender is the English treasury, would be sent out of the country, and be a clean loss to it, thus reviving the old evil of absenteeism.

Suppose the timid citizens are prepared to face this and pay anything rather than do their own police work! Their paid military police will then be a Pretorian Guard which, when its work of restoring order is done, no Government will dare discharge, for the excellent reason that instead of taking its discharge and then, in its destitution, also taking to the hills and beginning the Republican struggle all over again, the army would simply remove the Government and replace it by one friendly to the soldiers. Even as it is, there is nothing but General Mulcahy's conscience to prevent him from making himself President tomorrow by a *coup d'état;*[2] and his successors may be less conscientious and more ambitious than he, especially with no enemy in the field to steady them. The inevitable end of the Pretorian business must be either a legalized military despotism whose tax collectors' little fingers will be thicker than Mr de Valera's loins, or a civilian revolution in which the citizens will have to face regular troops illegally as the penalty for having shirked the job of facing irresponsible gunmen with the support of the Government. Surely it is better to take the bull by the horns at once instead of piling up a gigantic debt for new soldiers, and feebly trusting to amnesties (each positively the very last) which only strengthen the Republicans by purging their ranks of the half-hearted.

I may add that if all civilized countries had the sense to make it blasphemy for anyone to take an official oath, beginning with their coronation oaths, amnesties would become much more hopeful, and peace made easier for this war-tortured world.

2. General Richard James Mulcahy, Free State minister of defense, succeeded Michael Collins as commander in chief of the Free State army.

SAFE HOLIDAYS IN IRELAND

To *The Times*, London, 31 July 1923

Sir,—Several persons have complimented me on my courage in venturing into the South of Ireland for my summer holiday.[1] These people feel safer in the friendly atmosphere of Poincaresque France, or in the land of the bottomless mark chute, where merchants chain up their typewriters with Krupp chains overnight, only to miss them, chains and all, in the morning. They are not afraid even of being dosed with castor-oil in Italy by Anglophobe Fascists. But they dare not set foot in Ireland. I admit that there is some excuse for them. The Irish Government has just passed a Coercion Act which would make Trotsky gasp, and which makes the history of Dublin Castle under English rule seem like freedom broadening down from precedent to precedent. It contains a flogging clause, directed specially against robbery under arms, of such savagery that foreigners may well be led to believe that no man's property or person is safe.

The truth is that Cork and Kerry are much safer, in respect of both person and property, than the Administrative County of London. A year ago no owner of a bicycle in Ireland risked riding it out of call of a barrack, as it was sure to be stolen "under arms"; and even the cheapest motor cars were hidden more carefully than illicit stills. Today not only Fords, but Vauxhall 38s and Crossley 25s career over the mountain roads as carelessly as over the Surrey hills. The tourist's heart is in his mouth when he first crosses a repaired bridge on a 30 cwt. car, for the repairs are extremely unconvincing to the eye; but after crossing two or three in

1. Although de Valera had ordered all Republican commands to cease activities on 30 April 1923, he and a number of other Republican leaders refused to surrender personally, and occasional acts of violence continued to mar the peace of the country. During the general elections in August 1923, de Valera came out of hiding to stand for his old constituency of Ennis, County Clare, but was arrested by Free State soldiers when he attempted to address a public rally in Ennis. He was elected by an overwhelming majority yet spent the first eleven months after his election in prison. When he was released in July 1924, he was prevented from taking his seat in the Dáil by his refusal to take the oath of allegiance required under the Anglo-Irish Treaty.

safety he thinks no more of them. Since I arrived I have wandered every night over the mountains, either alone or with a harmless companion or two, without molestation or incivility. Naturally there is plenty of room in the hotels; and the quality of the potatos, the butter, and the milk is such as to make one feel that one can never eat the English substitutes again. In short, there is not the smallest reason why Glengarriff and Parknasilla should not be crowded this year with refugees from the turbulent sister island and the revolutionary Continent, as well as by connoisseurs in extraordinarily beautiful scenery and in air which makes breathing a luxury. However, the dock strike must be reckoned with. The passengers must unload the ship, and must therefore leave Saratoga trunks behind. It is hard on the dockers to have to look on idly whilst potential employers whose rate of pay varies from twelve to thirty shillings an hour handle their own luggage and evidently enjoy it for once in a way as a holiday lark; but it need not hinder the passenger traffic from Paddington to Cork via Fishguard.

Perhaps I should explain that though the Coercion Act empowers every superintendent of police or army captain to seize any man's property, even to his clothes, leaving nothing on him but the onus of proving that he ever possessed them or had any right to possess them, this power (in force for one year only) is not exercised at the expense of the errant Englishman, and exists only because the loot from plundered houses has to be redistributed by rough-and-ready methods for which the permanent law is too slow and contentious. Ireland is at present in a reaction of quiet, with the hands of its Government reinforced by extraordinary temporary measures, and is therefore at this moment probably the safest country in the world for visitors.

Yours truly,
G. Bernard Shaw.

ON THROWING OUT DIRTY WATER

The Irish Statesman, new series, Dublin, 15 September 1923

When I was a complex Irish youth some half-century ago I was warned never to throw out dirty water until I had got in fresh. As I had only one bucket, the advice did not prove practicable. I turned to another precept, and cast my bread on the waters, not once but many times, with the result that it did indeed return to me after many days provided I worked pretty hard in the meantime.

But I remained an attentive observer of the dirty water business, and found that those who were so anxious to prevent their neighbors from throwing it out prematurely were giving themselves a good deal of trouble for nothing, because the real difficulty is not that people will not wait for the fresh water before they throw out the dirty, but that they will not throw it out at all, and just pour the fresh water into it when they are lucky enough to get any.

To drop the metaphor, men are not averse to new ideas: on the contrary, they are too greedy and credulous in pursuit of them; but nothing is rarer in nature than a man who, on accepting a new idea, proceeds to overhaul his old ideas and see how many of them must be scrapped to make logical room for the newcomer. It has often been my professional business to develop new ideas after their introduction by others, and on such occasions my most furious assailants have been the very persons whose discoveries I was vindicating. They had hit on the idea, but they had not perceived all its consequences. They were holding simultaneously the new truth and the old error that had become ingrained in them before the new light dawned. That is what men do. They are born to a belief in a flat earth, with a flat ceiling and heaven on the first floor. They are converted to a belief that the earth is a ball spinning on its axis and flying through boundless space, and are proud of this advance in scientific culture; but they go on believing in the flat ceiling and the first floor just as if nothing had happened in their minds. And if you press them too hard on the point, you run the risk of unhinging them to such an extent that they will empty the baby out with the bath, and refuse to believe in anything at all, like the Cork voter at the late General Election, who, having suffered a few disillusions in politics, marked his voting paper "To Hell with the Whole Lot."

Now, Ireland is at this moment a regular rag-and-bottle shop of superseded ideas, or superstitions, as they were accurately called when words were something more than reach-me-downs from the newspapers. There are formidable vested interests in our huge national stock of junk and bilge, glowing with the phosphorescence of romance. Heros and heroines have risked their lives to force England to drop Ireland like a hot potato. England, after a final paroxysm of doing her worst, has dropped Ireland accordingly. But in doing so she has destroyed the whole stock-in-trade of the heros and heroines. The heros and heroines cannot realize it. The rallying of the Irish against English tyranny has long since become a reflex action with them; and they cannot control their reflexes. They will die calling for a forlorn hope to storm Dublin Castle. It has surrendered; but even were it demolished as completely as the Bastille they would never notice it.

The reason English rule produced oppression in Ireland was that England had herself to take care of. Her internal poverty, and the pressure of her industrial disorder on her foreign policy, occupied all her political energy and administrative machinery, leaving Ireland and India to force themselves on her reluctant attention by violent insurrection. Yet it seems to be quite a common opinion in Ireland that the Cabinet in London, untroubled by English problems, and indifferent to the adventures of M. Poincaré, Signor Mussolini, and the fall of the mark, occupies itself wholly with sending orders to President Cosgrave[1] to arrest and torture that devoted local patriot, Padraig (*ci-devant* Patrick) Soandso, of Ballysuchandsuch. This is no doubt partly the egotism of lunacy, which is incurable; but it is also largely a combination of childish ignorance of how the world is really governed, with the careless practice of pouring the fresh water of the Free State into the dirty water of Dublin Castle.

I have to deal in crude and glaring instances, but I am quite aware that our worst troubles will not be with the most obvious superstitions. Mere

1. William T. Cosgrave became president of the Free State government after the assassination of Michael Collins in August 1922.

surfeit is already disposing of them. Our improvized governing class is spewing them out vigorously enough; but it needs traditions to keep its routineer ministers steady (it has to fill up with routineers when it is short of Solons), and in its work of building traditions it will have to keep abreast of modern political science or it will find itself with nothing but a shelf-ful of tinpot Napoleonisms which are useful only for emergencies. Now, a Government which comes out strong only in emergencies will be tempted to create and maintain a state of chronic emergency as Napoleon had to create a state of chronic war, or as the doctor who would cure fits and nothing else began his treatments always by trying to induce epilepsy. Let our strong men, our pilots who weathered the storm, our men of one idea and that only the very old one of victory and order at any price, remember that when there is no longer anything particular the matter, they may share the fate of the man who puts his foot down after he has reached the bottom of the stairs.

Nationalism must now be added to the refuse pile of superstitions. We are now citizens of the world, and the man who divides the race into elect Irishmen and reprobate foreign devils (especially Englishmen) had better live on the Blaskets, where he can admire himself without much disturbance. Perhaps, after all, our late troubles were not so purposeless as they seemed. They were probably ordained to prove to us that we are no better than other people; and when Ireland is once forced to accept this stupendous new idea, goodbye to the old patriotism. We must realize that National independence is now impossible. What the British Empire, the French Republic, and the United States of America cannot achieve, Ireland cannot achieve except by becoming so insignificant that her independence would not matter. Nobody disputes the independence of the Kingdom of Dalkey.[2] So much the worse for Dalkey. Ireland as a constituent of a big Commonwealth with its veins heavily charged with her blood— Ireland speaking and writing the language of a quarter of the human race, and speaking and writing it specially well, is something to be reckoned with. As anything less she would be a beetle among mammoths. What is England but such a constituent? What would she be as a tight

2. An uninhabited island in Dublin Bay, once the scene of a mock "Kingdom of Dalkey."

little island now? Then let us pension off all our old Nationalists, since we cannot without ingratitude drown them.

As to Labor, I have not space left for its superstitions, though there is no real future for anything but Labor. Mere Trade Unionism is only Capitalism applied to Labor from Labor's point of view. It has only one weapon: the strike, idealized as the General Strike. Now, the strike means starving on your enemy's doorstep. It may terrify an Oriental if he happens to believe that your death will bring the wrath of Allah on him; but the modern capitalist snaps his fingers at Allah: he simply calls the police to remove your body to the mortuary. In Cork the other day Labor tried a general strike, and had actually succeeded in starving out Cork when it suddenly realized that it was part of Cork itself, and was hungry. At which point it had to turn to and work the bread business, which at once reduced the theory of the General Strike to absurdity. The doorstep plan is dirty water, and must be thrown out before Labor can get a step further. Labor for everybody, and idleness for nobody, rich or poor, is the only policy that can make a country economically sound, and its people physically and morally healthy. In a truly Free State nobody can be free until he has earned his keep, and nobody can be considered a gentleman if he is mean enough to stop at that.

As to Republicanism, there was a Republican party at the late election opposing a Free State party. But every Free State candidate, outside Trinity College, began his speech (after the obligatory collect in a tongue equally unintelligible to himself and his audience, but useful in reducing the most turbulent assembly to depressed silence) by claiming that he had been a Republican before his opponents were politically born. If he could add that he had fought for the Republic in Easter 1916, so much the better. To distinguish themselves, the Republicans had to turn back a leaf and call themselves Shinners. They differed as to two forms of an oath. One was an intelligent, sensible, and consequently binding form drafted by Mr de Valera. The other was an archaic absurdity which lost all meaning four hundred years ago at the battle of Bosworth Field, and could not possibly bind anybody nowadays. President Cosgrave concluded, like Touchstone confronted with the marriage service, that the less binding it was the easier it would be to break on occasion. Mr de Valera insisted on being properly bound. But the oath, as an institution, is a superstition, and a very annoying one. There should be no question of abolishing this oath or that oath. The Free State should abolish all oaths and all tests of that kind. If Canada and Australia and South Africa and Britain still ask for an oath to allay their dread of this poor little island, why, let them have what form they prefer, even if they wish the President to drink symbolic claret from a *papier maché* skull; but let our own life be free of such follies.

Finally, let it be made a misdemeanor for any man or woman to allege or imply that the Irish race is any better than any other race, or indeed that races exist at all. Let all the romantic ladies be engaged compulsorily as actresses in a national theatre, and all the drunken doctors be transported to America. Let the fisherman who strays on Lough Neagh's bank[3] when the clear cold eve's declining be thrown into it. And then Ireland will have a chance at last.

3. See p. 93, note 2.

IRELAND'S FORGOTTEN PRISONERS

To *The Manchester Guardian*, 20 October 1924

Sir,—It is a blessed thing, and still a delightful novelty, for Englishmen to face a General Election without having their own heavy grievances thrust into the background by the comparatively bearable ones of Ireland; but I have just come across an Irish document which directly concerns the British taxpayer, and which may as well be dealt with before any change of government which may possibly result from the election.

In the year 1922 the Ulster Government had to resort to that policy of Frightfulness *(Schrecklichkeit)* for which we strenuously reproached the Germans without finding ourselves able to refrain from it ourselves under due provocation. The British electorate no doubt believes that in this particular instance it is in a position to say to Ulster "What is that to us? See thou to that." But this is a mistake. The thrifty Protestants of Belfast, always more than a match for the British lamb, not only dealt out the most appalling sentences of imprisonment of all the insurgent Republicans and Anti-Partitionist Free Staters they captured, but, on the plea that they had no convict prisons, dumped their catch on the British taxpayer, who, instead of simply saying, "Well, if you have no prisons, why dont you build some?" feebly allowed the prisoners to be shoved into Peterhead Gaol, and then apparently forgot about them. At all events there they are at present, much against their own wills, being fed, lodged, clothed, and duly made miserable at the expense of this most gullible of islands.

From the list which has come into my hands I find that we are entertaining unawares thirtysix men, sentenced to 233 years of imprisonment (an average of six and a half years apiece), made up of eight comparatively tenderhearted sentences of three years (now expiring), and the rest culminating in two sentences of ten years, two of fifteen, and one of twentyone on a gentleman from Galway whose presumably monstrous malefactions baffle the imagination; for how a man could deserve twentyone years' imprisonment and yet be fit to live is a question beyond answering.

It is clear that these sentences were mere incidents of a White Terror, the necessity for which need not now be disputed. What admits of no dispute is that as the Terror has served its turn and is done with, and the leaders in the conflict have been released, there is no excuse for detaining these less noted guests of Britain, as reluctant as they are unwelcome, any longer. The three-year sentences having been served all alike, the sentences of seven, eight, ten, fifteen, and twentyone years are now barbarous nonsense and should be remitted, with apologies for the stern necessities of civil war, at once.

I suggest that the British Government should politely but firmly announce that the limits of its hospitality have been reached and that Ulster must take back its prisoners unless it would prefer an exercise of the King's prerogative of mercy. There may be people in Ulster who would like to keep the Galway gentleman in prison for twentyone years; but as these kill-hards would obviously burn him alive if our criminal code permitted that extreme, their opinion will not weigh with reasonably good-natured folk.

Every act of grace that can sweeten the atmosphere for the discussion of the Irish boundary difficulty is opportune just now, no matter what Government may come into power next month. The boundary question is a very dangerous one, because, as there is not the slightest real excuse for fighting over it, everyone will make melodramatic excuses with a sense of fervent and noble disinterestedness. The sensible thing for the Irish people to do is just exactly nothing. Leave things as they are, and the Ulster employers will soon be driven by organized Labor into the arms of the Southern agriculturists. They will prefer a Dublin Parliament to a Belfast Soviet. And the Free State cannot take part in the settlement of a boundary without recognizing and sanctioning partition, by which it will compromise its own Anti-Partitionist principles and incur reasonable reproach from the otherwise sometimes unreasonable followers of Mr de Valera.

As to the British Prime Minister, his position will be a most uncomfortable one unless the Commission has sense enough to report that, as no rational boundary is discoverable, the present one will do as well as another, and had better be left as it is.

But the Commission may not have that much sense. It may be obsessed with the notion that its business is to change the boundary, and that it has no other reason for existing. Now, if it changes the boundary by one yard, there may be an immediate Custom-house collision on that yard, developing into a riot, developing into a collision between the Northern and Southern police forces, developing into a collision between troops called out on both sides, developing into civil war. In that case, what is the wretched British Prime Minister to do? If he leaves the combatants to fight it out, what becomes of the Pax Britannica and the treaty? If he rains bombs impartially on both sides until they stop fighting he will have to police the new frontier with English troops, and will find himself between two fires from North and South, execrated by both as another and more murderous Cromwell, and committed to another generation of odious and never sufficiently resolute coercion, with England again unable to gain a moment's attention for her own affairs, and much worse hampered in her foreign policy than even the Germans imagined her to be in 1914.

The practical moral is unmistakeable. Let the prisoners be amnestied under whatever constitutional form is most convenient; and let the Boundary Commission either delay its report until Ulster comes in, or else decide in favor of the present boundary.[1] Meanwhile, the Anti-Partitionist inhabitants of Tyrone and Fermanagh may be depended on to keep quiet, amply consoled for the Protestantism of their rulers by the relative cheapness of provisions and postage which accompanies it.

Yours, &c.,
G. Bernard Shaw.

1. The Boundary Commission, which sat during 1924 and 1925, could not reconcile its differences and was dissolved after one member resigned, leaving the boundary as it was, and is.

THE IRISH CENSORSHIP

Time and Tide, London, 16 November 1928;
The Irish Statesman, Dublin, 17 November 1928

It is a convention to assume that there is nothing people like more than political liberty. As a matter of fact there is nothing they dread more. Under the feeble and apologetic tyranny of Dublin Castle we Irish were forced to endure a considerable degree of compulsory freedom. The moment we got rid of that tyranny we rushed to enslave ourselves. We gave our police power to seize any man's property and to put upon him the onus of proving that it belonged to him. We declared that as prison would not deter Irishmen from evil-doing they must be savagely flogged; and when the evil-doers were flogged they were imprisoned for long periods lest the flogging should provoke them to commit fresh crimes. When gunmen were all over the place we made it a crime for anyone to possess a weapon to protect himself against gunmen. We are too much afraid of our peaceful citizens to arm them, and too much afraid of brawlers not to suspect a brawler in every peaceful citizen. We are afraid to let a fellow citizen practise fine art because he (or she) might take advantage of our ignorance of art to cheat or corrupt us. Miss Mia Cranwell, the Irish Benvenuto Cellini (I am not referring to her private life),[1] is to be driven out of the country by the sellers of the dullest and commonest English silver goods under a regulation which a medieval guild in the last stage of decay would have refused to believe possible in a sane community.

We shall never be easy until every Irish person is permanently manacled and fettered, gagged and curfewed, lest he should punch our heads or let out the truth about something. It is useless to remonstrate. As Mark Twain said, the average man is a coward. The latest demonstration of Irish abjectness is the supplanting of constitutional law by the establishment of a Censorship, extending in general terms to all human actions, but specifically aimed at any attempt to cultivate the vital passion of

1. Mia Cranwell was a Dublin worker in precious metals, a book illustrator, and a designer of jewelry (including a ring for Charlotte Shaw).

the Irish people or to instruct it in any function which is concerned with that passion.[2] It is, in short, aimed at the extermination of the Irish people as such to save them from their terror of life and of oneanother. The Jews aspired to a state in which "none should make them afraid"; but they proposed to live to enjoy it, each Jew sitting up, alive and hearty, under his own vine and fig tree. We hope for no peace until we lie dead, each under his own headstone, forgetting that when it comes to the point we shall be afraid to die lest the devil should use us worse than even our dreaded fellow creatures.

Since it would be in vain to appeal to the Irish people, I turn to the Church, which is not Irish, but Catholic. Is it going to submit to this amateur Inquisition which is eliciting triumphant chuckles of "We told you so" from Ulster? Does it realize the ghastly change that threatens its temples in the Unfree State at the suggestion of Sir William Joynson-Hicks,[3] the most resolute No Popery man in England, and of a raving Orangeman[4] who supplies Ireland with English papers and declares that he would rather murder his children than trust them uncensored. I am on cordial personal terms with both of these sturdy Protestants, but I hardly expected to see the Catholic Church coming to heel at their whistle.

All those figures of the dead Christ, with their strong appeal to the pity and love of Irish girls (who has not seen them weeping and praying before such figures?), must be melted or smashed, and the girls referred to St Thomas Aquinas for instruction in purely intellectual religious emotion. All the handsome brave St Joans must be chopped up for firewood. The boys who feel that they can pray to St Joan when they cannot pray

2. The Censorship of Publications Act (1929) provided for the banning of two kinds of books: (a) those that are "indecent or obscene" and (b) those that advocate abortion or promulgate methods of birth control by artificial means. An amendment of 1945 provided to publishers and authors the right of appeal to a separate appeal board. Some of Shaw's apprehensions about the possible applications of the act were premature, since the act was still being debated in the Dáil at the time he was writing.

3. William Joynson-Hicks, politician and lawyer, was prominent in the Protestant evangelical movement and wrote books on censorship and morals.

4. Presumably this was John Charles Malcolm Eason, Irish bookseller and newspaper distributor, who encouraged literary and film censorship and made a submission to the Committee on Evil Literature, which presaged the 1929 Censorship of Publications Act.

with any heart to the distantly august Trinity will cease to pray, and interest themselves in getting rich quickly. The Catherines and Margarets with
their long tresses, teaching the young to associate loveliness with blessed-
ness, will be torn down, leaving their adorers to associate loveliness with
debauchery, like all Censors. The Mother of God herself will be spared
only on condition that she be made repulsively ugly lest she should "excite sexual passion," a course which must end in her complete banishment
lest the ugliness should excite abhorrence. The Faith will wither at the
root and perish. The Iconoclast will rejoice and exult.

Then what of the priest? Clearly his splendid vestments at the altar
cannot be tolerated by the Censors: his carnal good looks must be masked
in Genevan black. The gilded shrine must be replaced by a cricket pavil-
ion locker and the incense replaced by asafetida; for did not Mahomet say,
"There are three supremely delightful things: perfume, woman, and
prayer; and the greatest of these delights is prayer" [Sir William Muir,
Life of Mohammad, 1923]. And what is incense but perfume? Clearly if
Mahomet had been an Irishman he would not have wasted his time praying when he could get all his soul's troubles settled for him by a Censorship.

As to singing in churches, its sensuous appeal must be severely censored under the Act. In London the contrast between the virility and
charm of the singing in Westminster Cathedral and the wretched bawling
of the opera choruses has struck everyone who has compared them; and I
cannot believe that the Irish cathedrals do not equally eclipse the Gaiety
Theatre. But under the Censorship the Mass will be sung in Ireland by the
choristers of the musical-comedy stage, because their efforts could not
possibly warm the most susceptible female heart.

These fleshly and artistic snares of the devil are, however, mere trifles.
What of the priest as confessor, counselor, spiritual adviser, teacher of
youth? If innocent youths or maidens going from a sheltered home into
the world are warned by their pastor of the perils of venereal disease,
away with him to prison for corrupting the young. If the wives and husbands of his congregation come to him for help in the domestic troubles
brought on them by their ignorance, and he brings the ancient wisdom of
his Church to their relief (his supply of modern scientific treatises on the
subject being cut off), away with him at once: the priest who would mention such things in conversation with a lady is no better than Dr. Marie

Stopes.[5] If, in his counsels to schoolboys, he makes any reference to homosexuality, unfrock him and cast him forth to share an eternity of burning brimstone with Miss Radclyffe Hall.[6]

And when all these monstrous follies are being perpetrated by way of purifying Ireland, the Church will be blamed for it. Already it is said on all hands that the Censorship Bill is the Church's doing. It will certainly be the Church's undoing unless the Church stands openly by its anti-Puritan tradition. The notion that Raphael was less inspired, or otherwise inspired, when he painted the history of Cupid and Psyche, than when he painted the Transfiguration, has no warrant in Church doctrine.

(By the way, what is to be done with the National Gallery under the Act?)

What we have to consider in judging the special aim of the Bill is that life, especially married life, is unnecessarily troubled and occasionally wrecked because we have no technique of marriage; and this ignorance is produced by the deliberate suppression of all responsible information on the subject. England has an expert instructress in the person of Dr Marie Stopes; and the result is that—quite apart from the special technique of Birth Control, which she has at all events rescued from the uncontradicted, and in Ireland presently to become the legally uncontradictable, advertisements of the underground trade in "specialities"—numbers of needlessly unhappy marriages have been set right by her instruction. The Irish people will not be allowed to consult either Dr Stopes or their spiritual directors. Of clandestine instruction there will be plenty; but as nobody will be allowed to criticize it, or even to mention it, everything that is evil in it will be protected and nourished, and everything that is honest and enlightened in it will be discredited and suppressed.

But we must not let our vision be narrowed by the specific and avowed objects of the Act, which are, to prevent our learning the truth about the various methods of Birth Control (some of them in urgent need of criticism) now in irresistible use, and to hide from us the natural penalties of prostitution until we have irrevocably incurred them, often quite innocently at second hand. The matter of Censorship as opposed to constitu-

5. Stopes was cofounder of the mothers' clinic for constructive birth control and author of many books on marriage and contraception.

6. Hall was the author of *The Well of Loneliness* (1928), a sympathetic study of lesbianism.

tional law is bigger than these, its meanest instances. Ireland is now in a position of special and extreme peril. Until the other day we enjoyed a factitious prestige as a thorn in the side of England, or shall I say, from the military point of view, the Achilles heel of England? We were idealized by Pity, which always idealizes the victim and the underdog. The island was hymned as one of saints, heros, bards, and the like more or less imaginary persons. Every Don Quixote in Europe and America, and even actually in China, made a Dulcinea of Kathleen ni Houlihan and the Dark Rosaleen. We thought ourselves far too clever to take ourselves at the Quixotic valuation; but in truth even the most cynically derisive Dubliners (detestable animals!) overrated us very dangerously; and when we were given a free hand to make good we found ourselves out, with a shock that has taken all the moral pluck out of us as completely as physical shell-shock.

We can recover our nerve only by forcing ourselves to face new ideas, proving all things, and standing by that which is good. We are in a world in which mechanical control over nature and its organization has advanced more in a single century than it had done before in a whole epoch. But the devil of it is that we have made no corresponding advance in morals and religion. We are abject cowards when confronted with new moral ideas, and insanely brave when we go out to kill oneanother with a physical equipment of artificial volcanos and atmospheres of poison, and the mental equipment appropriate to stone axes and flint arrowheads. We incite our young men to take physical risks which would have appalled the most foolhardy adventurers of the past; but when it is proposed to allow a young woman to read a book which treats sexual abnormalities as misfortunes to be pitied instead of horrors to be screamed at and stoned, an Irishman arises in the face of England and madly declares that he is prepared in the interests of family life to slay his children rather than to see them free to read such a book. What sort of family life his daughter has led him since he made this amazing exhibition of Irish moral panic is a matter for shuddering conjecture; but, however dearly he has paid at his own fireside for his terrors, he can hardly have got worse than he deserves.

The moral is obvious. In the XIX century all the world was concerned about Ireland. In the XX, nobody outside Ireland cares twopence what happens to her. If she holds her own in the front of European culture, so much the better for her and for Europe. But if, having broken England's grip of her, she slips back into the Atlantic as a little green patch in which a few million moral cowards are not allowed to call their souls their own, by a handful of morbid Catholics, mad with heresyphobia, unnaturally combining with a handful of Calvinists mad with sexphobia (both being in a small and intensely disliked minority of their own co-religionists), then the world will let "these Irish" go their own way into insignificance without the smallest concern. It will no longer even tell funny stories about them. That was what happened to so mighty a Power as the Spanish Empire; and in magnitude we are to the Spanish Empire what a crumb is to a loaf.

By the way, the reality behind that poetic fiction, "the Irish race," has a good deal of Spanish blood in it. The seed of Torquemada is in the Irish soul as well as the seed of Calvin.

Let Ireland beware!

SHAW TALKS OF IRELAND

A questionnaire by Andrew E. Malone.
The Manchester Guardian, 16 August 1932

Three years ago in Malvern you said, "I know nothing about the future of Ireland. Neither does anyone else." Is that your feeling still?

I was not expressing a feeling. I was stating a fact. It remains a fact.

But have you any views about the Oath?[1]

I have very decided views about it. I think Mr de Valera, in his preoccupation with the British Island, missed a chance there. All these oaths are ridiculous superstitions: their total abolition is long overdue. If Ireland had given a lead to civilization by abolishing the oath as an institution, and taking the ground that in a progressive community no citizen can bind his political or spiritual future and that experience has proved that all attempts to do so by oaths are as futile as they are absurd, I can see no position which England could have taken to the contrary except one of pure perversity. And the Senate would not have had a leg to stand on.

You said in 1929, "England may be driven to make a desperate struggle for independence of the Commonwealth. In that case Ireland and the Dominions will probably resist the attempt by force, as the Northern States of America did in 1861."[2] Would you believe Irish Republicans, now very vociferous, likely to take a share in the resistance?

Well, look at Ottawa![3] When England arrived there in her usual attitude of condescending self-complacency the Dominions set on her like a pack of hounds on a fox. The thing I foretold is being enacted before your eyes.

1. See "The Irish Crisis," pp. 268–72 (especially the note on the Anglo-Irish Treaty), and the penultimate paragraph of "On Throwing Out Dirty Water," p. 289.
2. Interview with Andrew E. Malone, August 1929; not located.
3. At a conference in Ottawa in 1932, member states of the British Empire undertook to satisfy their import needs, wherever possible, from within the Empire. Ireland gained no benefit from the conference.

The Irish are comparatively friendly. As to the Irish Republicans, they will take a share in anything that is directed against England. They have not yet learnt how to take some little interest in Ireland. But the I.R.A. is useful. It frightens tourists away from Ireland; and as so much of Ireland is beautiful but barren, and is much more valuable as a great sanatorium than as a means of working very poor men to death in the effort to drag a livelihood out of it, there is a real danger that the country may become too dependent on foreign tourists and valetudinarians. The fear of being shot up by the I.R.A. acts as a salutary check on such development.

What is your opinion on the matters in dispute between the Irish Free State and British Governments? Do you think the land annuities should continue to be paid?[4]

I dont know. The case is *sub judice,* and I have not gone into it myself. But it is clear that Ireland has as much right to demand a judicial revision of the treaty which founded the Irish Free State as Germany has to challenge the Treaty of Versailles, or France to repudiate eighty per cent. of her debt to British and Irish subscribers to her War Loan, or England to demur to her financial obligations to the United States. But England can never understand why anyone should question what seems to her to be her obvious right to be judge, jury, and executioner in every case to which she is a party; and this ridiculous infatuation led her to behave with gross stupidity when Mr de Valera raised the question of the annuities.

If Mr Thomas[5]—or rather the Cabinet which is behind Mr Thomas— had had an ounce of gumption or any objective grasp of the situation it would have at once recognized Ireland's right to a judicial inquiry, but would also have insisted that the judges or arbitrators should be impartial foreigners unattached to the British Empire; for it was clear that if Mr de Valera was left free to choose inside the Empire he would either choose a team of Afrikander Republicans or nominate Mrs Sarojini Naidu and Ma-

4. De Valera, who became prime minister in February 1932, almost immediately put into action a preelection pledge to withhold land annuities that hitherto had been paid to the British government as repayment of loans made to Irish tenant farmers to purchase the land. This measure led to an economic war that was not resolved until the Anglo-Irish agreement of 1938.

5. James Henry Thomas, British labor leader and politician, was secretary of state for the colonies from 1930 to 1935.

hatma Gandhi.[6] Instead, the Irish Government's perfectly correct assumption that the inquiry should be disinterested was met by a peremptory demand that Mr de Valera should confine his choice to the British Empire, in every province of which there is a violently anti-British party. The most recalcitrant Irish pig would have been ashamed of such a blunder.

But worse remained behind. Mr MacDonald[7] would have been perfectly in order in asking Mr de Valera to deposit the annuities, pending the inquiry, in the International Bank in Basle. But what did he actually do? He allowed Mr de Valera to make a second journey to London under the impression that the Cabinet had come to its senses and was prepared to discuss the matter reasonably, and then met him on the threshold with the direct and intolerable insult of a refusal to discuss anything until the annuities were deposited in England's own pocket. What are you to do with men who behave like this in responsible positions? What could Mr de Valera do but go home and add his traveling expenses and the value of his wasted time, plus an adequate solatium for Ireland's wounded dignity, to the claims to be adjudicated?

Do you believe that the whole matter should go to arbitration? And, if so, what do you think ought to be its composition?

Well, there is the International Tribunal at the Hague.[8] What is it for, if not to deal with such cases? Ireland claims representation at Geneva, and thereby implies that she is willing to do what she can to further existing attempts at internationalism. Neither Ireland nor England can pack the court. Both of them probably dislike it on that account. But that is precisely why the public opinion of the rest of the world should press them to resort to it. Arbitrations are unsatisfactory substitutes for any permanent courts of justice.

Do you believe that Mr de Valera's self-sufficing State is either possible or desirable? Particularly for Ireland?

6. Naidu, Indian poet and reformer, was the first Indian woman president of the Indian National Congress. She and Mohandas Gandhi represented the congress in the second Round Table Conference (London) in September 1931.

7. James Ramsay MacDonald, longtime leader of the Labor Party, was prime minister of a coalition government from 1931 to 1935.

8. The Permanent Court of Arbitration (League of Nations).

It is so desirable that all the nations are struggling towards it, because all wars are now settled not by fighting but by blockade. But they are confused by their bankers and foreign traders, who fill the papers with assumptions that prosperity is directly proportionate to the volume of trade. The truth is the exact contrary. The nearer the consumer is to the producer the greater is the prosperity. Only in the cases, now exceptional, where home production is impossible—for example, tea and tigers in Ireland—or where the natural conditions enable a foreign country to produce luxuries so much more easily and cheaply that the expenses of transport are worth incurring and the risk of blockade negligible, is foreign trade an advantage. But as Ireland can at a pinch do without tea and tigers, and modern production is so artificial that it can be established almost anywhere, the old case for Free Trade is greatly weakened. Still, dont suppose that this justifies tariff wars. It justifies total prohibition of commercial imports; and it may involve the purchase of dumped goods en bloc by the Government for distribution at regulated prices when prohibition produces a temporary shortage; but the game of retaliatory tariffs is like throwing a dead cat back and forward over a garden wall.

It is suggested that you are interested in the foundation of an Irish Academy and that you will be one of its members. Do you really believe in such things?

Man alive, it exists already, and I am a member. Mr Yeats and I elected one another. I see the Irish press is almost as far behind the times as the English.

THE IRISH ACADEMY OF LETTERS

W. B. Yeats approached Bernard Shaw in 1932 with a proposal that
they jointly found an academy to honor Irish literary achievement and
to organize writers to wage war against censorship by the Catholic Church
in Ireland. Shaw agreed, principally for the second purpose. The initial
meeting of a provisional council was convened in Dublin on 14 September
1932, its members consisting of Yeats, George Russell, Lennox Robinson,
Seumas O'Sullivan (pseudonym of James S. Starkey), Oliver St. John
Gogarty, Frank O'Connor (pseudonym of Michael O'Donovan), and
F. R. Higgins. Shaw (the only absentee) was unanimously voted
president, Yeats vice president, and Russell secretary-treasurer. A letter
to nominees drafted by Shaw was read and approved, with the proviso
that copies be sent as well to members of the provisional council.
The printed letters, forwarded to London for Shaw's cosignature,
were posted, undated, from England in September 1932.
Of the seventeen nominated academicians, five (including James
Joyce, Sean O'Casey, and George Moore) declined, Joyce informing
Yeats that he wished for the academy "the success it aims at," though he
saw no reason why his name "should have arisen at all in connection
with such an Academy," feeling "quite clearly that I have no right
whatsoever to nominate myself as a member of it" (Joyce,
Letters, ed. Stuart Gilbert [New York: Viking, 1957], 325).

Dear Sir,

We have at present in Ireland no organisation representing *Belles
Lettres,* and consequently no means whereby we Irish authors can make
known our views, nor any instrument by which action can be taken on
our behalf.

There is in Ireland an official censorship possessing, and actively exer-
cising, powers of suppression which may at any moment confine an Irish
author to the British and American market, and thereby make it impossible for him to live by distinctive Irish literature.

As our votes are counted by dozens instead of thousands and are therefore negligible, and as no election can ever turn on our grievances, our
sole defence lies in the authority of our utterance. This, at least, is by no
means negligible, for in Ireland there is still a deep respect for intellectual

and poetic quality. In so far as we represent that quality we can count on a consideration beyond all proportion to our numbers, but we cannot exercise our influence unless we have an organ through which we can address the public, or appeal collectively and unanimously to the Government.

We must therefore found an Academy of *Belles Lettres*. Will you give us your name as one of the founder members?

In making this claim upon you we have no authority or mandate beyond the fact that the initiative has to be taken by somebody, and our age and the publicity which attaches to our names makes it easier for us than for younger writers.

Please send your reply to the Provisional Hon. Secretary, GEORGE RUSSELL, ESQ., 17 Rathgar Avenue, Dublin.

Yours faithfully,
G. Bernard Shaw.
W. B. Yeats.

ON ST PATRICK'S CATHEDRAL

A reply to Mrs. N. Kilkelly, secretary of a Dublin committee
initiated to seek a friendly settlement for the restoration of Christ's
Church Cathedral or St. Patrick's Cathedral to the Catholics.
East Anglian Daily Times, Ipswich, 23 January 1935.

Dear Madam

I cannot join the Committee, as it happens to be my personal opinion
that all our medieval cathedrals should be catholic in the sense of belonging to all human beings—Christian, Mahometan, Hindu, Buddhist, Par-
see, Sinn Fein, or what not—who desire a suitable place for contempla-
tion and the making of their souls.

But I remember very well how, on returning to Dublin after an absence
of thirty years, I went to see St Patrick's Cathedral,[1] and found it as ugly
as if the devil had built it, and on the same day went into Christ's Church
and found it absolutely empty—not even a verger or a charwoman in
charge. I thought how sensible it would be for the Ecclesiastical Commissioners to offer to exchange this unused temple, in which one can still feel
the Presence of God, for the St Patrick's structure, which could then be
deconsecrated and demolished, and its site let lucratively for commercial
purposes—a good Protestant bargain. I do not remember whether I expressed this feeling at the time; probably I did. If so, I may be the origina-
tor of the movement you represent.

My own family and antecedents are ultra-Protestant, and I am a bit to
the left of Protestantism myself; but when there are two cathedrals available within a stone's-throw of oneanother, it seems rather dog-in-the-
mangerish to deny its use to the catholic majority, in whose hands no visi-
tor could at any hour find it completely deserted, as I did.

Faithfully,

G. Bernard Shaw.

1. In the text published in the *East Anglian Daily Times* the name inexplicably
appeared as St. Paul's Cathedral. In a letter of apology published in *The Irish Times*,
Dublin, on 22 March 1935, Shaw complained that "some Handy Andy . . . had altered
the name in my letter, thereby reducing it to revolting absurdity and discrediting the
whole project."

EIRE—ULSTER—AND BRITAIN

Extract from an interview or questionnaire by Sean MacBride, former chief of staff of the IRA, who, after a political career, became chairman of Amnesty International (1961–74) and, in 1977, recipient of the Nobel Prize for peace. Published in *The Sunday Chronicle*, Manchester, Irish edition, 13 March 1938. In an introductory paragraph the editor noted that "Mr. Shaw was one of the first [in Britain] formally to register as a citizen of Ireland under the recently enacted Irish Citizenship Act."

The British Government claim that the Irish question was finally settled by the Treaty of 1921. Mr. de Valera claims that the 1921 Treaty was imposed on the Irish people under a threat of "immediate and terrible war"; that it caused the Irish Civil War; that its provisions restrict Ireland's freedom and that the Irish people do not consider that they are bound by it. Do you consider that the 1921 Treaty is a final settlement of Anglo-Irish relationship?

There is no such thing as a final settlement in this changing world. Herr Hitler has torn the Treaty of Versailles to rags and thrown the pieces in the teeth of the Allies. The Treaty of 1921 is no more sacred than the Treaty of Limerick.[1] So Mr de Valera need not bother about that.

Mr. de Valera claims that there is an overall majority in four of the six counties under the rule of Lord Craigavon's Government,[2] which is definitely opposed to the Partition of Ireland. The British Government claim that the Partition of Ireland is essential from a strategic point of view and also that it is necessary in order to safeguard Protestant interests. Are you in favor of the continuance of the Partition of Ireland?

In 1914 England immediately occupied all the Greek islands that for one reason or another were necessary to her in the war, without the slightest regard for the neutrality of Greece. In any future war, England will do the same to Ireland, partition or no partition. She must. Consequently, whilst Eire cannot prevent this, the strategic point is purely platonic.

1. See p. 196, note 2

2. Sir James Craig, created First Viscount Craigavon in 1927, was prime minister of Northern Ireland from 1921 until his death in 1940. See also p. 150, note 4

[What about] the question of the occupation of certain Irish ports by British troops?

I have no objection to the spending of British money by British troops in Eire, nor to the additional security they give against foreign invasion, to which Eire is very vulnerable. As they do not interfere in the government of the country nor prevent the development of native defence I do not bother about them. . . .

ON IRISH NEUTRALITY

I

Liberty, New York, 29 July 1939; *The Sunday Chronicle*, Manchester, 30 July 1939

I have been asked to say what in my opinion would be Ireland's attitude in the event of war. And it is suggested that neutrality would be quite unlikely to save her from invasion.

I reply that neutrality would make invasion a certainty.

From the military and naval point of view, Ireland, England, and Scotland are one country. This is not a matter of opinion, but a fact. An invader can choose between Harwich and Galway. Let us consider Galway.

When I was a child, Galway was defended by an exciseman with a wooden leg. If it has any more formidable defences now, I am not aware of them.

The magnificent natural harbors on the west coast of Ireland, of which the Irish make no use, are very tempting—as tempting as those on the west coast of the Adriatic Sea.

The difference between Irishmen and Englishmen would trouble an invader no more than the difference between Czechs and Slovaks troubled Herr Hitler.

Eire, as they call her now, has a population of three millions and an army of six thousand, which she could increase to twenty-seven thousand by calling up her reserves and volunteers. Northern Ireland has a population of a million and a quarter.

What is the plain conclusion to be drawn? In the event of a war, England would have to come to the rescue of Ireland with a considerable military reoccupation of the country and a thorough naval blockade.

But—and this is of the gravest importance—if England is ever tactless enough to attempt to conscript Ireland, the fat will be in the fire.

Ireland must conscript herself.

II

A questionnaire by Emrys Hughes in *Forward*, Glasgow, 30 November 1940

What would be your advice to de Valera?

To stop talking obvious nonsense about Ireland defending herself—four million disunited Irish against forty million British, eighty million Germans, fortyfour million Italians, and 130 million Americans! For if Germany invades her, and Ireland becomes the cockpit of the war, she will have to defend her neutrality against the lot. Until Mr de Valera admits that Ireland can do nothing for herself by herself except commit suicide nobody will waste time listening to him.

And to the Government of Ulster?

Nothing but O.K.: go ahead. The Protestant boys are carrying the drum all right.

What would you think should be done if Eire persists in her refusal to allow the British navy to use the ports it requires?

The British MUST take the ports if the German submarine campaign threatens to starve them out. They took Eubea from the Greeks in 1914 to secure their supply of a mineral needed for their blast furnaces. Do you suppose they will hesitate to take the Irish ports to secure their supply of bread?

What do you think would happen to Eire if Hitler won the war?

I dont know. Probably the Führer will adopt the view that the Irish are the lost tribes of Israel and treat them accordingly. At any rate, neither Protestants nor Catholics of the Irish variety can expect any mercy from him.

Would Ireland stand to gain by coming in on our side?

No country stands to gain in the long run by war. Ireland would be right to keep out of the war if that were possible. If she were to come in and choose the German side it would mean that she had turned Nazi or else was simply backing Germany to win—on terms, of course. In that case, as the odds are at present, it looks as if she would be backing the wrong horse. She could not possibly unite the Irish on it. It would mean civil war.

AN APPEAL TO THE IRA

The self-proclaimed "Government of the Republic of Ireland" (that is,
the IRA) issued a leaflet, *George Bernard Shaw Appeals to the I.R.A.: Friendship with Britain,* signed by its secretary, Patrick Fleming, and dated 25 July
1940, in which it printed and responded to an undated appeal by Shaw calling
for the IRA's wartime cooperation with Britain. The published source of
Shaw's statement is undetermined; but a carbon typescript with holograph
revisions and corrections survives in the Shaw archive in the British Library
(Add. Mss. 50698, fols. 158–62). The only known copy of the leaflet is in the
Laurence/Shaw Collection, University of Guelph Library.

[PRELIMINARY REMARKS BY PATRICK FLEMING]

Mr George Bernard Shaw, known to Europe and America as the greatest
publicist of British Imperialism, surveys Ireland's position in the World
War from the new point of view imposed upon England by the colossal
victories of Germany, and the certainty of the neutral nations of the
world that the British Empire has crumbled.

He believes that with the aid of African Negroes, Indian Gurkhas, and
Irish Legionaries, English supremacy over the black races might still be
maintained, provided all these could be induced to fight for the Empire
against Herr Hitler. The Negroes and Indians should, he urges, be encouraged to die for Britain because Germany wishes a pure European
race in the Reich, and the Irish should join them because Germany, unlike
the British-supported regime of Craigavon, is anti-Catholic.

Here is Mr. Shaw's contribution to the squeals of the trapped rats of
British Imperialism.

[SHAW'S SURVEY OF THE IRISH POSITION]

Our country is out of luck in this war. In the last one the Germans could
not invade us for the simple reason that from the Baltic sea coast, the only
one at Germany's disposal, it was a long way to Tipperary. England
could afford not only to leave Ireland undefended, but to amuse herself
by bombarding Dublin in sheer devilment under pretext of capturing a

single building occupied by a handful of men who in England would have been starved out by the police in a few days.

The English are kindly enough until they are frightened; but when they are frightened they are capable of every heroism and every atrocity. And they forget all about both, the moment the emergency is over, whereas we forget nothing, and are too busy remembering the Treaty of Limerick to consider where we stand with Adolf the Conqueror, whose claims on our attention are much more pressing than those of Brian Boru or Sarsfield.[1]

Ever since his conquest of France,[2] Adolph commands the seaports of France; and Brest is not such a very long way from Tipperary. All the wonderful natural harbors of our west coast are open to him as far as we are concerned; for our four millions of Irish are no more able to stop him than Pearse and Connolly, de Valera and Cosgrave, Collins and Griffith were able to silence the British batteries or wipe out the Black and Tans[3] in 1916 and after. All we could do was to burn oneanother's houses, break down our own bridges, and shoot Collins.

If England had not been dependent on the United States for victory she could have exterminated those of us who were left after our efforts to exterminate oneanother. We might have been exterminated by the Black and Tans but for the revolt of the conscience of Mr Churchill and other Englishmen against this logical end of the campaign.

When the situation became too wicked to be endured, our demand that the British Government should get out and stay out, leaving us to govern ourselves, was agreed to; but as the British rule had reduced our man

1. Patrick Sarsfield, seventeenth-century Jacobite and soldier, is credited with raising the siege of Limerick (1690) and negotiating the final Jacobite surrender of the town in 1691. He died in battle with Louis XIV's army in the Spanish Netherlands in 1693.

2. The French armistice with Germany was declared on 25 June 1940, establishing the earliest date for Shaw's draft of the commentary.

3. To downgrade for world opinion the Anglo-Irish War of 1919–21 to the level of a police action rather than a rebellion, the British recruited over 9,000 war veterans to form a special police force to oppose the Irish republicans. However, because of a shortage of proper police uniforms, the recruits wore makeshift uniforms consisting of khaki military trousers and very dark green police tunics. The Irish called them Black and Tans after the name of a celebrated Galway hunting pack despite the inaccuracy in the colors. The English in turn called their Irish opponents Shinners after their nationalist political party Sinn Féin.

power to a point at which we could not defend our island against any of the Great Powers, it was a necessary condition of the bargain that the British fleet and army should guarantee us against foreign invasion.

Unfortunately this bargain contained two ideas: "Get out and stay out" and the contrary idea "See that no other Power comes in and grabs us." Now, Ireland, though mostly strong in common sense, always produces a minority of heros whose ardor and devotion make them incapable of entertaining two ideas at once. Inferiority of numbers means nothing to them; they are ready to fight King George, or Mr Hitler, or Signor Mussolini, all together or one-down-and-t'-other-come-on, in the sacred cause of Ireland. They want to die for Ireland. They enumerate unpleasant ways of dying, and sing "What matter if for Ireland dear we fall?"

Mr de Valera, whose job it is to be a practical statesman and not a brainless hero, has to reply that it may not matter to them, but that it matters a good deal to Ireland whether she is to be occupied by corpses lying on the battlefield or swinging from the gallows, or by men who live for Ireland, work for Ireland, and think for Ireland all the time, and occasionally fight for Ireland when it cannot be helped, and not to die if they can possibly avoid it.

The Orangeman cannot sing "What matter if for England dear we fall?"; for if I were to call him an Englishman he would feel more insulted than if I called him a savage; but he will profess a businesslike attachment to the British Commonwealth of Nations, and even call it the Empire, provided its capital is understood to be Belfast. He also believes that the Catholic soul will go to hell when it dies, which gives him an unfair advantage; for the Catholic, thanks to the Christian wisdom of Pope Pius IX, is obliged to let the Orangeman off in that last extremity on the ground of his invincible ignorance.

What are we, the sane Irish, who are after all the majority, to do between these irreconcilable heros whose heads have not room for two ideas at the same time? It would seem that we need not trouble about the Orangemen; for they want to hold England to her bargain and flood Eire with British troops, and even to resume her rule there in its present form of complete Military Communism. The IRA is the bother; its "get out and stay out" is a Monroe doctrine that forbids both the German Reich and the British Empire to set foot on our sacred soil. It borrows the Orange slogan "We wont have it," forgetting that it was at Gladstonian

Home Rule that the Orangemen hurled it, with the result that Northern Ireland is the only province in the world that is Home Ruled in the Gladstone manner.

They also forget or overlook the fact that they will not be consulted by Mr Hitler or Mr Churchill, either of whom (or both, for they will cooperate heartily for this purpose) can shrivel up the IRA heros like moths with their flame-throwing tanks, riddle them with their machine-gunning planes, blast them into smithereens with their high explosives; for what can a few thousand mostly penniless men do against sixty million Germans plus forty million British? No doubt they can still sing "No matter if for Ireland dear we fall." But I repeat, it does matter most damnably. The IRA must wake up from the futile Fenianism of the eighteen-sixties, and not merely consent to a military re-occupation of Ireland by the London Government for the duration of the war, but demand it energetically as the fulfilment of the British guarantee under the Treaty.

Whether it consents or not, the thing will happen if Germany attacks or threatens to attack from the west as surely as it happened in Finland when the capitalist Powers threatened to attack Russia from the north. Ireland is the British Finland; and unless we make up our minds as to which side we will take, it will be the worse for us. Neutrality is no use; it has not helped Norway nor Holland nor Belgium.

The IRA may grant this; but as the question which side we should take is an open one from the Army's point of view, it may say "Better Hitler than de Valera and the Dail." Roger Casement, who was a trained diplomat and no fool, believed that an independent Ireland under the protection of a victorious Germany was the best available solution of the Irish problem. Germany was not victorious and Casement was hanged for backing the wrong horse.

Anyhow, Casement's argument no longer applies. The protection of the Hohenzollern monarchy after a victory over England achieved on its Continent is not the same as the invasion of Ireland by a Hitler autocracy denounced by the Pope for its merciless persecution of Catholics in Poland. The Kaiser never claimed that the Germans have a divine right as a chosen race to dominate the rest of the world and dictate to us our religion and our politics. In fact, Hitlerism rivals the Vatican as a secular Catholicism with Mr Hitler as its Pope. He calls this National Socialism, and points to the Socialist work he has done in Germany to support the assumption. I give him due credit for such work, because I was a National Socialist before he was born, and have not changed my views in that respect. But this chosen race business is not Socialism in any sense, but as my late literary colleague Charles Dickens expressed it, "so far from it on the contrary quite the reverse."[4] An Orangeman might possibly favor it as long as it confined its persecutions to Catholics and Jews; but as it is out to kill him as a Britisher he has to fight a German invasion for his life. But that a Catholic Irishman should fight for Hitler, or against his only western opponent, or be neutral in the conflict, is conceivable only on the assumption that he is hopelessly muddle-headed. Most heros are, unfortunately.

But the clearest head does more harm than good if its eyes are at the back instead of in front, and it cannot see such staggering contemporary facts as the German conquest of France and its possible consequence in a German conquest of England. What is to become of Ireland in that case? To call for three cheers for Germany as we used to call for three cheers for the Boers thirty years ago will not now serve our turn. If Finland, Albania, Latvia, Estonia, Besarabia, Czechoslovakia, Poland, Norway, Belgium, Holland, and even mighty France itself have been gathered like so many daisies by the bigger Powers, what can a little cabbage garden like Ireland do with nothing but its brains, which it mostly refuses to use, imagination being easier. Nothing at present but attach itself to whatever bigger Power seems most likely to let it call its soul its own. The choice is not large. Russia and Japan are too far off, and hardly know that there is such a country as Ireland. Germany persecutes Catholics, the Nazi State being a rival Church. Italy does tomorrow what Germany does today. France is conquered. There is left the British Commonwealth and the United States of North America. Ireland has been protected for years against the worst that the Union Jack majorities in England dare have done to it in the face of Ireland beyond the seas, which is a part of the United States, and the British Overseas Empire. Now, if we take the part of Mr Hitler against Britain we instantly lose the protection and sympathy of the United States, and make the British Commonwealth our active and infuriated enemy.

The choice is really Hobson's choice. We must back the British if Germany attacks them from the west.

4. *Pickwick Papers*, chapter 16.

"IRELAND'S ANSWER" [THE IRA RESPONSE, SIGNED BY PATRICK FLEMING]

Thus opportunely Mr. Shaw pleads with his fellow countrymen to forget their foolish heroics of the past, as England has done, and for the maintenance of their religious and economic liberties to throw in their lot with the British Empire, bulwark of Christianity, and defender (at odd intervals) of the faith and of small nations.

The continued persecution of the Catholic minority in British occupied territory in Northern Ireland is merely a suitable topic on which to sharpen the famous Shavian wit. In his delineation of Herr Hitler and Signor Mussolini as the instigators of a new series of Penal Laws against Irish Catholics, he ignores their recent efforts to establish a Catholic Government in Spain against the opposition of Britain and Germany and Italy's serious breach of the British Imperial tradition in withdrawing their forces and waiving all claims, territorially and otherwise, on the fortunate recipient of their aid.

Mr. Shaw's urgent call to the Irish Government to appeal for help from Britain as the only big power likely to let them call their souls their own, is a continuation of the futile game of politics that made France and Belgium, Norway and Holland, so many protective barriers for a decaying empire. He may draw comfort from the assurance that his native country has less to fear from a German invasion than his adopted country.

The consistent policy of the progressive European Powers during many centuries has favored the restoration of Ireland to the comity of nations as a mother country with a distinctive lingual, cultural and social history and outlook. Spain, France, the Vatican, have sent expeditionary forces to Ireland to rescue her from the military and economic tyranny of Britain. Germany has given her not only the support of her armed forces, but the help of her ablest sons to restore the civilization which Britain deliberately destroyed.

The Third Reich, as the guardian and energizing force of European policy, is inevitably interested in the continuity of these principles of national freedom enunciated in the past by Germany and the other Great European Powers and if, in the prosecution of the present war German forces should land in Ireland, they will land as they did in 1916, as friends and liberators of the Irish people.

Germany desires in Ireland neither territory nor the fruit of economic penetration; her reward for any help that she may accord, directly or indirectly, is the freedom of civilized nations from the intolerable yoke of Britain and Britain's satellites and the reconstruction of a free and progressive Europe.

Why is it in the face of the known and proven attitude of Germany that Mr. de Valera, while sprinkling himself and his followers with the blood of the Irish Republican Cabinet of 1916, reverses their policy, denies their wisdom, attacks their patriotism and their honesty? Every one of them, according to Mr. de Valera (and Lord Craigavon) was a Dermot Mac Murrough,[5] for not only did they invite German aid for Ireland, but boasted of it and as recently as 1922 Mr. de Valera was still asking for German support. Is German aid less valuable now than it was in 1916 because the Kaiser has been succeeded by Herr Hitler or because modern Germany has proven that she can and will smash Britain here. Just as she has already smashed her from Spain to the Balkans and from Iceland to Africa. For 25 years Mr. de Valera has claimed to be a Separatist and a Republican and has sworn solemnly that he kept the faith of Tone,[6] Pearse, and Casement. Why then is it that when the Republic could have been achieved almost without the firing of a shot, Mr. de Valera finds that a Republic is not desirable and that Tone and Casement were really traitors? Why do Mr. de Valera, Lord Craigavon, and Mr. Churchill adopt exactly the same attitude to Irish Republicanism? Why does Mr. de Valera appoint to his Government ignorant and willful men whose allegiance is to Britain? Why are the key positions in the Civil Service staffed with Britishers? Why is the Defence Council composed solely of men who have publicly and repeatedly advised the Irish people to support Britain in this war? Why is Mr. de Valera's own newspaper [The Irish Press] so pro-British that it published a series of articles on Germany

5. MacMurrough was a feuding king of Leinster who was driven from Ireland in 1153 after abducting the wife of a rival ruler. He returned a year later, aided by a force of Anglo-Norman nobles, an involvement that led to the conquest of Ireland.

6. Theobald Wolfe Tone, father of Irish republicanism, was a member of two French expeditions that attempted unsuccessfully to invade Ireland at Bantry Bay, County Cork, in 1796, and at Killala Bay, County Mayo, in 1798. Captured by the British and under sentence of death, he cut his throat with a pen knife the night before he was to be hanged.

written by an American—articles that were so vile that they were boycotted even in England?[7] Why are the key positions in the newspaper
held by a succession of British hacks from editors to sports writers? Why
have we the British Censorship, the British A.R.P. [Air Raid Precautions],
the British blackout, the secret deals with the British police and the British
Government? Why, in short, is the present Government of the 26 counties more meanly, malevolently pro-British than Cosgrave when he was
murdering Irish prisoners or the Redmond and Dillon party when they
were cheering in the House of Commons for the murder of the 1916 leaders? Why, in short, is the Government of the 26 counties doing exactly
the same things in the same way and with the help of the same people as
the Government of 1914? The same class of mugs (sometimes the same
mugs) are guarding the bridges as in 1914–15. The same class of foxy
English army officers and shopkeepers with a little money to lose are advising people to join the British forces. The special police of that date are
the local security (Carey Column)[8] of today.

The answer to all these questions is obvious: Mr. de Valera was never
sincere in anything. When appealing to the people to elect his party to
power he promised:—

To establish the Republic.

To eliminate unemployment.

To reduce taxation.

To purify public administration.

To restore the Irish language.

To build up a defence force and a mercantile fleet.

What he did was:—

He finally disestablished the Republic of 1916 (in so far as his
Free State parliament could do it).

He increased unemployment.

He increased taxation.

He appointed to the administration ruffians that even Cosgrave
rejected.

He insisted that Irish was necessary for boiler cleaners but not for
teachers and propagandists.

7. Not located.
8. Unidentified.

He instituted an army composed mainly of wastrels and ex-tommies armed with English guns.

His public life has been an unbroken series of broken promises, of hypocritical patriotism, of weakness masked by obstinacy and poisoned by fear.

SIGNED ON BEHALF OF THE
GOVERNMENT OF THE REPUBLIC.
P[ATRICK]. FLEMING,[9]
Runaidhe [secretary].

25 July 1940

9. Patrick Fleming, who served with the IRA contingent in the Spanish civil war (despite a Dáil edict against participation in the conflict), later was one of a dozen young members selected for "field training" in bomb squads, his base being Manchester. Around 1940, under chief of staff Sean Russell, he was one of a handful of the IRA's surviving Second Dáil who helped to reestablish a formal link between the IRA and Sinn Féin. On 9 March 1946 he was arrested with several of his fellows in a raid in Ardee Street, Dublin, and was imprisoned for a year. Beyond this, nothing is known of his activities.

ÉAMON DE VALERA AND
THE SECOND WORLD WAR

Forward, Glasgow, 1940–44

I

7 December 1940

The interview given by Mr de Valera to the United Press of America gives a tragic complexion to the Irish difficulty. It is in its way admirable, clearheaded, full of character and brains, and, given Mr de Valera's point of view, inevitable. Nothing could be more straightforward and logical. The ports are Ireland's; he will not give them up. He will not throw Ireland into the cockpit to be bombed and "blacked-out" in a war declared by England without consulting her. If any Power, under whatever flag, violates Irish neutrality, he will throw a quarter of a million Irish soldiers into the field to fight it. He can understand Britain's position, and if he could do anything to relieve the sufferings of the British people he would do so. But it is primarily with the welfare of his own people that he must concern himself.

There you have the great Irishman; and he will not swerve from his line. First and last a Catholic Republican Separatist, and as such chosen to be Prime Minister by the Catholic majority of his countrymen. Nobody can say a word against the choice from their point of view. He has all the academic distinctions, and has given all the proofs a man could give of his devotion and personal courage, staking his life at impossible odds, being sentenced to death, and going through two imprisonments. He opposed the Treaty as an out-and-out separatist, but finally consented to make the best of the new Constitution, which recognized Ireland as "a sovereign independent State in the name of the Most Holy Trinity, from Whom is all authority and to Whom, as our final end, all actions both of men and States must be referred." In short, he is a marvel of integrity in public and private life.

But his integrity is also his limitation. He is a Paoli, a Garibaldi, not a Cavour. What is Mr Churchill to do if Britain's exclusion from the Irish ports gives Germany command of the sea? In that case he must reply: "I see your position; but I feel about England exactly as you do about Ireland, and I will not allow forty million Britons to be starved and defeated to save the paper neutrality of a few million hostile Irish. If and when the situation becomes grave enough to convince America that I have no alternative, I will reoccupy your ports and leave you to do your damnedest."

If I were in Mr Churchill's place I should put it more philosophically. I should say: "My dear Mr de Valera, your policy is magnificent, but it is not modern statesmanship. You say the ports belong to Ireland: that is what you start from. I cannot admit it. Local patriotism with all its heroic legends is as dead as a doornail today. The ports do not belong to Ireland: they belong to Europe, to the world, to civilization, to the Most Holy Trinity as you might say, and are only held in trust by your Government in Dublin. In their name we must borrow the ports from you for the duration. You need not consent to the loan, just as you did not consent to the Treaty; and you will share all the advantages of our victory. All you have to do is to sit tight and say: 'I protest.' England will do the rest. So here goes."

II

On 21 December 1940 the editor of *Forward,* Emrys Hughes, published what was ostensibly Shaw's reply to an Associated Press interview with de Valera in response to Shaw's foregoing article. In actuality Hughes had reproduced only a third of Shaw's remarks, expunging the first three paragraphs. The omissions have now been restored from Shaw's shorthand draft and a transliteration by his secretary Blanche Patch. We are indebted to the Harry Ransom Humanities Research Center, University of Texas at Austin, for permission to publish the full text from the manuscript in its collections.

I stand paralyzed before Mr de Valera's innocence. The late Lord Craigavon was right: there is no use talking to him. I found him, as it were, walking through a field deep in thought and apparently unconscious of the fact that the cattle in the field included at least four bulls. In the most courteous terms I warn him that in a certain dangerously probable event one of the bulls will certainly go for him, and that if he fails to appease it all four may go for him. Instead of thanking me for the warning Mr de Valera accuses me of inciting the bull to attack him, and expresses the lowest opinion of me personally. He adds that he offered to feed the bull, and that the bull preferred to get its food elsewhere. And with that he resumes his walk and his meditations as if he had dealt exhaustively with the situation.

What are we to do with such a man? To drop the metaphor does Mr de Valera believe that if the German submarines reproduce the 1917 famine in England the British Government will need any incitement from me to re-occupy the Irish ports? For 60 years I have been inciting the British government to do all sorts of sensible things. Has it ever paid the smallest attention to my incitements? Granted that all the faults Mr de Valera finds in my character, and worse, are provable up to the hilt, will his indictment paralyze Mr Churchill, disable Herr Hitler, pacify Signor Mussolini, and substitute Mr Willkie for Mr Roosevelt[1] at the White House?

Granted that Mr de Valera's good feeling towards England is not reciprocated, and that the tract recently published by Lord Alfred Douglas,[2] in which the Black and Tans are represented as Galahads and the Shinners as abandoned scoundrels is typical of the feeling roused in England by the bombing exploits of the IRA and its satisfaction by the sentences passed on the bombers, does that make the seizure of the ports less likely or more? Granted ten times over everything that Mr de Valera says, what difference does it make? None that I can see.

So Mr de Valera dismisses me with an unprovoked kick in my Protestant pants, and stands for making Eire a Western Switzerland. Eire has her Alps: the Galtees, the Kerry Reeks, the Twelve Pins of Connemara, the Wicklow Sugarloaf and the Dublin Three Rock. She has a three million population, the traditional ten per cent. of which will give her more than the promised army of 250,000 fighters. The word is "Come the four quarters of the world in arms and we shall shock them."[3]

1. Wendell L. Willkie, the Republican candidate for the U.S. presidency in 1940, was defeated by President Franklin D. Roosevelt, who had run unprecedentedly for a third term. Shaw misspelled the name as "Wilkie" in his manuscript.

2. Poet, man of letters, and friend of Oscar Wilde, Douglas had sent to Shaw a vehemently anti-Irish pamphlet, *Ireland and the War against Hitler,* whose cost he had underwritten. See Shaw's correspondence with Douglas in *Collected Letters, 1926–1950* (London: Max Reinhardy, 1988) 586–88.

3. Shakespeare, *King John,* 5.7.117, substituting "four quarters" for "three corners."

It is simple, heroic, and academically quite correct.

Well, England has smashed the invasion threat, and may possibly smash the submarine offensive without troubling the Irish ports. If she does, Mr de Valera will get away with it, and I shall have made a fuss for nothing.

I hope so. We shall see.

III

11 January 1941

In 1939 all the Powers and nations, including Ireland and the United States of America, were thrown into a position of pressing difficulty and danger when the British Empire, according to its invariable custom, declared war on the German Reich without consulting the League of Nations, the House of Commons, or in fact anybody, the immediate provocation being dissatisfaction with the re-partition of Poland by the Reich and the U.S.S.R.

Some of the consequences were unforeseen. Germany, having driven the British Expeditionary Force into the sea and forced the French, Belgian, Danish, Dutch, and Norwegian Governments to capitulate, occupied all the ports on the Channel and the North Sea and threatened to invade the British Isles. This forced the British Government to take the unprecedented step of inviting the United States to occupy and defend the British West Indian ports. When Italy entered the war on the side of Germany, the Greeks invited Britain to occupy and defend the ports of Crete and the Dodecanese. The U.S.S.R. had already reoccupied by force the ports in the Gulf of Finland. In fact, all the strategically vital ports in the world changed hands with one exception. That exception was the Irish ports. When the German submarine campaign achieved some blockading successes it became apparent that, if the sinkings off the Irish coast went much further, the Irish ports and the great natural harbors of Eire's west coast must be occupied and defended either by the British Empire, the United States—or both.

The Irish Taoiseach (Premier), Mr de Valera, made no move; and Admiral Beamish, M.P. for Lewes, began pressing the British Prime Minister to occupy the Irish ports. Mr de Valera declared that as he could not take any step in favor of one or other of the belligerents without pushing Eire into the war, Eire must remain strictly neutral. In case of invasion by any foreign Power, including the British Commonwealth, he, with an army of quarter of a million men, would take the field and resist as Poland had resisted, as Finland has resisted, as Norway, Belgium, and Holland had resisted, as Denmark had not resisted, and as Greece was resisting. This decision implied that Eire was not a part of the British Commonwealth, but a sovereign independent State in the fullest sense, a position which England, then very strongly on the appeasement tack, thought it best to overlook as long as she could do without the ports, and the danger of a German attack through Eire seemed negligible.

So the matter stands at present. It will stay put unless and until the question of Irish neutrality is taken out of Mr de Valera's hands by Herr Hitler, Mr Churchill, or even President Roosevelt, under pressure of circumstance. But the situation is perilous. Admiral Beamish's demand for seizure of the ports is received with unanimous acclamation in the House of Commons; and though Mr Churchill is evidently anxious to avoid trouble with Eire, a bad week or two in the submarine blockade may force his hand. In that case, if Mr de Valera throws his quarter of a million soldiers into the field to fight the British Commonwealth he will be virtually throwing Eire into the war on the side of Germany and against the Pope and making a catastrophic end of Irish neutrality.

Would Catholic Eire, to say nothing of her Protestants, support him in such a policy? Does he seriously contemplate it himself?

In any case, his position is one of extreme responsibility. By the 1921 treaty which constituted the Irish Free State, Eire was a dominion of the British Commonwealth of Nations, and was entitled to claim the protection of the Commonwealth for her ports. But the new Irish Constitution of 1937, which passed almost unnoticed in England, made Eire a sovereign independent, theocratic State, belonging not to the Commonwealth but "to the most Holy Trinity."

Mr de Valera is placed by it in the odd position of having presently to decide, if Eire's neutrality is violated, whether the Trinity is for or against Herr Hitler. If he decides that it is pro-Hitler, he declares war on the Commonwealth, on the Pope, on Northern Ireland, and must prepare for war with America too. If he decides that the Trinity is true-blue British, he secures the warm assent of Lord Halifax and, let us hope, backs the winning horse as against Signor Mussolini and Monsieur Laval; but to the Irish Republican Army he will seem to be holding a candle to the devil. Whichever side he chooses his neutrality will be finished by the first shot he fires; if he hits a British soldier Eire will, in effect, be in the war on the side of the Axis. If he hits a German, Eire will be in the war on the side of Britain and America.

If I were in Mr de Valera's dilemma, I think I should take care not to fire a shot. I should interpret the Trinity as saying to the German and Italian dictators and to Mr Churchill: "Sirs, ye are brothers; wherefore do ye wrong one to another?" I should do what the Government of Denmark has done by letting the belligerents do their worst without any help or hindrance from her people, and should carry on as best might be under the circumstances, making what formal protest is proper against the breach of neutrality.

My own *locus standi* is only that of an absentee Irish landlord who has lived twenty years in Ireland and sixtyfive in England; but as the Irish climate has worked on my stock for some centuries, I can claim to be at least as indigenous as a half-Spaniard like Mr de Valera or a half-American like Mr Winston Churchill, though I regard their cross-breeding as all to the good. But I can get nothing relevant out of Mr de Valera. He says I am inciting England to seize the ports. His notion that England needs any incitement to an act of self-preservation, or that I, who have spent all my life inciting the English to act sensibly without for a moment gaining their confidence, could produce any effect on the British Government, seems to me to prove that he knows very little about me and less about England.

He qualifies my conduct as contemptible. I cannot think why, except it be part of a general misanthropic conviction that all human conduct is contemptible; for I had regarded myself self-complacently as an Irishman of some eminence, entitled to my opinion in a grave political crisis. He accuses me of morally justifying war tactics. Far be such an impossibility from me! Though England, like other nations, likes to claim that her tactics are all exemplary moral gestures, war is a competition in atrocity in which victory goes to the competitor who kills and destroys most. But, in any case, what the world wants to know is not Mr de Valera's valuation of me. It wants to know definitely which side he will come down on if Eire is pushed off the fence into the field.

Very old-fashioned Irish people like myself may regard Ireland as the first flower of the earth and the first gem of the sea; but Ireland belongs, always has belonged, and always will belong to (in Bunyan's phrase) "him that can get her." Whether his name be Brian Boru or Strongbow,[4] Hitler or Mussolini, de Valera or Churchill, she can make Irishmen of any or all of them. Mr de Valera might give this a moment's thought, and also ask himself what he would do if he were in Mr Churchill's place and the U-boat score were running up again.

Meanwhile, Herr Hitler's inept airmen have mistaken Eire for Northern Ireland and bombed it. The Führer, whilst expressing his regret for the error, has no doubt made a private note that Mr de Valera now understands what will happen to him if he comes down on the wrong side from the German point of view.

Suppose the United States, which are quite as much New Ireland as New England, were to ask for the Irish ports for the duration, what then?

IV

1 April 1944

When the Irish Free State was established I took it as a matter of course that, in the event of a second Punic War, England would have to reoccupy Ireland militarily, either to forestall or repel an invasion by the enemy. When that war actually came, England was very loth to do this lest it should offend the U.S.A., whose intervention, as the German Bernhardi had vainly warned the Kaiser, would determine the event. I, not depending on this, and not believing that Eire, as the Free State now calls itself, could keep out of the war anyhow, suggested that she should stand in with the Commonwealth.

Mr de Valera described the suggestion as contemptible, and declared that with his army of 40,000 (say three divisions) he would fight any and every Power that dared to invade his country. This in the then quite possible event of Germany invading Eire on the west and south, and En-

---

4. Richard Fitz Gilbert (d. 1176), Earl of Pembroke, was called Richard Strongbow. He was the Anglo-Norman son-in-law, military ally, and heir of Dermot MacMurrough, king of Leinster.

gland necessarily throwing in an army on the north and east "to defend Ireland," Mr de Valera, caught between the "fell incensèd points of mighty opposites,"[5] would be obliged to fight the British Commonwealth and the German Reich with his three divisions unless they allowed him to intern their puissant armies.

It seemed a crack-brained line to take; yet Mr de Valera got away with it. England, still with an eye on America, pocketed his refusal of the ports and decided to be content with Northern Ireland. Thus he was saved by the Partition which he abhorred.

Pearl Harbor changed the situation completely. The U.S.A. came thundering into the war; and now it is not Mr Churchill asking for the ports and putting up with a defiant refusal, but President Roosevelt peremptorily ordering Mr de Valera to declare war on Germany at once.

It is Mr Roosevelt's first really stupid mistake. The Eirish leader, with all Ireland, Protestant and Catholic, behind him, Mr de Valera will tell the President, in fact, to go to hell. And he will get away with it again.

Can it be that Mr Roosevelt is overworked and is catching too many colds? Or is he determined to shew that the U.S.A. can be as unilateral in respect of Ireland as the Soviet in respect of Poland, Finland, and Italy?

Howbeit, that powerless little cabbage garden called Eire wins in the teeth of all the Mighty Powers. *Erin go bragh.*

5. Shakespeare, *Hamlet,* 5.2.61–62.

THE GREATEST LIVING IRISHMAN?

A "Special Interview" by an unidentified correspondent, ostensibly
obtained in Shaw's home in Ayot St. Lawrence, but apparently
a written questionnaire. *The Irish Times,* Dublin, 6 December 1941,
subcaptioned "Who Is the Greatest Living Irishman?"

Do you think Ireland's wisest course in 1921 was to agree to Dominion status?

I do not. Wisdom has nothing to do with nationalism, which is in many
ways a curse, and is wise only when it is a beginning of Catholicism. It is
an instinct that must be satisfied wisely or unwisely, like birth, marriage
and death. Eire is not allowed to call herself by her great historic name—
Ireland,[1] and she governs herself far more tyrannically than ever Dublin
Castle or the old Grand Juries dared to govern her. Fascism and Nazism
are merely pale copies of the present "Eiric" Constitution. But it had to be.

It is a queer business. The English are arrogant mongrels, and so are we,
but we pretend that we are pedigreed animals of the purest uncrossed race.

I have often prophesied that some day England will try to break loose
from her domineering Dominions, and be once more a self-governed,
tight little island. If she does, Ireland will head the Unionist war to chain
her to the Commonwealth, with the President in the *rôle* of Abraham Lincoln.

*What do you think would have happened to Ireland if the [Irish] Treaty del-
egates had refused to sign?*

I think Ireland would have got better terms. Churchill, to his strict credit,
could not stand the Black and Tans business, and the British Government
generally could not afford to alienate the United States by going on with it.
However, it is well enough as it is. When we get really free in our minds—
free from our own past—we shall see that Ireland is not big enough for our

1. In January 1922, under the ratification by the parliament of southern Ireland of
the peace agreement with Britain, the new dominion became known as the Irish Free
State. Under the Constitution of 1937 the name was abolished, being supplanted by
Éire. See p. 268, note 1.

brains, and that our business is to compete with Westminster for the direction of the Commonwealth. If Ulster alone could bully England, what could not a solid Ireland do? I, a single Irishman, do it myself. Meanwhile, the irresistible joke in the business is that Ulster is left with Gladstonian Home Rule. When her capitalists find that only by combining with the agricultural Twenty-six Counties can they stand against the Socialism of their industrial proletariat they will probably end as anti-Partitionists. So there is no need to hurry about that question.

Do you think the Irish language drive since the Treaty, intensified in recent years, will make Ireland bilingual ultimately?

I hope not. I have no patience with this atavistic folly of planting a dead language on Irish schools as Latin verse is planted on English ones. Our greatest achievement in this field has been our conquest and annexation of the English language, which we handle more easily than the English do. It gives us power over the minds and imagination of the human race in all the continents. It is read and spoken everywhere, and this school Gaelic is read and spoken nowhere.

What would you think of the English if they proposed to abolish Shakespear and go back to Anglo-Saxon? Well, that is what I think of the idiots who want to abolish Swift and Shaw and go back to Gaelic. It is an attempt to make the Irish still more Irish, whereas what is wrong with us is that we are a great deal too Irish and too little European. Its fanciers are provincials who want us to be parochials, and parochials who want us to be nobodies. If we want to be bilingual, let us learn Russian or some other live language.

Whom do you think to be the greatest living Irishman?

I tell you the great man is a fabulous monster like the unicorn. If you must have a greatest living Irishman you can choose between me and Mr de Valera.

EIRE AND HITLER

To *The Times*, London, 18 May 1945

Sir,—The correctness of the Taoiseach's action when the death of the head of the German State was reported has been vindicated by Commander A. MacDermott.[1] But his letter does not cover the whole story. In 1943 the Allies called upon the neutrals to deny asylum to Axis refugees, described for the occasion as war criminals. Portugal refused. The rest took it lying down, except Mr de Valera. He replied that Eire reserved the right to give asylum when justice, charity, or the honor or interest of the nation required it. That is what all the neutrals ought to have said; and Miss Hinkson, as an Irishwoman, will, on second thoughts, be as proud of it as I am. The voice of the Irish gentleman and Spanish grandee was a welcome relief from the chorus of retaliatory rancor and self-righteousness then deafening us.

I have not always agreed with the Taoiseach's policy. Before the ink was dry on the treaty which established the Irish Free State I said that if England went to war she would have to reoccupy Ireland militarily, and fortify her ports. When this forecast came to the proof the Taoiseach nailed his colors to the topgallant, declaring that with his little army of 40,000 Irishmen he would fight any and every invader, even if England, Germany, and the United States attacked him simultaneously from all quarters, which then seemed a possible result of his attitude. And he got away with it triumphantly, saved, as Mr Churchill has just pointed out, by the abhorred partition which gave the Allies a foothold in Ireland, and by the folly of the Führer in making for Moscow instead of for Galway.

Later on I hazarded the conjecture that Adolf Hitler would end in the Dublin Viceregal Lodge, like Louis Napoleon in Chislehurst and the Kaiser in Doorn. If the report of the Führer's death proves unfounded this is still a possibility.

1. When Hitler's death was reported in May 1945, de Valera, as *taoiseach* of Ireland, called upon Eduard Hempel, German minister in Dublin, and offered condolences. Commander MacDermott's letter on protocol appeared in *The Times*, London, on 15 May, as did a letter from writer Pamela Hinkson.

It all sounds like an act from Victor Hugo's Hernani rather than a page of modern world-war history; but Eamon de Valera comes out of it as a champion of the Christian chivalry we are all pretending to admire. Let us recognize a noble heart even if we must sometimes question its worldly wisdom.

Faithfully,
G. Bernard Shaw.

A FILM INDUSTRY FOR IRELAND

I

Extract from a written interview submitted to the anonymous author
of the daily "London Letter." *The Irish Times*, Dublin, 31 January 1945

*I asked Mr. Shaw whether he thought . . . there was a future for film productions
on Irish locations, or for an Irish film industry.*

Ireland is an ideal country for modern film work. It has mountains that
look twice as high as they really are, the most picturesque atmosphere in
the world, natural colors in Sligo Bay and elsewhere that are unbelievable
by anyone who has not seen them, magical, haunted islands like Skellig
Michael,[1] Atlantic waves, colossal cliffs, desert bogs, battlefields, prehis-
toric forts, ancient castles that cannot be reproduced in pasteboard, green
and scarlet sunsets, firmaments fretted with golden fires, and everything
the cinematographer can need or desire. Ceylon is only a next best.[2] Unfortunately, Ireland is short of capital. What has the government of Eire to
say to this, in view of the enormous educational and propagandist power
of the film?[3]

*I asked Mr. Shaw if he thought the Irish revival would be accelerated by films
in the native tongue shown in schools and picture houses to the rising genera-*

1. An immense rock, 700 feet high, with twin peaks rising from the sea off the coast
of Kerry, Skellig Michael is famous for its early monastic remains. See Shaw's graphic
description, in a letter to Frederick Jackson on 18 September 1910, of his visit to the
Skelligs the previous day (Shaw, *Collected Letters, 1898–1910*, 1972).

2. Ceylon, another candidate at that moment for development of a film industry,
was familiar to Shaw, who had visited the island on a round-the-world cruise in January 1933.

3. Shaw designedly avoided suggesting any personal interest here, although he
and film producer Gabriel Pascal entertained very shortly afterward the possibility of
creating, with the blessing of de Valera, an independent, government-sponsored film
company and studio, one half of which would be used exclusively for their own
productions and the balance for documentary and educational films. The enterprise
foundered.

tion, or if the anglici{ing influences of the Press, the BBC, Denham[4] and Hollywood will be too strong even for Mr. de Valera's iron determination to restore the language.

Mr de Valera's unfortunate addiction to the hopelessly effete foreign language called Gaelic is almost as deplorable as Hitler's prejudice against the Jews. English is Ireland's native tongue. The English cannot speak it as well as we do, and our command of it in literature is a command of more than a quarter of the globe. Without it we should shrink into the most negligible of cabbage gardens. Gaelic is segregational, which means that it is anti-Catholic. More than any other single cause, it has kept the Irish enslaved for centuries by the English-speaking Protestant ascendancy. All members of the Gaelic League should be shot as the worst enemies of their country. I should, however, recommend Mr de Valera to mercy.

II

Typescript draft; dated 10 September 1947 by Shaw's assistant
Dr. F. E. Loewenstein and posted to Reuter's Press Bureau on 12 September.
Publication not located. Shaw's manuscript is in the Harry Ransom
Humanities Research Center, University of Texas at Austin.

I have had in mind for a long time the fitness of Ireland for a film industry. The climate, the scenery, the dramatic aptitudes of the people, all point that way. The present domination of Hollywood over the mind of the world is to me deplorable: it is creating a barbarous sock-on-the-jaw morality from which Ireland must be rescued. Having already municipalized my Irish landed property,[5] I am ready to give Ireland the first call on my

4. Denham was the British movie studio, proximate to London, where Shaw's *Major Barbara* (1941) and *Caesar and Cleopatra* (1945) were filmed.

5. In May 1944 Shaw proposed to the Carlow Urban Council that he hand over to the municipality, for the common welfare, the Carlow properties he had inherited in 1899 on the death of his maternal uncle Walter John Gurly. Though the council was prompt to accept the offer, it discovered there was no law in Ireland enabling them to accept on the terms required by Shaw, through the creation of a civic improvements fund. Shaw appealed in early June 1945 to the prime minister, de Valera, in response to whose request the Dáil quickly passed a Local Authorities (Acceptance of Gifts) Bill. The gift of seventeen land parcels was conveyed to the council on 13 August 1945. A smaller gift of property was made to Wexford on the same terms.

valuable film rights. I have in fact executed an agreement which will have that effect if the project meets with the necessary public approval and financial private support. Already I have been met more than half way in both respects. An experimental company, to be known presently as Irish Screen Art Limited, is now in existence with sufficient Irish capital to exploit certain film rights of mine until it is in a position to build the necessary studios to operate exclusively in Ireland: a work which might well be undertaken by the Irish State. This is as far as the matter has gone at present.

My friend Arthur Rank[6] has no part in the affair, all the capital being Irish; but I hope his many picture houses, in which his strength lies, will be filled with Irish films to make up for the threatened restrictions on the import of Hollywood ones. Hollywood itself may prove a good customer.

6. J. Arthur Rank, the British film titan who became the most powerful film creator in Britain, had recently financed Pascal's production of Shaw's *Caesar and Cleopatra*.

SHAW SPEAKS TO HIS NATIVE CITY

A questionnaire by James Whelan on the occasion of Shaw's being offered the Honorary Freedom of Dublin. *New York Journal-American,* 17 and 18 March 1946; *Leader Magazine,* London, 23 March 1946

You spent a boyhood which was a singularly free and imaginative one. You taught yourself to swim in Killiney Bay?

Yes, I found that I simply couldnt learn to swim in shallow water, for my feet would insist upon touching the ground. So I went to what is called the White Rock, and jumped in where I could not reach the bottom—and thereby was forced to swim ashore.

In your world traveling since, have you ever seen anything to equal the view of Killiney Bay? Is there anything in Britain to touch Irish scenery?

The Torca shoulder of Dalkey Hill, the Telegraph Hill overlooking the two bays from Dalkey Island northward to Howth and southward to Bray, is not surpassed in its view of mountain, sea, and sky (Shakespear's "majestical roof fretted with golden fire" is to be seen there), anywhere I have been. For brilliancy of color—making rocks, rain pools, and herbage look like terrestrial jewelry, I have seen nothing like the heights above Sligo Bay. And, for magic that takes you far out of this time and this world, there is Skellig Michael, ten miles off the Kerry coast, shooting straight up six hundred feet sheer out of the Atlantic. Whoever has not stood in the graveyards at the summit of that cliff, among those beehive dwellings and their beehive oratory, does not know Ireland through and through. Until the motor boat existed, this supernatural outpost was accessible only in a fishing boat with nine rowers, on a sea too calm for sailing. Even a motor boat dare not rub sides with the piers of the tiny harbor; but it's worth while being swung ashore by a derrick—as the lighthousemen often are.

It is the beauty of Ireland that has made us what we are. I am a product of Dalkey's outlook; and the scenery has infected the architecture. The railway station of Dun Laoghaire (Kingstown), and some of the old provincial court houses, would be impossible in England. When the intelligent Englishmen come to Ireland they burn their boats and never return, in spite of the charm of their Midlands and the beauties of the Malverns and of Wales. Fortunately for us, few of them are intelligent.

The revival of the Gaelic language in the schools and as the everyday language of the people has been pressed by both the Cosgrave and de Valera Governments since 1922, and much progress has been made. Hasn't Mr. de Valera, in achieving complete independence from Britain, been of the greatest benefit to future generations of the Irish race?

Nonsense! How can we be completely independent of our next-door neighbor? Are we not Europeans and citizens of the world?

The English language, our most priceless acquisition and conquest, gives us three-quarters of the world for our audience. Would you throw it away for a scholastic exercise which was never common speech in any country on earth, like V century Latin? And torture Irish children with three languages: English, school Gaelic, and vernacular village Irish? It would be much saner to teach them the bagpipes and the pirouetting Highland dancing which attract us to the Scottish gatherings.

One of the members of the Corporation of Dublin declared you were not a fit mentor for the youth or the adults of Ireland.

Who is?

Mr. Jim Larkin suggested that you should be asked: What about coming home and taking six feet or more of Irish soil?

I have not left myself even six feet of Irish soil to be buried in; I gave the last sod of my Irish property to Eire a month ago, and had to get an Act of Parliament passed to enable me to do it. But, as the nephew of the founder of Mount Jerome cemetery, I know too much about earth burial to contemplate such a horror. It should be made a criminal offence. My ashes will be mixed inseparably with those of my wife, which are being kept for that purpose; and when that is done, neither of us will concern ourselves with what happens to them afterwards. After seventy years in a country so much less happy and oppressed than my own, I can hardly grudge it the handful of clean, harmless cinders which will be all that will remain of us two presently.

Has the influence of mothers on famous men in world history been the most decisive one?

My parents never consciously provided me with anything except clothes and bread and butter, which was always left within my reach because my father held that a child should never be hungry. Bread was bread in those days; and I greatly preferred it to beef. I found myself in a house where there were books, pictures, a piano at which my mother sang, a trombone on which my father could vamp a rum-tum bass, a pet dog, occasionally a cat, and servants who lived in the basement and dusted and made the beds and washed up for £8 a year, had no holidays, went "to chapel" instead of "to church," and could neither read nor write. Parental duties were as far as possible left to them.

We were fond of the dog, and the dog was fond of us. I was such a nuisance that I was sent as a "day-boy" to a prison called a school where I learnt nothing until I was fifteen, when I went into an office, where I sang operas with the apprentices when the principals were out of hearing. Thousands of children are brought up like that, without pianos, trombones, or books, but born of the same younger-son stock, and consequently being ladies and gentlemen without the necessary incomes. They alone know how much worse impecuniosity is than poverty. They have children without instruction in parental duties, just as they have votes without civic instruction. My mother sang and my father talked in my hearing without the least suspicion that they were educating me.

Another Dublin councillor asked what you had done for Ireland. "An occasional long-distance wisecrack—that is all I can find," he said.

English journalists often reproach me with ingratitude to their country, to which they attribute all my success and reputation. It is hardly polite on my part to assure them that when I came to England I got nothing for nothing, and very little for a halfpenny; that I was abused, vilified, censored, and suppressed to the limit of possibility, until my successes in Germany and America convinced my detractors that there was some money in my evil doctrine. When my seventieth birthday was celebrated, the English Government prohibited the reporting of my speech before it was delivered. But the people in the market-places and at the street corners stood by me, and I bear no malice. Now that I am ninety, British Cabinets are no longer so desperately afraid of me.

Alderman Butler, of Dublin, said that your intellectualism had brought the world to the sad state it was in today. He added that it was an intellectualism that scoffed at the existence of God, scoffed at revealed religion, and was in conflict with the intellectualism of Thomas Aquinas.

When I was adolescent a very eminent Irish physicist, John Tyndall, declared in Belfast that he saw in matter the promise and potency of all science. Since then, there has been a mighty swing spirally upward from Materialism to Creative Evolution; now Thomas Aquinas is on the map again, and Tyndall quite off it. I have been in the vanguard of that movement all through. Saint Thomas was the intellect of the Church in the days when the latest science was Aristotle's. Alderman Butler has not read me often enough.

Don't you think that this recognition by your native city is rather belated, and that the Irish race has always been most ungrateful to its greatest sons, e.g., the way in which it threw out Parnell?

I do not belittle the Freedom as belated. I like to think that nobody can yet be sure of what I will be up to next or whether I shall die in my bed or be hanged. Parnell is now only an example of that risk; the old gang of Gladstonian Nationalists hardly bear comparison with Griffith and Collins, much less with de Valera. And for heaven's sake, dont talk to me about that hackneyed myth, the Irish race. There is no Irish race. We are a parcel of mongrels: Spanish, Scottish, Welsh, English, and even a Jew or two. My remotest known ancestor was Macduff; but my later forbears have breathed Irish air for centuries; and Irish air will change even an English man or woman so usefully that two years of it should be made part of their compulsory education, just to make their minds flexible.

The Freedom will presumably be conferred by a special delegation of the Corporation, who will travel to Ayot St. Lawrence. Would you like this method?

It would kill me stone dead, though the delegates would be personally very welcome. But what would they find here? A dotard who, after a pitiable effort to rise to the occasion and speak as he could ten years ago, would fall asleep in their faces. He could not entertain them on his vegetarian ration. The village has no hotels, no trains, no buses, no shops, no cinemas, no Woolworths, consequently no domestic service, nothing to shew to the envoys of a great capital but its oldest inhabitant.

How could the Delegation get here? How would it get away? Never, unless I arranged it: and how should I survive the effort?

Do not terrify me.

IRELAND ETERNAL AND EXTERNAL

The New Statesman, London, 30 October 1948;
Atlantic Monthly, Boston, February 1949

Eternal is the fact that the human creature born in Ireland and brought up in its air is Irish. Whatever variety of mongrel he or she may derive from, British or Iberian, Pict or Scot, Dane or Saxon, Down or Kerry, Hittite or Philistine: Ireland acclimatizes them all. I have lived for twenty years in Ireland and for seventytwo in England; but the twenty came first, and in Britain I am still a foreigner and shall die one.

External is harder to define; and until Mr Costello bounced it into the headlines the other day[1] it meant nothing for me except house repairs that the landlord and not the tenant has to pay for. When I was born, Ireland was governed by Dublin Castle and by grand juries of Protestant country gentlemen. They were as Irish as Irish could be, though the figurehead was Queen Victoria, an Englishwoman married to a consort then frequently alluded to in Reynolds Newspaper as a pudding-faced German. The royal pair were represented in Ireland by a British Lord-Lieutenant. But he too was an Irish institution, and when his term of office expired his wife wept publicly in her open carriage as she drove through the streets from the city in which she was an Irish queen to the foggy neighboring island where she was a nobody.

Not that this intense Irishness meant Irish unity. Irish faction to the verge of civil war, and sometimes over it, never ceased for a moment. North and South, Protestant and Catholic, Republican and Vice-Royalist, each holding the other to be eternally damned, were irreconcilable. Mr St John Ervine's Fabian political apprenticeship in London could not wash out of him the Orange dye of his native Belfast. He can hardly write the words Southern Ireland without spitting as my Orange mater-

---

1. The Republic of Ireland Act (1948), passed by a coalition government under Prime Minister John A. Costello, dissolved Ireland's connections with the British Commonwealth and declared that the official description of Ireland henceforth would be the Republic of Ireland.

nal grandfather used to spit when he uttered the word Papist. But call Mr Ervine an Englishman and he will knock you down.

This grandfather, by the way, living midway between north and south, had a sister who was a Catholic Abbess.[2]

Such is the eternal Ireland. Certain English historians, and even some Irish Gaelic Leaguers, have tried to steal Swift and Berkeley, Sheridan and Yeats (to say nothing of myself) as Anglo-Irish. There never was any such species as Anglo-Irish; and there never will be. It is hard to make Englishmen understand this, because America can change an Englishman into a Yankee before his boots are worn out. But America has never changed an Irishman. I am not for a moment implying that this is not greatly to the Englishman's credit: I am only stating an ethnological fact. Nor when I add that the Irish leave Hitler and Houston Chamberlain nowhere in their conviction that the Irish are The Chosen Race am I defending that illusion. I can only say that it exists, and that I share it in spite of reason and commonsense.

Now as to external relations. I am by birth a British subject. I have always so described myself when applying for passports, though I never stood up nor took my hat off while the English national anthem was being played until Ireland became a so-called Irish Free State. I am also a registered citizen of my native Ireland. When Mr Costello shot out of the blue his intention to abolish external relations, a wild hope arose in me that as a citizen of Nowhere I might be able to escape taxation Anywhere. This would not matter to me in Ireland, where I have municipalized my property and pay no taxes. But in England, where I am being beggared by surtaxes called Capital Levies to humbug the Labor Left (which ought to know better), my citizenship is all-important.

Why on earth has the question been raised? We were getting along quite comfortably as citizens of the Commonwealth. To me it seemed that Mr Costello and his Coalition were anxious to shew that they were even more Irish, more Nationalist, more Anti-Partition than Mr de Valera, and could think of nothing else that would do the trick than knocking off the Crown. As the King will be more comfortable in his bowler hat, I do not think he will greatly care provided he can still sell me

2. Hannah Gurley, a Catholic convert, as Mother Mary Augustine headed a Presentation Convent at Stradbally, County Lalos, in 1860.

up if I do not pay British taxes. Beyond this I can make neither head nor tail of the move.

As to Partition, I have always held that when the Labor Movement is fully developed in Ireland, the manufacturers and shipbuilders of the North, finding themselves, like all plutocratic régimes, unable to carry on without the support of a predominant agricultural Catholic vote, will themselves join up with Eire.

Partition saved Mr de Valera's neutrality in the war; for without it England would have had to reoccupy Ireland from the east, and the U.S.A. invade it from the west. The possession by these allied and irresistible Powers of bases in Northern Ireland saved the situation for once; but if it recurs and finds Ireland an independent Republic right in the fairway and open to enemy invasion, a British re-conquest will be inevitable. Such independence was Roger Casement's aim, and England promptly hanged him for it. He hoped that the jealousies of the Powers would secure the neutrality of Ireland, as it had so long secured the neutrality of the Netherlands; but that is now a forlorn hope. As the Conference of Prime Ministers has just declared unanimously for arming to the teeth, some Anglo-Irish link must be contrived, were it only to confer Commonwealth citizenship on the Irish as privileged lunatics. So I shall not bother myself about it. I shall not even say "I told you so" when the trick is done.

ULSTER AND PARTITION

Questionnaire interview, believed to have been written for P.J.A.
Scott-Maunsell, secretary of the London Area Council of the Anti-
Partition of Ireland League, published as "Ulster Always Able to
Bully Westminster." *Anti-Partition News*, June 1949

Do you agree that the British Government was responsible for creating the Partition of Ireland and that it is solely Britain's responsibility to end it?

No. Ulster has always been able to bully Westminster into doing whatever it wants. The trick was done when Lloyd George announced that it was "impossible to control Ulster."[1]

If, in your opinion, it is not solely Britain's responsibility, from whom do you consider the initiative should come for a practical move to end it?

Partition will end itself when labor is sufficiently organized in Belfast to make the electoral support of the agricultural Catholic South indispensable to the employers.

At present, Ireland is governed by two parliaments and two civil services. Do you agree that economically this is ridiculous, and that the money thus wasted could be used to uplift the social services of the whole country under a single government?

No. At present parliaments and civil services are biting off more than they can chew. Great Britain urgently needs more parliaments and services, and is setting them up in all directions.

The Six-County Government claims that because it has a majority in the six partitioned counties it has the right to divide itself off from the rest of Ireland. Is it not completely illogical, therefore, for the Six-County Government to hold on to the counties of Fermanagh and Tyrone, each of which adjoins the twenty-six counties and voted a majority against Partition at the last election?

What has logic to do with administrative ability? The world is not governed by syllogisms.

1. Not located.

If you agree, do you consider that the British Government could with justice refuse to consent to the inclusion of these constituencies with the rest of Ireland if such a demand were to be made upon it?

I dont agree. The discussion of such questions is mere shadow boxing.

Do you agree that the Irish people have good grounds to mistrust Britain's protestations of democracy and desire for international justice while she denies the same democratic rights and justice to Ireland?

All governments make the same protestations. No capable statesman is imposed on by them.

Have you any suggestions as to how the unity of Ireland can speedily be brought about?

Unity is a carrot run after by donkeys. Nationalism united Ireland. Anti-Partition is nationalism in its last ditch. When that is crossed, as it will be, United Ireland will split into dozens of creeds and sects, commercial interests and aesthetic tastes, village politics and world politics, Cobdenists and Marxists, Materialists and Creative Evolutionists, industrialist trade unionists and agricultural husbandmen, and groups and sects of all sorts. And a good job too.

ENVOI

On 26 July 1950 the representative of the Irish Republic in London, Mr. John
Dulanty, under a new agreement between Great Britain and Ireland,
was officially proclaimed Ireland's first ambassador to the United
Kingdom. By a happy coincidence this was Shaw's 94th birthday.
His congratulatory message to Mr. Dulanty was published
in *The Times*, London, 25 July 1950.

My birthdays are an unmitigated curse to me, and the people who persist
in reminding me of them exhaust my capacity for hatred. This one is
worse than ever; but it has one consolation: it has been chosen for giving
John Dulanty official recognition of the position he really occupies, that
is, of Ireland's Ambassador to England. His Excellency has been a fact so
long that it is only diplomatic decency to make it a form as well.

INDEX

DAN H. LAURENCE, literary and dramatic adviser to the Estate of Bernard Shaw from 1973 to 1990, is Shaw's official bibliographer. He is the editor of *Collected Letters of Bernard Shaw* (four volumes), general editor of *Bernard Shaw: Early Texts, Play Manuscripts in Facsimile* (sixteen volumes), and coauthor with Leon Edel of *A Bibliography of Henry James*. He has been a professor of English and drama at a number of colleges, principally New York University.

DAVID H. GREENE, New York University professor emeritus, is the coauthor of *J. M. Synge, 1871–1909* and editor of *An Anthology of Irish Literature* and *1,000 Years of Irish Prose: The Literary Revival*.